FC_12/06/18_11:00_Press Conference and Special Tour with Poligonal
@ Czech Centre / IBeB / Frizz23 / Metropolenhaus

FC_14/06/18_14:00_New Coalitions for the Cooperative City with Keynote Levente Polyak
@ Czech Centre

MCO_15/06/18_17:00_Berlin 3000 with Ortner & Ortner Baukunst and Berliner Ensemble
@ Bertold-Brecht-Platz

MCO_16/06/18_15:00_Guided by Paradoxies with Grün Berlin
@ Spreepark

MCO_16/06/18_11:00_Children Shaping the City with kleine baumeister and Stadtgestalten
@ afilii

MCO_17/06/18_14:00_An Ethnographic and Culinary Walk between Conflict and Affirmation with Poligonal @ Thai Park

MCO_18/06/18_11:00_The First Robot Manufactured Heritage with HG Merz
@ State Opera Berlin

MCO_18/06/18_18:00_Building in a Hot Climate with Indigo Architects
@ LoBe Block

HUB_18/06/18_16:00_Happy Owners with Soazic Guezennec
@ Alte Münze, 2 OG

MCO_19/06/18_13:00_Construction Site Visit
@ Axel-Springer-Neubau

ST_19/06/18_13:00_Frankie & Johnny Revisited with Holzer Kobler Architekten
@ EBA51

MCO_19/06/18_10:00_Site Visit with Zanderroth Architekten
@ ze05

ST_20/06/2018_19:00_Common Archipelagos with Imke Woelk and Partner
@ Unité d'Habitation

This publication was made possible by the Senate Department for Urban Development and Housing

Senate Department
for Urban Development
and Housing

Editor/Herausgeberin:
Francesca Ferguson, Make_Shift

Make City

A Compendium of Urban Alternatives

Stadt anders machen

jovis

2.
Governance, Strategic Alliances and Negotiating the City
Governance, strategische Allianzen und Stadt neu verhandeln

3.
Typologies, Third Spaces and the Porosity of Mixed Use
Typologien, dritte Räume und Mischnutzungen

Embracing Multiplicity

We embarked upon the MakeCity Festival of 2018 with a multitude of partners and a resolutely trans-disciplinary and trans-sectoral agenda: one that brought together architects and landscape architects; urban planners, designers and makers; cultural institutions and civic groups; and municipal decision-makers – all of whom are defining innovative strategies and new coalitions for changing cities.

Emerging from Berlin, an urban context where land and property speculation has, between 2010 and 2018, driven up the cost of land by up to 500 percent and where civic initiatives are forging new alliances with municipal administrations in order to re-shape local districts and re-vitalise existing structures, the motivation of the MakeCity Festival has been to seek out and consider architecture and urban planning that is founded – above all – upon social and spatial innovation.

Beginning with the central notion of a contemporary urban discourse that should go well beyond the architect to include developers, landowners and public bodies, we also take seriously the premise that ownership entails responsibility, a concept grounded in the German constitution. In efforts to curb ongoing and relentless short-term, profit-driven land speculation, and to halt outright sales of public land to the highest bidder, advocates of such fundamental changes at the political level have been laying the foundation for a kind of social contract for cities: a shared agenda that upholds cooperative forms of ownership, that seeks to devise concrete architectural models for mixed use and that leverages ground floor spaces for public or private enterprises – all of which are geared towards the greater goal of developing resilient neighbourhoods.

Urban change begins with a questioning of the structures and processes that underlie decision-making, construction and collaboration: now is the time to look to cities as sites for deep, systemic and transformative processes. To do this requires taking a close look at innovative strategies for cooperation between urban policy makers, citizens and designers. Municipal administrators responding to, and managing this civic

Der Vielfalt gerecht werden

Mit vielen verschiedenen Partner*innen und einem entschlossen transdisziplinären und bereichsübergreifenden Programm begingen wir im Sommer 2018 das zweite MakeCity Festival: Es brachte Expert*innen aus Architektur, Landschaftsarchitektur, Stadtplanung, Gestaltung und Produktion sowie aus Kulturinstitutionen, zivilgesellschaftlichen Gruppen und Stadtverwaltungen zusammen. Gemeinsam diskutierten und entwarfen sie neue Strategien und Bündnisse für Städte im Wandel.

Das Festival ist in Berlin entstanden, einem urbanen Kontext also, in dem Land- und Immobilienspekulation die Preise zwischen 2010 und 2018 um bis zu 500 Prozent in die Höhe getrieben haben. Um Bezirke umzugestalten und bestehende Strukturen wieder zu beleben, gehen zivilgesellschaftliche Initiativen hier neue Bündnisse mit Kommunalverwaltungen ein. Das gemeinsame Ziel des Festivals war, die Bedeutung von Architektur und Stadtplanung für gesellschaftliche und räumliche Innovation bewusst zu machen und zu hinterfragen.

Eigentum bedeutet Verantwortung. Dieser Grundgedanke ist in der deutschen Verfassung verankert und bestimmt den gegenwärtigen Diskurs um das Urbane. Neben der Architektur sollte er auch für Entwicklungsfirmen, Grundbesitzer*innen und öffentliche Stellen gelten. Um die andauernde und schonungslose, kurzfristig gewinnorientierte Bodenspekulation einzudämmen und den Ausverkauf öffentlicher Grundstücke an höchstbietende Investor*innen aufzuhalten, ist auf politischer Ebene bereits die Grundlage für eine Art städtischer Gesellschaftsvertrag entstanden. Er unterstützt genossenschaftliche Eigentumsformen ebenso wie die Entwicklung architektonischer Modelle der Mischnutzung, wobei Erdgeschossflächen von öffentlichen wie privaten Unternehmen genutzt werden – alles mit dem großen Ziel, resiliente Nachbarschaften entstehen zu lassen.

Für städtischen Wandel ist es notwendig, zunächst die Strukturen und Prozesse zu hinterfragen, die Entscheidungsfindungen, Bau und Kooperationen zugrunde liegen: Es ist an der Zeit, Städte als Orte tiefgreifender systemischer und transformativer Prozesse zu begreifen. Das erfordert einen genauen Blick auf neue Strategien der Zusammenarbeit zwischen Menschen, die städtische Politik gestalten,

imperative are clear in declaring that there is an emergent political mandate of co-creation to be taken seriously, one that requires new levels of transparency, participatory models and shared accountability. The leading proponents of an urban governance that takes into account our digitised society, such as Francesca Bria, are calling for "a new deal on data": a deal that acknowledges that data sovereignty should be placed firmly in the hands of the people to be administered as a public good - a reformulation of democracy. Though such far-reaching concepts of governance are often proclaimed within the rhetoric of smart cities - but are rarely, if ever, fully implemented - many of the self-managed and collectively financed projects featured in this compendium as innovative and workable models and prototypes have drawn on new technological possibilities, and as a result, as Daniel Dahm writes, some established hierarchical organisational structures have given way to pluralistic models of governance, galvanising civic agency.

Shared cooperative ownership, or co-investment models, are shaping the architecture of mixed-use and housing developments featured in these pages. Crucial to the success of these cooperative models for development is that the resulting prototypes for new living and working models in cities have been conceived by the architectural profession itself: it is the architects as developers who are pressing beyond the design briefs they are presented with. By curating and designing mixed financing models, developing floor plans to accommodate a maximum diversity of use, and injecting a sense of community into what would otherwise be standard office builds, architects are assembling new and shared social agendas. In addition to celebrating the architectural quality of such projects, we recognise and salute those first-time developers who are bold enough to manoeuvre risk-averse financing in order to innovate. The process itself - often immediate and with the tangential conceptual drive determined by a certain urgency - leads to third spaces where, as Joanne Pouzenc declares, "voluntary commitment and self-empowerment are considered a raw material". The end product reaches far beyond the formal structures and architectural elements themselves, with such third spaces becoming central to the ongoing evolution of communities.

Fundamental to the positions assembled here - from the foundational statements to the case studies that underscore them - is the conviction that in the current climate, when it comes to

und denjenigen, die an Stadtplanung beteiligt sind und in der Stadt leben. Die Stadtverwaltungen reagieren auf diesen zivilgesellschaftlichen Imperativ, mit dem sie umgehen müssen, machen aber auch deutlich, dass ihnen ein politischer Auftrag, der gemeinsame Gestaltung ernst nimmt, mehr Transparenz, partizipatorische Modelle und geteilte Verantwortung abverlangt. Herausragende Fürsprecher*innen einer Stadtregierung für die digitale Gesellschaft, wie Francesca Bria, rufen zu einem „New Deal on Data" auf: zu einer politischen Reform des Umgangs mit Daten, die anerkennt, dass Datensouveränität fest in den Händen der Menschen liegen und als öffentliches Gut gehandhabt werden muss. Das entspricht – kurz gesagt – einer Neudefinition von Demokratie. Solche weitreichenden Regierungskonzepte werden in der Rhetorik der intelligenten Stadt zwar häufig eingefordert, aber selten – wenn überhaupt – umgesetzt. Dennoch beziehen sich viele der selbstverwalteten und kollektiv finanzierten Projekte, die wir in dieser Sammlung als innovative und machbare Modelle oder Prototypen vorstellen, auf die neuen technologischen Möglichkeiten. Im Ergebnis, so schreibt Daniel Dahm, haben so manche der etablierten hierarchischen Organisationsstrukturen pluralistischeren Modellen des Regierens Platz gemacht; die zivilgesellschaftliche Handlungsfähigkeit ist wieder wachgerüttelt.

Gemeinschaftseigentum oder kombinierte Investitionsmodelle prägen die Architektur der Mischnutzungs- und Wohnprojekte auf den folgenden Seiten. Entscheidend für den Erfolg dieser kooperativen Formen ist, dass die so entstehenden Prototypen für neue städtische Wohn- und Arbeitsmodelle aus dem professionellen Blickwinkel der Architektur selbst hervorgegangen sind. Denn es sind Architekt*innen als Entwickler*innen, die auf Entwürfe bestehen, welche weit über die ursprünglichen Aufträge hinausgehen. Indem sie gemischte Finanzierungsmodelle kuratieren und gestalten, Etagenpläne für eine möglichst vielseitige Nutzung entwickeln und – ansonsten standardmäßigen – Bürogebäuden einen Gemeinschaftssinn einpflanzen, übernehmen Architekt*innen gleich mehrere neue gesellschaftlich bedeutende Aufgaben. Wir gratulieren gleichermaßen zur architektonischen Qualität solcher Projekte wie auch zum Mut, mit risikoscheuer Finanzierung innovativ zu bauen. Der Prozess selbst – oft unmittelbar und mit sprunghaftem konzeptuellem Antrieb –, der von einer gewissen Dringlichkeit bestimmt ist, führt zu dritten Räumen, für die – in Joanne Pouzencs Worten gesprochen – „freiwilliges Engagement und Selbstermächtigung als Rohstoff" gelten. Das Endprodukt reicht weit über die formalen Strukturen

devising real solutions for the urban realm, we are no longer in a position to think within the comfort of sectors and specialisations. Diversity and collaborative thinking are vital and necessary as the systemic change we need requires multiple perspectives and shared responsibilities.

This volume, "Make City", sets out to reflect the heterogeneity of positions that are actively moving in new directions and shaping urban alternatives at every level, from urban governance to our use - and re-use - of resources. The urgency of our diminishing natural and spatial resources and the resulting need for shared practices and cooperative, socially just city-making are at the heart of the pioneering discourse featured throughout this compendium.

For the many new typologies that are currently emerging, such as those inspired in part by the nineteenth-century avant-garde model of the Berlin courtyard that allowed for a multiplicity of uses, it is clear that negotiation is essential: whether this relates to agencies like Plateau Urbain harnessing large, obsolete structures for temporary use; to municipalities offering developers an extra floor for curated ground floor sites offering socio-cultural use within a newly developed district; or to architects manipulating every possible loophole that exists within regulatory parameters. The results are unique - or better yet, proto-typical - and they are marked by bursts of ingenuity that are often prompted by radical propositions, engendering something greater than any defined building type can offer: schools become open plan concepts, for instance, mirroring the most innovative approaches to learning and they can be anchored onto other parts of the urban infrastructure or they can offer spaces that are open for local activities. A terraced building for studios and small businesses leads to shared gardening and cooperative ownership of livestock, and thereby generates a sense of community around working hours. An art project evolves into a key identifier for migropolitanism and an entirely new civic agenda. Sometimes architecture is stripped of its vanities, and, as naked infrastructure, is re-negotiated and re-conceived for a range of incomes and uses. And in each instance, dialogue and hard-won bargaining between all of the protagonists are critical to extracting the maximum possibilities from what might otherwise appear to be spatial, financial and material limitations.

Although dialogue-driven design is often seen by developers and local administrations as

und architektonischen Elemente selbst hinaus: Solche dritten Räume sind für die laufende Evolution von Gemeinschaften von zentraler Bedeutung.

Grundlegend für die hier versammelten Positionen – von den Grundlagentexten bis hin zu den Fallstudien, die sie unterstützen – ist die Überzeugung, dass wir im gegenwärtigen Klima nicht länger in der Komfortzone von Sektoren und Spezialisierungen denken dürfen, wenn wir konkrete Lösungen im urbanen Bereich finden wollen. Weil systemischer Wandel vielfältige Perspektiven und geteilte Verantwortlichkeiten erfordert, sind Vielseitigkeit und kollaboratives Denken entscheidend und notwendig.

„Make City" spiegelt daher die Heterogenität der Positionen, die sich in neue Richtungen bewegen und auf allen Ebenen urbane Alternativen prägen: von der Stadtregierung bis hin zu unserer Nutzung – und Wiederverwendung – von Rohstoffen. Die Dringlichkeit unserer schwindenden natürlichen und räumlichen Ressourcen und die daraus hervorgehende Notwendigkeit einer gemeinsamen Praxis und der kooperativen, gesellschaftlich gerechten Stadtgestaltung bilden den Kern eines wegweisenden Diskurses in diesem Sammelband.

Die vielen aufkommenden Typologien – beispielsweise jene, die zum Teil vom Avantgarde-Modell des Berliner Hinterhofs aus dem 19. Jahrhundert inspiriert sind, der eine Vielzahl von Nutzungen zuließ – zeigen klar, dass es ums Aushandeln geht: von Büros wie Plateau Urbain, die große, ausgemusterte Strukturen temporär nutzbar machen, bis hin zu Stadtverwaltungen, die Entwickler*innen eine zusätzliche Etage überlassen, wenn sie im Gegenzug Erdgeschossflächen in einem neu entwickelten Bezirk soziokulturell bespielen, oder Architekt*innen, die jedes rechtliche Schlupfloch kreativ (aus)nutzen. Die Ergebnisse sind einzigartig oder vielmehr: prototypisch. Ihr Einfallsreichtum ist mitreißend und oft von radikalen Entwürfen inspiriert, die Größeres hervorbringen, als irgendein (vor)bestimmter Bautypus es je bieten könnte: Schulen werden zu Großraumkonzepten, in denen sich innovativste Ansätze von Lernen widerspiegeln. Sie können mit anderen Teilen der städtischen Infrastruktur verbunden werden oder selbst Raum für nachbarschaftliche Aktivitäten bieten. Ein Terrassengebäude für Ateliers und kleine Unternehmen schließt sogar Gemeinschaftsgärten und kollektive Viehhaltung ein. Aus dem Arbeitsalltag erwächst Gemeinschaftssinn. Ein Kunstprojekt entwickelt sich zu einem Symbol für Migrationspolitik – und zeugt von einer gänzlich neuen zivilgesellschaftlichen Agenda. Manchmal werden der Architektur

time-consuming, risky and costly, at the heart of the conversations and statements that form the backbone of this compendium, we find that particular attention is being paid to creating added value throughout engaged design processes. The pioneering spirit that underlies collaborative design testifies to the value of extending any commission: staking out lesser-known opportunities in order to contribute to society building while at the same time testing the instruments of civic entrepreneurship. Whether or not the spaces that result can be defined as third spaces, it is clear that the process of accommodating a multiplicity of interests and paying attention to particular needs and identities that are too often overlooked can generate value that is simply unquantifiable in monetary terms.

With "Make City", we have sought out and commissioned essential statements and case studies that take into account the urgent need to synthesise a wide range of knowledge on urban resources. At the level of resource and material flows, cities are the most important sites for the fundamental re-think that is required; we need to move from linear economic and production systems that simply produce waste to establishing and embracing circular economies and systems, and we need to break the pattern of built-in obsolescence that determines our current economic system. As Anupama Kundoo highlights in her practice, our dwindling material resources require listening to and reflecting upon collective wisdom across specialised fields, oftentimes returning to local or multi-generational wisdom, in particular when it comes to building for climate change. Whether advocating for the environmental advantages of wood-built architecture, plant-based cooling systems or radical re-use strategies, the statements and case studies that follow in this book coalesce to form a position in which urban realms and resource cycles are resolutely interconnected.

Urban alternatives also encompass the crucial interplay between urban spaces and nature, itself a spatial and material resource. Martin Rein-Cano points out that "architectural movements have tended to separate, organise and sort experience and typologies into distinct categories". Just as it is no longer tenable to build monostructural or monocultural urban districts, so the landscape architecture featured here liberates design and moves beyond grey and green infrastructures: the time has come to hybridise! By interweaving nature with the built environment and by regarding infrastructure as a resource that has the ability

ihre Eitelkeiten entzogen, und sie wird als nackte Infrastruktur für eine Bandbreite von Einkommenssituationen und Nutzungsmöglichkeiten neu verhandelt und neu konzipiert. In jedem Fall sind der Dialog und mühsame Aushandlungen zwischen allen Beteiligten entscheidend, um ein Maximum an Möglichkeiten aus dem herauszuholen, was sonst räumlich, finanziell und materiell beschränkt erscheint.

Obwohl dialogorientiertes Planen von Entwicklungsfirmen und lokalen Verwaltungen oft als zeitraubendes, risikoreiches und kostenintensives Unterfangen angesehen wird, finden wir im Kern der Gespräche und Erklärungen in diesem Band eine besondere Aufmerksamkeit dafür, welche zusätzlichen Werte in solchen engagierten Gestaltungsprozessen geschaffen werden. Das wegweisende Engagement, das kollaborativer Planung zugrunde liegt, belegt den Wert erweiterter Gremien. Weniger bekannte Möglichkeiten einzusetzen, trägt zu einer Form des gesellschaftlichen Aufbaus bei. Zugleich werden so die Instrumente des zivilgesellschaftlichen Unternehmertums erprobt. Ob die daraus hervorgehenden Räume nun als dritte Räume, auch bekannt als Mischnutzungsprojekte, definiert werden können oder nicht – eines ist klar: Die Berücksichtigung einer Vielzahl von Interessen und die Achtsamkeit für bestimmte, viel zu oft übergangene Bedürfnisse und Identitäten erzeugen einen Wert, der monetär schlicht nicht erfassbar ist!

Für „Make City" haben wir Grundlagentexte und Fallstudien ausgesucht bzw. in Auftrag gegeben, die die dringende Forderung nach der Zusammenfassung einer größeren Wissensbandbreite hinsichtlich urbaner Ressourcen berücksichtigen. Auf der Ebene der Rohstoff- und Materialflüsse sind Städte die wichtigsten Orte für ein grundlegendes Umdenken, das notwendig ist. Wir müssen uns von linearen Wirtschafts- und Produktionssystemen, die Einwegabfall produzieren, verabschieden und stattdessen Kreislaufökonomien und -systeme errichten und fördern. Wir müssen auch mit dem Schema der eingebauten Obsoleszenz brechen, das unser gegenwärtiges Wirtschaftssystem bestimmt. Wie Anupama Kundoo in ihrer Praxis betont, verlangen unsere schwindenden materiellen Ressourcen, dass wir über Nischen hinaus auf die kollektive Weisheit hören und ihr folgen, was uns häufig zu lokalem und älterem Wissen zurückführt, insbesondere, wenn es um Bauprojekte gegen den fortschreitenden Klimawandel geht. Egal, ob sie die ökologischen Vorteile des Baustoffs Holz herausarbeiten, sich für Kühlsysteme auf Pflanzenbasis oder radikale Wiederverwendungsstrategien aussprechen: Die zitierten Aussagen und vorgestellten Fallstudien eint ihre Position, nach der

to open and extend the aesthetic potential of urban natures, landscape architects and engineers play a key role in formulating new narratives for urban spaces and mobility. Urban food production also becomes one of the building blocks of urban development by merging landscape design with supply systems and infrastructure. The pragmatism of the engineer combined with the multi-faceted approach of the landscape designer can lead to unique solutions for public spaces that are increasingly compromised by extreme rainfall; it can turn residual landscapes into gathering places, and obsolete buildings into new hybrids, including foodscapes such as Berlin's Thai Park, urban jungles like those found in the Taitung Ruin Academy of Taiwan, or recreational sites such as Flussbad Berlin that are inserted at unexpected junctures within the urban fabric.

Finally, whom are we addressing with this compendium? We hope that these statements, exhortations, prototypes and case studies make clear that the best examples of resilience and the need for change in our increasingly overpopulated cities involve everyone. Architecture, landscape architecture and urban planning are about climate, land speculation, making the most of our public spaces and infrastructure, and building for diverse identities and cultures. Heterogeneity is something to be embraced and fostered; it is only through multiple perspectives and a broad range of positions that we can imagine and implement new urban models for living together.

alle urbanen Bereiche und Ressourcenkreisläufe miteinander verbunden sind.

Urbane Alternativen umfassen auch das wichtige Zusammenspiel zwischen städtischem Raum und Natur, das selbst eine räumliche und materielle Ressource darstellt. Martin Rein-Cano stellt heraus, dass Architekturströmungen dazu neigten, Erfahrungen und Typologien in getrennte Kategorien aufzuteilen, zu organisieren und zu sortieren. Die Zeit für Hybridisierung ist aber reif! So wie es nicht mehr tragbar ist, ganze Stadtviertel mit einer einzigen Baustruktur oder für eine einzige Bevölkerungsgruppe zu planen, kämpft sich die hier vorgestellte Landschaftsarchitektur aus den Designvorgaben frei und geht über graue und grüne Infrastrukturen hinaus. Sie verwebt die Natur mit der baulichen Umgebung und betrachtet die Infrastruktur als Ressource, die das ästhetische Potenzial städtischer Natur eröffnen und erweitern kann. Dadurch spielen Landschaftsarchitekt*innen und -ingenieur*innen eine entscheidende Rolle. Sie formulieren neue Narrative für urbane Räume und Mobilität. Auch die städtische Lebensmittelproduktion wird zu einem der Bauelemente urbaner Entwicklung, indem Landschaftsplanung mit Liefersystemen und Infrastrukturen gestalterisch verwoben wird. Die Kombination aus dem Pragmatismus des Ingenieurwesens und den vielseitigen Ansätzen der Landschaftsplanung kann zu einzigartigen Lösungen für öffentliche Räume führen, die zunehmend extremen Niederschlägen ausgesetzt sind. Sie kann Wohngebiete in Treffpunkte verwandeln und veraltete Gebäude in neue Hybride. „Esslandschaften" – sogenannte Foodscapes – wie der Berliner Thai-Park, urbane Dschungel wie der in der Taitung Ruin Academy oder Freizeitflächen wie das „Flussbad" mitsamt Parklandschaft schaffen unerwartete Verbindungen im städtischen Gebilde.

Wen wollen wir mit diesem Kompendium des Andersmachens ansprechen? Wir hoffen, dass alle enthaltenen Erklärungen, Mahnungen, Fallstudien und Prototypen deutlich machen, dass die besten Beispiele der Resilienz und der Notwendigkeit für Veränderung in unseren zunehmend überbevölkerten Städten uns alle angehen. Architektur, Landschaftsarchitektur und Stadtplanung drehen sich ums Klima und um Bodenspekulation, versuchen, aus unseren öffentlichen Flächen und Infrastrukturen das Beste zu machen und für vielfältige Menschen und Kulturen zu bauen. Heterogenität müssen wir begrüßen und fördern; denn nur durch multiple Perspektiven und eine große Bandbreite an Positionen finden wir zu neuen urbanen Modellen des Zusammenlebens.

Land, Ownership, Financing Models and Developing the City

Grund und Boden, Eigentum, Entwicklungs- und Finanzierungsmodelle

1

Land, Ownership, Financing Models and Developing the City

Grund und Boden, Eigentum, Entwicklungs- und Finanzierungsmodelle

Berlin has sold off 220,000 publicly owned residential units since the 1990s at a value of 1.3 billion euros. Since 2017, 260,000 residential units of social housing have been planned for 2030.

Berlin hat seit den 1990er Jahren 220.000 Wohnungen aus öffentlichem Eigentum im Wert von 1,3 Milliarden Euro verkauft. Im Jahr 2017 wurde der Bau von 100.000 neuen Sozialwohnungen beschlossen, die bis 2030 entstehen sollen.

Since 2001, more than 6,000 plots of publicly owned land in Berlin, totalling over 14 million square metres, were sold off. In Amsterdam, no public land is sold, as all land is owned and leased through the municipality.

Seit 2001 wurden in Berlin mehr als 6.000 Grundstücke (über 14 Millionen Quadratmeter) aus öffentlichem Besitz verkauft. Amsterdam verkauft 0 Prozent öffentliches Land. Das gesamte Land bleibt im Besitz der Gemeinde und wird von ihr vermietet.

Between 2015 and 2018, Berlin repurchased 28 residential properties with a total budget of 100 million euros to remove rental housing units from the property market.

Seit 2015 hat Berlin 28 Wohnimmobilien zurückgekauft, um dem Spekulationsmarkt Mieteinheiten zu entziehen. Hundert Millionen Euro Gesamtbudget stehen dafür bereit.

After 25 years of financial mismanagement and speculation in the Netherlands, the 2015 "New Housing Act" stipulates that only non-profit enterprises are eligible to build social housing.

Nach 25 Jahren finanzieller Misswirtschaft und Spekulation beschließen die Niederlande 2015 einen „New Housing Act". Er sieht vor, dass nur gemeinnützige Unternehmen Sozialwohnungen bauen dürfen.

Sources / Quellen:
Knight Frank Global Residential Cities Index Q4 2017, Guthmann Estate, Guardian, UK Department for Communities and Local Government, New Economics Foundation, Berliner Morgenpost, Guggenheim, City of Amsterdam, Handelsblatt Global, German Constitution, Housing Europe, Amsterdam Federation of Housing Associations

In 2018, Berlin was the number one city worldwide for real estate speculation.

2018 war Berlin weltweit die Nummer eins im Bereich Immobilienspekulation.

Between 2008 and 2023, Berlin apartment prices will increase by 450 percent. Within the district of Neukölln, values will increase by 800 percent.

Zwischen 2008 und 2023 stiegen und steigen die Berliner Wohnungspreise um das 450-Fache. Im Bezirk Neukölln beträgt das Wachstum 800 Prozent.

Article 14 of the German Basic Law states: "Property entails obligations. Its use shall also serve the public good."

Artikel 14 der deutschen Verfassung sagt: „Eigentum verpflichtet. Sein Gebrauch soll zugleich dem Wohle der Allgemeinheit dienen."

80 percent of homes built in London are affordable for only the city's wealthiest 8 percent.

Achtzig Prozent der in London gebauten Häuser sind nur für die reichsten acht Prozent der Stadt erschwinglich.

In October 2018, Alphabet's plans to develop a 3,000-square-metre Google campus in the Kreuzberg district of Berlin were abandoned after three years of community protest.

Im Oktober 2018 wurden, nach drei Jahren Protest der Bevölkerung, die Pläne von „Alphabet", in Berlin einen 3.000 Quadratmeter großen Google-Campus zu errichten, aufgegeben.

As housing prices continue to rise faster than income, millennials will be the first generation to be at a disadvantage. In the UK, parents have become the ninth largest mortgage lender.

Millennials sind als erste Generation von steigenden Immobilienpreisen und verlangsamtem Einkommenswachstum betroffen. Ihre Elterngeneration wird zum neuntgrößten Hypothekengeber Großbritanniens.

British targets to build 160,000 residential units will be reached twelve years late if public land continues to be sold off at a rate of 813 residential units per month. Between 2015 and 2017, 127 plots of public land were sold off to the highest bidder.

Das Ziel des Vereinigten Königreichs, 160.000 neue Wohneinheiten zu bauen, wird nach zwölf Jahren erreicht, während öffentliches Land weiterhin mit 813 Wohneinheiten pro Monat verkauft wird. Zwischen 2015 und 2017 wurden 127 Grundstücke an Meistbietende verkauft.

Overcoming Old Dependencies

Empathic Economy and Co-operative Urban Transformation

The political and social mainstream - flanked by the media - continues to drive a resource-intensive economy. In the economic paradigm of the twentieth century, people and societies are being reduced to their functionality. Doubts, however, are mounting because neither the findings of the Intergovernmental Panel on Climate Change (IPCC) nor socio-economic developments can be ignored any longer. The global repercussions of climate change, economic development and the movements of displaced people - all of which extend beyond borders - are changing our understanding of the world. Income and wealth disparities, exacerbated by low income levels and a lack of ownership on real value and material assets, have led to dangerous levels of societal inequality that range from unequal access to education and a lack of opportunities for the young in an increasingly precarious job market and exacerbated poverty among the aged. Rapidly increasing material deprivation contributes enormously to the inequalities in our society. The possibility of home ownership, as well as access to material assets and social security, is now depleted, resulting in a destabilisation of societal participation. As a consequence, social cohesion and peace are eroded, as well as democratic participation and self-motivated agency. The principal strength and capacity of civil society to support inclusion, integration and adaptibility - to create and stabilise the common good - depends on the extent to which people are self-motivated and able to contribute to their community at large.

What is happening in cities, beyond the administrative and political levels? A research project I led together with Gerhard Scherhorn, financed by the German Federal Ministry of Education and Research (Bundesministerium für Bildung und Forschung), yielded representative data on the sector of community-oriented urban subsistence. The research showed that around five billion unpaid hours per year are spent voluntarily carrying out community-oriented work in the public realm in Germany,with around two thirds of our citizens contributing to this statistic. However, the opportunity to empathetically contribute to the greater good continues to dwindle. Increasingly, the rising pressures to earn adequate salaries are

Alte Abhängigkeiten überwinden

Empathische Ökonomie und kooperativer Stadtwandel

Der politische Mainstream konsolidiert, medial flankiert, eine ressourcenintensive Wirtschaft. Darin werden Menschen und Gesellschaften auf ihre ökonomische Funktionalität in einem Entwicklungsparadigma des 20. Jahrhunderts reduziert. Zwar mehren sich Zweifel, denn weder die Befunde des Weltklimarats IPCC noch die sozioökonomische Entwicklung lassen sich dauerhaft ignorieren. Die Erfahrung globaler grenzüberschreitender Wirkungen durch Klimawandel, Wirtschaftsentwicklung oder Fluchtbewegungen verändern das Verständnis unserer Welt. Die Einkommens- und Vermögensdisparitäten durch niedrige Lohnniveaus bei fehlenden Sachwerten haben eine gefährliche gesellschaftliche Ungerechtigkeit erschaffen, die von Bildungs- und Chancenungleichheiten für Junge über prekäre Beschäftigungsverhältnisse bis hin zu Altersarmut reicht. Die wachsende materielle Deprivation erhöht die Ungleichheiten unserer Gesellschaft erheblich, indem sie aufgrund fehlenden Wohneigentums, fehlender Sachwerte, fehlender sozialer Sicherheit die Möglichkeit zur gesellschaftlichen Teilnahme verstellt. In der Folge erodieren sozialer Frieden und Zusammenhalt, demokratische Teilhabe und eigenmotiviertes Handeln. Kraft und Fähigkeit einer Bürgergesellschaft zu Inklusion, Integration, zu Widerstands- und Anpassungsfähigkeit, zur Schaffung und Stabilisierung des Gemeinwohls hängen davon ab, wieweit Menschen sich eigenmotiviert in die Gemeinschaft einbringen können.

Was passiert in Städten jenseits dessen, was kommunal und politisch realisiert wird? Aus einem BMBF-Forschungsprojekt, das ich bis 2004 mit Gerhard Scherhorn leitete, ergab sich eine repräsentative Empirie zur gemeinschaftsorientierten – urbanen – Subsistenz. Rund fünf Milliarden Stunden werden jährlich freiwillig und unbezahlt gemeinschaftsorientiert im öffentlichen Raum in Deutschland geleistet. Dazu tragen rund zwei Drittel unserer Bürger*innen bei. Doch die Möglichkeiten, sich empathisch gemeinwohldienlich einzubringen, schwinden. Der Erwerbsdruck prägt immer dominanter die Biografien von Menschen, und Zeit wie Raum für Gemeinschaftsorientierung werden knapper. Städte sind kaum mehr inklusions- oder integrationsfähig. Noch sind sie in der Lage, kulturelle Identitäten zu stärken oder Veränderungsprozesse zu ermöglichen. Seitens der westlich-europäischen Industriestaaten wurde der Rest der Welt

impacting human biographies. Time and space for community-oriented activities is being reduced. The cities of the present are now scarcely capable of facilitating inclusion or integration; nor do they have the capacity to encourage cultural identities or for transformative processes to unfold. For generations, the rest of the world has been misused to supply Western European countries' hunger for land, resources and productivity, as well as becoming a sinkhole for our waste, emissions and social costs - our negative externalisations. We abuse the planet, other cultures and economies, and now it is our turn. Migratory movements are one consequence; another is the weakened fabric of our civil society. Our population has never experienced such high income and wealth disparity. And in Berlin, we are experiencing this process in fast forward.

Seldom do we discuss whether it is useful for our society that ever-increasing tracts of living space serve to benefit an ever-smaller, excessively high-income sector of the population, while at the same time, a social worker, a nurse, a cashier, a mechanic, a primary school teacher, a scientist or even a professor pay off the equivalent of two or three apartments by way of rental costs. At the end of their professional lives they have no property and are threatened by poverty. Our national economy must compensate for the costs of social inequality, old-age poverty, low reserves etc., even though, in effect, these socio-economic consequences are the results of the externalisation (equal to passing on the burden) of costs by private economic interests, namely, for cheap labour, for low unit wage costs, for the commercial utilisation of public spaces, building plots and real estate.

Our formerly social market economy has been displaced by an expansionist form of finance capitalism. At the regulatory level, nothing has been done to lessen this - quite the contrary. In recent decades, the Enlightenment's notion of a market economy that maintains and strengthens its production base and that, in principle, is capable of facilitating market participation for all has been almost completely destroyed by profit-oriented thinking. Whosoever dares to address this damaging dynamic of finance capitalism - an ideology that threatens both life and society - risks very quickly being stigmatised.

The founder of ordoliberalism, Walter Eucken, wrestled with the problem of marrying unimpeded development with community good: "Whoever benefits must also carry the costs." Regu-

generationenlang als Quelle unseres Land-, Rohstoff- und Produktivitätshungers missbraucht und als Senke unserer Abfälle, Emissionen und sozialen Kosten – umfassender negativer Externalisierungen (= Abwälzungen) – entwürdigt. Wir missbrauchen den Planeten, andere Kulturen und Volkswirtschaften, und nun sind wir selbst an der Reihe. Migrationsbewegungen sind eine der Folgen, ebenso wie unsere geschwächte Bürgergesellschaft. Wir haben so hohe Einkommens- und Vermögensunterschiede wie noch nie zuvor. In Berlin erleben wir dies im Zeitraffer.

Wenig wird diskutiert, ob es gesellschaftlichen Nutzen bringt, dass immer mehr Wohnraum einer immer kleineren, übermäßig verdienenden Bevölkerungsgruppe zugutekommt, während Sozialpädagog*innen, Krankenpfleger*innen, Kassierer*innen, Handwerker*innen, Grundschullehrer*innen oder auch Wissenschaftler*innen in ihrem Berufsleben zwar den Wert von zwei bis drei Eigentumswohnungen über Mietzahlungen abstottern, doch am Ende keine davon besitzen und von Altersarmut bedroht sind. Die sozioökonomischen Folgekosten von Ungleichheit, Altersarmut, fehlenden Rücklagen usw. muss die Volkswirtschaft – an günstigen Arbeitskräften, niedrigen Lohnstückkosten, öffentlichen Flächen, Baugrundstücken oder Immobilien – ausgleichen, obwohl diese Externalisierungen aus privatwirtschaftlichen Interessen resultieren.

Unsere ehemals soziale Marktwirtschaft wurde von einer expansiven, finanzkapitalistischen Wirtschaftsform verdrängt und ordnungspolitisch dem nichts entgegengesetzt, im Gegenteil. Die Profitorientierung hat den aufklärerischen Gedanken einer Marktwirtschaft, die ihre Produktionsgrundlagen erhält und stärkt und prinzipiell allen Menschen die Teilnahme ermöglicht, fast vollständig zerstört. Wer die lebens- und gesellschaftsschädigende Dynamik der Ideologie des Finanzkapitalismus angreift, wird schnell stigmatisiert.

Der Begründer des Ordoliberalismus, Walter Eucken, rang damit, freiheitliche Entfaltung und Gemeinschaftsorientierung zusammenzubringen: „Wer den Nutzen hat, muss auch die Kosten tragen." Ordnungspolitik sollte staatliche Raison ersetzen und der Erweiterung von Freiheitsgraden dienen. Dass Liberalismus und Marktwirtschaft ursprünglich ein Gegenentwurf zur demokratiefeindlichen Figur eines entgrenzten, unregulierten Kapitalismus waren, ist vielen Wirtschaftspraktiker*innen – und -theoretiker*innen – heute nicht mehr präsent. Der stark medial legitimierten Aufladung einer per se verrückten Vorstellung wirtschaftskonformer Gesellschaftsentwicklung steht die klimaökologische und sozio-

latory policy should replace state interests and serve the expansion of degrees of freedom. The combined notions of liberalism and the market economy – which both originated as counter-projects to the spectre of a borderless, unregulated and fundamentally anti-democratic capitalism – are currently, for many market practitioners and theorists, no longer on the table. A highly mediated, loaded and essentially insane projection of societal development conforming with economic development is set in opposition to the ecological, climate-based and socio-economic reality, with empirical findings either ignored or trivialised. Short-term profits for a societal minority are prioritised, to the detriment of disproportionately high semi- and longterm costs and burdens for citizens, national economies and entire regions. We are destroying natural and social spaces in order to avoid conflict with a small number of asset-holders. We have more than enough cause to reorient ourselves politically. The economy should serve the greater good for people and communities in order to have legitimacy – this is enshrined in our Basic Law. And yet the private sector's obligation to serve the common good is still not legally enforceable. A political order with a regulatory policy that serves the common good would be one that facilitates the justicie of public shared interests against private economic interests, so that negative externalisations no longer reward the companies at fault with higher profits and competitive advantage. Instead, the market order should support the externalisation of sustainable and social benefits.

However, until today, the political system insists on subsidising the welfare system through taxable income from an economy built on earnings. In order to keep pace with constant growth in productivity, it is necessary to maintain constant economic growth together with a consistent growth in demand in order to generate an adequate amount of taxable income. Because of this, an economy built on earnings is forced to rely on the continual supply of energy, resources and cheap labour – as well as the externalisation of negative social and ecological repercussions – in order to reduce costs and remain competitive. The consequence of this is that ecological and social commons (our shared assets) become overburdened and degraded. This mode of securing our welfare is fatefully dependent, through its economic praxis, on depriving itself of its material and immaterial requirements for existence (and production) – and in this sense, it is destined to fail. The capitalist economic paradigm debunks itself of its own accord in that

ökonomische Wirklichkeit gegenüber, deren empirische Befunde weiterhin mühsam ignoriert oder bagatellisiert werden. Kurzfristige Gewinne für gesellschaftliche Minoritäten werden priorisiert, zuungunsten überproportional hoher mittel- und langfristiger Kosten und Belastungen für Bürger*innen, Volkswirtschaften und ganze Regionen. Wir zerstören Natur- und Sozialräume, um nicht mit einer Minderheit von Vermögenden in Konflikt zu geraten. Dass Ökonomie dem Gemeinwohl der Menschen dienen muss, um sich zu legitimieren – das steht in unserer Verfassung. Doch justiziabel ist die Gemeinwohlverpflichtung des Privatgutes bislang kaum. Eine gemeinwohldienliche Ordo muss die Justiziabilität gemeinschaftlicher Interessen gegenüber privatwirtschaftlichen Interessen ermöglichen, sodass negative Externalisierungen für die verursachenden Unternehmen nicht mehr mit höheren Profiten und Wettbewerbsvorteilen belohnt werden, sondern umgekehrt die Marktordnung die Externalisierung von ökologischem und sozialem Nutzen unterstützt.

Doch bislang finanziert die Politik das Wohlfahrtssystem aus steuerlichen Erträgen der Erwerbswirtschaft. Um mit den stetigen Produktivitätszuwächsen Schritt zu halten, erfordert dies stetiges Wirtschaftswachstum sowie eine stetig steigende Nachfrage, um ausreichend Erwerbsarbeit und dadurch besteuerbares Erwerbseinkommen zu generieren. Damit ist die Erwerbswirtschaft zwanghaft auf beständige Zufuhr von Energie, Rohstoffen, billige Arbeit angewiesen sowie auf die Externalisierung negativer sozialer und ökologischer Effekte, um Kosten zu senken und wettbewerbsfähig zu bleiben. Die Konsequenz sind die Überlastung und Degradation der ökologischen und sozialen Grundlagen und Ressourcen – unserer Gemeinschaftsgüter. Diese Wohlfahrtssicherung beruht darauf, dass sie sich mittels der Wirtschaftspraxis ihre materiellen wie immateriellen Lebens- (und Produktions-) grundlagen selbst entzieht. Sie ist zum Scheitern verurteilt. Das kapitalistische Wirtschaftsparadigma widerlegt sich selbst:

1) Es vernichtet die eigenen Produktionsgrundlagen, ohne ihre Regenerationsbedingungen zu berücksichtigen,
2) überführt ihren Nutzen in Finanzkapital und akkumuliert dieses bei immer wenigeren, sodass
3) die Möglichkeit zur Teilnahme am Marktgeschehen der Mehrzahl der Menschen verstellt ist.

Auf diese Weise wird der Kapitalismus zum Gegenteil der Marktwirtschaft und verunmöglicht zugleich Zukunftsfähigkeit. Wirtschaft soll den Menschen zur Verwirklichung gemeinschaftlichen und

1) it destroys its own production bases, without taking into account the conditions required for regeneration;
2) it transfers its use into finance capital, which is accumulated into the hands of ever-fewer players, such that
3) the possibility for participating in market activity is out of reach for the majority of people.

In this way, capitalism is transformed, becoming the absolute opposite of the market economy, and rendering future sustainability redundant. Economies should serve people in the development of shared and individual well-being. Like politics and justice, economy is a subsystem of society, legitimised through societal agreements. Instead, the political order facilitates the destruction of production bases. Bit by bit, economic praxis is withdrawing each and every foundation of life, and is pushing ever-more players from the market. In this way, we are destroying the functionality of markets, our civil society and nature, which support us all. This is the main result of our politics, which has allowed this process to continue for years, has regulatorily and strategically encouraged and legitimised it - and internationally exported it. Trapped in the fossils of models of thought from the twentieth century, Western European-influenced industrial societies insist on their path dependencies, even as they are no longer capable of fulfilling the promise of limitless progress and increasing prosperity.

However, new understandings of the economy are forming, particularly among the young, that are geared towards overcoming old dependencies, drawing on new technological possibilities. New technologies are capable of repressing established hierarchical organisational structures and facilitating pluralistic models of governance. Indicators of these possibilities include the testing and training of new social communities, in which borders along the lines of nations, cultures and languages are increasingly dissolved. The sharing economy is proving to be far more useful and resource-friendly than the relentless accumulation of owned goods and capital. Entrepreneurial approaches to making use of collaboration and decentralisation as competitive factors are coming to the fore, with digital infrastructures such as blockchain, the internet of things, and Artificial Intelligence using and strengthening subsidiarity. Here, a new relationship between humans and the economy is forming, in which plurality, difference and subsidiarity repress and dissolve the old, moribund hierarchies and governance models.

individuellen Wohlstandes dienen. Sie ist wie Politik und Recht ein Subsystem der Gesellschaft, legitimiert durch gesellschaftliche Übereinkünfte.

Doch der ordnungspolitische Rahmen ermöglicht die Vernichtung der Produktionsgrundlagen. Die ökonomische Praxis entzieht allen schrittweise die Lebensgrundlagen und verdrängt immer mehr Akteure von den Märkten. So zerstören wir die Funktionalität von Märkten, unserer Bürgergesellschaft und der Natur, die uns trägt. Dies ist das Hauptergebnis unserer Politik, die diese Prozesse seit Jahren ermöglicht, regulativ und strategisch befördert und legitimiert – und international exportiert. Verfangen im fossilen Denken des 20. Jahrhunderts verharren die westlich-europäisch geprägten Industriegesellschaften in ihren Pfadabhängigkeiten, obwohl sie die Verheißungen grenzenlosen Fortschritts und stetigen Wohlstandszuwachses nicht mehr erfüllen.

Doch besonders bei Jüngeren zeichnet sich ein anderes, neues Verständnis von Ökonomie ab, das alte Abhängigkeiten überwinden will. Neue Technologien sind in der Lage, etablierte hierarchische Strukturen zu verdrängen und pluralistische Governancemodelle zu ermöglichen. Indikatoren sind etwa die Ausbildung neuer Communitys, die nationale, kulturelle und sprachliche Grenzen immer weiter auflösen. Sharing Economy erweist sich als nützlicher und ressourcenschonender als grenzenlose Güter- und Kapitalakkumulation. Unternehmerische Ansätze, die Kollaboration und Dezentralität als Wettbewerbsfaktoren nutzen, sind dabei, sich durchzusetzen; digitale Infrastrukturen wie Blockchain, Internet of Things, Artificial Intelligence nutzen und stärken Subsidiarität. Hier bildet sich ein neues Verhältnis zwischen Menschen und Wirtschaft heraus. Pluralität, Differenz und Subsidiarität beginnen, alte erstarrte Hierarchie- und Governancemodelle zu verdrängen und abzulösen.

In diesen Dynamiken verändern sich auch die nun veralteten Vorstellungen von Eigentum und ökonomischer Teilhabe. Während die Rolle des Staates als Treuhänder natürlicher, sozialer und kultureller Gemeinschaftsgüter nicht gut funktionierte, setzten sich zunehmend neue Konzepte von Eigentümerschaft durch. Etwa eine demokratische Eigentümerschaft mittels Wiederaneignung öffentlicher Güter, um diese vor der Kurzsichtigkeit, Inkompetenz und Profitgier politischer Akteure und ökonomischer Interessengruppen zu schützen und unter die Governance der beteiligten Menschen statt von Staaten und Regierungen zu stellen.

Das alte Menschenbild ist nicht geeignet, Empathie in Freiheit zu befördern. Es fehlt am institutionellen

In the dynamics traced here, outdated notions of property and economic participation are changing. While the role of the state as custodian of natural, social, and cultural common goods has not functioned well, new concepts of property are increasingly emerging. For example, a democratic notion of ownership reappropriates public goods in order to protect them from the short-sightedness, incompetency and greed of political players and economic interest-groups, bringing them under the governance of the people involved, instead of states and governments.

The old understanding of human nature is not well-suited to encouraging empathy in freedom and institutions lack a fundamental faith in people's capability for responsibility and collaboration. But life experience teaches us otherwise. If you create a clearing - a void - in a monocultural forest, it will, in time, be populated by a multiplicity of species - as 3.8 billion years of evolution has shown us.

Zutrauen in einen verantwortungs- und kollaborationsfähigen Menschen. Doch die Erfahrung des Lebendigen lehrt uns anderes. Schafft man innerhalb eines Monokulturwaldes eine Freifläche, Lichtung – einen Leerraum –, wird diese von einer Vielzahl unterschiedlicher Arten besiedelt und bespielt werden – und das ganz von allein, wie 3,8 Milliarden Jahre Evolution uns zeigen.

A laboratory for cultural use in an historic urban fabric: Alte Münze at Molkenmarkt

Die Alte Münze am Molkenmarkt: Zivilgesellschaftliches Labor für kulturelle Nutzung historischer Bausubstanz

"Land is not a commodity that can be multiplied at will. And scarce, urban land must be used in such a way that it serves the common good as comprehensively and substantially as possible."

„Boden ist keine Ware, die man beliebig vermehren kann. Und gerade knapper, städtischer Boden muss so eingesetzt werden, dass er dem Gemeinwohl möglichst umfassend und substanziell dient."

Frauke Burgdorff

Hold onto Land and Shape It!

A New Land Policy on Good Grounds

For cities worldwide, land speculation is increasingly unsustainable. One of the consequences is that low-income households spend too much money on rent, often more than 40 percent of their income. In Berlin, between 2008 and 2018, prices for land slated for construction rose by 350 percent. Frauke Burgdorff is committed to addressing questions around community-oriented urban and real estate development. In light of this detrimental situation, she demands an end to speculation. Land should be controlled - permanently - by the public hand and community-oriented owners.

Land is the basis for each and every urban development and it is the question I have been dealing with for around the last ten years. Without land, spaces for living - for providing the basis of existence - and for free and green areas would no longer exist. Land is a special commodity and it cannot be reproduced. It is in short supply, and those who own it give it back only rarely, if at all. Land policy is shaped above all by those who own land. Today, this primarily means the private sector.

With ownership comes responsibility: the federal government, the states, and the municipalities own land. They are also subject to - at the very least - the same responsibilities as private owners, if not greater ones. However, the public sector has been generous with land in recent history. It has sold land in order to rehabilitate its budgets, either directly or through the privatisation of public and non-profit companies.

Holding onto land is a fundamentally conservative project

Selling off land in accordance with this "one-way street principle" means relinquishing it from the public sphere forever - and with it, relinquishing the most important lever for good urban development. The public hand must therefore hold onto its land! When used to replenish the public

Boden halten und gestalten!

Für eine neue Politik aus gutem Grund

Die weltweite Spekulation mit Boden wird für Städte zunehmend untragbar. Eine der Folgen: Haushalte mit niedrigem Einkommen geben zu viel für die Miete aus – häufig mehr als vierzig Prozent. In Berlin sind die Baulandpreise seit 2008 um 350 Prozent gestiegen. Frauke Burgdorff engagiert sich in Fragen der gemeinwohlorientierten Stadt- und Immobilienentwicklung und fordert aufgrund dieser belastenden Situation ein Ende der Spekulation. Boden gehört dauerhaft in öffentliche und gemeinwohlorientierte Hände.

Seit ungefähr zehn Jahren beschäftige ich mich mit der Bodenfrage. Boden ist die Basis jeglicher Stadtentwicklung. Ohne ihn gibt es kein Wohnen, keine Daseinsvorsorge, keine Frei- und Grünräume. Boden ist eine ganz besondere Ware. Er lässt sich nicht vermehren, er ist knapp, und wer ihn einmal hat, gibt ihn nur selten wieder her. Bodenpolitik gestalten können vor allem diejenigen, die ihn besitzen – und das sind heute überwiegend Private.

Eigentum verpflichtet: Der Bund, das Land wie auch die Kommunen besitzen Boden. Sie unterliegen damit mindestens der gleichen Verpflichtung wie private Eigentümer*innen – wenn nicht sogar einer größeren. Allerdings war die öffentliche Hand in den letzten Jahren besonders freigiebig. Sie verkaufte Boden, um ihre Haushalte zu sanieren – direkt oder über die Privatisierung öffentlicher und gemeinnütziger Unternehmen.

Boden halten ist ein ursächlich konservatives Projekt

Boden nach diesem „Einwegprinzip" zu veräußern, bedeutet, ihn für immer aus der Hand zu geben – und damit auch den wichtigsten Hebel für gute Stadtentwicklung. Die öffentlichen Hände müssen ihren Boden deshalb behalten! Er lässt sich nur einmal für die Haushaltssanierung verwenden. Danach ist er weg! Nehmen wir uns doch hier ausnahmsweise einmal die katholische Kirche zum Vorbild, die schon seit Hunderten Jahren ihren Boden nicht verfrühstückt, sondern selbst nutzt, verpachtet und

budget, land can only be used once - then it is gone! For once, let us take the Catholic Church as a guiding example. For hundreds of years, the Church has not frittered away its land, but rather has used it, leased it out and secured it. Holding onto land is not an invention of modernity or the Left. It is a causatively conservative project.

When it comes to housing, land is one of the key drivers of cost. The acquisition of property can incur increases of up to 50 percent. This presents a challenge on a national level. How might increasing land prices be curbed? And how can land be secured permanently as a basis for affordable housing?

First of all, the public hand must be called upon to lead by example. In particular, the federal government must dampen speculation and cost-cutting with the land it still owns. The 470,000 hectares controlled by the German Federal Agency for Real Estate (BImA) and the Federal Ministry of Finance would be a step in the right direction. What if this resource were to be turned into a foundation, and made available for innovative, affordable housing, with its long-term returns freed up to fund municipal infrastructure? Stefan Rettich and Jochen Lang presented this proposal before the last general election in Germany and were met with a surprising amount of resistance. Today, I would rather focus on what Basel has initiated by means of a referendum: we must focus our attention on the municipalities and their sovereignty over land. If they are allowed to sell off land, it should be on the condition that they must acquire land of the same value elsewhere. The basic public stock would then be secured. In Germany, this model would mean that the BImA transfers its land to the municipalities. After all, municipalities are best positioned to look after public land - as long as they are not allowed to use it to replenish their budgets.

There is a catch, however. In Germany - at least since the establishment of private pension funds - retirement provisions rest on the pillar of land and property values. A property of your own is a good precautionary measure against the financial challenges of old age. An attack on private property is thus an attack on security. As long as this is the case, it will be difficult to dissuade people from the notion of ownership and enforce a different, public welfare-oriented policy. Another solution is co-operatives, which usually offer their members an adequate return and lifelong housing rights. Co-operative members are not

sichert. Boden halten ist keine Erfindung der Moderne oder der Linken. Es ist ein ursächlich konservatives Projekt.

Beim Wohnungsbau ist Boden einer der wichtigsten Kostentreiber. Der Erwerb des Grundstücks kann mit bis zu fünfzig Prozent zu Buche schlagen. Das ist eine Herausforderung nationaler Dimension. Wie lassen sich steigende Bodenpreise eindämmen? Und wie kann Boden dauerhaft als Basis für bezahlbare Wohnungen gesichert werden?

Zunächst einmal sind die öffentlichen Hände aufgerufen, mit bestem Beispiel voranzugehen. Gerade der Bund muss mit seinen Flächen dazu beitragen, Spekulation und Kostentreiberei zu dämpfen. Die 470.000 Hektar, die der Bundesanstalt für Immobilienaufgaben (BImA) und dem Bundesfinanzministerium unterstellt sind, wären doch schon mal ein Anfang! Was wäre, wenn diese Ressource in eine Stiftung überführt würde und für innovativen, preisgünstigen Wohnraum und dessen langfristige Renditen der kommunalen Infrastruktur zur Verfügung stünde? Den Vorschlag haben Stefan Rettich und Jochen Lang vor der letzten Bundestagswahl vorgestellt. Er hat erstaunlich viel Gegenwehr verursacht. Ich würde heute eher das fordern, was Basel mittels Volksentscheid auf den Weg gebracht hat: Wir müssen unseren Blick auf die Kommunen und ihre Gestaltungshoheit in Bodenfragen richten. Sie dürfen keinen Boden mehr verkaufen beziehungsweise nur unter der Voraussetzung, ihn in gleichem Umfang zu erwerben. Der öffentliche Grundbestand wäre dann gesichert. Auf Deutschland übertragen, bedeutete dies, dass die BImA ihren Boden den Kommunen überträgt. Denn: Kommunen sind die besten Bodensteuerer, sofern sie die wertvollen Flächen nicht für eine Haushaltssanierung ver(sch)wenden dürfen.

Einen Haken gibt es allerdings: In Deutschland ruht die Altersvorsorge spätestens seit der Riester-Rente auch auf dem Pfeiler aus Boden und Immobilie. Eine eigene Immobilie gilt als gute Vorsorge gegen finanzielle Probleme im Alter. Der Angriff auf das Privateigentum ist somit ein Angriff auf die Sicherheit. Solange das so ist, wird es schwierig bleiben, Menschen von der Eigentumsidee abzubringen und eine andere, gemeinwohlorientierte Politik durchzusetzen. Eine alte und neue Lösung sind Genossenschaften, die ihren Mitgliedern in der Regel eine sehr auskömmliche Rendite bieten und lebenslanges Wohnrecht. Dafür stehen die Genoss*innen keineswegs in der Pflicht, den Wert der Immobilien persönlich zu erhalten. Auch gibt es ein erstes Modell, Wohneigentum in gemeinwohlorientierte Fonds einzubringen, die dann ebenfalls eine kleine

obliged to personally cash in on the value of real estate. There is also already a model for integrating home ownership into charitable funds, which then facilitate a small private return. This is already being tested by a company called WEG-Damit GmbH in Hamburg.

We need a far-sighted land policy

One thing is certain: we need a far-sighted land policy. We need to stop responding to short-term market cycles and we need to take advantage of the inertia of land itself, as has been done in Vienna or by the over 250 Community Land Trusts (CLT) in the United States and Belgium.

Another land policy is possible. CLTs secure land in order to generate affordable residential and commercial rents, among other things. Although civil society brings together the necessary funds, state institutions also fund CLTs in order to counter gentrification and price increases. The CLTs assign land exclusively via leaseholds. Fortunately, this instrument is also attracting attention in Germany: private foundations (such as Trias or Edith-Maryon), publicly financed institutions (such as the Klosterkammer Hannover) and, of course, the churches use it in order to follow community-oriented goals or generate small but constant incomes.

The solutions are already at hand. Every square metre of land that we now sell, we lose forever. Land belongs in the public hand - to civil society - and it should be 100 percent community-oriented! Wouldn't it be incredible if all of the land held by the BImA (federal agency for real estate) were to be extracted from speculative forces of the market - forever? The time is ripe for fundamental change!

private Rendite ermöglichen: Die WEG-Damit GmbH praktiziert es bereits in Hamburg.

Wir brauchen eine Bodenpolitik der langen Linien

Sicher ist: Wir brauchen eine Bodenpolitik der langen Linien. Wir müssen aufhören, auf kurzfristige Marktzyklen zu reagieren, und uns die Trägheit des Bodens zunutze machen.

Eine andere Bodenpolitik ist möglich. Das zeigt das Beispiel Wien. Das zeigen die Community Land Trusts (CLT) in Belgien oder in den USA, wo über 250 solcher CLTs existieren. Sie halten den Boden, um unter anderem günstige Wohn- und Gewerbemieten zu erzeugen. In der Regel ist es die Zivilgesellschaft, die die erforderlichen Mittel aufbaut, aber auch staatliche Institutionen fördern CLTs, um Gentrifizierung und Verteuerung entgegenzutreten. Die CLTs vergeben ihren Grund ausschließlich im Erbbaurecht. Dieses Instrument findet glücklicherweise auch in Deutschland wieder Beachtung: Private Stiftungen (z. B. Trias, Edith Maryon), öffentlich getragene Gesellschaften (z. B. Klosterkammer Hannover) und natürlich die Kirchen nutzen es, um gemeinwohlorientierte Zwecke zu verfolgen oder eine ruhige und stetige Rendite zu erwirtschaften.

Die Lösungen sind also da. Keinen Quadratmeter Boden, den wir jetzt verkaufen, bekommen wir jemals zurück. Boden gehört in öffentliche und zivilgesellschaftliche Hand und zwar zu hundert Prozent gemeinwohlorientiert! Wäre es nicht großartig, wenn der gesamte Grund der BImA (Bundesanstalt für Immobilienaufgaben) für immer den spekulativen Kräften des Marktes entzogen würde? Die Zeit ist reif für eine bodenständige Entscheidung!

From Co-ignorance to Co-creation

Shaping Alliances with Civil Society

Worldwide, new strategies are urgently required in order to realise community-oriented projects in cities that are experiencing explosive increases in land and building values. Aside from returning to a tradition of urban planning where specific, already existing legal instruments in some European countries can be implemented, experiments with new constellations of use, financing and stakeholders are creating an influence in many locations. Berlin offers countless examples of experimentation, because here, an unexpected real estate boom has challenged a city with a vital civil society that has long – and successfully – tested out models that oppose market-oriented urban development. Manfred Kühne, the head of the Department for Urban Planning and Projects in the Senate Administration for Urban Development and Housing, makes a plea for a new culture of co-production.

Berlin has – perhaps surprisingly, but nonetheless vehemently – been drawn into the circle of booming metropolises, meaning that it now shares many of the problems of Munich, Frankfurt or Hamburg. Because of this, debates in Berlin's state and municipal political circles are particularly dynamic. Hence it was, and remains, imperative that we learn from the experience in this city, particularly in our approach to the classic instruments at our disposal: from funding new price-fixed housing, to rent control and land use. Such measures, however, are far less likely to calm the political situation than in other cities: not only due to the aggravated situation, but also because the potential for experimental alternatives is so vast.

Berlin: a city of tenants

Berlin is not a city of tenants due to neoliberal measures. The construction of tenement housing in the nineteenth century and 70 years of mostly socially democratic and socialist housing policy – combined with stultified privatisation after the German Democratic Republic came to an end –

Von Ko-Ignoranz zu Ko-Produktion

Neue Allianzen mit der Zivilgesellschaft

Für die Umsetzung gemeinwohlorientierter Projekte auch in Metropolen mit explodierenden Grundstücks- und Gebäudepreisen werden weltweit dringend neue Strategien gesucht. Neben einer Rückbesinnung auf rechtliche Instrumente der Stadtplanung, die zumindest in vielen europäischen Ländern Tradition haben, prägen aktuell an vielen Orten Experimente mit neuen Nutzungs-, Finanzierungs- und Akteurskonstellationen die Planungspraxis. Berlin bietet zahlreiche Beispiele für diese Tendenz, weil hier gerade ein unerwarteter Immobilienboom eine vitale Zivilgesellschaft herausfordert, die Gegenmodelle zu einer marktgetriebenen Stadtentwicklung schon erfolgreich erprobt hat. Manfred Kühne, Leiter der Abteilung für Städtebau und Projekte in der Senatsverwaltung für Stadtentwicklung und Wohnen, plädiert für eine neue Kultur der Ko-Produktion.

Seit Berlin überraschend, aber dafür umso heftiger, in den Kreis der boomenden Metropolen gerückt ist und jetzt viele Probleme Münchens, Frankfurts oder Hamburgs teilt, entwickeln sich die Debatten der Berliner Landes- und Bezirkspolitik besonders dynamisch. Es war und ist deshalb naheliegend, intensiv vom Erfahrungsschatz dieser Städte zu lernen: beim Umgang mit klassischen Steuerungsinstrumenten bei der Förderung preisgebundener Neubauwohnungen über Mietpreisdämpfung und Milieuschutz im Bestand bis hin zum Ankauf von Wohnungsbeständen und Baugrundstücken. Doch werden solche Maßnahmen wahrscheinlich sehr viel weniger als in den Vergleichsstädten zu einer politischen Beruhigung führen: aufgrund der verschärften Lage, aber auch, weil das Potenzial für experimentelle Alternativen so groß ist.

Berlin: Stadt der Mieter*innen

Nicht erst durch neoliberale Machenschaften ist Berlin zur Mieter*innenstadt geworden. Der Mietskasernenbau des 19. Jahrhunderts, siebzig Jahre überwiegend sozialdemokratische und sozialistische Wohnungspolitik in Verbindung mit der ausgebliebenen Privatisierung nach dem Ende der

culminated in an astoundingly drawn-out phase of empty housing stock. This, together with low rents, created new facts and new expectations. A rental quota of over 90 percent means that the overwhelming majority of residents are more likely to be afraid of a real estate boom than to profit from it. The crisis in housing - and therefore in land policy - is also particularly deep-seated in comparison to elsewhere in the European region, since Berlin is the only capital city and economically booming metropolis in which income lies significantly below the national average. Despite decreasing unemployment, long-term residents have profited little from a strong increase in highly qualified and well-paid jobs.

The legacy of austerity

The crisis has only been intensified by the fact that, on the back of 15 years of intense austerity measures implemented both at the state and municipal levels, politics has called for a return to state-backed investment for the past decade, meaning that larger budgets have again been freed up - for the foreseeable future. However, the drastically reduced municipal administration is no longer capable of effectively unrolling the plethora of public and private investments that are now possible. The everyday experience of failure extends the deep crisis of trust in the legitimacy of government. The most palpable expression of this failure is in the successful referenda regarding large-scale development planning, which have affected high-rises in the Friedrichshain-Kreuzberg district, the Tempelhof and Tegel Airports, and the supply of water and bicycle infrastructure.

Thanks to the special tradition and strength of local civil society, this widespread mistrust, accompanied by protest, has not led to the success of right-wing populist groups. This strength is derived not only from the strong 1968 movement in the former West, but also the 1989 movement in the former East. A generation of new arrivals, too, have influenced this legacy, strengthening an image of Berlin as a metropolis with a vital and creative civic society, in which new lifestyles and branches of the economy form - from club and designer culture, to tourism, to housing and the economic innovation of its start-ups.

Members of civil society have put two and a half decades of stagnation to use, developing Berlin's

DDR, gefolgt von einer erstaunlich langen Phase des Wohnungsleerstands und niedriger Mieten haben Fakten und Mentalität geprägt. Bei einer Mieter*innenquote von über neunzig Prozent muss die überwiegende Zahl der Bewohner*innenschaft den Immobilienpreisanstieg mehr fürchten, als von ihm profitieren zu können. Die wohnungs- und damit auch bodenpolitische Krise ist auch im europäischen Vergleich besonders tiefgreifend, weil Berlin die einzige Hauptstadt und wirtschaftlich boomende Metropole ist, in der das Einkommen deutlich unter dem nationalen Durchschnitt liegt. Die länger ansässige Bevölkerung profitiert trotz stark sinkender Arbeitslosigkeit kaum vom enormen Zuwachs an hoch qualifizierten und hoch bezahlten Arbeitsplätzen.

Das Erbe der Sparpolitik

Krisenverschärfend wirkt, dass die Politik auf Senats- und Bezirksebene nach 15 Jahren härtester Sparpolitik zwar ein Jahrzehnt der Investitionen ausgerufen hat und auf absehbare Zeit wieder große Budgets bereitstellen kann. Die drastisch reduzierte Verwaltung ist aber nicht mehr angemessen leistungsfähig, um die Vielzahl der möglichen öffentlichen und privaten Investitionen effektiv abzuwickeln. Das alltäglich erlebbare Versagen verlängert die tiefe Vertrauens- und Legitimitätskrise. Ihr spürbarster Ausdruck sind die erfolgreichen Referenden zu großen Planungsvorhaben. Sie reichen von Hochhäusern in Friedrichshain-Kreuzberg über die Flughafenstandorte Tempelhof und Tegel bis hin zu Wasserversorgung und Fahrradverkehr.

Dass ein so weit verbreitetes Misstrauen, begleitet von Protesten, in Berlin nicht zu rechtspopulistischen Erfolgen führt, dürfte der besonderen Tradition und Stärke der lokalen Zivilgesellschaft zu verdanken sein. Sie speist ihr Selbstbewusstsein nicht nur aus der enorm starken 68er-Bewegung im ehemaligen Westteil und der 89er-Bewegung im früheren Ostberlin. Auch die jüngste Zuwanderergeneration prägte auf der Basis dieses Erbes das Bild Berlins als einer Metropole der vitalen und kreativen zivilgesellschaftlichen Kräfte, in der neue Lebensstile und Wirtschaftszweige entstehen: von der Club- und Designkultur über den Tourismus bis hin zum Wohnungsbau und den ökonomischen Innovationen seiner Start-ups.

Zivilgesellschaftliche Akteur*innen konnten die anderthalb Jahrzehnte der Stagnation nutzen, um Berlins Baugruppen- und Clubkultur zu entwickeln,

co-op and clubbing cultures, which resonate far beyond the city itself. As a result, civil society has been able to profit from a persistent co-ignorance between civil society and the administration. Many actors were able to secure a niche for themselves in central locations in the city. Politicians and administrators observed and tolerated such developments without disrupting them. A large number of experimentally oriented individuals and groups were able to occupy various places and gather experiences by finding their own investment sources, implementing their own building plans and creating their own economic solutions. At the same time, the unchecked privatisation of municipal land was - correctly - seen as a threat with long-term consequences. Through this, reform-oriented land policy initiatives such as "Stadt neu denken" (Rethinking the city) found a political platform.

On rebellious acquisition and places of experimentation

Positive resonance in media and politics eased the transition to a form of "rebellious acquisition", with prominent representatives of co-ops and initiatives announcing their plans to take on and develop land or build on public land. More complex and attractive projects were realised in this way than through the conventional private or municipal project developers. These co-ops and initiatives inaugurated innovations in architecture, in mix of use and in community-oriented finance models. Exemplary in this sense are projects such as the building plans at the "Blumengroßmarkt" - a major site at a former flower market -, which developed out of an improvised concept process, or "Holzmarkt", - a private and co-operative development at the River Spree - whose stakeholders profited directly from the awarding of municipal land.

What happens if the political decision is made to refuse to sell off any further municipal land? How might alternative actors finance and realise their plans if they are not able to become owners and can no longer obtain loans against the assets of their land? Is it possible and necessary, under such conditions, for urban initiatives to co-operate with the city's housing or building management associations? The first experiments have already begun: currently, members of the contemporary art and culture sector have taken

die weit über die Stadt hinaus Vorbildwirkung errungen hat. Sie profitierten dabei von einer anhaltenden „Ko-Ignoranz", bei der sehr viele Akteur*innen in sehr zentralen Lagen der Stadt räumliche Nischen fanden. Politik und Verwaltungen beobachteten und duldeten die Entwicklungen, störten sie aber nicht. So konnte eine große Zahl von experimentell orientierten Akteur*innen Standorte besetzen und im Umgang mit eigenen Investitionen, Bauvorhaben und Bewirtschaftungslösungen Erfahrungen sammeln. Die ungebremste Privatisierung kommunaler Grundstücke wurde dabei zu Recht als latente langfristige Bedrohung empfunden. So entstanden bodenpolitisch orientierte Initiativen wie „Stadt neu denken", die Gehör finden.

Von rebellischer Akquisition und Orten des Experiments

Positive Resonanz in Medien und Politik begünstigte den Übergang zu einer Art „rebellischer Akquisition": Prominente Vertreter von Baugruppen und Initiativen bekundeten unüberhörbar, dass sie Grundstücke oder Gebäude aus öffentlichem Besitz übernehmen und entwickeln wollten. Es gelang der Nachweis, komplexere und attraktivere Projekte verwirklichen zu können als konventionelle private oder auch kommunale Projektentwickler*innen: Sie konnten Innovationen in der Architektur, beim Nutzungsmix und bei gemeinwohlorientierten Finanzierungsmodellen belegen. Dafür stehen Projekte wie die Baugruppen am Blumengroßmarkt, die aus einem improvisierten Konzeptverfahren hervorgegangen sind, oder der „Holzmarkt", dessen Akteur*innen von einer Direktvergabe der kommunalen Grundstücke profitierten.

Was aber passiert, wenn die politische Grundsatzentscheidung getroffen ist, kommunale Grundstücke nicht mehr zu verkaufen? Wie können alternative Akteur*innen ihre Vorhaben finanzieren und betreiben, wenn sie nicht Eigentümer*innen werden und ihre Grundstücke nicht beleihen können? Ist es unter diesen Umständen möglich und nötig, dass Initiativen gemeinsam mit kommunalen Gesellschaften des Wohnungsbaus oder Gebäudemanagements Projekte kooperativ entwickeln? Die ersten Experimente haben begonnen: Gerade ist in die denkmalgeschützte Alte Münze ein zeitgenössischer Kunst- und Kulturbetrieb eingezogen; im Leuchtturmprojekt Haus der Statistik koaliert die zivile Bürgerschaft mit der Stadtregierung, im Dragonerareal wurde nach langen Streitigkeiten der Verkauf an ei-

on the heritage-listed Alte Münze; the flagship project Haus der Statistik has been formed out of a coalition between civil society and the city's administration; and the sale of the Dragonerareal - publicly owned former barracks - to a private investor has, after long dispute, been cancelled. Further fields are emerging, both in central locations slated for reconstruction, and in sites the size of small suburbs, such as the former Tempelhof airport. Here, the level of engagement is a way of testing out new forms of co-production, spurred on by coalitions between civil society and public associations. These are subject to an exceedingly dense set of guidelines for dealing with land and buildings in the public hand, as well as the use of funds on a European and national level. This must be aided by taking into account large-scale participatory processes and the everyday interests of a highly diverse population. Rules are needed to ensure the co-operative programming of functional and socially mixed use, allowing for varied and combined finance models and guiding principles for urban planning, free spaces and rights of use. The allocation of contracts for planning and rights of use must also be regulated. Projects from other cities inside and outside Germany could provide input. The results must be communicated on a municipal and state level to legitimise the realisation of experimental projects and newly applied processes. In future, new impulses could arise for the vast and growing stock of communally owned buildings. Only then will it be evident: that many free spaces, mixed-use buildings and land with potential for development - such as the surroundings of the Fernsehturm (TV Tower) - are municipally owned. Such places offer the singular opportunity to develop one of Berlin's two central zones so that it is oriented towards community and public use.

New forms of co-production are also increasingly becoming imperative, as real estate and rental costs rise due to profit-oriented owners and project developers. The use of street-level spaces through shops and gastronomy, studios and galleries - which enliven many of Berlin's traditional streets and squares - should also apply to new urban quarters built by private consortiums. The Europacity, north of the main central station, is a test site for how a privately financed and organised ground floor management might be put into use - one that might also secure space for social initiatives and artists. If this succeeds, it will clear the way for new projects.

nen Privaten rückgängig gemacht. Weitere Felder sind absehbar, an extrem zentralen Neubaustandorten und auch in Komplexen von Stadtteilgröße wie dem Flughafen Tempelhof. Hier wird mit Engagement getestet, wie die „Ko-Produktion" von organisierten zivilgesellschaftlichen Initiativen und kommunalen Gesellschaften aussehen kann, die einem überaus dichten nationalen und europäischen Regelwerk für den Umgang mit Grundstücken und Gebäuden im öffentlichen Besitz sowie beim Mitteleinsatz unterliegen. Darüber hinaus sollen breit angelegte Partizipationsverfahren auch die Alltagsinteressen einer sehr diversen Bürger*innenschaft berücksichtigen helfen. Es braucht Regeln für die gemeinsame Programmierung von funktional und sozial gemischten Nutzungen, unterschiedliche, kombinierbare Finanzierungsmodelle und Gestaltungsregeln für Städtebau, Freiraum und Gebäude. Auch die Vergabe von Planungsaufträgen und Nutzungsrechten muss geregelt sein. Projekte aus anderen Städten im In- und Ausland können Anregungen geben. Im Ergebnis muss erfolgreich für politische Beschlüsse auf Bezirks- und Senatsebene geworben werden, um die Umsetzung der experimentellen Projekte und neue Prozessstandards zu legitimieren. Perspektivisch können sich daraus auch Impulse für den Umgang mit den großen und wieder wachsenden Gebäudebeständen im kommunalen Besitz ergeben. Dann könnte auch die erstaunliche Tatsache sichtbare Wirkung entfalten, dass beispielsweise im Umfeld des Fernsehturms ausgedehnte Freiräume, gemischt genutzte Gebäude und entwicklungsfähige Grundstücke kommunaler Besitz sind. Sie bieten die international einzigartige Chance, einen der beiden Zentrumsbereiche weitgehend gemeinwohlorientiert zu entwickeln.

Neue Formen der Ko-Produktion werden bei steigenden Immobilien- und Mietpreisen im Gewerbebereich zunehmend auch in der Kooperation mit renditeorientierten Eigentümer*innen und Projektentwickler*innen dringlich. Erdgeschossnutzungen durch Läden und Gastronomie, Ateliers und Galerien, die in vielen Gründerzeitquartieren Berlins Straßen und Plätze beleben, soll es auch in Neubauquartieren geben. Für die Europacity nördlich des Hauptbahnhofs wird gerade erprobt, wie ein privat finanziertes und organisiertes Erdgeschossmanagement entstehen kann, das auch sozial und künstlerisch arbeitenden Akteur*innen Raum sichert. Sollte dies gelingen, wird das Beispiel Schule machen.

The Politics of Mapping

Revealing and Reshaping Civic Initiatives

The Vivero de Iniciativas Ciudadanas (VIC) platform was set up by the architecture firm estudio [SIC] to support citizens' projects in Madrid by making them visible and accessible to each other. Based on this mapping process and related research, VIC joined forces with the Madrid municipality and six other partners to develop Mares de Madrid, a project mapping urban initiatives that are part of the social and solidarity economy, positively impacting mobility, food, recycling, energy and care. Out of this widespread resistance, numerous initiatives continue to come together, positively impacting the city of Madrid, including Los Madriles, a platform that makes critical and active citizenries visible. Make City in conversation with VIC co-director Mauro Gil-Fournier.

Make City: Advocates of civic engagement and those who see a need for self-initiated projects to be acknowledged as an alternative economy by municipal administration often emphasise the need for visibility as a means to establishing a collective awareness of the extent of such initiatives within the urban fabric. Can you tell us more about the initial impulse that led to the Los Madriles project and what that cartography developed into?

Mauro Gil-Fournier: VIC's first mission has always been to map innovative civic initiatives. For ten years we have been mapping and updating maps of Madrid in various formats that include seminars and research. This means that we are constantly updating knowledge and recognising existing and newly formed communities in the city. Over the past five years we have expanded our own mandate to do this in 28 cities throughout the Ibero-American region. During this time, the city has undergone several economic, political, housing and eviction crises, and we have been growing and mapping alongside these developments.
Los Madriles is the result of a seven-year process that included public and official communication about the process itself. It is a tool for the city and its communities that is being continually updated.

Die Politik der Kartierung

Zivilgesellschaftliche Bündnisse festigen

Das Architekturbüro estudio [SIC] hat 2008 die digitale Plattform Vivero de Iniciativas Ciudadanas (VIC) eingerichtet, um zivilgesellschaftliche Projekte in Madrid zu unterstützen. Hier sind sie für alle sichtbar und zugänglich. Basierend auf diesem Kartierungsprozess und den damit verbundenen Forschungsarbeiten entwickelte VIC in Zusammenarbeit mit der Stadt Madrid und sechs weiteren Partner*innen Mares de Madrid, ein Projekt, das städtische Initiativen erfasst, die Teil der Sozial- und Solidarwirtschaft sind und sich positiv auf Mobilität, Ernährung, Recycling, Energie und Pflege auswirken. Aus dem breit aufgestellten Bündnis zivilgesellschaftlichen Widerstands sind weitere Initiativen entstanden, die seither positiven Einfluss auf die Stadt nehmen. Make City sprach mit Mauro Gil-Fournier, dem Leiter von VIC.

Make City: Vertreter*innen von zivilgesellschaftlichen Initiativen und alle, die eine größere Anerkennung der Kommunalverwaltung für selbstorganisierte Projekte als alternative Ökonomie erreichen wollen, betonen häufig, wie bedeutend Sichtbarkeit als Mittel ist, um ein kollektives Bewusstsein für die Verbreitung solcher Initiativen im urbanen Geflecht zu schaffen. Können Sie uns mehr über den ursprünglichen Impuls erzählen, der zum Projekt Los Madriles und dessen Weiterentwicklung führte?

Mauro Gil-Fournier: Oberstes Ziel von VIC war es immer, zivilgesellschaftliche Innovation zu kartieren. Zehn Jahre lang haben wir auf verschiedenen Karten von Madrid unterschiedliche Formate verzeichnet und aktualisiert, einschließlich Seminar- und Forschungsangeboten. Wir erneuern den Wissensstand also kontinuierlich und machen bestehende und neu gebildete Gemeinschaften in der Stadt kenntlich. Über die letzten fünf Jahre haben wir unseren eigenen Auftrag erweitert und tun dies nun in 28 Städten der gesamten iberoamerikanischen Region. Während dieser Zeit hat Madrid mehrere wirtschaftliche, politische, Wohnungs- und Räumungskrisen durchlebt, an denen wir gewachsen sind. Wir haben die entstandenen Projekte kartiert.
Los Madriles ist das Ergebnis eines siebenjährigen Prozesses mitsamt Öffentlichkeitsarbeit und amtlicher Kommunikation. Es ist ein Werkzeug für die

MC: How are the civic initiatives categorised and how are the programmes and projects made tangible in relation to one another?

MGF: With or without cartography, citizen initiatives are always there; there is no city without them. On the civics.cc website platform there are more than 5,000 initiatives in 28 cities; to simplify this, we had to group initiatives - a taxonomic process - into various interests. What we have now is the dynamic result of modifying this taxonomic process through workshop after workshop. Ultimately, it helps pinpoint categories and thus engender new alliances.

MC: What are the frameworks or conditions that qualify an initiative for inclusion, or visibility, on the map?

MGF: Perhaps it is better to answer with the conditions that would disqualify an initiative. Then the answer is very simple. We do not accept initiatives that encourage expressions of hatred or intolerance on issues of gender, race, ethnicity, social position, sexual orientation, religion or origin. To foster accessibility, the registration is free. The system itself is modifiable by the user, allowing one to create an organisation panel of activities that then categorises the initiative.

MC: Why does one not include the public/private initiatives that might develop alternative economic models (which include private ownership or private capital) as opposed to public subsidies which may or may not be sustainable? Here, in particular, I am thinking about the commons movement ...

MGF: I think that today it is not necessary to define everything in a binary opposition such as public or private; this has already been demonstrated by feminist theory. What we are trying to define is how a public-social link can be formulated by independent initiatives. The fourth sector, including the co-operative world, social economy and feminist economies, are showing us answers to these questions, from places that are distinctly not publicly administered or subsidised.

MC: Often, it seems that the initiatives are working to replace urban public services that are lacking. Could you outline some of these?

MGF: I do not think it's exactly like that. I think what many of the initiatives do is to modify our perspective of the problem at hand. So, for instance, civic initiatives do not do the work of the

Stadt und ihre nachbarschaftlichen Zusammenhänge, das immer weiter aktualisiert wird.

MC: Wie werden die zivilgesellschaftlichen Initiativen kategorisiert und wie werden die Programme und Projekte füreinander greifbar?

MGF: Ob dokumentiert oder nicht: Zivilgesellschaftliche Initiativen gibt es immer. Es gibt keine Stadt ohne sie. Auf der Plattformwebseite civics.cc sind mehr als 5.000 Initiativen in 28 Städten verzeichnet. Um das zu vereinfachen, mussten wir Initiativen nach verschiedenen Interessen bündeln – ein taxonomischer Prozess. Aus der stetigen Änderung dieses Prozesses durch viele Workshops hindurch ist ein dynamisches Ergebnis entstanden, das nun dabei helfen kann, herauszufinden, wer sich als potenzieller Verbündete*r für bestimmte Aktionen eignet.

MC: Nach welchen Maßgaben oder Bedingungen eignen sich Initiativen für die Aufnahme und damit Sichtbarkeit auf der Karte?

MGF: Vielleicht ist es besser, dies umgekehrt mit denjenigen Kriterien zu beantworten, die eine Initiative für uns ausschließen würde. In diesem Fall ist die Antwort nämlich sehr einfach: Wir akzeptieren keine Initiativen, die zu Hass oder Intoleranz bezüglich Geschlecht, sozialer Position, sexueller Orientierung, Religion oder Herkunft ermutigen. Um den Zugang zu fördern, ist die Registrierung kostenfrei. Das System selbst ist durch die Nutzenden veränderbar, sodass sie Aktivitäten nach einem eigenen Raster organisieren können, nach dem die Initiativen dann kategorisiert werden.

MC: Warum werden keine öffentlich-privaten Initiativen aufgenommen, die womöglich alternative wirtschaftliche Modelle entwickeln (die privates Eigentum oder Kapital beinhalten) und den – manchmal nachhaltigen und manchmal weniger nachhaltigen – öffentlichen Subventionen entgegenstehen? Hier denke ich besonders an die Gemeingutbewegung ...

MGF: Ich denke, dass wir heute nicht mehr unbedingt alles in einem diametralen Gegensatz – öffentlich oder privat – definieren sollten; das hat die feministische Theorie bereits gezeigt. Wir versuchen zu erkennen, wie unabhängige Initiativen eine Verbindung zwischen Staat und Gesellschaft herstellen. Der vierte Sektor, einschließlich der Kooperativen, der Sozialwirtschaft und der feministischen Ökonomien, bietet uns Antworten – von Stellen aus, die eben keine öffentliche Verwaltung oder Subvention darstellen.

administration, but through their practice, they provide us other positions from which to observe reality as it is and as it could be. They give us clues about what other paths we could experience, such as bicycle mobility in the city or circular recycling systems. This is different in cases of extreme vulnerability, such as evictions. The platform created for those affected by the mortgage crisis and supported by citizen resources supplemented specific needs that the administration did not attend to, including provision of psychologists, lawyers and, sometimes, simply neighbours. This was a critical support to so many people who were - and continue to be in - extremely vulnerable positions.

MC: What is the political outcome of this mapping, this creating of networks between neighbourhoods, on the civic projects and initiatives themselves?

MGF: There is no direct, or perhaps measurable, result. A mapping generates local urban knowledge around specific issues. It also generates a history of connections that are reflected in the different prototypes, tests, projects and programmes that can be carried out in collaboration. These processes are often unpredictable, but mapping helps to create an awareness of an existing and resilient citizen ecosystem, in which things are not only being done, but many different projects co-exist simultaneously. As a project, the map is successful when the initiatives begin to collaborate and mingle together, and the resulting projects exceed the limits of what was previously possible.

MC: What effects have the act of mapping and the resulting maps had on the perception of these alternative civic economies? For example, at the level of municipal government?

MGF: Each city is a world of cities. There are already many cities that can talk about their own experiences of collaboration through concrete learning. After mapping, citizen laboratories are the best tools to share and transfer these learnings. The urban laboratories that we developed from VIC are an example for specific cases of city development, such as MarinaLab, LegazpiLab or CCDLab. As an urban co-production programme, Mares de Madrid is one of the best tools to experiment in the city and has transferred real knowledge towards an innovation in public policies. Other projects with which we collaborate include MediaLabPrado, Intermediae in Madrid or SantaLab in Rosario, Argentina, MVDLab in

MC: Es scheint oft, als würden die Initiativen fehlende städtische öffentliche Dienste ersetzen. Könnten Sie einige davon skizzieren?

MGF: Meines Erachtens ist das nicht ganz richtig. Ich denke, dass viele der Initiativen unsere Perspektive auf das jeweils vorliegende Problem verändern. Zivilgesellschaftliche Innovationen machen keine Verwaltungsarbeit, aber durch ihre Praxis bieten sie uns andere Positionen, aus denen wir die Wirklichkeit betrachten können – wie sie ist und wie sie sein könnte. Sie geben uns Hinweise, welche anderen Pfade wir einschlagen könnten, zum Beispiel Fahrradmobilität in der Stadt oder Kreislaufsysteme der Wiederverwertung.
In Fällen der extremen Verletzbarkeit – etwa bei Räumungen – ist das anders. Die Plattform war für all jene da, die von der Hypothekenkrise betroffen waren, und hat mit Unterstützung der Stadtbevölkerung Angebote zur Befriedigung von Bedarfen bereitgestellt, um die die Stadtverwaltung sich nicht gekümmert hat: psychologische, rechtliche und manchmal bloß nachbarschaftliche Begleitung. Das war eine entscheidende Unterstützung für so viele Menschen, die in extrem verletzlichen Positionen waren – und es weiterhin sind.

MC: Was ist das politische Ergebnis der Kartierung – dieser Vernetzungsarbeit zwischen Nachbarschaften – für die zivilgesellschaftlichen Projekte und Initiativen selbst?

MGF: Es gibt kein direktes oder messbares Ergebnis. Eine Kartierung erzeugt lokales städtisches Wissen über bestimmte Themen. Es erzeugt auch eine Geschichte der Verbindungen. Sie spiegeln sich in Prototypen, Tests, Projekten und Programmen wider, die in Zusammenarbeit durchgeführt werden können. Diese Prozesse sind häufig unvorhersehbar, aber ihre Kartierung hilft dabei, ein Bewusstsein über ein bestehendes, belastbares zivilgesellschaftliches Ökosystem zu schaffen, in dem nicht nur etwas vollbracht wird, sondern in dem viele verschiedene Dinge zur gleichen Zeit geschehen. Als Projekt ist die Karte dann erfolgreich, wenn die Initiativen beginnen, zusammenzuarbeiten und sich zu verbünden, und wenn die daraus hervorgehenden Projekte über das hinausgehen, was bis dahin möglich war.

MC: Welche Auswirkungen hat der Akt der Kartierung und haben die so entstandenen Karten auf die Wahrnehmung von diesen alternativen, zivilgesellschaftlichen Ökonomien – zum Beispiel auf der Ebene der kommunalen Regierung?

MGF: Jede Stadt ist eine Welt aus Städten. Es gibt

Montevideo, Uruguay; the list goes on. There are many places where these transfers happen and generate international protagonists in civic action.

MC: What do you see as the effects of connecting these initiatives and communication?

MGF: It is not only about connecting initiatives, it is about thinking together about which prototypes or pilot projects we need in the city. What programmes can we produce? What are the changes that we want to see in the city? By asking these questions we can find a way to co-produce projects that we need and want. Sometimes this happens independently, sometimes from public support, in yet other cases from more hybrid places. There are plenty of possibilities available in the city at any given time. In the most concrete example, Mares de Madrid enables different devices to move from civic innovation to processes of circular and resilient economies. This happens through citizen competency laboratories, learning communities, support for communication projects, pilot projects, legal capacity and an overall understanding of the urban. The initiatives often arrive at a junction which the municipal administration and the market has not reached. That is the gap that we must find and support.

bereits viele Städte, die von ihren Erfahrungen der Zusammenarbeit durch ganz konkretes Lernen erzählen können. Nach der Kartierung sind zivilgesellschaftliche Werkstätten das beste Instrument, um solche Erkenntnisse zu teilen und weiterzugeben. Die städtischen Labore des VIC sind Beispiele für spezielle Fälle der städtischen Entwicklung – etwa das MarinaLab, LegazpiLab oder CCDLab. Als Programm der urbanen Ko-Produktion ist Mares de Madrid eines der besten Werkzeuge, um in der Stadt zu experimentieren. Es hat schon echtes Wissen für Innovationen in die öffentliche Gesetzgebung eingespeist. Andere Projekte, mit denen wir zusammenarbeiten, sind das MediaLab Prado, Intermediae in Madrid sowie das SantaLab in Rosario, Argentinien, und das MVDLab in Montevideo, Uruguay; die Liste ist fortsetzbar. Es gibt viele Orte für diesen Wissenstransfer, die selbst eine Rolle als zivilgesellschaftliche Akteur*innen übernehmen.

MC: Wie wirkt sich die Verbindung dieser Initiativen und ihrer Kommunikation aus?

MGF: Es geht nicht nur darum, die Initiativen zu verbinden, sondern auch darum, gemeinsam zu überlegen, welche Prototypen oder Pilotprojekte wir in der Stadt brauchen. Welche Programme können wir herausbringen? Welche Veränderungen wollen wir sehen? Indem wir diese Fragen stellen, können wir einen Weg finden, Projekte mitzugestalten, die wir benötigen und schaffen wollen. Manchmal passiert das unabhängig, manchmal mit staatlicher Unterstützung, manchmal aus hybrideren Situationen heraus. In der Stadt gibt es immer so viele Möglichkeiten, wie das konkrete Beispiel zeigt: Mares de Madrid hat verschiedene Instrumente, die Bürger*innen erfunden haben, in die Prozesse der robusten Kreislaufwirtschaften eingebracht. Das geschieht durch Kompetenzlabore für Bürger*innen, Lerngemeinschaften, Unterstützung für Kommunikationsprojekte, Pilotprojekte, rechtliche Kompetenzen und ein allgemeines Verständnis vom Urbanen. Die Initiativen kommen oft weiter. Sie gelangen an Orte, die Verwaltung und Markt noch nicht kennen. Das ist die Lücke, die wir finden und schließen müssen.

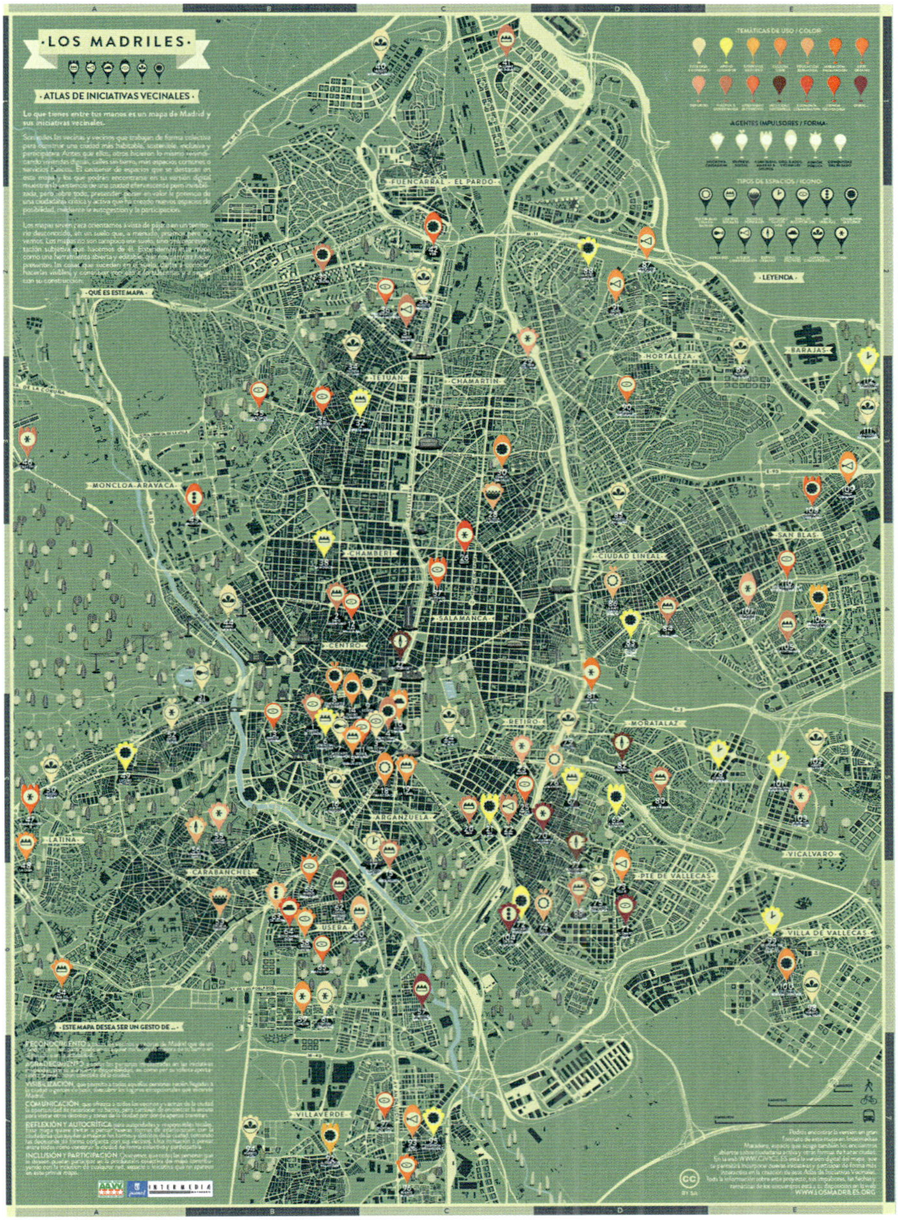

Los Madriles: cartography showing 112 initiatives across Madrid that pinpoint civic initiatives and socially engaged entrepreneurs

Los Madriles: Kartierung und Sichtbarmachen von 112 in Madrid aktiven Zivilinitiativen und sozial engagierten Unternehmen

"The time is ripe for architects to shake things up, to take control and responsibility for realising dreams for the future in the cities where they live. We deserve a new and imaginative architectural heritage."

„Es ist Zeit, das Joch des Alltäglichen abzuschütteln und die Kontrolle und Verantwortung für die Zukunft der Stadt wieder zu übernehmen! Wir verdienen ein neues und fantasievolles Architektur-Erbe."

Roger Zogolovitch

Fill the Gaps!

The Architect as Artisanal Developer

Roger Zogolovitch is an architect and developer who deftly transforms infill – i.e., gap – sites into artful, light-filled, open-plan homes. Here, he argues for a redefinition of the limited, traditional role of the architect and the developer. Architects who are trained to identify spaces that can be transformed into something new have an expertise that market driven investors and real estate developers often do not have. As an architect-developer, Zogolovitch is the champion of an architectural movement that uses ingenuity to make new developments on forgotten fragments of land at the heart of our cities. Zogolovitch appeals to city governments and urban planning authorities to use this potential in our cities, seeking out gap sites "that release inspiration".

In the city grid, if you are looking, you can find forgotten fragments of land and buildings. These gap sites are stumbled upon, discovered or arrived at simply by walking the streets of cities, peering around corners and examining backland sites. Gap sites need inquisitive eyes, like those of the independent developer, to find them.

The city is peppered with these small sites, all of which are improvable. The historic manufacturing sites of cities are becoming redundant as technological advances herald alternative work patterns. New uses of the city are the order of the day. These emptied structures – the remains – become opportunities for imaginative development and reconfigurations; a new category of independent development. Old structures combine with new opportunities, while the results counter larger scale developers whose corporate buildings and commercial interests currently dominate the city skyline.

Like gathering rocks

The MakeCity Festival in June 2018 demonstrated this. It brought together a variety of independent thinkers and practitioners. From their collective experience a consistent theme emerged: each participant showed how they had identified

Lücken füllen!

Das architektonische Potenzial der Nische

Roger Zogolovitch ist Architekt und Immobilienentwickler. Er verwandelt Baulücken geschickt in kunstfertige Wohnhäuser mit offenen Räumen und viel Licht. Er plädiert für eine Neubestimmung der eingeschränkten traditionellen Rolle von Architektur und Entwicklung. Architekt*innen, die dazu ausgebildet sind, Orte aufzuspüren und in etwas Neues zu verwandeln, besitzen eine Expertise, die marktorientierten Investor*innen und Immobilienentwickler*innen oft fehlt. Zogolovitch steht für eine architektonische Strömung, die mit Einfallsreichtum aus vergessenen Flächen im Herzen unserer Städte neue Bauprojekte entstehen lässt. Er ruft städtische Regierungen und Planungsbehörden dazu auf, dieses Potenzial zu nutzen und jede gefundene Baulücke „zur Inspiration freizugeben".

Wenn wir genau hinschauen, können wir im Raster der Städte jede Menge vergessener Grundstücks- und Gebäudeteile finden. Über diese Baulücken stolpere ich, entdecke oder finde sie, einfach indem ich durch die Straßen spaziere, um die Ecken sehe, dahinter- und dazwischenliegende Grundstücksflächen erkunde. Baulücken zu finden, erfordert neugierige Blicke wie die von unabhängigen Entwickler*innen.

Diese kleinen Flächen sind im gesamten Stadtgebiet zu finden. Und sie alle sind ausbaufähig. Die historischen Handwerksorte und Werkstätten der Städte werden überflüssig, wenn der technologische Fortschritt alternative Arbeitsmuster hervorbringt. Neue Nutzungen sind das Gebot der Stunde. Die (sinn)entleerten Strukturen, die zurückbleiben, bieten dann Gelegenheiten für ideenreiche Ausbauten und Umgestaltungen: eine neue Kategorie unabhängiger Entwicklung. Alte Strukturen kombiniert mit neuen Möglichkeiten schaffen im Ergebnis etwas anderes als die Projekte der großen Entwicklungsbüros, deren Firmengebäude und kommerzielle Interessen derzeit die städtische Skyline dominieren.

a gap site project. It was like lifting stones on a beach; unearthing the prospects hidden below.

This new breed of creative developer seems closer to a filmmaker than a traditional developer. In their capable and experimental hands, each scheme becomes a creative endeavour. Using imagination and artistry, sites previously deemed impossible become viable. Through persistence and dedication, these developers produce rich, beautiful projects. In this creative gesture, each developer reveals their own unique experience and skills; as architects, curators and engaged residents. They all create schemes without compromise.

The leap of faith and independent development

City administrations and their administrators could and should learn from such examples of successful, independent development. They should support and foster these tailored and community-led enterprises. Cities and their administrators should identify their own gap sites, offering those from 0.05 hectares and upwards (for example) to new developers. In this way, a new kind of creative experimentation and innovation can begin.

The potential of these sites is without limit - they can serve so many different communities and address a range of pre-existing needs of a place: affordable housing; maker spaces for crafts people and artisans; performing spaces; cultivated landscapes; spaces for learning.

The scale and diversity of these projects encourage the introduction of patient capital. Crowd-funding, intervention and philanthropy can contribute to both the project development and retention of community interest. Most of our cities face the same problem: a shortage of affordable housing. The role of the independent developer is therefore to demonstrate new possibilities and bring a passion for development that is not simply motivated by profit. Enterprise, enthusiasm, determination and artistry can bring further independent and inspiring developments from the urban centres of our cities.

Wie Steinesammeln am Strand

Das MakeCity Festival im Juni 2018 hat dies deutlich gemacht. Es brachte eine Vielfalt unterschiedlicher Denker*innen und Praktiker*innen zusammen. Ein Thema bestimmte die gemeinsame Erfahrung aller Beteiligten: Alle berichteten von Baulückenprojekten, die sie entdeckt hatten. Es war wie Steine-Sammeln am Strand; als hätte man versteckte Schätze gehoben.

Dieser neue Typus kreativer Entwickler*innen scheint den Filmemacher*innen ähnlicher zu sein als der traditionellen Entwicklungsbranche. In ihren kompetenten und experimentierfreudigen Händen wird jedes Projekt zu einer kreativen Unternehmung. Mit viel Fantasie und Kunstfertigkeit werden Orte wieder nutzbar, die zuvor als untauglich galten. Mit Ausdauer und Einsatz schaffen sie es, bereichernde, wunderbare Projekte durch- und umzusetzen. Jede dieser kreativen Gesten zeugt von einzigartigen Erfahrungen und Fähigkeiten – als Architekt*innen, Kurator*innen und engagierte Bewohner*innen. Sie alle entwerfen Pläne – ohne Kompromisse.

Mut zur Lücke und zur unabhängigen Entwicklung

Stadtverwaltungen und ihre Verwaltungsbeamt*innen könnten und sollten von solchen Beispielen erfolgreicher unabhängiger Entwicklung lernen. Sie sollten diese maßgeschneiderten und gemeinschaftlich geleiteten Unternehmungen unterstützen und fördern. Städte und ihre Verwalter*innen sollten ihre eigenen Baulücken ausfindig machen und alle, die (beispielsweise) 0,05 Hektar aufwärts messen, den neuen Entwickler*innen anbieten. Das kann der Beginn einer neuen Art kreativen Experimentierens und städtischen Neugestaltens sein.

Das Potenzial dieser Flächen ist grenzenlos. Sie können vielen verschiedenen Gemeinschaften zugutekommen und eine Vielfalt bestehender Bedürfnisse erfüllen: bezahlbarer Wohnraum, offene Werkstätten für Kunsthandwerk und Handwerkskunst, Räume für darstellende Künste, Kulturlandschaften, Lernorte.

Umfang und Vielfalt dieser Projekte ermutigen dazu, geduldiges Kapital einzusetzen. Crowdfunding, Intervention und Philanthropie tragen dann sowohl

The potential is borderless: gap-sites as unlimited inspiration

The ability to blend vision and pragmatism is the skill of an architect guided by value rather than cost. It is passionate commitment and enthusiasm that can affect the status quo and trigger a wave of change. All in all, the dissemination of these small but innovative interventions will foster debate and clarify meaning. This, in turn, will amplify their impact, leading to greater demand for this type of development from the wider public. Together, we need to encourage and amplify the message that the city needs independent developers. We must support them as they seek out the gaps which can be used to renew. It is imperative we do this, as it will enrich the city of the future.

dazu bei, die Projekte zu entwickeln, als auch, nachbarschaftliche Interessen zu wahren. Die meisten unserer Städte stehen demselben Problem gegenüber: Es mangelt an bezahlbarem Wohnraum. Die Rolle der unabhängigen Entwickler*innen ist es, neue Möglichkeiten aufzuzeigen und dabei eine Leidenschaft für Entwicklung mitzubringen, die nicht bloß von Profit motiviert ist. Unternehmungslust, Enthusiasmus und Kunstfertigkeit können aus den urbanen Zentren unserer Städte wieder unabhängige und inspirierende Entwicklungen hervorbringen.

Das Potenzial ist grenzenlos: Baulücken zur Inspiration freigeben

Die Kunst der Architekt*innen ist die Fähigkeit, Vision und Pragmatismus zu verbinden und sich in der Arbeit mehr von Werten als von Kostenfragen leiten zu lassen. Ähnlich wie in der Brotbackkunst sind sie so leidenschaftlich in ihrem Einsatz und Enthusiasmus, dass sich das auf den Status quo auswirken und eine Welle der Veränderung anstoßen wird. In der Summe wird die Verbreitung dieser kleinen, aber innovativen Interventionen zu Debatten anregen und ihre Bedeutung klarmachen. Das wiederum wird ihren Einfluss vergrößern, der zu einer größeren Nachfrage der breiten Öffentlichkeit nach dieser Form von Bauprojekten führen wird. Gemeinsam müssen wir die Botschaft senden und stärken, dass die Stadt unabhängige Entwickler*innen braucht. Wir müssen sie auf ihrer Suche nach den Lücken unterstützen. Das ist dringend notwendig und bereichert die Stadt der Zukunft.

With Ownership Comes Responsibility!

"Its use shall also serve the public good."

With the selling off of our cities and the increasing economisation of our environment, society is facing a host of new challenges. Land and housing are being demoted to assets for investment, ownership of which governs access to the environment, whether urban or rural. Olaf Grawert calls for a more conscious architectural concept that recognises these economic and political realities and provides answers. As part of the MakeCity Festival, he moderated the panel "Does Ownership Come with Responsibility?" with Verena von Beckerath, Frauke Burgdorff, Daniel Dahm, Barbara König, Manfred Kühne, Stephan Reiß-Schmidt and Sascha Zander.

10.09.2018, Wedding district court:

A property of 482 square metres on Grüntaler Straße in Berlin, not far from the district court in Wedding, is to be auctioned. Until now, it has been used as a car repair yard and contains a shed. The property is now destined to host a five-storey building offering up to 723 square metres of living space. The commercial value of the land is 224,000 euros, including demolition costs: today's auction opens with a starting price of 174,000 euros.

I am one of around one hundred interested parties squeezed into the courtroom. I recognise a few faces: young architects who are bidding partially for their own use, partially for contractors. We all begin with the same calculation: the "land price set according to development potential" predicts a price of around 240 euros/m^2 of buildable space.

After some 25 minutes the auction closes. The land changes hands for 1,100,000 euros, plus taxes and fees. The audience leaves the courtroom in a mix of speechlessness, amusement and horror, speculating about the intentions of the buyer. Out of curiosity, I linger in front of the court in order to ask him about his plans for the project; now with a burden of 1,550 euros/m^2 of buildable space. His answer is curt: "It's an

Eigentum verpflichtet!

„Sein Gebrauch soll zugleich dem Wohle der Allgemeinheit dienen."

Angesichts des Ausverkaufs unserer Städte und der fortschreitenden Ökonomisierung unserer Umwelt sieht sich die Gesellschaft mit neuen Herausforderungen konfrontiert. Grund und Boden sowie Wohnraum werden zu Anlagegütern degradiert, deren Besitz den Zugang zu unserer Umwelt, egal ob Stadt oder Land, und Gesellschaft regeln. Olaf Grawert plädiert für einen bewussteren Architekturbegriff, der diese ökonomischen und politischen Realitäten anerkennt und architektonische Antworten darauf liefert. Im Rahmen des MakeCity Festivals moderierte er hierzu die Veranstaltung: Eigentum verpflichtet? mit Verena von Beckerath, Frauke Burgdorff, Daniel Dahm, Barbara König, Manfred Kühne, Stephan Reiß-Schmidt und Sascha Zander.

10.09.2018, Amtsgericht Wedding:

Versteigert wird ein 482 Quadratmeter großes Grundstück in der Grüntaler Straße unweit des Gerichtes im Berliner Wedding. Bis dato wird es als Autowerkstatt genutzt und ist mit einem Schuppen bebaut. Jetzt soll auf dem Grundstück ein fünfgeschossiges Haus mit bis zu 723 Quadratmetern (Wohn-)Fläche entstehen. Der Verkehrs-(Markt-)wert des Objekts beträgt 224.000 Euro, abzüglich der Abrisskosten: Bei 174.000 Euro startet die Auktion an diesem Tag.

Ich bin einer von rund einhundert Interessierten, die sich im Gerichtssaal drängen. Neben mir einige wenige bekannte Gesichter: junge Architekt*innen, die teils zur Eigennutzung, teils für Auftraggeber*innen mitbieten. Wir alle starten mit der gleichen Rechnung in das Rennen: „Grundstückspreis durch bebaubare Fläche" ergibt eine anfängliche Belastung von rund 240 Euro pro Quadratmeter projizierter Wohnfläche.

Nach rund 25 Minuten ist die Auktion beendet. Das Objekt wechselt für 1.100.000 Euro, zuzüglich Steuern und Gebühren, den Besitzer. Die Anwesenden verlassen den Saal in einer Mischung aus Sprachlosigkeit, Belustigung und Entsetzen. Im Treppenhaus schallt das Geschehen nach, bis sich

investment. For now, nothing will be built there."

What happened on that Thursday morning is not an isolated incident. It represents a general trend in Berlin's real estate market. Access to land is becoming a privilege for those few who - operating outside any sense of social responsibility - consider land and living space solely for investment purposes. Article 14 of the German Basic Law (or Grundgesetz, GG) seems to have been forgotten: "Property entails obligations. Its use shall also serve the public good" (Art. 14.2 GG). The question of landownership - the "basis of all urban development" (see Frauke Burgdorff, MakeCity Festival, 18 June 2018) - lies at the heart of every debate around alternative models for architecture and the city. This debate has been present since the 1970s and is, at its core, an originally conservative project (see Frauke Burgdorff), even if all efforts to reform the land law are mainly associated with the Social Democrats, above all with Hans-Jochen Vogel and his campaign to end land speculation and herald land reforms.

"Who owns the land? - and with it, the city?" These questions are fundamental if we want to have an understanding of our built environment. Land ownership and property influence not only our understanding of society but also our relations to one another. Economisation - and with it, the increasing privatisation of our cities - increasingly create imbalances in the availability and accessibility of public and shared spaces. A systematic debate around new forms of management and construction models, as well as new architectures, is necessary - a discussion that must move beyond simply describing current circumstances, in order to generate real alternatives to existing norms in society and the built environment. We need new models in which, beyond the large enterprises, non-commercial investors get the opportunity to develop and structure our cities.

-

The most valuable city in Germany

A quick glance at the framing conditions reveals how difficult it is for (private) investors to create affordable living space in Berlin: according to the communal real-estate assets, Berlin is the most lucrative city in Germany - but its citizens earn far less in comparison to other cities. This financial asset increases in value due to pressure from external capital. Berlin today, and even five years

die Menschenmenge vor dem Gerichtsgebäude auf einige wenige ausdünnt, die über den Käufer und seine Absichten spekulieren. Aus Neugierde warte ich, um ihn nach seinen Plänen für das mit 1.550 Euro je Quadratmeter vorbelastete Projekt zu fragen. Seine Antwort lautet knapp: „Investition, gebaut wird erst mal nichts."

Was an diesem Donnerstagvormittag passierte, ist mehr als eine Momentaufnahme. Es ist ein Sinnbild des Berliner Immobilienmarktes. Der Zugang zu (Bau-)Land wird zum Privileg weniger, die – jenseits einer gesellschaftlichen Verantwortung und Notwendigkeit – Grund und Wohnraum als Investitionsgut begreifen und beanspruchen. Vergessen scheint der Artikel 14 des Grundgesetzes, der unter anderem besagt: „Eigentum verpflichtet. Sein Gebrauch soll zugleich dem Wohle der Allgemeinheit dienen." (Art 14.2 GG). Die Bodenfrage als Basis jeder Stadtentwicklung steht dabei im Zentrum jeder Debatte um alternative Handlungsmodelle für Architektur und Stadt, einer Debatte, die seit den 1970er Jahren präsent und im Kern ein ursächlich konservatives Projekt (vgl. Frauke Burgdorff, MakeCity Festival, 28.06.2018) ist; auch wenn Bestrebungen zur Reformierung des Bodenrechts vorwiegend mit der Sozialdemokratie – allen voran dem politischen Kampf gegen Bodenspekulation von Hans-Jochen Vogel – assoziiert werden.

Die Fragen „Wem gehört der Boden – wem gehört die Stadt?" sind grundlegend für das Verständnis unserer gebauten Umwelt, denn Grundbesitz und (Immobilien-)Eigentum prägen sowohl unser Verständnis von Gesellschaft wie auch unser Miteinander. Die Ökonomisierung und zunehmende Privatisierung unserer Städte aber stellt die Verfügbarkeit und Zugänglichkeit von öffentlichen und gemeinschaftlichen Räumen zusehends infrage. Eine systemische Debatte über neue Betreiber*innen- und Bauherr*innenmodelle sowie neue Architekturen ist nötig – eine Auseinandersetzung, die über die bloße Beschreibung des Ist-Zustandes hinausgeht und Alternativen zu bestehenden gesellschaftlichen und baulichen Normen aufzeigt. Wir brauchen Modelle, in denen nicht kommerzielle und großunternehmerische Investor*innen die Chance bekommen, unsere Städte zu gestalten.

-

Die wertvollste Stadt Deutschlands

Wie schwierig es ist, als (private) Investor*innen leistbaren Wohnraum in Berlin zu schaffen, wird bei einem Blick auf die Rahmenbedingungen deut-

ago, was the number one European city to produce the highest turnover both for international, and national, local developers (see the survey by the architect Sascha Zander, MakeCity Festival, 28 June 2018) with an ownership rate of 15 percent, in comparison to the rest of Germany at 50 percent. The constant flow of capital into the real estate market means that the few properties available rise in value; in the last decade, by 1500 percent (see Sascha Zander, MakeCity Festival, 28 June 2018: "2005: 167 euros/m^2 vs. 2018: 2,500 euros/m^2"). This growth by far exceeds other capitals such as Paris or London, which share a similar legacy: the sell-out of public properties to private investors, under the paradigm of popular capitalism and the free market.

Along with land prices, building costs have increased, leading to market-optimised, efficient architectures in which public and shared spaces no longer have a place. In order to guarantee the middle class - now itself threatened by displacement - access to living space in our cities, the last way out for architects seems to be the reduction of the apartment size itself.

The complete economisation of space

As a consequence, we can observe a homogenisation of contemporary architecture, following the same economic logic, reproducing the ever-same spaces and milieus. Various private stakeholders - from individuals to companies and investment funds - substantiate their belief in private property by contributing to the complete economisation of our living spaces. The responsibility of making the built environment - as well as to the city and its land - is being shifted, from the public domain (represented by politics) to private parties who are operating with an unclear agency. Under the credo of "no-alternative", these spaces degrade residents to so-called "users", rendering homogeneity the guiding principle of society.

What needs to be done? Architects and planners are challenged to develop alternative models with their contractors which might provide spatial and economic answers to the situation. Alternatives dreamt up through collaborations such as the "IBeB" at the former Blumengroßmarkt Berlin by ARGE ifau | HEIDE & VON BECKERATH must be explained and understood, so that they find

lich: Nach der Bewertung des kommunalen Immobilienvermögens ist Berlin die wertvollste Stadt Deutschlands, bei vergleichsweise niedrigen Durchschnittseinkommen. Dieser Vermögenswert steigt durch den Kapitaldruck von außen. Berlin ist heute, wie schon vor fünf Jahren, die europäische Stadt mit den höchsten Renditeerwartungen, sowohl für internationale Projektentwickler*innen als auch für nationale und lokale Projektentwicklungen (vgl. Recherche von Sascha Zander, MakeCity Festival, 28.06.2018). Eine überdurchschnittlich niedrige Wohnungseigentumsquote von 15 Prozent (versus fünfzig Prozent im deutschen Mittel) nährt den stetigen Kapitalfluss in den Immobilienmarkt und lässt die wenigen noch vorhandenen Grundstücke im Preis steigen; in den letzten zehn Jahren um rund 1.500 Prozent (vgl. Sascha Zander, MakeCity Festival, 28.06.2018: „2005: 167 Euro/m^2; 2018: 2.500 Euro/m^2"). Das ist eine Steigerung, die selbst Hauptstädte wie Paris oder London in den Schatten stellt und in ähnlichen Historien gründet: dem Ausverkauf städtischer und privater Liegenschaften im Höchstbieterverfahren auf dem freien Markt.

Neben den Grundstückskosten verteuern die gestiegenen Errichtungspreise die Baukosten und produzieren marktoptimierte und effiziente Architekturen, in denen öffentliche und gemeinschaftliche Räume keinen Platz haben. Letzter Ausweg für Architekt*innen scheint nur die Reduktion der Wohnungsgrößen zu sein, um einer von Verdrängung bedrohten Mittelschicht weiterhin Zugang zu Wohn- und Lebensraum in unseren Städten zu gewährleisten.

Die vollkommene Ökonomisierung unseres Lebensraums

Was wir in der Folge beobachten können, ist eine Homogenisierung der Architekturen unserer Städte. Sie folgen den immer gleichen wirtschaftlichen Logiken, reproduzieren die immer gleichen Räume und Milieus. Die unterschiedlichen Parteien und Kräfte – ob Einzelpersonen, Unternehmen oder Fonds – folgen der festen Überzeugung von Individualbesitz und tragen so zur vollkommenen Ökonomisierung unseres Lebensraums bei. Die Gestaltungshoheit über unsere gebaute Umwelt, sowohl über die Stadt als auch über das Land, verlagert sich von der Öffentlichkeit (vertreten durch die Politik) hin zu privaten Parteien, deren Agenda meist unklar ist. Mit dem Credo der Alternativlosigkeit zur freien Marktwirtschaft entstehen so Räume, die Bewohner*innen zu Verbraucher*innen degradieren

their way into a more widespread practice as an argument and guide for further action – because it is these architectural success stories that offer an alternative to the market.

With ownership comes responsibility!

und Homogenität zum gesellschaftlichen Leitbild bestimmen.

Was tun? Architekt*innen und Planer*innen sind gefordert, gemeinsam mit privaten Bauherr*innen alternative Modelle zu entwickeln, die räumliche und wirtschaftliche Antworten auf die Situation geben. Gemeinschaftlich gedachte Alternativen wie das Projekt am Blumengroßmarkt der Architekt*innen ARGE ifau | HEIDE & VON BECKERATH müssen erklärt und verstanden werden, damit sie als Handlungsanleitung und Argument Einzug in eine weitergehende Praxis finden. Denn es sind diese Erfolgsgeschichten der Architektur, die ein Gegenangebot zur Alternativlosigkeit des Marktes bieten.

Eigentum verpflichtet!

-> Case Study 03 pp. 70 f. IBeB

Celebrating the Amateur

The Business of Shaping the Social

In the summer of 2018 in Berlin, three unique buildings, Frizz23, IBeB and LoBe, spanning an array of architectural styles, from design vocabularies to investment models, opened their doors. Particularly unique are their different models of operation and the stories of how the buildings came into being, which are always directly linked to the people behind them. Olaf Grawert recounts fragments of the story of the LoBe Block Terrassenhaus and its developer Olivia Reynolds attempting a categorisation of the private and public, the economic and social.

This text is not about the end of the city and its public spaces. Certainly, it is clear that our cities are being sold off: their land, living spaces, squares and infrastructures. This text is, however, about a new reality in which private individuals assume the tasks of the public hand in order to provide answers to problems such as the lack of housing, displacement and the homogenisation of our living spaces. These are stories of - and about - amateurs who are willing to take financial and social risks in order to make a contribution to the common good. They do this with the hope of making a small change to society: stories of success, failure, renegotiation and adaptation, which should serve as encouragement to follow them in their footsteps or to do things differently.

"What planet am I on here ...?"

Searching for architects in the spring of 2014, gallerist and entrepreneur Olivia Reynolds met with architects Brandlhuber+ Emde, Burlon, in their studio building at Brunnenstraße 9 in Berlin. Their building proposal was the closest to what Reynolds believed architecture is - and what she imagined it could do. It was for this reason that she wanted to develop their concept, together with the architects, for her property in Berlin's Wedding district.

Bought with private capital, the land - formerly an informal car park and then a wasteland - was unattractive to conventional investors for a num-

Privat handelt öffentlich

Über die Vereinbarkeit von wirtschaftlich und sozial

Im Nebeneinander der Architekturen, zwischen Formensprachen und Investitionsmodellen, öffneten in Berlin im Sommer 2018 drei besondere Häuser ihre Türen: Frizz23, IBeB und LoBe. Besonders daran: die unterschiedlichen Betreiber*innenmodelle und Entstehungsgeschichten, die immer auch in direktem Zusammenhang mit den Menschen hinter den Projekten stehen. Olaf Grawert erzählt in Auszügen die Geschichte des Terrassenhauses LoBe Block und seiner Bauherrin Olivia Reynolds und unternimmt den Versuch einer erzählerischen Einordnung zwischen privat und öffentlich, wirtschaftlich und sozial.

In diesem Text geht es nicht um das Ende der Stadt und ihrer öffentlichen Räume. Zwar können wir ihn alle beobachten: den Ausverkauf unserer Zentren, des Baulands, Wohnraums, der Plätze und Infrastrukturen; in diesem Text geht es um eine neue Realität, in der private Akteur*innen die Aufgaben der öffentlichen Hand übernehmen, um Antworten auf Probleme wie die Wohnraumverknappung, die Verdrängung und Homogenisierung unserer Lebensräume zu finden. Es sind Geschichten von und über Amateur*innen, die bereit sind, finanzielles und gesellschaftliches Risiko einzugehen, um einen gemeinwohlorientierten Beitrag zu leisten – in der Hoffnung, gesellschaftlich etwas verändern zu können: Geschichten von Erfolg, von Scheitern, von Nachverhandlung und Anpassung, die zugleich ermutigen und aufklären sollen, es genauso, anders und besser zu machen.

„Entschuldigung, bin ich hier richtig ...?"

Auf der Suche nach einem Architekturbüro traf die Galeristin und Unternehmerin Olivia Reynolds im Frühjahr 2014 die Architekt*innen Brandlhuber+ Emde, Burlon in dem von ihnen geplanten Atelier- und Bürogebäude „Brunnenstraße 9" (Berlin). Das Haus kam den Vorstellungen der Bauherrin, was Architektur ist und leisten sollte, am nächsten. Deshalb wollte sie das Konzept für ihr Grundstück im Berliner Wedding gemeinsam mit den Architekt*innen entwickeln.

ber of reasons. Not so to its current owner, who recognised the hidden potential of gaps in the urban fabric, and insisted on a playful way of dealing with laws and restrictions on construction in Berlin. The resulting design surpassed her expectations and highlighted her sense of social responsibility. Reynold's wishes for shared green spaces and an open architecture were to accommodate various uses and users via the terraced house typology. Intended to house studios and small-scale enterprises, the design fulfilled existing construction laws and norms, while also allowing for the possibility to transform the building into housing units in the future. The design simultaneously demanded that the owner rethink her own position, taking more risks and assuming more responsibilities - a challenge that Reynolds rose to. She decided on the project, taking into account its business model and future potential uses, as well as the possibilities offered by the piece of land itself and the increasing demand for spaces for studios and light industry. Together, all of these arguments made the financing of the project possible.

"Okay, but ... "

The realisation of the design - both its architecture and its business model - revealed hidden difficulties. The economic and social norms of our society were and are decisive in this context, operating under the paradigm of the free market. Reynolds found herself continually confronted with others' understanding of what is "normal" or what constitutes "the rules". Banks asked her where the "man at her side" was - a question that had nothing to do with the responsibility the branch holds towards its shareholders, and one of countless examples of normative thinking. Only after the ninth try was Reynolds able to secure financing with GLS Bank - a socially and ecologically oriented bank that looked beyond her economic and financial plan, recognising and valuing the social potential of her project.

The stumbling blocks presented by the market also played a role in the building process. Increasing demand for living space means that across Germany, and above all in Berlin, there is a boom in building and a scarcity of construction labour. The result is a growing lack of alternatives. As a result of increasing demand, construction companies have the power to pick their projects, pushing prices up and contributing to the general price increase. This is a widespread

Das mit Eigenkapital finanzierte Grundstück – eine ehemalige Brache, die bis dahin als Autoabstellplatz genutzt wurde – war aufgrund zahlreicher Einschränkungen für klassische Investor*innen unattraktiv. Nicht so für die Bauherrin, die das Potenzial der Lücke erkannte und auf den spielerischen Umgang der Architekt*innen mit Gesetzen und Baunormen hoffte. So entstand ein Entwurf, der die gesellschaftliche Verantwortung der Eigentümer*innenschaft herausstellt. Reynolds Wünsche nach gemeinschaftlichen Grünflächen und einer für verschiedenste Nutzer*innen offenen Architektur konnte die Typologie des Terrassenhauses erfüllen. Gedacht als Atelier- und Gewerbebau, schaffte es der Entwurf, die bestehenden baulichen Normen zu erfüllen und zudem eine mögliche zukünftige Nutzung als Wohngebäude mitzudenken. Gleichzeitig forderte der um ein Vielfaches umfangreichere Entwurf die Bauherrin auf, ihre eigene Position zu überdenken und mehr Risiko und Verantwortung zu übernehmen – eine Forderung, der Reynolds nachkam. Sie entschied sich für das Projekt, auch im Hinblick auf dessen Betreiber*innenmodell und zukünftige Nachnutzungen. All das waren Argumente, die zusammen eine Finanzierung des Projekts auf Grundlage des vorhandenen Grundstücks und steigender Nachfrage nach Atelier- und Gewerbefläche ermöglichten.

„Okay, aber ..."

Die Umsetzung der Planung – sowohl der Architektur als auch des Betreiber*innenmodells selbst – entpuppte sich als durchaus schwieriger als gedacht. Ausschlaggebend waren und sind in diesem Zusammenhang die wirtschaftlichen und sozialen Normen unserer Gesellschaft unter dem Paradigma des freien Marktes. So sah sich Reynolds, trotz konkreter Planung, wiederholt mit den Vorstellungen von dem, was „normal" und „die Regel" ist, konfrontiert. Die Nachfrage der Banken nach „dem Mann an ihrer Seite" hatte dabei nichts mit einer Verantwortung der Branche gegenüber ihren Anleger*innen zu tun, sondern ist lediglich eines von zahllosen Beispielen normativen Denkens. Erst im neunten Anlauf gelang Reynolds die Finanzierung mit einer sozial ausgerichteten Bank, die über ihren Wirtschafts- und Finanzierungsplan hinaus das gesellschaftliche Potenzial ihres Projekts erkannte und wertschätzte.

Die Tücken des Marktes spielten auch im Bauprozess eine Rolle. Die steigende Nachfrage nach Lebensraum führt deutschlandweit, vor allem aber in Berlin, zu einem Bauboom und einer Verknap-

problem that, in combination with low average incomes (in Berlin), leads to the homogenisation of architecture in our cities. Architects must choose between refusing to compromise or following the same economic logic that reproduces the same spaces and milieus.

In the case of the LoBe Block, a protracted process of negotiation between owner, planning and operating architects - Brandlhuber+ Emde, Burlon/Muck Petzet - and third parties led to adjustments of the framing conditions in order to remain faithful to the original concept, both in its form and its content.

"Finally, now we can ... "

The opening of the building has already demonstrated the venture was well worth the expense and risk that Reynolds put on the line. Together with cultural studies scholar Elke Falat, Reynolds founded "LoBe Block GmbH", which is intended to facilitate negotiations between economic and shared social interests. The company takes on the programming and maintains the building. Today, the building is operated on a cross-financing model: temporary, profitable units are necessary in order to balance out additional costs, guaranteeing an average long-term rent, making further building investments in the external spaces possible. In return, the commercial tenancies and studios gain access to a new way of living on layered street spaces that together have created a new public paradigm.

In the mid-term, ownership of the building is to be transferred to a foundation, which will not counteract the pressure to be profitable but it won't exacerbate market pressure. Naturally, self-interest also plays a role in this context. However, first and foremost, the LoBe Block provides us with an example of how private and public interests can be brought together, proving that a building for businesses as a socially oriented project - even when conceptualised by a small, private team - can be set in motion.

pung von Arbeitskraft. Die Folge ist eine wachsende Alternativlosigkeit. Aufgrund der steigenden Nachfrage haben Firmen die Wahl. Sie können teuer anbieten und tragen zum Kostenanstieg bei – ein weitverbreitetes Problem, das in Kombination mit den niedrigen Durchschnittseinkommen (in Berlin) zu einer Konformität der Architekturen unserer Städte führt. Die Architektur muss wählen: Entscheidet sie sich für die Kompromisslosigkeit oder folgt sie den immer gleichen wirtschaftlichen Logiken, die immer gleiche Räume und Milieus reproduzieren?

Im Falle des LoBe Blocks folgte ein langwieriger Anpassungsprozess zwischen Bauherrin, den planenden und ausführenden Architekt*innen (Brandlhuber+ Emde, Burlon / Muck Petzet Architekten) und den involvierten Drittparteien: ein Adjustieren der Rahmenbedingungen, um dem Ursprungskonzept sowohl baulich als auch inhaltlich weitestgehend treu zu bleiben.

„Endlich, jetzt können wir ..."

Mit der Eröffnung des Gebäudes wurde eines klar: Der Aufwand und das Risiko, das Reynolds als private Bauherrin auf sich genommen hatte, waren es wert. Gemeinsam mit der Kulturwissenschaftlerin Elke Falat gründete Reynolds die „LoBe Block GmbH", die zwischen Wirtschaftlichkeit und Gemeinwohlinteresse zu vermitteln versucht. Die GmbH übernimmt die Programmierung und unterhält den Block. Heute wird der Gewerbebau im Querfinanzierungsmodell betrieben: temporäre Rendite-Einheiten wurden nötig, um die Mehrkosten auszugleichen, eine marktübliche Miete langfristig zu gewährleisten und das Weiterbauen und Gestalten der (Außen-)Räume zu ermöglichen. Was die Nutzer*innen dafür bekommen, ist eine neue Form von Zusammenleben, die an gestapelte Straßen erinnert und in die Öffentlichkeit programmatisch eingeschrieben ist.

Mittelfristig soll das Gebäude in eine Stiftung überführt werden, was den Renditedruck zwar nicht aushebelt, aber auch nicht fortschreibt. Denn natürlich spielen in diesem Zusammenhang auch Eigeninteressen eine Rolle. Doch ist der LoBe Block ein Beispiel für die Vereinbarkeit von privaten und öffentlichen Interessen und der Beweis, dass ein privates gemeinwohlorientiertes Gewerbebauprojekt nur mit viel Risiko und Aufwand sowie im Team gedacht, geleistet und geschaffen werden kann!

A wider perspective: the LoBe Block; an iconic symbol for a more civic agenda defies difficult conditions between railway lines, transport noise and global investment pressures

Ausrichtung mit Weitblick: Der LoBe Block als ikonenhaftes Sinnbild für gemeinschaftliche Initiative trotzt den schwierigen Bedingungen zwischen Bahntrasse, Straßenlärm und globalem Investitionsdruck

Mix of uses at all levels: offices, gastronomy and residential amongst vegetable patches and beekeeping

Nutzungsmix auf allen Ebenen: Büros, Gastronomie und Wohnen vereint mit Gemüsebeeten und Bienenzucht

01. Midway Artist Studios

Project: Midway Artist Collective (MAC)
City: Boston (USA)
Client: Midway Artist Studio residents
Planning: N/A
Status: 2013-current

This Sale Will (Not) Affect You
A Social Finance Model

In 2013, Midway Artist Studios - a 67,000 square-metre brick loft in Boston's Fort Point neighbourhood that provided living and working space for 100 artists - was put up for sale. Discovering that there would be no mechanism for rent control beyond income-qualified studios, and with Midway poised to become a luxury rental building, a concerned group of tenants anticipated that they were likely to be evicted and decided to buy the building themselves. They created the Midway Artist Collective (MAC), a non-profit corporation, to compete with commercial developers attempting to purchase the property. MAC began raising money internally. Within five days, residents raised 540,000 dollars, convincing a local developer to partner with them through a unique ownership model involving a combination of rent and investment. Together they submitted a 20 million dollar bid; it was labelled "non-competitive" and denied.

With 91 percent of the residents on board, they launched an aggressive overnight letter writing campaign to any and all stakeholders, and in a frenetic 14-day period, they secured 1.1 million dollars from investors towards the required deposit. Next, MAC secured 1 million dollars in support from the Neighbourhood Housing Trust and a further 3 million dollars from the non-profit community development financial institution Boston Community Capital. With the weight of the community behind them, they were able to assume a 14.5 million dollar mortgage from Oppenheimer Finance. MAC submitted an adjusted, and ultimately successful, 20 million dollar bid, ensuring affordable rent for the resident artists in perpetuity.

The story of Midway Artist Studios is remarkable, but it is not unique; it is the transferrable story of a group of people whose stake in maintaining their ability to live and work compelled them to show investors, community lenders, neighbourhood housing trusts, big banks, mortgage funders, city authorities - and themselves - that a different type of funding model for mixed-use developments is both possible and achievable.

Dieser Verkauf hat (keine) Folgen
Ein sozialer Finanzplan

2013 wurden die Midway Artist Studios – ein 67.000 Quadratmeter großer Backsteinspeicher in Bostons Viertel Fort Point, der hundert Kunstschaffenden Lebens- und Arbeitsraum bot – zum Verkauf angeboten. Die betroffenen Mieter*innen erkannten, dass es, abgesehen von einkommensbezogenen Studiomieten, keinerlei Mechanismus geben würde, die Mieten zu kontrollieren, und dass Midway ein Luxusmietshaus werden würde. Daraus folgerten sie, dass die Wahrscheinlichkeit einer Räumung enorm war, und entschlossen sich, selbst aktiv zu werden und das Gebäude zu kaufen. Sie gründeten das Non-Profit-Unternehmen Midway Artist Collective (MAC), um mit kommerziellen Entwicklungsfirmen, die versuchten, die Immobilie zu erwerben, in den Wettbewerb treten zu können. Das MAC begann, intern Geld zu sammeln. Innerhalb von fünf Tagen hatten die Bewohner*innen 540.000 Dollar beisammen und überzeugten einen örtlichen Projektentwickler, sich mit ihnen zusammenzutun. Zusammen konnten sie ein Gebot in Höhe von 20 Millionen Dollar platzieren; es wurde jedoch als „nicht wettbewerbsfähig" abgelehnt.

Mit 91 Prozent der Mieter*innen an Bord starteten sie kurzfristig eine Kampagne, in der sie sich schriftlich an alle Interessengruppen und Entscheidungsinstanzen wandten. So konnten sie in zwei Wochen 1,1 Millionen Dollar von Investor*innen für die erforderliche Kaution sichern. Als weitere Unterstützung sicherte sich das MAC eine Million Dollar von der örtlichen Wohnungsbaugesellschaft und weitere drei Millionen von einer nicht-gewinnorientierten Finanzinstitution für lokale Entwicklung. Mit der Kraft der Nachbarschaft im Rücken wurde eine Hypothek in Höhe von 14,5 Millionen Dollar übernommen. Das MAC konnte so ein erneutes – und schließlich erfolgreiches – Gebot in Höhe von 20 Millionen abgeben und so auf Dauer bezahlbare Mieten für die Künstler*innen sichern.

Die Geschichte der Midway Artist Studios ist bemerkenswert, aber nicht einzigartig; es ist die modellhafte Geschichte einer Gruppe von Menschen, deren Interesse am Erhalt ihrer Arbeits- und Wohnsituation sie dazu bringt, Investor*innen, lokalen Kreditgeber*innen und Wohnungsbauinstitutionen, Banken, Hypothekengeber*innen und städtischen Behörden – sowie sich selbst – zu zeigen, dass ein alternatives Finanzierungsmodell für Mischnutzungsentwicklungen möglich und erreichbar ist.

"Midway has proved to be an enduring financial and social model, giving rental residents the benefits of ownership control."

„Midway hat sich als dauerhaftes finanzielles und soziales Modell erwiesen, das den mietenden Bewohner*innen die Vorteile der Eigentumskontrolle verschafft."

Raber Umphenour

The mix of individualised studios and workshops coalesced into communality, as tenants galvanised co-ownership thorough intense collaborative action

Die individualisierten Studios und Werkstätten fügten sich zu einer Gemeinschaft, als Mieter*innen den kooperativen Besitz durch intensive kollaborative Aktion errangen

02.

Project: **Plateau Urbain**

City: Paris (FR)
Client: City of Paris
Planning: Plateau Urbain with Yes We Camp, Aurore
Status: 2013-current

The Agency of Temporary Use A Socio-political Tool

Since 2013, Plateau Urbain has been initiating temporary uses of vacant office buildings, shopping centres and former industrial complexes throughout France. Their largest and most famous project is Les Grands Voisins (the Big Neighbours), located in Paris's fourteenth arrondissement. Together with the charity association Aurore and the architectural collective Yes We Camp, a programme was developed for the 3.2-hectare site of the former children's hospital Saint-Vincent-de-Paul. The concept: an emergency shelter for the homeless and refugees became a housing project for more than 600 people. People of different social milieus are brought together, while the public spaces of the site are used for social projects aimed at solidarity. Around 1,000 people come to work here every day, with more than 300 organisations, social sponsors, artists, activists and start-ups coming together within the 20,000 square metres of the site.

In the meantime, Plateau Urbain has launched about 20 projects - ranging in scale from less than 530 square metres of space to those covering more than 21,000 square metres - all located in the metropolitan areas of Paris, Lyon and Marseille. The goal is always to provide temporary non-commercial spaces that allow diversity in urban coexistence, thereby initiating a political debate on real estate speculation. However, Plateau Urbain not only creates urban spaces but also provides tools for users and offers a large portfolio of support: legal foundations, insurance advice, digital tools and access to a comprehensive network. Co-operatively organised, Plateau Urbain determines a discourse on temporary use and provides the impetus needed for alternatives in urban development. Politicians now see temporary projects as instruments of innovation and support such alternatives. This endorsement also contributes to the consolidation of Plateau Urbain's initiatives, both spatially and socially: communities are being strengthened and jobs created - not only temporarily, but sustainably.

Die Kraft der Zwischennutzung Ein soziopolitisches Werkzeug

Seit 2013 initiiert Plateau Urbain Zwischennutzungen in leer stehenden Bürogebäuden, Einkaufszentren oder ehemaligen Industrieanlagen in Frankreich. Das bekannteste und größte Projekt ist Les Grands Voisins – die großen Nachbarn – im 14. Pariser Arrondissement. Gemeinsam mit dem sozialen Träger Aurore und dem Architekturkollektiv Yes We Camp wurde ein Programm für das 3,2 Hektar große Terrain des ehemaligen Kinderkrankenhauses Saint-Vincent-de-Paul entwickelt. Die Idee: Eine Notunterkunft für Obdachlose und Geflüchtete wird zum Wohnprojekt für 600 Personen. Menschen verschiedener sozialer Milieus werden zusammengebracht, dabei die Freifläche des Geländes für soziale und solidarische Projekte genutzt. Auf 20.000 Quadratmetern fanden so über 300 Organisationen, soziale Träger, Künstler*innen, Aktivist*innen und Start-ups zusammen. Bis zu 1.000 Menschen arbeiteten täglich vor Ort.

Inzwischen hat Plateau Urbain rund zwanzig Projekte – von 530 bis 21.000 Quadratmetern Fläche – im Großraum Paris, Lyon und Marseille angestoßen. Das Ziel ist immer das gleiche: vorübergehend nichtkommerzielle Räume zur Verfügung zu stellen, die eine Vielfalt im städtischen Miteinander ermöglichen, und dabei eine politische Debatte über Immobilienspekulation anzustoßen. Plateau Urbain schafft allerdings nicht nur Raum. Die Aktivist*innen stellen auch Werkzeuge für die Zwischennutzenden zur Verfügung und bieten ein großes Portfolio an Unterstützung an: rechtliche Grundlagen, Versicherungsberatung, digitale Tools oder auch ein umfassendes Netzwerk. Genossenschaftlich organisiert, bestimmt Plateau Urbain den Diskurs über Zwischennutzungsmöglichkeiten und gibt Impulse für Alternativen in der Stadtentwicklung. Die Politik steht dahinter und sieht temporäre Projekte als Elemente der Innovation an. Dieser Rückhalt trägt auch zur Verstetigung der Initiativen von Plateau Urbain bei, sowohl räumlich als auch sozial: Gemeinschaften werden gestärkt und Jobs geschaffen – nicht nur temporär, sondern nachhaltig.

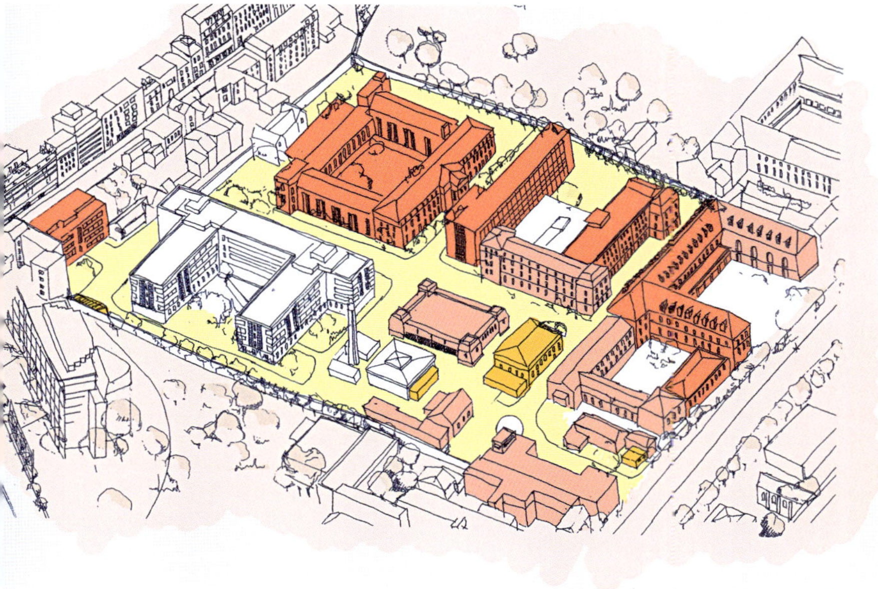

NGOs, educational programs, crafts and arts define the mix

NGOs, Bildungsprogramme, Handwerk und Kunst prägen den Mix

Temporary structures for overnight visitors designed by the architecture collective Yes We Camp

Übernachtungsmöglichkeiten für Kurzzeitbesucher*innen geplant vom Architekturkollektiv Yes We Camp

03.

Project: **IBeB**

Integrated building project in the former wholesale flower market (IBeB), Berlin-Kreuzberg

City: Berlin
Client: N/A
Planning: ARGE ifau | HEIDE & VON BECKERATH, Self-building co-operative Berlin eG
Status: Completed 2018

Form Follows (Cross-)Finance Architecture Shaped by Alternatives

In 2018 the living and studio building next to the Blumengroßmarkt (wholesale flower market) in the Kreuzberg district of Berlin was completed as the result of an innovative concept and collaborative procedure. By using stark architectural language, the project illustrates essential building policy issues, while questioning alternative urban developments through the negotiation of civil society issues and essential housing questions. As one of three projects, the IBeB was the result of a dialogue between the district, the Berlin Senate, and residents - with the goal of keeping development for residential purposes out of the grasp of the highest bidder and, instead, available to developers with concepts most appropriate for the site.

It was the architectural firms ifau and HEIDE & VON BECKERATH, together with the baugruppe, who were most convincing with their concept of a mixed-finance construction and development model. Spatially and programmatically linking residential space with studio spaces, units can be either rented by co-operatives or purchased as property. The property was sold by the Berlin Real Estate Fund at a discounted price, with the difference to the market value of the property included as an allowance in the purchasing price of the condominiums, thereby being credited to the co-operative units so that a favorable rent can be realised (see diagram). The assembly consists of privately owned residential units, with 25 percent of the units held by the Selbstbaugenossenschaft Berlin eG and a smaller part by a social sponsor. The result is a building that architecturally reflects the diversity of its users as well as the quality of negotiated decisions. The structure of the building projects this effortlessly: an internal horizontal access road - the Rue Intérieure - that is bright as daylight leads to courtyards, creating inner neighbourhoods and structuring the nesting of the typologically diverse housing units. The ground floor is primarily occupied by commercial, studio and production facilities that activate the public space as two-storey units.

The house as an encyclopaedia: the IBeB showcases concept procedures and exemplifies the possibilities of architecture as a collaborative endeavour. The question of reproducibility is obvious. However, this does not mean copying this

Form folgt (Quer-)Finanzierung Wie Alternativen Architektur prägen

Das im Rahmen eines Konzeptverfahrens entstandene Wohn- und Ateliergebäude am Blumengroßmarkt in Berlin-Kreuzberg wurde 2018 fertiggestellt. Mittels klarer Architektursprache veranschaulicht das Projekt essenzielle baupolitische Themen, Fragen zu alternativer Stadtentwicklung und der Verhandlung zivilgesellschaftlicher Belange der Wohnungsfrage: Als eines von drei Projekten resultierte das IBeB aus einem Dialog zwischen Bezirk, Senat und Anwohner*innen und dem Ziel, verfügbare Bauflächen nicht an Meistbietende zu vergeben, sondern an Bauträger*innen mit standortadäquaten Ideen.

Die Architekturbüros ifau und HEIDE & VON BECKERATH in Kooperation mit der Selbstbaugenossenschaft eG überzeugten mit ihrem Konzept einer mischfinanzierten Baugruppe, die Wohn- und Atelierfläche räumlich und programmatisch verknüpft, wobei die Einheiten genossenschaftlich gemietet oder als Eigentum erworben werden können. Das Grundstück wurde vom Berliner Liegenschaftsfonds zu vergünstigten Konditionen vergeben. Die Differenz zum Marktwert des Grundstücks ist als Zulage im Kaufpreis der Eigentumswohnungen enthalten und wird den genossenschaftlichen Einheiten gutgeschrieben, sodass eine günstige Miete realisiert werden kann (siehe Diagramm). Die Baugruppe besteht aus privaten, selbstnutzenden Eigentümer*innen; 25 Prozent der Einheiten hält die Selbstbaugenossenschaft Berlin eG und einen kleineren Teil ein sozialer Träger. So entstand ein Gebäude, das auch architektonisch die Vielfalt seiner Nutzer*innen und räumlich die Qualität der Verhandlungsentscheidungen widerspiegelt. Die Gebäudestruktur lässt dies mühelos zu: Eine innenliegende horizontale Erschließungsstraße – die „Rue Intérieure" – die durch eingefügte Lichthöfe taghell ist, schafft Nachbarschaften und strukturiert die Verschachtelung der typologisch vielfältigen Wohneinheiten. In den Erdgeschossflächen befinden sich vorrangig Gewerbe, Ateliers und Produktionsstätten, die als zweigeschossige Einheiten und über großzügige Tore den öffentlichen Platz aktivieren.

Ein Haus als Enzyklopädie: Das IBeB avancierte zum Vorzeigeprojekt des Konzeptverfahrens und zeigt modellhaft die Möglichkeiten von Architektur in gemeinschaftlich-integrativen Projekten auf. Die Frage nach der Reproduzierbarkeit liegt daher auf der Hand. Modellcharakter meint in diesem Fall jedoch

highly complex, site-specific constellation elsewhere. Instead, what is exemplary in this project are the many options and variables that can serve as a blueprint for an integrated urban development, a viable alternative in resisting speculative housing developments.

nicht, die ortsspezifische, hoch komplexe Konstellation anderenorts zu kopieren. Vorbildhaft sind vielmehr die vielfältigen Optionen und Aspekte, die auch isoliert betrachtet als Blaupause für integrative Stadtentwicklung und spekulationsresistenten Wohnungsbau dienen können.

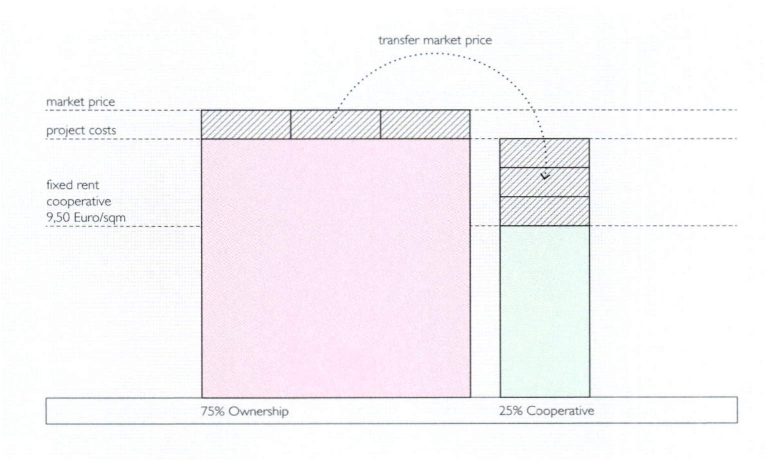

Cross-financing of co-operative residential and studio spaces facilitate affordable rents

Projektinterne Querfinanzierung von genossenschaftlichen Wohn- und Atelierräumen: So können günstige Mieten realisiert werden

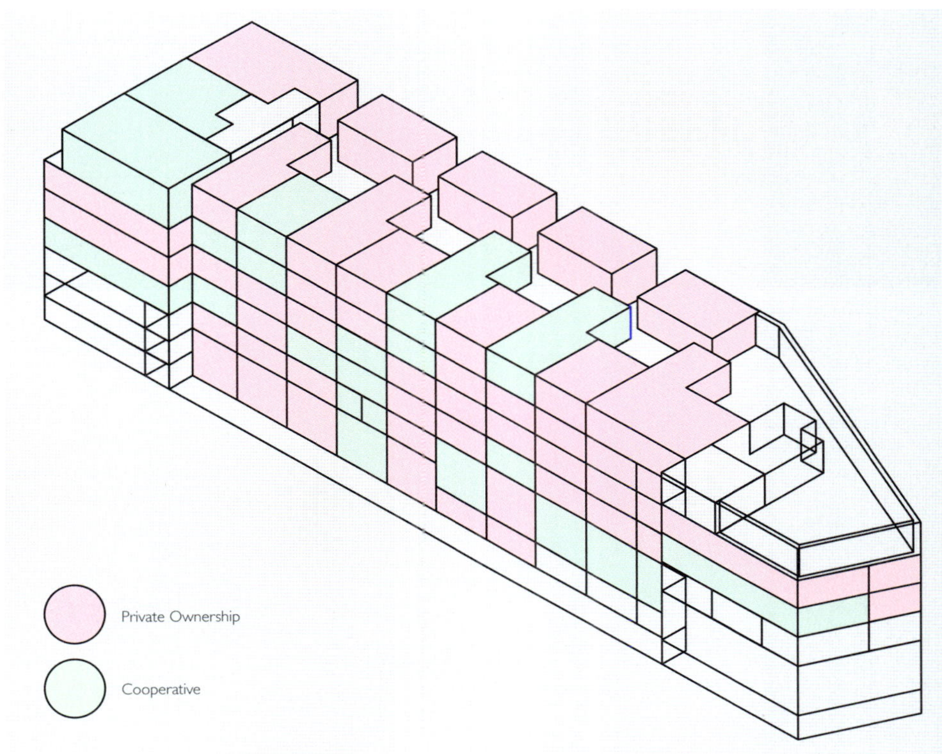

Courtyards shape the roofscape, form neighbourhoods and allow for "plugged-in" apartments

Lichthöfe formen die Dachlandschaft, erzeugen Nachbarschaften und erlauben durchgesteckte Wohnungstypen

A textbook for architectural approaches: post-war modernism, critical reconstruction and concept-based land sale at Blumengroßmarkt

Architekturlehrbuch Blumengroßmarkt: Nachkriegsmoderne, kritische Rekonstruktion und Konzeptverfahren

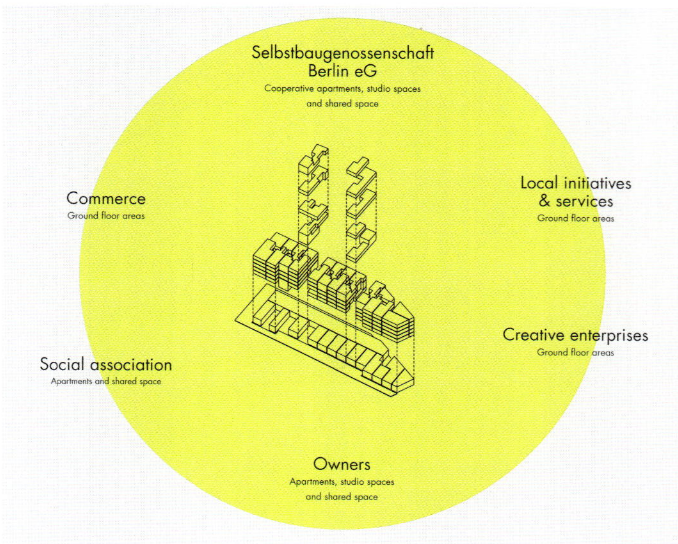

Options and variables translate to mixed floor plans

Gemischte Grundrisse: hell, groß-zügig und variabel nutzbar

04.

Project:

Kraftwerk1/Zwicky Süd

City: Zurich
Client: Bau- und Wohngenossenschaft Kraftwerk1
Planning: Schneider, Studer, Primas
Status: Completed 2016

The Co-operative as Developer The Zurich Model

Since its founding in the 1990s, the Kraftwerk1 co-operative has been aiming to contribute to urban development through innovative housing projects. Their third project, created on the premises of the Swiss spinning mill Zwicky, houses an extraordinary constellation of clients and is a radical statement for densification and urban life on the periphery of the city. With the settlement Zwicky South, the co-operative is daring to become involved in this urban agglomeration by investing in an area that has good access to public transportation to Zurich City as well as the airport, despite being difficult to develop due to high levels of noise pollution and no neighbourhood infrastructure. This area was effectively a no man's land between three separate municipalities and required a willingness to take risks and implement innovative ideas.

Together with interested members, the co-operative developed ideas for land use, approaching the site through a series of local events, while linking networks and the surrounding communities. The architects developed three building types with different qualities: the pane, the block and the hall. These types complement each other, enabling a broad mix of uses with different forms of living, from mini-studios to 14.5-room co-operative housing clusters, commercial units and accommodation services. The robust architectural language is reminiscent of shell buildings: an aesthetics of the unfinished. Appropriation and co-creation by the inhabitants are desired, leaving space for the articulation and creation of individual identities. The ambitious cost targets are anchored in the planning together with the contractor, who has been involved since the beginning.

The inhabitants are socially mixed in terms of age, income and education, and for many, the organisation of the co-operative is something new. Orchestrating a self-organised co-existence in this heterogeneity of everyday life is a challenge but for Kraftwerk1 this means assuming the social responsibility enshrined in its statutes: sustainable urban development means divesting collective property from speculation, enabling long-term low-cost rents, living in solidarity and inviting residents to take responsibility for their own living environment so that together they can shape the emerging neighbourhood.

Die Genossenschaft als Entwicklerin Ein Zürcher Weg

Seit ihrer Gründung in den 1990er Jahren verfolgt die Genossenschaft Kraftwerk1 das Ziel, mit innovativen Wohnprojekten einen Beitrag zur Stadtentwicklung zu leisten. Ihr drittes Projekt, das auf dem Areal der Schweizer Spinnerei „Zwicky" entstanden ist, zeigt eine außergewöhnliche Konstellation von Auftraggeber*innen und ist ein radikales Statement für Verdichtung und urbanes Leben an der Peripherie der Großstadt: Mit der Siedlung Zwicky Süd wagt die Genossenschaft den Schritt in die Agglomeration. Die Investition in ein Areal, das zwar durch eine gute Nahverkehrsanbindung an Flughafen und Zürich City verfügt, andererseits aber aufgrund starker Lärmbelastung schwierig zu bebauen ist und im Niemandsland zwischen drei Gemeinden keine Quartierinfrastruktur aufweist, erfordert Mut zum Risiko und gute Ideen.

Gemeinsam mit interessierten Mitgliedern entwickelt die Genossenschaft Nutzungsideen, nähert sich über Veranstaltungen dem Ort an und knüpft Netzwerke in die umliegenden Gemeinden. Die Architekt*innen entwickeln drei Gebäudetypen mit unterschiedlichen Qualitäten: die Scheibe, den Block und die Halle. Sie ergänzen sich ideal und ermöglichen einen breiten Nutzungsmix mit verschiedenen Wohnformen vom Mini-Studio bis zum 14,5-Zimmer-WG-Cluster, Gewerbeeinheiten und Quartiersdienstleistungen. Ästhetik des Unfertigen: Die robuste Architektursprache erinnert an Rohbauten. Aneignung und Mitgestaltung durch die Bewohner*innen ist ausdrücklich erwünscht und schafft so Identität. Die ambitionierten Kostenziele werden gemeinsam mit der Totalunternehmung, die ebenfalls von Beginn an beteiligt ist, in der Planung verankert.

Die Bewohner*innen sind in Bezug auf Herkunft, Alter, Einkommens- und Bildungsniveau breit durchmischt, für viele ist die Organisationsform der Genossenschaft neu. In dieser Heterogenität des gelebten Alltags ein selbstorganisiertes Zusammenleben zu orchestrieren, ist eine Herausforderung. Für Kraftwerk1 bedeutet das, die in ihren Statuten verankerte gesellschaftliche Verantwortung zu übernehmen: Nachhaltige Stadtentwicklung heißt, kollektives Eigentum der Spekulation zu entziehen, langfristig günstige Mieten zu ermöglichen, Solidarmodelle zu leben und die Bewohnenden dazu einzuladen, Verantwortung für die eigene Lebensumwelt zu übernehmen und das Quartier mitzugestalten.

A distinct typological mix: urban industrial scale interspersed with micro squares

Typologische Mischung: urban-industrieller Maßstab mit eingestreuten Mini-Plätzen

Scaffolding-like arcades span the spaces and generate common areas

Baugerüstartige Laubengänge umspannen die Volumen und generieren Gemeinschaftliches

The construction of social space is ever present

Die Konstruktion des Sozialen bleibt auch nach Fertigstellung im Aufbau

05.

Project: **SESC**
(Serviço Social do Comércio)
City: Rio de Janeiro, other cities in Brazil
Client: Brazilian society
Planning: N/A
Status: Ongoing

Direct Taxes for Culture
A Metropolitan Social Contract

The Serviço Social do Comércio (SESC) is an unparalleled arrangement that exists between the Brazilian state and the free economy. Initiated by the business community and instituted in 1946 in Rio de Janeiro, the SESC was a social welfare-oriented cultural and educational initiative for a country that was just beginning the processes of urbanisation and industrialisation while welcoming post-war refugees. Brazilian cities were experiencing unprecedented growth, with new labour forms and alliances emerging. In response, a Letter of Social Peace was drafted, promising that industry would make a mandatory percentage-based financial contribution based upon their payrolls. Today this takes the form of a 1.5 percent tax on all service-based firms in the country. The more money raised, the more culture is produced.

Since its inception, the SESC has spread to 572 sites in all 27 of Brazil's states. The money is collected and then redistributed to autonomously operated SESC subsidiaries, the principle being that a compulsory and multi-organisational collection system ensures the foundation is not beholden to the promotional interests of any single contributor. This independent-but-guaranteed financial stream has removed the marketing or promotional pressure that so often burdens similar organisations or initiatives elsewhere, with such interests set aside in favour of fostering social welfare; advancing artistic production; promoting autonomy, advancement and communal living; and nurturing solidarity.

Although the notion of a tax-based collection and distribution of cultural funding is not new, the immediacy, simplicity and autonomy of SESC are unique. As a private institution with resolutely inclusive public commitments, SESC does not limit its programming, and the resulting cultural diversity of the programmes means that it addresses the entire spectrum of Brazilian society. Facilities for culture, sports and crafts are available for everybody, everywhere. Even after five decades, this model is still groundbreaking. However, president-elect and right-wing populist Jair Messias Bolsonaro currently questions the system.

Kulturraum auf direktem Weg
Ein städtischer Gesellschaftsvertrag

Der Serviço Social do Comércio – SESC – ist ein Übereinkommen zwischen dem brasilianischen Staat und der freien Wirtschaft, das seinesgleichen sucht. Von der Wirtschaft initiiert und 1946 in Rio de Janeiro gegründet, war der SESC eine soziale, wohlfahrtorientierte Initiative, die sich um Kultur und Bildung eines Landes kümmerte, das gerade am Anfang des Prozesses der Urbanisierung und Industrialisierung stand und zugleich Nachkriegsflüchtlinge aufnahm. Die brasilianischen Städte erlebten im Zuge neuer Arbeitsformen und Bündnisse einen unvorhergesehenen Wachstumsboom. Als Reaktion darauf wurde ein „Brief für den sozialen Frieden" entworfen, der versprach, dass die Industrie einen prozentual festgelegten finanziellen Beitrag auf Grundlage ihrer zu entrichtenden Lohnsteuer machen würde. Heute bedeutet dies, dass alle Dienstleistungsfirmen des Landes eine 1,5-prozentige Steuer zahlen. Mehr Geld, mehr Kultur.

Seit seines Inkrafttretens hat der SESC mittlerweile 572 Firmen in allen 27 brasilianischen Bundesstaaten in der Pflicht. Das Geld wird gesammelt und an die selbstständig verwalteten Tochtergesellschaften des SESC verteilt. Dabei stellt ein obligatorisches, vielschichtig organisiertes Einzugssystem sicher, dass die Förderinteressen einzelner Beitragszahler*innen nicht über die Förderung von Projekten entscheiden. Diese unabhängigen, aber verlässlichen Zahlungen reduzieren den Marketing- oder Förderdruck, der in anderen Ländern häufig auf ähnlichen Organisationen oder Initiativen lastet. Stattdessen werden die soziale Wohlfahrt, das künstlerische Schaffen, die Autonomie, die Weiterentwicklung und das gemeinschaftliche Leben unterstützt und die Solidarität gefördert.

Obwohl die Idee einer steuerbasierten Kultursubvention nicht neu ist, ist das SESC in seiner Direktheit, Einfachheit und Autonomie ein einzigartiges Modell. Als private Institution mit einem konsequent öffentlichen Bekenntnis beschränkt der SESC sein Programm und die daraus entstehende kulturelle Vielfalt nicht und richtet sich so an die ganze Bandbreite der brasilianischen Gesellschaft. Orte der Kultur, des Sports und des Kunsthandwerks sind für alle überall zugänglich. Selbst nach fünf Jahrzehnten ist dieses Modell noch immer wegweisend. Der neu gewählte rechtspopulistische Präsident Jair Messias Bolsonaro stellt das System jedoch infrage.

SESC Pompeia Sao Paolo: Lina Bo Bardi's cohesive cultural oasis of urbanity manifests both cultural heterogeneity and social living

SESC Pompéia, São Paulo: Lina Bo Bardis kulturelle Oase der Urbanität manifestiert kulturelle Heterogenität und Soziales

The architect Lina Bo Bardi envisioning SESC Pompeia, 1986: together with Andre Vainer and Marcelo Ferraz outside the cultural industrial icon

SESC Pompéia in der Vorstellung der Architektin, 1986: Lina Bo Bardi, André Vainer und Marcelo Ferraz vor der kulturellen Industrie-Ikone

The SESC complex hosts count-less facilities and events, from sports to concerts, libraries and dance venues

Der SESC-Komplex beherbergt unzählige Einrichtungen und Veranstaltungen von Sport über Musikkonzerte bis hin zu Bibliotheken und Tanzstätten

Governance, Strategic Alliances and Negotiating the City

Governance, strategische Allianzen und Stadt neu verhandeln

2

Between 2014 and 2018, an unprecedented influx of 1.8 million refugees arrived in the EU. More than 1.2 million of these refugees arrived in Germany, of which over 600,000 have been settled since 2017.

Eine noch nie da gewesene Zahl von 1,8 Millionen geflüchteten Menschen traf seit 2014 in der EU ein – mehr als 1,2 Millionen davon in Deutschland. 600.000 Menschen aus Fluchtgebieten haben sich seit 2017 hier niedergelassen.

Up to 20 percent of healthcare workers in the British National Health Service are non-UK nationals.

Bis zu zwanzig Prozent der Menschen in Gesundheitsberufen im britischen National Health Service haben nicht die britische Staatsbürgerschaft.

Sweat equity is the non-monetised "contribution to a project or enterprise in the form of effort and toil."

Sweat Equity ist der nicht-monetarisierte „Beitrag zu einem Projekt oder Unternehmen in Form von Anstrengung und Arbeit".

Nearly 15 million German citizens over the age of 14 spend 5 billion hours volunteering annually.

Knapp 15 Millionen Bundes-bürger*innen ab dem 14. Lebens-jahr engagieren sich zusammen-genommen jährlich fünf Milliarden Stunden freiwillig.

Community land trusts deliver almost 50 percent of the 250,000 new homes needed every year in the UK.

Fast fünfzig Prozent der 250.000 neuen Wohnungen, die jedes Jahr in Großbritannien benötigt werden, stellen Community Land Trusts.

Between 2007 and 2018, over 150 Berlin self-initiated building groups (Bau-gruppen) have developed projects at a cost of 25 per-cent less than developers within the last 10 years.

Zwischen 2007 und 2018 haben über 150 selbst initiierte Baugruppen in Berlin Projekte entwickelt, deren Kosten um 25 Prozent niedriger waren als die der Immobilienentwickler*innen.

Sources / Quellen:

UNHCR Institute for Employment Research IAB, UK National Health Service, Generali Zukunftsfonds, The Cooperative City, Wohnungsbaugenossenschaften Deutschland, Baunetzwoche #319, Neue Zürcher Zeitung, City Lab, Plateau Urbain, change.org

With continental Europe's highest real estate prices, Zurich has stipulated since 2011 that 33 percent of new residential tenancies must be rented at prices no higher than the cost of construction and maintenance.

In Zürich, der Stadt mit den höchsten Immobilienpreisen in Kontinentaleuropa, gilt seit 2011, dass 33 Prozent der neuen Mietwohnungen zu Preisen vermietet werden müssen, die nicht höher liegen als die Kosten für Bau und Instandhaltung.

Association Plateau Urbain offers over 55,000 square metres of temporary space for co-working and housing in vacant Parisian properties.

Die Organisation Plateau Urbain bietet über 55.000 Quadratmeter temporären Raum für Zusammenarbeit und Wohnen in leer stehenden Pariser Immobilien.

In the UK, it takes 100,000 signatures by registered voters to compel a parliamentary debate on an issue. In Germany, only 50,000 signatures are required.

Im Vereinigten Königreich sind 100.000 Unterschriften registrierter Wähler*innen erforderlich, um eine parlamentarische Debatte zu einem Thema zu erzwingen. In Deutschland sind nur 50.000 Unterzeichner*innen erforderlich.

In Berlin, 20,000 signatures of registered voters can bring a motion to the floor in the house of representatives.

20.000 Unterschriften registrierter Wähler*innen reichen, um im Berliner Repräsentantenhaus einen Antrag zu stellen.

Since 2017, over 31,000 petitions have been successful on the platform change.org.

Seit 2017 waren über 31.000 Petitionen auf der Plattform change.org erfolgreich.

50,000 signatories collected within four months can halt a legal change already passed by Berlin's house of representatives.

50.000 Unterschriften, die innerhalb von vier Monaten gesammelt wurden, können eine Gesetzesreform stoppen, die das Berliner Repräsentantenhaus bereits verabschiedet hat.

In December 2018, tenant groups on Karl-Marx-Allee campaigned and gathered the 170,000 signatures required within four months to force a referendum with the aim of expropriating Deutsche Wohnen's 700 apartments and halting their profit-driven resale.

Stand Dezember 2018: Mietergemeinschaften in der Karl-Marx-Allee sammeln 170.000 Unterschriften, die innerhalb von vier Monaten für ein Referendum benötigt werden, um 700 Wohnungen von der Deutsche Wohnen zu enteignen und den gewinnorientierten Wiederverkauf zu stoppen.

Learn Economics, the Rest Will Follow!

The Case for Civic Capitalism

Civic capitalism means that emancipation is only complete when we learn how to manage our own economic affairs. Citizens of a civil society who are not capable of managing their economic affairs remain in a state of dependency. This applies not only to the independence of companies and finance capitalism or online monopolies but also, of course, to the public sector. Creatives and freelancers tend to give up their economic autonomy – they convince themselves that subsidised funding is better than participating in the market. This is a fundamental mistake. As a result, such individuals fall into a state of dependency that they think they can control politically – this, however, is a misconception, as has been shown over and over again.

The reason: it is clear that public support is by no means neutral but dependent on political conditions – and these, in democracies, are subject to change.

Since when have bureaucracies been positive about change?

My opposing position is encapsulated in the key word of the 1968 movement: self-determination. The long march through the institutions was a mistake that may well have made a simple life possible for the marchers, but has done nothing to change fundamental conditions. This conversation has already been had, and it should again be integrated into a much-needed, broader discourse if we are serious when we say that self-determination and welfare do not work together. Austerity does not offer a solution. Co-ops do, as do co-operation and networks and greater autonomy. In the alternative milieus of the '70s and early '80s, this was far clearer than it is today. This is the reason for the confidence of many in the ecological field, which has held onto this legacy.

However, it is precisely these instruments of autonomy that are consistently discredited by the Left – as well as by economically conservative forces. It is clear that the main aim is to stabilise

Lernt Ökonomie, der Rest folgt!

Ein Plädoyer für Zivilkapitalismus

Zivilkapitalismus meint, dass die Emanzipation erst dann vollzogen ist, wenn wir lernen, mit unseren ökonomischen Angelegenheiten souverän umzugehen. Bürger*innen einer Zivilgesellschaft, die nicht in der Lage sind, ihre eigenen wirtschaftlichen Angelegenheiten zu regeln, bleiben abhängig. Und das gilt natürlich nicht nur für die Abhängigkeit von Konzernen und Finanzkapitalismus oder monopolistischen Plattformen im Netz, sondern auch für den öffentlichen Sektor. Gerade Kreative und Selbstständige neigen dazu, ihre wirtschaftliche Autonomie abzugeben – und sich einzureden, Subventionen und Förderungen wären besser als die Teilnahme an Märkten. Das ist ein fundamentaler Irrtum. Man begibt sich dadurch nur in eine andere Form von Abhängigkeit, von der man glaubt, man könne sie politisch kontrollieren – dies ist allerdings auch ein Trugschluss, wie sich immer wieder zeigt.

Denn natürlich ist die öffentliche Unterstützung keineswegs „neutral", sondern davon abhängig, wie die politischen Rahmenbedingungen sind – und die sind in Demokratien natürlich wechselhaft.

Seit wann sind Bürokratien Freundinnen der Veränderung?

Ich halte dagegen mit einem Kernwert der 68er-Bewegung, der Selbstbestimmung. Der lange Marsch durch die Institutionen war ein Irrtum, der zwar ein einfacheres Leben für die Marschierer*innen gebracht hat, aber die Verhältnisse nicht grundlegend geändert hat. Die Diskussionen darüber wurden geführt – und sollten wieder in einen großen Diskurs eingehen, den wir führen müssen, wenn wir ernst meinen, was wir sagen: Selbstbestimmung und Fürsorge passen nicht zusammen. Alimentation ist keine Lösung. Genossenschaften sind eine, Kooperationen, Netzwerke, mehr Selbstständigkeit. In den alternativen Milieus der 1970er und frühen 1980er Jahre war das klarer als heute. Darauf baut auch die Zuversicht vieler im ökologischen Bereich.

Allerdings werden genau diese Instrumente der Autonomie in der Linken konsequent diskreditiert (wie

dependency. This is unsurprising, particularly because many of those profiting from institutions have a need to retrospectively legitimise their positions. This is not a political or social or economic project but simply an attempt at biographical doctoring based on the deception of oneself and others. Nobody should be ashamed of receiving public funding. But the creation of independent, sustainable economic structures and the knowledge of elementary economic principles should be a source of pride - above all, the capacity to create sustainable structures that are independent in the long term. I place great value on this capacity.

Never before have individuals been able to achieve so much for themselves

Therefore, I would recommend directing energy towards the creation of independent structures. Even more so because self-employment is going to play a central role as a means of income in the coming decades. This has repercussions that encompass the development of mobility and urban spaces - but also social structures, which change as a result. Capitalism is no longer the sole domain of monopolies and oligarchs but, in particular, the domains of those who are able to invest in knowledge and personal ability. Never before could individuals achieve so much for themselves. The majority of self-employed workers are, however, afraid to think economically, except in terms of managing negotiations. They take cover under the protection of the state or public funding structures (where many people work who see things the same way as I do, which is a source of hope).

This is not the "exit from self-imposed immaturity" which Kant, correctly, identified as a fundamental principle of the Enlightenment. This is an unashamed mind-set of unashamed servitude. I am convinced that a civic-capitalist mode of action - meaning the development of self-determined economic structures - will unleash far more potential for resistance than adaptation to statist bureaucracies. Since when were bureaucrats friends of change?

Independence can only flourish where self-determination can arise, and this is probably simply a question of competency. When it is no longer

auch von ökonomisch konservativen Kräften). Es geht offensichtlich darum, Abhängigkeit zu stabilisieren. Das ist nicht überraschend, denn offensichtlich versuchen viele Marschierer*innen, durch die Institutionen ihre Position zu legitimieren, im Nachhinein. Das ist allerdings weder ein politisches noch ein soziales noch ein ökonomisches Projekt, sondern nur der Versuch der biografischen Selbst- und Fremdtäuschung. Man muss sich nicht für öffentliche Förderung schämen. Aber auf die Schaffung eigener, tragfähiger ökonomischer Strukturen, auf das Lernen elementarer wirtschaftlicher Kenntnisse könnte man sogar ein wenig stolz sein. Vor allen Dingen aber könnte man damit auch tragfähige Strukturen schaffen, die langfristig unabhängig sind. Ich halte das für einen Wert.

Noch nie konnten Individuen so viel für sich erreichen

Ich würde also die Energien eindeutig auf die Errichtung eigener Strukturen legen. Das gilt umso mehr, als Selbstständigkeit auch als Erwerbsfaktor in den nächsten Jahrzehnten die zentrale Rolle spielen wird. Das hat Auswirkungen: auf die Entwicklung der Mobilität, der Städte – aber eben auch auf die Sozialstrukturen, die sich ändern. Kapitalismus, das ist nicht mehr die Domäne der Monopolist*innen und Oligarch*innen, sondern eben auch und ganz besonders die der Investition in Wissen und persönliches Können. Noch nie zuvor war es möglich, dass Individuen in so großer Zahl so viel für sich erreichen konnten. Die meisten Selbstständigen haben aber Angst davor, wirtschaftlich zu denken, sei es nur, Verhandlungen zu führen, und ducken sich dann unter das Dach des Staates oder öffentlicher Förderungseinheiten (in denen es viele Menschen gibt, die das genauso sehen wie ich, was ich erfreulich finde).

Das ist eben nicht der „Ausgang aus der selbstgewählten Unmündigkeit", von der Kant zu Recht als Grundanforderung der Aufklärung sprach. Es ist eine unverhohlene Untertanenmentalität. Ich bin überzeugt, dass zivilkapitalistisches Handeln – also das Entwickeln von selbstständigen wirtschaftlichen Strukturen – weitaus mehr Widerstandspotenzial hat als die Anpassung an etatistische Bürokratien. Seit wann ist die Bürokratie eine Freundin von Veränderung?

Unabhängigkeit kann nur dort entstehen, wo auch Selbstständigkeit entsteht, und die ist vielfach

clear whether the market economy fundamentally works, it will become even more difficult – and this is often the case.

I long for more pragmatism in this discussion. Where does the principle of self-determination stand? This question is asked by civic capitalism. On the other hand, the question of whether one has legitimised existing relations is a question that civic capitalism has not yet posed.

Learn economics, the rest will follow.

schlicht eine Kompetenzfrage. Wo noch nicht mal klar ist, wie die Marktwirtschaft grundlegend funktioniert, wird es schwierig – und das ist sehr oft der Fall.

Ich wünschte mir mehr Pragmatismus in der Diskussion. Wo ist die Selbstbestimmung geblieben? Diese Frage stellt Zivilkapitalismus. Die Frage, ob man die Verhältnisse legitimiert, stellt Zivilkapitalismus nicht.

Lernt Ökonomie, der Rest folgt.

Vision and Pragmatism

Empowering Social Entrepreneurship

The public sector knows it should be supporting participation in the development of services as well as solutions to challenges. Yet, how often do we hear about visionary and pragmatic approaches to civic participation that are geared towards long-term change and rooted in the real lives of residents? And how often is participation connected to wider concepts, such as new economic models that provide value, catering directly to disadvantaged communities? Here, Sarah Prosser, special adviser in social entrepreneurship and innovation for the City District of Old Oslo, shares her hands-on experience of how the public sector continues to undertake community development in the Tøyen area of Oslo.

Despite having been mostly unaffected by the austerity seen in other parts of Europe, Oslo – the capital of Norway – is a city that has become markedly segregated in terms of wealth and social capital in recent years. There exists an implicit assumption amongst most of the population that the strong welfare system will take care of its citizens. Paradoxically, it is this very belief this may expose otherwise-excluded individuals and families to a lack of neighbourly support and solidarity. Tøyen is an area in central-east Oslo that has a diverse population of 14,000 and faces some of the greatest social-economic challenges in Norway. For example, over 60 percent of children are raised in low-income households, and measured health and education indices are considerably lower than in other areas of the city. The only anchoring institution in the area, the Munch Museum, will be moved away to a new building on the waterfront, scheduled to open in 2020 next to the Oslo Opera House. To compensate, and in response to residents' demands, a five-year urban renewal programme was started in 2013, funded by the city and the state. Simultaneously, housing prices have increased more than anywhere else in Norway; social inequality is now tangible, and signs of gentrification are obvious and increasing.

As part of the urban renewal programme and in an effort to combat issues that were both preceded and exacerbated by gentrification, a project was proposed to establish a community

Vision und Pragmatismus

Soziales Unternehmertum stärken

Dem öffentlichen Sektor ist längst klar, dass er Partizipation in der Entwicklung von Dienstleistungen und die Lösung gesellschaftlicher Herausforderungen unterstützen sollte. Doch wann hört man schon von visionären und pragmatischen Ansätzen der Bürger*innenbeteiligung, die langfristige Veränderungen hervorbrachten und dabei die wahren Bedürfnisse von Anwohner*innen berücksichtigten? Und wann wird Partizipation mit neuen Konzepten ökonomischer Modelle verbunden, die sich direkt in benachteiligten Gemeinden auswirken? Sarah Prosser, Sonderberaterin für Soziales Unternehmertum und Innovation in Oslo, berichtet von ihren Erfahrungen in der Kommunalentwicklung im Osloer Stadtteil Tøyen.

Obwohl sie von den Sparzwängen anderer europäischer Städte fast unbehelligt blieb, ist in der norwegischen Hauptstadt Oslo in den vergangenen Jahren eine immer größere Kluft zwischen Wohlstand und sozialem Kapital festzustellen. Der Großteil der Bevölkerung geht stillschweigend davon aus, dass sich das Wohlfahrtssystem des Landes schon um seine Bürger*innen kümmern wird. Paradoxerweise ist es genau dieser Glaube, der dazu führt, dass ausgegrenzte Menschen und Familien eben keine Solidarität und nachbarschaftliche Unterstützung erfahren. Tøyen ist ein Stadtteil im östlichen Zentrum von Oslo mit einer vielgestaltigen Bevölkerung von rund 14.000 Menschen und einigen der größten sozioökonomischen Herausforderungen in ganz Norwegen. So wachsen hier über sechzig Prozent der Kinder in Haushalten mit geringem Einkommen auf. Gesundheits- und Bildungsstand sind bedeutend niedriger als in anderen Gegenden der Stadt. Die einzige wichtige Institution, das Munch-Museum, wird in ein neues Gebäude am Wasser neben das Osloer Opernhaus umziehen. Die Eröffnung ist für 2020 geplant. Als Ausgleich und Reaktion auf die Bedürfnisse der Bewohner*innen wurde 2013 ein von Stadt und Staat finanziertes urbanes Erneuerungsprogramm über fünf Jahre gestartet. Gleichzeitig sind die Wohnungspreise stärker gestiegen als irgendwo anders in Norwegen; die soziale Ungleichheit ist spürbar, die Zeichen der Gentrifizierung sind deutlich.

Als Teil des städtischen Erneuerungsprogramms und als Versuch, gegen die Probleme der Gentri-

incubator to be run by Tøyen Unlimited (TU). The incubator started as a table and a logo in a vacant, unused office, which was slated to be the location of a future community centre. TU defined its mission as supporting local people who had innovative ideas about how to solve social issues - of which they had first-hand experience - through sustainable business models; in other words, through social enterprise. The model of support was inspired by a combination of UnLtd UK, Impact Hub, and other similar initiatives. However, unlike others, it was to maintain a strict focus on local people's talents within the geographical boundaries of the area while developing and fostering uniquely close ties with the public sector. TU started with a part-time position, funded by the public sector and filled by an individual with knowledge of social enterprise in community development. The only funding from the city was in terms of hours used by this post. Importantly, it came with a degree of freedom to try new approaches: TU was given room to experiment and take initiative. Local residents were invited to come with their ideas on how social problems could be solved in the area and were given access to the office which functioned as a micro co-working space. The TU representative coached them, linking an income-generating element to their idea and thereby creating a social enterprise to solve self-experienced challenges. Residents could drop in, linger and work, discuss, get coaching and/or be connected to relevant resources - financial or otherwise - inside and outside the public sector. This exchange of knowledge and network-building is how self-confidence and social capital are built.

After six months, Tøyen Unlimited established itself as an independent organisation outside of the public sector. The elements that made it successful - including close contact with city district employees, free office space in the community centre and the informal coaching - remained in place, but the addition of a degree of independence opened doors for new forms of support.

TU now provides support to individuals, referred to as Unlimiters, in the form of awards called "Try it", "Do it" or "Build it". Each award includes neighbourhood support in the form of funding, capacity building and network opportunities. To date, there have been around 20 Unlimiters and 18 young Unlimiters. Examples include Shamsa Moalin, who established Kulmis - a social meeting place with the mission of reducing levels of diabetes, cancer and social isolation amongst

fizierung vorzugehen, wurde ein Projekt ins Leben gerufen: der Gemeinschaftsinkubator von Tøyen Unlimited (TU). Alles begann mit einem Tisch und einem Logo in einem leer stehenden, ungenutzten Büro, das als zukünftiges Stadtteilzentrum dienen sollte. TU übernahm die Rolle der Unterstützerin für alle Anwohner*innen, die neue Ideen und nachhaltige Geschäftsmodelle gegen die selbst erlebten sozialen Probleme einbringen wollten. Mit anderen Worten: Es ging um die Gründung sozialer Unternehmen. Das Unterstützungsmodell wurde als Kombination aus UnLtd UK, Impact Hub und anderen ähnlichen Initiativen umgesetzt. Anders als andere Initiativen wollte das Projekt einen klaren Fokus auf die Fähigkeiten der Menschen vor Ort richten, innerhalb des Stadtteils bleiben und besonders enge Beziehungen mit der öffentlichen Hand knüpfen. TU begann mit einer mit öffentlichen Geldern finanzierten Teilzeitstelle. Besetzt wurde diese mit einer Person, die Kenntnisse von sozialen Unternehmen und der Entwicklung von Gemeinschaften hat. Die einzige finanzielle Unterstützung vonseiten der Stadt waren die Stunden für diese Stelle. Wichtig war, dass sie eine gewisse Freiheit hatte, neue Ansätze auszuprobieren: Sie erhielt Raum zum Experimentieren und eigenen Handeln. Anwohner*innen wurden eingeladen, ihre Ideen zur Lösung sozialer Probleme in der Gegend vorzubringen, und bekamen die Möglichkeit, das Büro als Mikro-Coworking-Space zu nutzen. Der TU-Mitarbeiter unterstützte sie darin, eine zur Idee passende Einkommensquelle zu etablieren: die Gründung eines sozialen Unternehmens. So konnten Herausforderungen angegangen werden, die sie in ihrem Alltag erfuhren. Anwohner*innen konnten einfach vorbeikommen, bleiben und arbeiten, diskutieren, Coachings in Anspruch nehmen und/oder Zugang zu relevanten Ressourcen finanzieller oder anderer Natur im öffentlichen Sektor und außerhalb bekommen. Dieser Wissensaustausch und die Netzwerkarbeit lieferten die Grundlage für Selbstvertrauen und soziales Kapital.

Nach sechs Monaten konnte sich Tøyen Unlimited als eigenständige Organisation außerhalb des öffentlichen Sektors etablieren. Die Elemente, die zum Erfolg geführt hatten, wie der enge Kontakt zu städtischen Beschäftigten, der kostenlose Büroraum im Gemeinschaftszentrum und das informelle Coaching, blieben bestehen. Aber die zusätzliche Unabhängigkeit eröffnete Wege für neue Formen der Unterstützung.

Heute vergibt TU an Personen – die „Unlimiters" – Preise fürs „Probieren, Machen oder Bauen". Zu jedem Preis gehören finanzielle Nachbarschaftshilfe, Kapazitätsentwicklung und Netzwerkmöglichkeiten.

women of Somalia and other backgrounds, funding her work through catering for local events. Another example is Ole Pedersen, who established Nedenfra (From Below), that works to democratise urban development through encouraging and enabling deeper participation, funded by consultancy services. Finally, Ayalew Desta established Independent Business Accelerator, which works to support small businesses through capacity-building in the areas of Tøyen and Grønland, so that they are stronger in the face of increasing gentrification. The ideas, solutions and impact of the Unlimiters reach far beyond normal public services through accessing excluded individuals and groups, as well as in the impact they make in connection with aspects of well-being, such as role-modelling, a sense of belonging and employment-readiness.

It is also worth mentioning projects outside of the TU community incubator that have been fundamental in the neighbourhood's work for change. These include the Tøyen Sport Club that is focused on inclusion as much as it is on sport, and two libraries that are as much wonderlands of cultural and educational activities as they are places to borrow books. These projects can be traced back to dedicated residents who have worked together, experimenting with new approaches and concepts to help realise their dreams for a better life and a better neighbourhood. The new libraries, play parks, gable murals and funds for neighbourhood projects have all made their positive mark on the community. So too, public service innovations around council housing - from tenant boards to urban gardening and art projects in the stairwells.

Leaving behind positive traces in the community

However, even as the TU model expands to other cities - with Stavanger Unlimited opening in January 2019 and youth-focused programmes under way in the neighbouring community of Grønland - there is still a long way to go before this approach will be understood and embraced by the majority of the public sector. The manner in which the incubator is supported continues to be vulnerable in the short term. It seems to fall between the world of shiny start-up co-working spaces, the welfare state and the non-profit sector. TU's decision to adopt an independent legal

Bis heute gibt es ungefähr zwanzig Unlimiters und 18 junge Unlimiters. Beispiele sind Shamsa Moalin, die „Kulmis" ins Leben gerufen hat, einen sozialen Treffpunkt, der Frauen aus Somalia und anderswo bei Diabetes, Krebs und sozialer Isolation Hilfe bietet. Ihre Arbeit finanziert sie mit Catering-Aufträgen für Veranstaltungen im Stadtteil. Ole Pedersen gründete „Nedefra" („von unten"), das, unterstützt durch Beratungsunternehmen, urbane Entwicklung demokratisieren und eine stärkere Teilhabe ermöglichen möchte. Ayalew Desta rief den „Independent Business Accelerator" ins Leben, der kleine Unternehmen durch Kapazitätsentwicklung in Grønland und Tøyen unterstützt und gegen die zunehmende Gentrifizierung stärkt. Die Ideen, Lösungen und der Einfluss der Unlimiters reichen viel weiter als der normaler öffentlicher Einrichtungen, denn sie erreichen ausgegrenzte Personen und Gruppen und haben wesentlich mehr Einfluss auf die gesundheitliche und soziale Situation. Sie sind Vorbilder, können Zugehörigkeit vermitteln und die Bereitschaft zur Arbeit unterstützen.

Auch Projekte außerhalb des TU-Inkubators waren maßgeblich an den Veränderungen des Stadtteils beteiligt. Darunter sind der Tøyen Sport Club, der sich genauso sehr um Inklusion wie um Sport bemüht, und zwei Büchereien, die, neben der Buchausleihe, auch magische Orte für kulturelle und pädagogische Angebote darstellen. Nicht zuletzt sind die Veränderungen Ergebnis der Arbeit engagierter Anwohner*innen, die zusammengearbeitet haben, neue Ansätze und Konzepte aufgenommen und damit experimentiert haben, um ihren Traum von einem besseren Leben und einer besseren Nachbarschaft zu verwirklichen. Die neuen Büchereien, Spielplätze, Giebelwandbilder und die Finanzierung von Nachbarschaftsprojekten haben positive Spuren in der Gemeinschaft hinterlassen. Das haben auch öffentliche Erneuerungen rund um die Sozialwohnungen geschafft – mit Mieter*innenvertretungen, gemeinsamen Gärten und Kunstprojekten in den Treppenhäusern.

Positive Spuren in der Gemeinschaft hinterlassen

Das TU-Modell wurde mittlerweile auf andere Städte übertragen. Stavanger Unlimited startet im Januar 2019 und in Tøyens Nachbarbezirk Grønland gibt es spezialisierte Programme, die sich an junge Leute richten. Trotzdem ist es noch ein langer Weg, bis der Ansatz von der Mehrheit der öffentlichen

status absolved the public sector of responsibility, leaving it dependent on a short-term partnership contract. The Stavanger municipality has decided to keep the management role in the public sector with three years of committed funding. In other words, as Unlimited Norway builds replications of community incubators in different cities, the co-creative relationship of social/public initiatives is still flexible and under evaluation.

Social enterprise solutions still feel quite radical in Oslo: to have conversations with citizens about cooperative forms of ownership, social enterprise, co-creation and co-production is a new concept. But whatever the form, solution or support mechanism, there seems to be little doubt that a new economy will come from people taking ownership of their future in every community in the country. A neighbourhood incubator such as that in Tøyen might be a solid, pragmatic place for any local government to start: find an empty room, invite local people in, listen to their ideas, build skills around social enterprise and see what blossoms.

Verwaltungen verstanden und unterstützt wird. Die Unterstützung des Inkubators ist weiterhin fragil und kurzfristig. Das Projekt scheint irgendwo zwischen glänzenden Start-up-Coworking-Spaces, Wohlfahrtsstaat und karitativem Bereich angesiedelt zu sein. Die Entscheidung von TU, rechtlich unabhängig zu sein, entband die öffentliche Verwaltung ihrer Verantwortung und machte das Projekt von einem befristeten Unterstützungsvertrag der Stadt Oslo abhängig. Die Stadtverwaltung von Stavanger entschied, dass sie die Verwaltung des Projekts behalten wird. Die Förderung ist für drei Jahre gesichert. Mit anderen Worten: Unlimited Norway vervielfältigt die Nachbarschaftsinkubatoren in verschiedenen Städten, allerdings ist die Beziehung von sozialen und öffentlichen Initiativen noch nicht gefestigt und muss evaluiert werden.

Sozialunternehmerische Lösungen fühlen sich in Oslo noch immer ziemlich radikal an: Gespräche über genossenschaftliche Formen von Besitz, soziales Unternehmertum und Zusammenarbeit mit den Bürger*innen sind ein neues Konzept. Aber welche Form, Lösung oder welche Unterstützung auch gefunden wird, es besteht nur wenig Zweifel daran, dass eine neue Ökonomie von Menschen ausgehen wird, die ihre Zukunft an jedem Ort des Landes selbst in die Hand nehmen. Ein Nachbarschaftsinkubator wie der in Tøyen kann ein guter und pragmatischer Anfang für eine Stadtverwaltung sein: Sucht einen freien Raum, ladet Anwohner*innen dorthin ein, hört euch ihre Ideen an! Nutzt die vorhandenen Fähigkeiten für soziale Unternehmen und seht zu, wie die Saat aufgeht.

"Bring your politicians and policy makers to Copenhagen, get them on a bike, and cycle through the city – it will change their perspective on everything."

„Bringt eure Politiker*innen und Entscheider*innen nach Kopenhagen, setzt sie auf ein Fahrrad und lasst sie durch die Stadt radeln – dies wird ihre Perspektive auf alles verändern."

Tina Saaby

A Seat at the Table

Co-creating Copenhagen

In recent years, a surge in the privatisation of Copenhagen's previously public and co-operative housing has led to the exclusion of many residents. And this, in one of the richest countries in the world. The highly celebrated welfare system, which is supposed to make life easier for marginalised groups, is often difficult to access. Despite these difficulties - or perhaps because of them - Copenhagen continues to experiment with how we build and experience cities. Tina Steiger and Nora Unger spoke with Tina Saaby, the city architect of Copenhagen until the end of 2018, about co-creation processes, and how we can take care of the city - and each other.

Tina Steiger: When you were appointed city architect of Copenhagen in 2010, city planners were using a "participation toolbox" whenever discussions for urban development were slated to start. Why has the city moved away from this approach?

Tina Saaby: Planners were not being reflective - they were simply taking a tool and applying it, without adding value to the process. Today, we go into urban spaces and count and observe citizens; we collect data in different ways, gathering knowledge about the needs of the city and its inhabitants. This adds crucial value to the process - in city-making, we must rely on observations, rather than our own opinions. This is participatory design.
This means that in neighbourhood improvement areas, we go on-site and, over the course of five years, initiate co-creation processes with stakeholders and professionals. This often involves temporary uses and the application of different methods including observation, dialogue, workshops and surveys to understand the site. In each neighbourhood improvement project, we experiment with new methods of co-creation, capturing knowledge from the local environment in new ways. It is a constant process of experimenting and learning.

Nora Unger: Today, officials in Copenhagen analyze the neighbourhood beforehand, rather than just asking locals at the end of the design process. This means using buildings and urban

Ein Platz am Verhandlungstisch

Die Mitgestaltung Kopenhagens

In den vergangenen Jahren hat der Anstieg der Privatisierung vormals öffentlicher und genossenschaftlicher Wohnungen in Kopenhagen dazu geführt, dass viele Einwohner*innen sogar in einem der reichsten Länder der Welt ausgeschlossen werden. Und die viel gefeierten Ansprüche auf soziale Sicherung, die das Leben in Kopenhagen für marginalisierte Gruppen möglich machen sollen, bleiben oft schwer durchsetzbar. Trotz – oder vielleicht auch wegen – dieser Schwierigkeiten experimentiert Kopenhagen weiterhin mit Alternativen für Städtebau und seiner Wahrnehmung. Tina Steiger und Nora Unger sprechen mit Tina Saaby, bis Ende 2018 Stadtarchitektin von Kopenhagen, über Prozesse der Zusammenarbeit und darüber, wie wir alle Sorge für die Stadt – und uns selbst – tragen können.

Tina Steiger: Als Sie 2010 zur Stadtarchitektin von Kopenhagen ernannt wurden, benutzten die Stadtplaner*innen eine Art Werkzeugkasten der Partizipation, wenn Diskussionen über die Stadtentwicklung aufkamen. Warum hat sich die Stadt von diesem Ansatz verabschiedet?

Tina Saaby: Die Stadtplaner*innen haben das nicht reflektiert – sie nahmen einfach ein Werkzeug und wendeten es an, ohne dem Prozess Bedeutung zu verleihen. Jetzt gehen wir in die urbanen Räume und beobachten die Bewohner*innen; wir sammeln auf verschiedene Weise Daten und Wissen über die Bedürfnisse der Stadt und ihrer Bewohner*innen. Das macht den Prozess viel wertvoller. In der Stadtplanung müssen wir uns stärker auf Beobachtungen als auf unsere eigenen Meinungen beziehen. Das ist teilnehmende Gestaltung.
In Gegenden, die verbessert werden sollen, sind wir vor Ort und stoßen über einen Zeitraum von fünf Jahren Prozesse der Zusammenarbeit zwischen Interessenvertreter*innen und Profis an. Das beinhaltet oft Zwischennutzungen und verschiedene Methoden, um die Gegend besser zu verstehen: Beobachtungen, Gespräche, Workshops und Umfragen. In allen Stadtentwicklungsprojekten experimentieren wir mit neuen Methoden der Zusammenarbeit – es ist ein ständiger Experimentier- und Lernprozess.

Nora Unger: Heute analysiert die Stadtverwaltung in Kopenhagen zuerst eine Gegend, anstatt die

spaces temporarily, often together with clients and developers, while liaising with local district and neighbourhood boards. How do you see this process evolving?

TS: In the future it could be interesting to engage citizens more in the building process, and for them to take part in the maintenance of a project afterwards. It would be interesting to see how this could push projects in other directions, putting the responsibility back onto ourselves, as citizens, to explore how we take care of the city.

TST: Participative practices are not a novelty in urban planning projects and are often critiqued for being slow and tedious, or inaccessible to marginalised groups. In the worst case, they are instrumentalised for the benefit of private interests. Can you talk more about why Copenhagen has invested in participation?

TS: City-making takes time, and we should accept that! This doesn't mean everything has to take ten years. Detailed plans take between 48 and 72 weeks. We have to accept that talking and learning together takes time. I'm convinced that if we take the time in the beginning, it will save us time in the long run.

TST: In Copenhagen, co-creation appears to be a political mandate and very much part of the strategic vision of city officials. Does this mean it has become part of everything planners do and implement?

TS: It helps us immensely to have this mandate as a political vision. Beyond doing citizen workshops, it means collaborating in every sense – involving all stakeholders, including businesses, citizens, volunteers and politicians. It is very important that every neighbourhood improvement area designs its own methodologies for co-creation with local stakeholders, rather than it being implemented from the top down. This also means that there is no single way of enacting urban participation, as it depends on the situation: the site, the context, the people around it. Many different circumstances are part of the reflections which go into crafting a participation process.
In recent years, schoolyards in Copenhagen's inner boroughs are being opened to their neighbourhoods. This is an important move towards stimulating participation amongst younger generations. In our open schoolyards, children learn to take responsibility. We learn how to be citizens while we teach children how to participate in the city.

Anwohner*innen erst im Anschluss an den Gestaltungsprozess zu befragen. Dies bedeutet, dass Gebäude und urbane Räume auch temporär genutzt werden, oft zusammen mit Kund*innen und Entwickler*innen, während zwischen der Bezirksregierung und Nachbarschaftsvertretungen vermittelt werden muss. Wie entwickelt sich dieser Prozess?

TS: In Zukunft könnte es interessant sein, Bürger*innen stärker in den Bauprozess und im Anschluss an ein Projekt auch in die Erhaltung einzubinden. Es wäre interessant zu sehen, wie dies ein Projekt in eine andere Richtung lenken kann und die Verantwortung wieder auf uns, die Bürger*innen, überträgt, also herauszufinden, wie wir uns um die Stadt kümmern.

TST: Partizipative Praktiken sind keine Neuheit in Stadtplanungsprogrammen und werden häufig kritisiert, langsam, mühsam und nicht für alle zugänglich zu sein. Im schlimmsten Fall werden sie von privaten Interessen instrumentalisiert. Warum investiert Kopenhagen in Partizipation?

TS: Städte zu bauen, braucht Zeit, und das sollten wir akzeptieren! Das heißt nicht, dass alles zehn Jahre dauern muss. Gründliche Pläne brauchen zwischen 48 und 72 Wochen. Wir müssen akzeptieren, dass es Zeit kostet, miteinander zu sprechen und zu lernen. Ich bin überzeugt, dass, wenn wir uns am Anfang Zeit nehmen, uns das aufs Ganze gesehen viel Zeit spart.

TST: In Kopenhagen scheint Zusammenarbeit politisch gewollt und Teil der strategischen Idee der Stadtvertreter*innen zu sein. Bedeutet das, dass sie Teil von allem wird, was Planer*innen tun und umsetzen?

TS: Es hilft uns ungemein, dass dies politisch so gewollt ist. Neben Workshops für Bürger*innen bedeutet dies, auf allen Ebenen zusammenzuarbeiten – alle Interessenvertreter*innen müssen beteiligt werden: Unternehmen, Bürger*innen, Freiwillige und Politiker*innen. Es ist sehr wichtig, dass jede Stadtentwicklungsgegend ihre eigenen Methoden der Zusammenarbeit mit Vertreter*innen vor Ort entwickelt und sie nichts übergestülpt bekommen. Es kommt immer auf die Situation an: auf die Umgebung, den Kontext, die Menschen. Viele verschiedene Umstände bestimmen den Partizipationsprozess. In den vergangenen Jahren wurden die Schulhöfe in der Innenstadt Kopenhagens für die Nachbarn geöffnet – ein wichtiger Schritt, um jüngere Generationen zu beteiligen. Auf den offenen Schulhöfen lernen die Kinder, Verantwortung zu übernehmen. Wir lernen, wie wir Bürger*innen sein

NU: Can you tell us about any projects that were created through the co-creation processes that you have been practising?

TS: There are different developments that led to unexpected outcomes. The development of the former Carlsberg Brewery was stalled due to the crisis in 2009, so we created a new plan. The area was opened up to the public, and people began using it temporarily for various cultural and artistic activities; Copenhageners began to explore the possibilities the area could offer. Likewise, as industry left Copenhagen's inner harbour, the former Paper Island became home to a lively street food market. While using the site, people began to realise it offered one of the sunniest waterfronts in the city. It ignited a movement of culinary start-ups: street food vendors and small businesses, all over the city. The success of the food stalls and the activities they catalysed ultimately influenced the functioning of the permanent plan. Rather than exerting control, we need to provide a framework for this to be possible throughout the city, using temporariness to permanently improve places.

TST: Ultimately, the question underlying the aspirations - and successes - of a participatory, co-creative city asks whose interests will be left standing at the end of the day? How are real estate developers and investors being held accountable? Ultimately, whose city is being realised?

TS: In many other cities, the discourse seems to be that developers come into the city; they propose a master plan for an area; and the city responds by making adjustments. In Copenhagen, we try to invite investors and real estate developers to the table before they start doing anything. We begin by telling them about our architectural policy and what is going on in the neighbourhood of interest. We ask them to talk to local stakeholders and we guide them through the process in light of current political mandates. They, in turn, help us by being able to make political visions come true. When investors or developers work with us, the approval process tends to be much easier than if they start their own project and we have to adjust it later. By inviting them to the table early on, the resulting plan becomes ours.

können, indem wir Kindern beibringen, wie sie sich in die Stadt einbringen können.

NU: Können Sie uns von Projekten berichten, die durch ihre Prozesse der Zusammenarbeit entstanden sind?

TS: Es gibt mehrere Projekte, die unerwartete Ergebnisse hervorgebracht haben: Die Entwicklung der früheren Carlsberg-Brauerei stagnierte wegen der Krise im Jahr 2009. Deshalb haben wir einen neuen Plan gemacht. Das Areal wurde für die Öffentlichkeit geöffnet, und Menschen nutzten es übergangsweise für verschiedene kulturelle und künstlerische Projekte; die Kopenhagener*innen begannen auszuloten, welche Möglichkeiten die Gegend zu bieten hatte. Oder: Als die Industrie den inneren Hafen von Kopenhagen verließ, wurde Paper Island zur Heimat eines lebendigen Streetfood-Marktes. Den Leuten wurde bewusst, dass die Gegend eines der sonnigsten Hafenviertel der Stadt ist. Das befeuerte eine Bewegung von kulinarischen Start-ups, Streetfood-Ständen und -Initiativen und kleinen Unternehmen in der ganzen Stadt. Der Erfolg beeinflusste den endgültigen Plan. Statt Kontrolle auszuüben, müssen wir einen Rahmen, in dem so etwas möglich ist, in der ganzen Stadt schaffen und Temporalität nutzen, um Orte aufzuwerten.

TST: Letztlich stellt sich die Frage, die allen Bemühungen – und Erfolgen – einer Stadt der Zusammenarbeit zugrunde liegt: Wessen Interessen bleiben am Ende übrig? Wie werden Immobilienentwickler*innen und Investor*innen zur Verantwortung gezogen? Und wessen Stadt wird hier verwirklicht?

TS: In vielen anderen Städten scheint der Diskurs so zu laufen, dass Projektentwickler*innen in die Stadt kommen, einen Masterplan für eine Gegend vorstellen und die Stadt nur reagiert, indem sie Anpassungen macht. In Kopenhagen laden wir Investor*innen und Immobilienentwickler*innen an unseren Tisch ein, bevor sie anfangen, irgendetwas zu tun. Wir berichten ihnen von unserer Architekturpolitik und was in dem betreffenden Bezirk gerade passiert. Wir fordern sie auf, sich mit Interessenvertreter*innen vor Ort zu treffen, und leiten sie durch den Prozess der aktuellen politischen Vorgaben. Sie helfen uns im Gegenzug dabei, politische Visionen wahr werden zu lassen. Wenn Investor*innen oder Entwickler*innen mit uns zusammenarbeiten, dann ist der Genehmigungsprozess zumeist sehr viel einfacher, als wenn sie ihre eigenen Projekte entwerfen, die wir anschließend anpassen müssen. Indem wir sie frühzeitig an den Tisch einladen, wird der Plan am Ende zu unserem.

Partaking in Participation

Legislating Co-operation

At MakeCity's podium discussion "Partaking in Participation", Berlin's senator for urban development and housing, Katrin Lompscher of Die Linke (the Left Party) called for guidelines that will integrate participation processes into democratic decision-making structures and promote participation in an intermixed city. What follows is a summary of her preliminary ideas about the tradition and future of participation from her keynote speech from the discussion "Partaking in Participation", 22nd June 2018, at the MakeCity Festival.

Participation in representative democracy

Article 20 of the German Basic Law states that "all authority is derived from the people". But in cities such as Berlin, with a population in the millions, there are countless issues that "the people" are not able to determine directly. Today, representative democracy and the separation of power is the foundational form of our polity with the majority of decisions made for the people by parliaments, governments and public administrations. Citizens are able to influence political decisions not only through their active and passive voting rights (such as through referenda and plebiscites), but also through civic engagement.

It is clear, however, that if decreasing numbers of people want to take part in such administrative and participatory forms of democratic engagement, the rule "of the people, for the people" loses its fundamental legitimacy in the long term. The danger exists that political decisions might be made in the people's favour less often, and increasingly in favour of vested interests - the authorities, or political and lobby groups. For this reason, every democracy is dependent on co-determination.

Beteiligung an der Beteiligung

Kooperation als Gesetz

Als Senatorin für Stadtentwicklung und Wohnen plädierte Katrin Lompscher von der Partei Die Linke in der MakeCity-Podiumsdiskussion „Beteiligung an der Beteiligung" für Leitlinien, die Beteiligungsprozesse in die Entscheidungsstrukturen der Demokratie integrieren und Teilhabe in einer durchmischten Stadt fördern. Über die Tradition und Zukunft von Partizipation – eine Zusammenfassung ihrer Auftaktrede beim Podium „Beteiligung an der Beteiligung" am 22.06.2018 des MakeCity Festivals.

Partizipation in der repräsentativen Demokratie

In Artikel 20 des Grundgesetzes heißt es: „Alle Staatsgewalt geht vom Volke aus." Aber in einer Millionenstadt wie Berlin kann das Volk nicht über sämtliche Angelegenheiten selbst entscheiden. Heute sind repräsentative Demokratie und Gewaltenteilung die Grundformen unseres Gemeinwesens. Die meisten Entscheidungen treffen Parlamente, Regierungen und öffentliche Verwaltungen für das Volk. Bürger*innen können durch ihr aktives und passives Wahlrecht (wie Bürger*innen- oder Volksbegehren und Volksentscheide), aber auch über ihr bürgerschaftliches Engagement politische Entscheidungen beeinflussen.

Fest steht: Wenn immer weniger Menschen an solchen demokratischen Amts- und Teilhabeformen mitwirkten, würde der Herrschaft des Volkes langfristig die Legitimationsgrundlage entzogen. Dann bestünde die Gefahr, dass politische Entscheidungen weniger für das Volk, sondern zunehmend im Eigeninteresse von Behörden, Politik oder Lobbygruppen getroffen werden. Daher ist jede Demokratie auf die Mitbestimmung angewiesen.

Civic participation in Berlin

In Berlin, civic participation has a long tradition, and in the West, the generation of 1968 were considered to be its originators. Student unrest was the trigger for strengthened citizen engagement. This was followed by intense debates regarding development and traffic planning. In urban development, this set into motion discussions around democratisation, a socially oriented political approach towards urban development and housing, and participation in planning processes. This movement led to the participation of those affected by modernisation processes in the 1970s, which, anchored into urban planning law, became a guiding principle for a more sensitive approach to urban renewal and the International Building Exhibition (IBA).

In Eastern Germany, the key roots of participation lie in the democracy movement before 1989, when people were dissatisfied with the centralised state. They demanded strengthened democratic influence and the salvaging of crumbling cities. This period led to the establishment of "Round Tables", where participation still takes place today, without a hierarchical structure.

Berliners like to be part of the civic conversation and, increasingly, representative institutions are being challenged by referenda. Since the referendum on the use of Tempelhofer Feld (the former Tempelhof airport), it is clear that when citizens are not in agreement with the plans of the Senate they are capable of defending their interests - vociferously. In 2014, they voted in favour of legislation drafted by the initiative 100 percent Tempelhofer Feld against proposed construction plans.

Social, functional, constructive

Berlin continues to grow and change. Despite this - or perhaps precisely because of this - we want to maintain a high quality of life for everyone. The famous "Berlin mix" - social, functional, constructive - should also be maintained during periods of growth. In the coming years, important decisions will be made. For the current coalition agreement governing Berlin that formed after the 2016 election, the SPD (Social Democratic Party), Linke (Left Party) and Grünen (Greens) decided to enter into an intensified dialogue with

Bürger*innenbeteiligung in Berlin

In Berlin hat Bürger*innenbeteiligung eine lange Tradition. Die 68er gelten in der Bundesrepublik als ihre „Erfinder*innen". Im früheren Westteil waren die Studierendenunruhen Auslöser für verstärktes bürgerschaftliches Engagement. Dazu kamen harte Auseinandersetzungen über die Bau- und Verkehrspolitik. In der Stadtentwicklung begannen als einem der ersten Politikbereiche die Diskussionen über Demokratisierung, über eine sozial ausgerichtete Stadtentwicklungs- und Wohnungspolitik sowie die Beteiligung an Planungsprozessen. Diese Bewegung führte beispielsweise dazu, dass die Beteiligung Sanierungsbetroffener in den 1970er Jahren im Städtebauförderungsgesetz verankert und zum Leitbild der behutsamen Stadterneuerung und der IBA wurde.

Für den Osten Deutschlands liegen wichtige Wurzeln von Partizipation in der Demokratiebewegung vor 1989. Die Menschen waren unzufrieden mit dem zentralistischen Staat, verlangten stärkere Einflussnahme und forderten die Rettung der dahinbröckelnden Städte. In dieser Zeit haben sich die „runden Tische" etabliert, an denen Beteiligung bis heute unhierarchisch stattfindet.

Die Berliner*innen reden gern mit. Zunehmend werden dabei repräsentativ gewählte Gremien von Bürger*innenentscheiden herausgefordert. Spätestens seit dem Volksentscheid zum Tempelhofer Feld ist klar, dass sich die Bürger*innen lautstark wehren, wenn sie mit Plänen des Senats nicht einverstanden sind. Sie stimmten 2014 für den Gesetzesentwurf der Initiative 100 % Tempelhofer Feld und gegen die Bebauung.

Sozial, funktional, baulich

Berlin wächst weiter und verändert sich. Trotzdem – oder gerade deshalb – wollen wir eine hohe Lebensqualität für alle erhalten. Die berühmte Berliner Mischung – sozial, funktional, baulich – soll auch im Wachsen erhalten bleiben. In den kommenden Jahren stehen wichtige Entscheidungen an. Im Koalitionsvertrag hat die Berliner Regierungskoalition aus SPD, Linken und Grünen 2016 beschlossen, in einen verstärkten Dialog mit der Stadtgesellschaft über die Zukunft Berlins zu treten. Wir wollen das bestehende System der Bürger*innenbeteiligung weiterentwickeln: mit Leitlinien für Bürger*innenbeteiligung, der

the city's public about the future of Berlin. We wanted to further develop the existing system of civic participation with guidelines: a binding participatory process for planning measures by municipal housing companies and more participation in urban planning, including the planning of free spaces and competitive architectural processes. I am convinced that good participation, integrated from the word go, makes better urban development possible.

Guidelines for civic participation in urban development

The guidelines for civic participation in urban development were formulated by the Senate in April 2017. A working group was established, consisting of ten citizens and representatives from the administrative and political levels, respectively. It is the aim of the working group to agree on shared standards, quality criteria and rules for civic participation, to give them binding force, to avoid future conflicts and to increase the acceptance of existing measures. These should apply to all projects and processes of spatial urban development and will be decided upon by the Senate and House of Representatives in the coming year.

What questions should we be asking ourselves?

How early is early? Clearly, participation must take place in the site analysis and goal-setting phases. This is where parameters for the planning process are set.
What projects and processes are we looking at? A "participation concept" represents the procedure of participation processes in detail. It clarifies the respective roles and responsibilities in the process and shows possible methods of participation.
What is fixed and what is variable? In order to avoid raising false hopes, the scope for action must be clearly established and explained before a participation process is set into motion. Within this remit, an open-ended outcome must be guaranteed.
How can as many people as possible be involved? Depending on the urban development

verbindlichen Beteiligung bei Vorhaben der landeseigenen Wohnungsbaugesellschaften sowie mehr Beteiligung an städtebaulichen, freiraumplanerischen und architektonischen Wettbewerbsverfahren. Ich bin überzeugt: Gute Partizipation von Anfang an ermöglicht eine bessere Stadtentwicklung.

Leitlinien für Bürger*innenbeteiligung an der Stadtentwicklung

Die Leitlinien für Bürger*innenbeteiligung an der Stadtentwicklung hat der Senat im April 2017 beschlossen. Ein Arbeitsgremium aus jeweils zehn Bürger*innen sowie Vertreter*innen aus Verwaltung und Politik entwickelt sie. Unser Ziel ist es, gemeinsame Standards, Qualitätskriterien und Regeln für Bürger*innenbeteiligung zu verabreden, Verbindlichkeit zu schaffen, Konflikte zu verhindern und Akzeptanz zu erhöhen. Sie sollen in allen Projekten und Prozessen der räumlichen Stadtentwicklung angewendet und im kommenden Jahr vom Senat und Abgeordnetenhaus beschlossen werden.

Welche(n) Fragen müssen wir uns stellen?

Wie früh ist früh? Klar ist, Beteiligung muss bereits in der Phase der Ortsanalyse und Zielfindung beginnen, weil hier die Weichen für die Planung gestellt werden.
Um welche Projekte und Prozesse geht es? Ein Beteiligungskonzept soll den Ablauf des Beteiligungsprozesses detailliert darstellen. Es klärt die jeweiligen Rollen und Zuständigkeiten im Prozess und zeigt mögliche Beteiligungsmethoden und -varianten auf.
Was ist fix, was variabel? Um falsche Erwartungen zu vermeiden, muss der Mitgestaltungsspielraum vor Beginn eines Beteiligungsprozesses offengelegt und geklärt sein. Innerhalb dieses Spielraums sollte Ergebnisoffenheit garantiert werden.
Wie beteiligen sich möglichst viele verschiedene Menschen? Abhängig vom jeweiligen Stadtentwicklungsprojekt wird geklärt, wer betroffen ist und welche Gruppen einzubeziehen sind. Eine zielgerichtete Ansprache, Öffentlichkeitsarbeit und aktive Werbung tragen dazu bei, möglichst viele verschiedene Bürger*innen zu mobilisieren.
Was passiert mit den Ergebnissen? Mit der sogenannten Rechenschaftspflicht ist eine verbindliche

project, people who should be involved in the planning process, such as those who will be affected, are identified. A target-oriented mode of address is used. Publicity work and targeted advertising contribute towards the mobilisation of as many citizens as possible from diverse groups.
What happens with the results? The so-called accountability principle means a binding answer is mandatory. It should be clear how the demands of citizens have contributed to decision-making. If demands have not been met, a reason must be provided.
How much does participation cost? In due course, an appropriate budget will be determined by the city for civic participation processes. Those bodies responsible for private construction plans will be encouraged by the political and administrative levels to also work such a budget into their planning.
How will the communication process work? Participation will be independently monitored and moderated, so that the positions of individual people or groups are dealt with in an equitable manner. All participants should come together to discuss matters respectfully, attentively and on an equal footing.
Who decides when and where the participation process takes place? Participation processes can be proposed by political stakeholders, the civic administration, companies, organisations from civil society and citizens. The point of contact should support citizens in the participation processes.
How might guidelines be improved? A newly set up monitoring body will examine the guidelines, develop them further and closely follow their implementation.

More transparency and easy access to information will also bring the possibility of online participation on the basis of open source technology. The platform mein.Berlin brings together all processes pertaining to participation. Alliances, opinions, budgets and development plans will be transferred to this platform.

Sustainable solutions can be reached if we succeed in bringing together everyday experience, creativity and professional competency. Participation brings acceptance. And that is something we have to work towards.

Rückmeldung vorgesehen. Dabei soll deutlich werden, wie die Belange der Bürger*innen in die Entscheidungen eingeflossen sind. Wenn Belange nicht berücksichtigt wurden, muss dies begründet werden.
Was ist uns Beteiligung wert? Für Bürger*innenbeteiligung wird im Landeshaushalt frühzeitig ein ausreichendes Budget eingeplant. Träger*innen von privaten Bauvorhaben werden von Politik und Verwaltung angehalten, ein solches Budget ebenfalls in Bebauungsplanverfahren einzubringen.
Wie reden wir miteinander? Partizipation wird neutral begleitet und moderiert, damit die Positionen einzelner Personen oder Gruppen ausgewogen behandelt werden. Alle Beteiligten sollen respektvoll, anerkennend und auf Augenhöhe miteinander ins Gespräch kommen.
Wer entscheidet, wann und wo die Teilnahme stattfindet? Partizipationsprozesse können von politischen Akteur*innen, der Zivilverwaltung, Unternehmen, zivilgesellschaftlichen Organisationen und Bürger*innen angeregt werden. Die Kontaktstelle für Bürger*innenbeteiligung sollte die Bürger*innen dabei unterstützen.
Wie können die Richtlinien verbessert werden? Eine neu eingerichtete Überwachungsstelle überprüft die Leitlinien, entwickelt sie weiter und überwacht ihre Umsetzung.

Mehr Transparenz und einen leichteren Zugang zu Informationen bringt nicht zuletzt die Möglichkeit der Online-Beteiligung auf Basis von Open Source. Auf der Plattform „mein.Berlin" sind alle Verfahren und Prozesse zur Bürger*innenbeteiligung im Land gebündelt. Allianzen, Meinungen, Bürger*innenhaushalte und Entwicklungspläne werden darauf umgesetzt.

Nachhaltige Lösungen entstehen, wenn wir Alltagserfahrung, Kreativität und fachliche Kompetenz erfolgreich zusammenbringen. Beteiligung bringt Akzeptanz. Und die müssen wir uns verdienen.

Data as a Big Deal

Can Digitalisation Reshape Democracy?

In collaboration with the City of Eindhoven, Linda Vlassenrood of Het Nieuwe Instituut (NL) curated a cultural programme on data and the notion of a smart society. The DATAstudio addressed the question of how we can build a smart society, rather than just a smart city. In other words, how can we use data and technology to benefit citizens and neighbourhoods? Francesca Bria, chief technology and digital innovation officer in the City Council for the mayor of Barcelona, Ada Colau, is tasked with transforming the workings of municipal government and public services. Both experts are fully invested in the development of technology and data for transforming cities and involving citizens in urban governance. Their conversation reflects upon the far-reaching implications of such technological evolution for civil and democratic societies.

Linda Vlassenrood: We have gleaned a number of conclusions from our DATAstudio project. Large-scale data collection yields numerous new insights and possibilities, including ways of improving efficiency and safety in cities. Yet it also constitutes the greatest imaginable threat to the democratic legal order, and to the relationships between governments, the private sector and citizens. We found that governments and businesses alike take their cues from the trends around datafication, without giving sufficient thought to the associated ethical issues and social consequences. The development of new social coalitions around the collection and use of data therefore calls for a critical approach.

Francesca Bria: Data has become the most valuable commodity in the world – it's the raw material of the digital economy. Companies in every industry are counting on artificial intelligence to drive growth over the next couple of years, and machine learning will increase their return on investment by between 10 to 30 percent. This massive transformation cannot be left to a handful of big US tech companies such as Google and Facebook. We need to strike a "New Deal on Data" to make the most out of data. Barcelona is betting on a new approach that we call "city data commons". We want Barcelona to have the most

Der neue Deal um Daten

Kann Digitalisierung Demokratie gestalten?

Linda Vlassenrood vom Het Nieuwe Institutut, Niederlande, hat in Zusammenarbeit mit der Stadt Eindhoven ein Kulturprogramm über Daten und die „Smart Society" kuratiert. Das DATAstudio befasste sich mit der Frage, wie wir eine effiziente, technologisch fortschrittliche, grüne und sozial inklusive Gesellschaft gestalten können, statt bloß eine Smart City – eine technologisch intelligente Stadt. Mit anderen Worten: Wie können wir Daten und Technik zum Vorteil von Bürger*innen und Nachbarschaften einsetzen? Francesca Bria, Beauftragte für technische und digitale Innovation im Stadtrat der Bürgermeisterin von Barcelona, Ada Colau, hat die Aufgabe, die Wirkungsweisen der kommunalen Regierung und öffentlichen Dienste zu verändern. Beide Expertinnen engagieren sich dafür, die Entwicklung von Technologien und Daten zur Transformation ihrer Städte mit der Einbeziehung von Bewohner*innen in die städtische Politik zu verbinden. Ihr Gespräch reflektiert die Auswirkungen solcher Entwicklungen für Zivilgesellschaft und Demokratie.

Linda Vlassenrood: Wir konnten eine Reihe von Schlussfolgerungen aus unserem Projekt DATAstudio ziehen. Groß angelegte Datensammlungen eröffnen zahlreiche neue Einsichten und Möglichkeiten, um die Effizienz und Sicherheit in Städten zu verbessern. Andererseits stellen sie auch die größte vorstellbare Bedrohung für die demokratische Rechtsordnung und die Beziehung zwischen Regierungen, Privatwirtschaft und Bürger*innen dar. Wir stellten fest, dass Regierungen wie auch Unternehmen ihre Schlüsse ausschließlich auf Grundlage des Datafizierungstrends ziehen, ohne die damit zusammenhängenden ethischen Probleme und gesellschaftlichen Folgen ausreichend zu reflektieren. Die Entwicklung neuer gesellschaftlicher Bündnisse rund um die Sammlung und Nutzung von Daten erfordert aber eine kritische Herangehensweise.

Francesca Bria: Daten sind zum wertvollsten Gut der Welt geworden. Tatsächlich sind sie der Rohstoff der digitalen Ökonomie. Unternehmen in jeder Branche zählen auf künstliche Intelligenz, um über die nächsten Jahre ihr Wachstum anzukurbeln. Ihre Kapitalrendite wird sich durch maschinelles Lernen um zehn bis dreißig Prozent erhöhen. Diese massive

dynamic, effective, and privacy-preserving data ecosystem in the world. We want Barcelona to make the most dynamic, efficient, and private data-ecosystem in the world.
Data is a new meta-utility, and a crucial piece of urban infrastructure. In our opinion it should be democratically controlled, and data sovereignty should be in the hands of the people once again.

LV: We also call for city governments that will act, more than ever, as guardians of collective conditions; keepers of an inclusive public sphere. They should be equal conversation partners on social innovations that will prioritise the city's value to its citizens. In this scenario, data is explicitly understood and administered as a public good, and citizens determine the uses to which their data will be put. Yet to achieve this, the relationship between government and citizens will have to change dramatically. Essentially, we must reinvent democracy. In cities that aim to become "smart", it will be vital to accelerate and sharply define the journey to social innovation, governmental reform and a responsible, high-quality use of data.

FB: Cities should indeed become the new custodians of the digital rights of their inhabitants. They need an ethical and democratic innovation strategy to preserve citizens' privacy and self-determination. This will help to ensure that intangible public resources and assets are retained, managed and distributed for the collective good. We are currently piloting new infrastructures to share data, provide encryption for the people and promote new ownership regimes to preserve citizens' social rights to data (see decodeproject.eu). Data commons will also enable cities to offer alternatives to predatory on-demand platforms such as Uber and Airbnb. Introducing fair regulation and algorithmic transparency to tame Big Tech – a course many cities are following – is simply not enough.

LV: I agree: many cities are still far from using technology in an inclusive way. Yet the existing gap presents tremendous opportunities. There is still room to shape the ways in which citizens take part in a critical conversation around data collection. Even a technology-driven city like Eindhoven acknowledges that technology should not be an end unto itself but should be used to solve local problems in society.
In reality, however, this proves to be problematic. Officials tasked with identifying challenges in a neighbourhood have usually done so from behind a desk. Furthermore, most of the relevant

Veränderung kann nicht einer Handvoll US-amerikanischer Technologie-Großunternehmen wie Google und Facebook überlassen werden. Wir brauchen einen „New Deal on Data", eine politische Reform zum Umgang mit Daten, um aus ihnen das Beste herauszuholen. Barcelona setzt auf einen neuen Ansatz, den wir „City Data Commons" nennen. Städtische Daten verstehen wir als Gemeingut. Wir möchten Barcelona zu einem der besten dynamischen, effizienten und die Privatsphäre wahrenden Datenökosysteme der Welt machen. Daten sind eine neue Meta-Versorgungsleistung („meta utility") und eine entscheidende städtische Infrastruktur. Unseres Erachtens sollten sie demokratisch gesteuert werden, und die Datensouveränität sollte wieder in den Händen der Menschen liegen.

LV: Auch wir fordern Stadtregierungen dazu auf, mehr als zuvor die kollektiven Bedingungen eines inklusiven öffentlichen Raums zu schützen. Sie sollten im Austausch über gesellschaftliche Innovationen als ebenbürtige Partner*innen agieren, die den Bürger*innen den Wert der Stadt vermitteln. In diesem Szenario werden Daten ausdrücklich als öffentliches Gut verstanden und verwaltet, wobei Bürger*innen über den Nutzen bestimmen, dem ihre Daten zugeführt werden. Um das zu erreichen, muss sich die Beziehung zwischen Regierung und Bürger*innen umfassend verändern. Im Grunde müssen wir die Demokratie neu erfinden. In Städten, die zur Smart City werden wollen, muss der Weg zur gesellschaftlichen Innovation, Regierungsreform und verantwortlichen, qualitativ hochwertigen Nutzung von Daten beschleunigt und klarer bestimmt werden.

FB: Städte sollten tatsächlich die neue Vormundschaft für digitale Bürger*innenrechte übernehmen. Sie brauchen eine ethische und demokratische Innovationsstrategie, um die Privatsphäre und Selbstbestimmung der Bürger*innen zu erhalten. Das wird dabei helfen, jene immateriellen öffentlichen Ressourcen und Vermögenswerte zum Wohle der Gemeinschaft zu erhalten, verwalten und zu verteilen. Unsere neuen Infrastrukturen sind Pilotprojekte, um Daten zu teilen, Verschlüsselung anzubieten und neue Eigentumsregelungen zu fördern, die die sozialen Rechte der Bürger*innen an ihren Daten erhalten (siehe etwa das decodeproject.eu). Daten als Gemeingut werden es Städten auch ermöglichen, Alternativen zu den räuberischen On-Demand-Plattformen wie Uber und Airbnb anzubieten. Der von vielen Städten verfolgte Kurs, gerechte Steuerung und transparentere Algorithmen einzuführen, reicht einfach nicht aus.

LV: Ich stimme zu: Viele Städte sind noch weit davon entfernt, Technologie auf inklusivere Weise zu

departments are working in parallel. How can a top-down decision to create a smart society be united with the kind of bottom-up movement that determines a participatory society?

FB: That's the main challenge. We need another culture and another way of working in public institutions. Transforming public procurement, introducing innovative clauses regarding ethics, gender and sustainability in the way we buy products and services in City Halls is a game changer. Public institutions are very hard to access if you are a community project or a small social enterprise. Rules are often complicated, and decision processes regarding funding allocation can be opaque. We need to create a culture of transparency and freedom of information. In Barcelona, we developed the Bustia Etica project, an encrypted whistleblowing infrastructure that allows citizens to denounce cases of corruption. With projects like this one, we are creating awareness regarding citizens' rights to access public information and knowledge.

LV: We found that these issues are intertwined with various assumptions about a participatory society and new forms of collaboration. With the many stakeholders and a plethora of interest groups involved – and their frequent resistance to criticism and interference – this process was a complex one. There were conflicting ideas on administrative and financial authority, the role of technology, alternative organisational forms and concepts like trust, transparency, exclusion and the concentration of power.
You are actually part of the government. What conditions and steps do you think are needed to really consider data as a public good, instead of only making the promise? And how have you tackled the difficulties with the bureaucratic system or upcoming elections, which might have significant consequences for your agenda?

FB: We need to reverse the neo-liberal model that has led to the privatisation and outsourcing of services and critical knowledge in the public sector; we need a culture where social impact is clearly measurable. This is the core of the current Barcelona model: promoting real participatory democracy and preserving the urban commons, which also means promoting, within public institutions, a culture of collaboration and partnership with citizens and communities. I believe that if we get engaged, the public sector can do a lot to empower communities and give people new tools and legal instruments to collectively self-organise. Self-determination will transform society.

nutzen. Doch die bestehende Lücke eröffnet enorme Potenziale. Es gibt noch Raum, um die Teilhabemöglichkeiten von Bürger*innen an einer kritischen Auseinandersetzung rund um Datensammlung zu gestalten. Sogar eine technikgetriebene Stadt wie Eindhoven erkennt an, dass Technologie kein Selbstzweck sein sollte, sondern genutzt werden muss, um lokale gesellschaftliche Probleme zu lösen.
In der Wirklichkeit erweist sich dies jedoch als problematisch: Die Beamt*innen, die die Herausforderungen in einer Nachbarschaft feststellen sollten, taten dies üblicherweise von ihrem Schreibtisch aus. Außerdem arbeiten die meisten zuständigen Abteilungen aneinander vorbei. Wie lässt sich eine Top-down-Entscheidung in einer smarten Stadt mit der Art von basisdemokratischer Bewegung verbinden, die eine partizipatorische Gesellschaft ausmacht?

FB: Das ist die zentrale Herausforderung. Wir brauchen eine andere Kultur und andere Arbeitsweisen in den öffentlichen Institutionen. Die öffentliche Beschaffung zu verändern, also innovative, ethische, geschlechterinklusive und nachhaltige Kriterien in Einkauf und Auftragsvergabe von Produkten und Dienstleistungen der Stadtverwaltungen einzuführen, würde einiges bewirken. Öffentliche Einrichtungen sind für Nachbarschaftsprojekte oder kleine soziale Unternehmen nur sehr schwer zugänglich. Die Regularien sind oft kompliziert und Entscheidungsprozesse bei der Mittelzuweisung intransparent. Wir müssen eine Kultur der Transparenz und Informationsfreiheit schaffen. In Barcelona haben wir hierfür das Projekt Bústia Ètica entwickelt, eine verschlüsselte Whistleblowing-Infrastruktur, die es Bürger*innen ermöglicht, Korruptionsfälle anzuzeigen. Mit solchen Projekten schaffen wir ein Bewusstsein für die Rechte der Bürger*innen auf Zugang zu öffentlichen Informationen und staatlichem Wissen.

LV: Wir stellten fest, dass diese Fragen mit verschiedenen Vorstellungen von einer partizipatorischen Gesellschaft und den neuen Formen der Zusammenarbeit verwoben sind. Mit den vielen verschiedenen Zielsetzungen und beteiligten Interessengruppen sowie deren andauernder Abwehr von Kritik und Einmischung war der Prozess sehr komplex. Es gab gegenläufige Ideen von administrativer und finanzieller Autorität, der Rolle der Technologie, von alternativen Organisationsformen und Konzepten wie Vertrauen, Transparenz, Ausschluss und Machtbündelung.
Du bist tatsächlich Teil der Regierung. Welche Bedingungen und Schritte sind deines Erachtens nach notwendig, um Daten wirklich als ein öffentliches

Gut zu begreifen, anstatt dies nur zu versprechen? Und wie seid ihr die Schwierigkeiten mit dem bürokratischen System oder mit den bevorstehenden Wahlen angegangen, die womöglich große Auswirkungen auf eure Agenda haben?

FB: Wir müssen das neoliberale Modell umkehren, das zur Privatisierung und Auslagerung von Diensten und entscheidendem Wissen im öffentlichen Sektor geführt hat. Wir brauchen eine Kultur, in der gesellschaftliche Wirkung deutlich messbar ist. Das ist der Kern des aktuellen Barcelona-Modells, das wirkliche partizipatorische Demokratie fördert und die städtischen Gemeingüter erhält. Das befördert innerhalb der öffentlichen Institutionen eine Kultur der Zusammenarbeit und Partnerschaft mit der Bevölkerung. Ich bin wirklich der Überzeugung, dass der öffentliche Sektor viel zur Stärkung nachbarschaftlicher Gemeinschaften beitragen und Menschen neue Werkzeuge und rechtliche Instrumente zur kollektiven Selbstorganisierung bieten kann, wenn wir uns dafür engagieren. Selbstbestimmung wird die Gesellschaft verändern.

Once part of the socialist GDR, the residential units of Karl-Marx-Allee were privatised in 1993 after German reunification. In a political move the Berlin Government used its primary right to buy back 700 residential units into public ownership in 2019

Einst Teil der sozialistischen DDR, wurde die Wohnbebauung der Karl-Marx-Allee 1993 nach der Wiedervereinigung privatisiert. In einem politischen Schritt hat die Berliner Landesregierung ihr Vorkaufsrecht 2019 geltend gemacht und 700 Wohneinheiten in öffentliches Eigentum überführt

Work the Democratic Tools!

New Coalitions for a Social City

Not so long ago, Berlin sold off much of its land and real estate to the highest bidder – in the name of liberalisation, and at bargain prices. Between 1990 and 2015, 220,000 publicly held flats were privatised, to investors from inside and outside of Germany, for example. Currently, the capital city is becoming more expensive at an astonishing rate, and is increasingly unaffordable for those on an average income.

Today, Berlin is buying back real estate: 100 million euros have been set aside for residential housing. In 39 designated protected areas, special permission is required for the demolition, change, or "change in use" of building sites. The sale of land must be approved by the district administration, which, in addition, has a right to pre-emptively buy housing. These instruments are employed to retain low-priced housing that is urgently needed in order to mitigate the displacement of tenants. If the legal structures are in place, the municipality exercises its pre-emptive rights for buyback from third parties – generally passing the property to one of Berlin's social housing associations. Those who acquire land, however, are able to avert pre-emptive buybacks in the designated protected areas. It is enough to adhere to the protected area's outlined aims, for example, by doing away with transforming rented apartments into owner-occupied ones, which is an effective means to avoid speculation.

Civil society and politics in cities can leverage legal instruments to nurture democracy. Pre-emptive buying rights is one of these instruments. It remains to be seen, however, how and to what extent these tools are also used. Only six of the twelve Berlin municipalities have applied pre-emptive buying rights to date. In order to alleviate undesirable developments, these legal instruments need to be applied vigorously and extensively. It is often lone fighters who set the pace at municipal and communal levels. Does the effectiveness of institutional instruments therefore depend only on the decisiveness of concrete initiatives and individuals?

Of the 28 repurchases and 60 preventions that Berlin has been able to set into motion, more than half have taken place in the municipality of

Demokratische Instrumente nutzen!

Neue Koalitionen für eine soziale Stadt

Vor nicht allzu langer Zeit hat Berlin seine Grundstücke und Immobilien verkauft: im Namen der Liberalisierung zu Spottpreisen und an Meistbietende. Zwischen 1990 und 2015 gingen 220.000 landeseigene Wohnungen in Privatbesitz über beziehungsweise an Investor*innen aus dem In- und Ausland. Aktuell wird die Hauptstadt im Eiltempo teurer und für Normalverdienende zunehmend unbezahlbar.

Jetzt kauft Berlin Immobilien zurück: Hundert Millionen Euro sind für Wohnungsrückkäufe bereitgestellt. In aktuell 39 Milieuschutzgebieten ist für den Abriss (Rückbau), die Änderung oder Nutzungsänderung baulicher Anlagen eine Genehmigung erforderlich; dem Verkauf von Grundstücken muss der Bezirk zustimmen. Er hat auch ein gesetzliches Vorkaufsrecht für Wohnhäuser. Damit soll der dringend benötigte preiswerte Wohnraum erhalten bleiben und so der Verdrängung von Mieter*innen entgegengewirkt werden. Liegen die gesetzlichen Voraussetzungen vor, übt der Bezirk das Vorkaufsrecht zugunsten Dritter aus – in der Regel zugunsten landeseigener Wohnungsbaugesellschaften. Wer Grundstücke erwirbt, kann die Ausübung des Vorkaufsrechts in Milieuschutzgebieten jedoch abwenden. Es genügt, die Ziele und Zwecke der Milieuschutzverordnung zu befolgen und beispielsweise auf die Umwandlung von Miet- in Eigentumswohnungen zu verzichten. Ein effektives Mittel, das Spekulation verhindert.

Stadtgesellschaft und -politik stehen also demokratiefördernde Instrumente zur Verfügung. Das Vorkaufsrecht ist eines davon. Die Frage ist jedoch, ob und mit welcher Entschlossenheit diese Werkzeuge auch genutzt werden. Nur sechs der zwölf Berliner Bezirke haben bis dato vom Vorkaufsrecht Gebrauch gemacht. Um Fehlentwicklungen entgegenzuwirken, müssen die zur Verfügung stehenden Instrumente aber flächendeckend aktiv angewandt werden. Häufig sind auf der Bezirks- und Kommunalebene jedoch Einzelkämpfer*innen tonangebend. Ist die Effektivität institutioneller Instrumentarien also nur von der Entschlossenheit konkreter Initiativen und Personen abhängig?

Von den 28 Rückkäufen und sechzig Abwendungen, die in Berlin bisher ausgeübt wurden, finden sich mehr als die Hälfte im Bezirk Friedrichshain-Kreuzberg. Der Bezirk hat ein rebellisches Image, wovon

Friedrichshain-Kreuzberg, setting a quasi-rebellious precedent. The recently successful prevention of the planned Google Campus in Kreuzberg's Umspannwerk bears witness to this. In city councillor Florian Schmidt (B'90/Die Grünen), the municipality has a decisive critic of a neoliberal housing market determined by speculators. Schmidt sees himself as an activist and representative of a broad civic-political scene, together with which he fights tirelessly against the displacement of tenants and industry. He stands for participation and dialogue between sectors within the Senate. Francesca Ferguson spoke with Florian Schmidt on the importance of broad alliances, the negotiation of interests and Berlin as a model city.

Francesca Ferguson: "Participating in participation" is one of our main topics of discourse. What does it mean to you?

Florian Schmidt: Increasingly, it is less about participation and more about real co-operation and involvement. A useful distinction to make would be between forms of civic engagement - information, consultation, cooperation and autonomy. Good projects develop when there is cooperation between politics, administration and community, and when specific ideas can be implemented through self-government.

FF: How do you see community empowerment being made sustainable, in terms of cities and urban development? How do we achieve participatory processes that function beyond special interests?

FS: We are committed to developing a new, up-to-date organisation by shifting our perspective and putting new phenomena in context. Ideally, the municipality would have as its goal the implementation of socially sustainable targets - through housing projects, neighbourhood development and city-wide frameworks - and would be conscious of the fact that the implementation of this will be undertaken in a hostile environment where the legal, economic and political climate is antithetical to social sustainability. In this model, market mechanisms are to be negated through socially sustainable initiatives by innovative property developers - co-operatives, foundations, housing associations such as the nationwide Miethäuser Syndikat (Apartment Housing Syndicate) and publicly owned housing organisations.
Neighbourhoods are another powerful category: a local community that wants not just to

nicht zuletzt die erfolgreiche Verhinderung des geplanten Google-Campus im Kreuzberger Umspannwerk zeugt. In Stadtrat Florian Schmidt (B'90/Die Grünen) hat der Bezirk einen entschlossenen Kritiker des neoliberalen – von Spekulation bestimmten – Wohnungsmarktes. Schmidt versteht sich als Aktivist und Repräsentant einer breiten zivilpolitischen Szene, an deren Seite er gegen die Verdrängung von Mieter*innen und Einzelhandel kämpft. Er steht für Partizipation und den transsektoralen Dialog zwischen Senatsverwaltungen. Francesca Ferguson sprach mit Florian Schmidt über die Bedeutung breiter Allianzen, die Verhandlung von Interessen und Berlin als Modellstadt.

Francesca Ferguson: Was bedeutet für Sie Beteiligung in der Stadtentwicklung?

Florian Schmidt: Es geht immer weniger um Beteiligung, sondern um echte Zusammenarbeit und Teilhabe. Information, Konsultation, Kooperation und Selbstverwaltung sind wirkungsvolle Formen der Einbindung. Gute Projekte entstehen, wenn kooperiert wird, wenn Politik, Verwaltung und Zivilgesellschaft also gemeinsam entscheiden und wenn bestimmte Themen in Selbstverwaltung umgesetzt werden können.

FF: Wie lässt sich die zivilbürgerliche Szene in Bezug auf Raum und Stadtentwicklung ermächtigen? Wie kommt man zu Beteiligungsprozessen, die jenseits von Partikularinteressen funktionieren?

FS: Wir setzen uns für eine zeitgenössische Konstellation von Akteur*innen ein, indem wir die Perspektive wechseln. Die Kommune kann in unserer Vorstellung durch Hausprojekte, Quartiersentwicklung und stadtweite Rahmenbedingungen für gesellschaftlich nachhaltige Ziele umsetzen und ist sich bewusst, dass dies in einem „feindlichen Umfeld" passiert, in dem Recht, Ökonomie und die politische Kultur einer gesellschaftlichen Nachhaltigkeit zuwiderlaufen. In diesem Setting wollen auch neuartige Bauherr*innen – Genossenschaften, Stiftungen, Hausvereine wie das bundesweite „Mietshäuser Syndikat" oder landeseigene Wohnungsunternehmen – durch gesellschaftlich nachhaltige Projekte den negativen Marktmechanismen entgegenwirken. Auch Nachbarschaften sind eine machtvolle Kategorie: eine lokale Community, die sich über ihre Zukunft verständigen und diese mitgestalten will. Bauprojekte können ein Anlass sein, eine solche nachbarschaftliche Verständigung herauszufordern. In den letzten zehn Jahren sind soziale Bewegungen besonders häufig als urbane Bewegungen mit dem Leitziel „Recht auf Stadt" auf den Plan getreten. Bedeutsam ist, dass es sowohl standort-

"Institutions are back at the frontline!"

„Institutionen sind wieder auf dem Vormarsch!"

Levente Polyak

have a say in its future but also to actively determine it. Property development projects can be opportunities to promote common understanding.

Over the past ten years, social movements have increasingly emerged as "right-to-the-city" urban movements. Significantly, there are both site-specific movements (e.g., Kotti & Co and the Haus der Statistik Initiative, both calling for the de-privatisation of large buildings in Berlin) as well as initiatives that address real estate policy. They are all socio-politically oriented, have the capacity to build a large network of partners and supporters and are able to engage in policy negotiation with strategic finesse.

FF: Given these developments, what is your vision for a Berlin model of urban development? What are the core ideas - the key building blocks that you are aiming for - to make the fair-city model different in Berlin?

FS: Today, buildings, neighbourhoods and even city-wide structures are particularly meaningful when they enable and ideally actively promote social participation. The starting point is allowing access to everyone. Because of a well-known flaw in the legal framework, combined with increasing demand for inner-city spaces and unscrupulous business deals, cities are degenerating into commercialised environments, where low-income and "marginalised" groups have no place. Resolute action must be taken wherever new developments are happening. New construction projects should be completely separate from speculation and free market activity.

spezifische Bewegungen gibt (wie z. B. Kotti & Co oder die Initiative Haus der Statistik – beide fordern die Rekommunalisierung von großen Häuserblocks in Berlin) als auch Initiativen, die sich mit Liegenschaftspolitik beschäftigen. Beide haben eine gesellschaftspolitische Ausrichtung und können auf ein großes Netzwerk von Partner*innen und Sympathisant*innen zurückgreifen. Sie verhandeln strategisch geschickt mit der Politik.

FF Was ist Ihre Vision für ein Berliner Modell der Stadtentwicklung? Welche Kernideen oder notwendigen Bausteine für ein gerechtes Modell streben Sie an, um in Berlin Stadt anders zu machen?

FS: Häuser, Quartiere oder auch gesamtstädtische Strukturen sind heutzutage insbesondere dann sinnvoll, wenn sie soziale Teilhabe ermöglichen und im besten Falle aktiv hervorbringen. Das beginnt damit, dass es keine Orte geben sollte, die bestimmten Gruppen den Zugang verweigern. Durch ein allseits bekanntes Versagen der rechtlichen Rahmenbedingungen in Kombination mit einer steigenden Nachfrage nach innerstädtischen Räumen und teils skrupellosen Geschäftemachereien degenerieren Städte zu durchkommerzialisierten Lebenswelten, in denen einkommensschwache Menschen und „Randgruppen" keinen Platz haben. Daher muss dort, wo neu gebaut wird, konsequent gegengesteuert werden. Neue Bauprojekte sollten der Spekulation und dem freien Marktgeschehen entzogen werden. Nur so können langfristig gesicherte bezahlbare Räume entstehen. Neue Orte sollten zudem möglichst die Werte des freiheitlichen und selbstbestimmten Miteinanders befördern und dem Zerfall des sozialen Zusammenhalts etwas entgegensetzen.

The occupation of Google Campus lasted two hours before the police evicted the activists and, as a result, the tech giant decided not to move in; for the next five years, however, Google will remain the official tenant of the building

Die Besetzung des Google-Campus dauerte zwei Stunden, bevor die Polizei die Aktivist*innen vertrieben hatte. Daraufhin entschied der Konzern, nicht einzuziehen. In den nächsten fünf Jahren wird Google jedoch der offizielle Mieter des Gebäudes bleiben

On Building Loopholes

Art as Strategy

Against the backdrop of shifting demographics, divisive politics and refugees fleeing into Europe, the Hamburg-based Kampnagel Theatre Company sees itself faced with a clear socio-political responsibility: the current political situation demands new measures and calls for the creation of platforms for participation and communication. In response, Kampnagel has opened up a theatre in an effort to create a space in which diverse communities and cultures come together to rehearse collaborative means of living together. Nadine Jessen explores the integration of refugees into Kampnagel's operations and programming as the company attempts to create equitable forms of exchange as well as collaborative working and living relations – all while providing ongoing support to independent artistic and cultural production carried out by refugees.

The Migrantpolitan is a small wooden building in the backyard of Kampnagel, an international independent centre for performing arts in Hamburg and Europe's largest production centre for contemporary performing arts. To tell its story, we must begin in 2014, when Kampnagel's International Summer Festival invited Baltic Raw, a Hamburg-based interventionist group of architects, to reflect on the city's relationship with its buildings, artists and residents. Baltic Raw responded by building a replica of the Rote Flora squat in Kampnagel's back yard. The opening of the building coincided with the twenty-fifth anniversary of the original occupation of Rote Flora on Schanzenstraße, which continues to be at the heart of an ongoing discussion about property speculation, artistic resistance and police intervention in Hamburg.

Shortly after, Lampedusa, a self-organised group of around 400 refugees and migrants from different African nations, had their right to asylum refused and were denied support or shelter by the Hamburg city government. The pressure to offer accommodation for thousands of people mounted, requiring urgent solutions. Kampnagel was asked to transform parts of its venue into temporary emergency shelter for refugees. Our days were filled with many discussions – finally, we de-

Das Spiel mit dem Schlupfloch

Kunst als Strategie

Vor dem Hintergrund demografischer Veränderungen, einer spaltenden Politik und weltweiter Fluchtbewegungen sieht sich das Theater Kampnagel in Hamburg in der klaren Verantwortung: Die Situation verlangt nach neuen Strategien und Plattformen für Partizipation und Kommunikation. Massenunterkünfte sind keine Lösung. Als Hamburgs Regierung 2015 der Gruppe Lampedusa das Bleiberecht verweigerte, öffnete Kampnagel sein Theater für Migrantpolitan und statuierte Kosmopolitismus kurzerhand zum Privileg. Nadine Jessen beschreibt den Wandel von einer temporären Kunstinstallation zum kosmopolitischen Programm-Macher für Kampnagel.

Das Migrantpolitan ist ein kleines Haus aus Holz. Es steht auf dem Hinterhof von Kampnagel, einem internationalen und unabhängigen Zentrum (und zugleich Europas größter Produktionsstätte) für zeitgenössische darstellende Kunst in Hamburg. Die Geschichte des Holzhauses beginnt im Jahr 2014, als Kampnagel zum internationalen Sommerfestival Baltic Raw eine Gruppe von Architekt*innen aus Hamburg einlud, das Verhältnis der Stadt zu ihren Gebäuden, Künstler*innen und Einwohner*innen zu reflektieren. Ergebnis war der hölzerne Nachbau der Roten Flora, der zum 25. Jubiläum des „politischen Störfaktors" eröffnete. Bis heute steht die Flora in der Schanze für künstlerischen Widerstand gegen Immobilienspekulationen.

Kurz darauf verweigerte Hamburgs Regierung Lampedusa, einer selbstorganisierten Gruppe von rund 400 Geflüchteten und Migrant*innen aus verschiedenen afrikanischen Staaten, das Bleiberecht. Der Druck, Unterkünfte für Tausende von Menschen zu finden, war hoch. Auch Kampnagel wurde gebeten, Räume als temporäre Notunterkunft zur Verfügung zu stellen. Nach vielen Diskussionen entschieden wir uns jedoch dagegen. Was wäre der Unterschied zu einem leer stehenden Supermarkt oder einer alten Fabrikhalle gewesen? Wir glaubten nicht an Massenunterbringung. Wir brauchten kleine Lösungen für große Probleme.

Anstatt das Holzhaus im Hof nach dem Festival abzubauen, machten wir es winterfest, sodass Lampedusa Teile davon als künstlerischen und sozialen Ort, als Schlupfloch und temporäre Unterkunft

clined. What would have been the difference between using an abandoned supermarket or our former factory halls? We didn't want to offer easy solutions and we didn't believe in the concept of mass accommodation - we needed to think of small solutions for big problems.

Instead of dismantling the replica after the festival, we made it suitable for winter habitation so that Lampedusa could use parts of it as an artistic and social space, a loophole and a temporary shelter. In close cooperation with refugees and future residents, the building was converted into a home. The Rote Flora replica was turned into Ecofavela Lampedusa Nord and included six multifunctional single-rooms, one collective living room, a kitchen, a shower and an eco-toilet. Six members from Lampedusa moved in. In Germany, the freedom of the arts is protected by law, with strict rules to follow - just like building permits. To make things work, you need ideas, money and structure - and, sometimes, you need to become a trickster.

Housing project? Permanent installation!

As the project progressed, a member of the AfD party reported it to the police as a "housing project for illegal people". Kampnagel's artistic director, Amelie Deuflhard, explained to the authorities that it was not a housing project per se but a durational performance installation that was being carried out for six months, every day, for 24 hours. I call this method art as camouflage. And it was through this artistic framing that the authorities accepted the construction. At the end of the six months, the project was over, and the Ecofavela performers were provided with private apartments. Some left Hamburg and some left the group. Lampedusa got smaller as refugees began to organise their own activist groups. Yet thousands of refugees were still stranded in camps. It became clear to us that if we wanted to continue to practise solidarity through the production of tricky loopholes, we would need to reinvent Ecofavela. We undertook a kind of needs-analysis with the refugees we knew through our networks. They needed safe space to gather, to hang out, a place to go to. A place to flirt, a place to party, a place to recover from the stress of life in the camps. A place to hide, a place to show off. They needed a place to experience new forms of community. Together with Larry Macaulay, a media activist from Nigeria

nutzen konnte. Gemeinsam mit den zukünftigen Bewohner*innen wurde das Gebäude in ein Zuhause verwandelt. Der Nachbau wurde zur Ecovavela Lampedusa Nord mit sechs Einzelzimmern, einem gemeinsamen Wohnzimmer, einer Küche, einer Dusche und einer Komposttoilette.

Hausprojekt? Dauerinstallation!

Ein Mitglied der Partei AfD zeigte das Projekt als „Haus für Illegale" bei der Polizei an. Die künstlerische Leiterin von Kampnagel, Amelie Deuflhard, erklärte den Behörden daraufhin, dass es sich keineswegs um ein Wohnprojekt, sondern um eine Dauerinstallation handelte, die sechs Monate lang jeden Tag für 24 Stunden bespielt würde. Die Behörden gaben das Okay. Ich nenne diese Methode Kunst als Tarnung. In Deutschland ist die künstlerische Freiheit gesetzlich geschützt. Es gibt strenge Auflagen. Manchmal muss man auch ein wenig tricksen. Am Ende der sechs Monate zogen die Künstler*innen der Ecovavela in private Wohnungen um. Manche verließen Hamburg, andere die Gruppe. Lampedusa wurde kleiner. Aber immer noch strandeten Tausende von Geflüchteten in Massenunterkünften. Uns war bewusst: Wir mussten die Ecovavela neu erfinden, um auch weiterhin künstlerische Schlupflöcher schaffen zu können. Was die Menschen brauchten, war ein sicherer Ort, wo sie hingehen, sich treffen und aufhalten konnten. Ein Ort zum Flirten und Feiern, an dem man sich vom Stress in den Flüchtlingsunterkünften erholen konnte. Ein Ort, um neue Formen von Gemeinschaft zu erleben.
Zusammen mit Larry Macaulay, einem Medienaktivisten aus Nigeria, der das Refugee Radio Network und zuvor auch Lampedusa selbst gegründet hatte, stellten wir Machthierarchien und soziale Zuschreibungen infrage. Alle wollten dem Status „Flüchtling" entkommen und anfangen zu leben. Wir lasen Texte von Thomas Nail, einem Philosophieprofessor aus Denver. Seine Gedanken wurden zu unserer Inspirationsquelle:

> „Die wahren Vertreter und Macher der kosmopolitischen Geschichte und Politik waren immer Migranten, und sie sind es bis heute […]. Wenn wir die Chance einer wirklich globalen Gesellschaft verstehen möchten, müssen wir die Kritik an Staatsbürgerschaft, Nationalismus und Liberalismus überwinden und einen Ansatz anbieten, der nicht Millionen von Migranten und Geflüchteten auf der ganzen Welt ausschließt. Wir müssen etwas schaffen, von dem ich vorschlage, dass

who is the founder of Refugee Radio Network and formerly of Lampedusa, we aimed to avoid reproducing power-gaps and social roles that we didn't choose ourselves; everybody wanted to escape "refugee status" and to start living. We read texts by Thomas Nail, a professor of philosophy at the University of Denver. His thoughts on Migrant Cosmopolitanism became our inspiration:

> The true agents and movers of cosmopolitan history and politics have always been, and continue to be, migrants. ... If we want to understand the prospects for a truly global community, we have to move beyond the critiques of citizenship, nationalism, and liberalism, and propose an approach that will not structurally exclude the millions of migrants and refugees of the world. We must create what I propose to call a migrant cosmopolitanism.[1]

Cosmopolitanism is a privilege

If you have the right papers, you can travel easily, and the world is yours. Our intention is to combine the positive aspects of cosmopolitanism with the political struggles of migrants and refugees. A bottom-up cosmopolitanism: migrantpolitanism. In 2015 Ecofavela transformed into Migrantpolitan. We rearranged the inside of the structure, removed walls and changed decorations. Without changing the outside of the wooden box in the backyard, we converted it into something new. The Migrantpolitan has since become a laboratory and a meeting place in which new forms of collaborative working and living are explored and developed. Here, the social categorisations of refugee and local are abandoned and participants collaborate to create cosmopolitan visions.

That same year, Anas Aboura, a political activist and professional networker from Syria, joined our team and began to spread the word through diasporic communities. Together, we formulated concepts, applied for funding, got bigger and created jobs, including one for Anas, who became a curator. This constellation of people and opinions, of artistic and political practices, has led to the creation of concepts that are now making their mark on the Kampnagel programme.

1 See Thomas Nail, "Migrant Cosmopolitanism", Public Affairs Quarterly 29, 2 (2015): 187–188.

wir es einen migrantischen Kosmopolitismus nennen." [1]

Kosmopolitismus als Privileg

Wer die nötigen Papiere hat, kann einfach reisen. Die Welt gehört ihm. Wir verbanden die positiven Aspekte von Kosmopolitismus, Migration und Flucht zu einem Kosmopolitismus von unten: dem Migrantpolitanismus. Im Jahr 2015 verwandelten wir die Ecovavela in Migrantpolitan. Wir veränderten dazu nur das Innere der Holzkiste im Hof, entfernten Wände und änderten die Einrichtung. Das Migrantpolitan ist seitdem zu einem Labor und Treffpunkt geworden, in dem neue Formen des gemeinschaftlichen Arbeitens und Lebens erprobt werden. Hier sind die sozialen Kategorien „Flüchtling" oder „Einheimische*r" aufgehoben. Die Teilnehmer*innen arbeiten an kosmopolitischen Visionen.

Im gleichen Jahr kam Anas Aboura, ein politischer Aktivist und professioneller Netzwerker aus Syrien, in unser Team. Er machte das Projekt in der Diaspora-Community bekannt. Zusammen formulierten wir Konzepte, beantragten Förderungen, wurden größer, schufen Jobs (darunter einen für Anas, der einer der Kuratoren wurde). Aus dieser Konstellation von Menschen und Meinungen, von künstlerischen und politischen Praktiken sind Konzepte entstanden, die heute das Programm Kampnagel prägen.

Seit seiner Eröffnung hatte Migrantpolitan 10.000 Besucher*innen: Ein Produktionsapparat mit migrantischer Perspektive ist entstanden, der das Kampnagel-Programm prägt. Zu den Beiträgen gehören arabischer Techno, eine neue Performancegruppe, regelmäßige Jam-Sessions, Filmabende und eine queere Geflüchtetengruppe. Um unsere unabhängige „Migrantpolitische Bank" zu unterstützen, veranstalten wir regelmäßige Events wie „Soicasino", bei denen Geldverlieren ein Akt der Solidarität ist. Auch ein Café ist entstanden. Wie Trickbetrüger*innen finden wir kreative Lösungen für strukturelle Probleme. Unser Mantra lautet: Denke kriminell, handle künstlerisch. So hat sich der Ort ohne Umbau immer wieder verwandelt: Er ist zur Perspektive geworden. Denn wir ermutigten Menschen, ihre eigenen Ideen und Jobs um unser

1 Siehe Thomas Nail: „Migrant Cosmopolitanism", zit. in: Public Affairs Quarterly, Vol. 29, No. 2, 2015, 187–188.

Since its opening it has seen around 10,000 visitors. As a label, Migrantpolitan works as a production device and enriches the programme with highlights that have been shaped by a migrant perspective, including new adventures in Arab techno and the establishment of a performance group, with regular events including jam sessions, film clubs and a queer refugee group. To feed our independent, self-organised "Migrantpolitan Bank" we hold regular events like "Solicasino", where losing money becomes an act of solidarity. Others opened up a café inside Migrantpolitan. We start from the needs of our members and find creative solutions for structural problems. Trickster-style. "Think like a criminal, act like an artist" is our mantra. Once again, this space shifted without modification: it became more than a place. To some, it became a perspective. But this was not enough. We figured out how to empower more people by encouraging them to create their own visions and jobs around our action centre. Every year we fear that the local authorities will not extend the permissions needed for the next year. And every year we have to claim our own vision; what does not fit is made to fit. Self-empowerment through self-invention. We make virtue out of necessity. We continue to write applications to enlarge our team. Those in the team who are in need of 'Bleibeperspektive', i.e. prospects of permanent residence, are given an honorary post that is almost as valuable as employment, because it too counts toward the application for their permanent residence status.

Building society, not buildings

Today, Migrantpolitan continues to exist. We recently won the Hamburg Nord Kulturpreis and were nominated for the Tabori Prize. And we have big plans for the future.

From the outside, it is still the same small wooden box, our replica of Rote Flora. But in its short life, it has been transformed from a temporary festival architecture into a home, a home into a community action centre, and now, a concept larger than the building itself: an autonomous self-made institution. Maybe we, as migrantpolitans, are architects of society, not of buildings.

Aktionszentrum zu schaffen. Wer eine Bleibeperspektive benötigt, bekommt ein Ehrenamt, das beinahe so viel wert ist wie eine Anstellung. Was nicht passt, wird passend gemacht. Jedes Jahr fürchten wir, dass die Behörden uns die Erlaubnis entziehen. Und jedes Jahr schreiben wir Anträge und tragen unsere Vision (und Version) vor.

Gesellschaft bauen, nicht Gebäude

Migrantpolitan existiert noch immer. Erst kürzlich erhielten wir den Kulturpreis Hamburg-Nord und waren für den Tabori-Preis nominiert. Für die Zukunft haben wir große Pläne.

Von außen betrachtet ist es immer noch die gleiche Holzkiste: unser Nachbau der Roten Flora. Aber in seinem kurzen Leben ist aus temporärer Festivalarchitektur ein Zuhause, ein gemeinschaftliches Aktionszentrum und schließlich eine autonome Institution geworden, die größer ist als das Gebäude selbst. Und wir? Wir sind Architekt*innen, die Gesellschaft bauen, und nicht Gebäude.

-> Chapter 3 pp. 139 ff. Third Spaces. The Production of Communities

A space for arrival and self-empowerment with language courses, solidarity events and exchange of experiences

Raum für Ankommen und Selbstermächtigung mit Sprachkursen, Solidaritätsveranstaltungen und Erfahrungsaustausch

01.

Project: **Every One Every Day**

City: London
Client: Borough of Barking and Dagenham, London, UK
Planning: Participatory City
Status: 2017-ongoing

By and for Everyone Participatory City

There exists a general belief that people working together - rather than against each other - will make our lives better. Despite this, today participation in neighbourhood projects is low, with widespread participation remaining difficult to achieve; although 60 percent of people in the UK say they want to be involved in a neighbourhood project, only 3 percent of people are engaged in projects in their own community.

Why is there such a gap?

Over the course of six years, Participatory City has been researching and prototyping new ways to support widespread practical participation. This work has led to the development of a case study on the scale of an entire neighbourhood in London - which aims to complete the full cycle of research, design, evaluation and codification necessary to create a blueprint for change. Participatory City is creating new structures designed to scale up practical participation, building collaborative activity into the fabric of everyday life and changing how all stakeholders - civic, private and municipal - work together to achieve a more equal society.

Every One Every Day is growing a network of residents, projects and collaborative businesses across Barking and Dagenham over the next four years which launched in the borough in the autumn of 2017. It is an ambitious project that aims to work with the creativity and energy that already exists in both areas. Every One Every Day will invite people to suggest ideas for projects and businesses they would like to create together, providing the support needed to bring hundreds of these ideas to life quickly and with minimal complications for residents. Every One Every Day will open five high street shops and a central warehouse. From these core spaces the team will work with local residents to create projects, arrange insurance, ensure health and safety, facilitate the use of smaller functional spaces for relevant projects, set up websites, produce newspapers and hold festivals, workshops, and business development incubator programmes.

Every One Every Day's ability to work in this way depends on a strong collaboration with the local authority, which acts as funder and partner,

Von allen, für alle Die partizipatorische Stadt

Es gibt die allgemeine Überzeugung, dass unser Leben besser wird, wenn Menschen zusammenarbeiten – anstatt gegeneinander. Die tatsächliche Beteiligung an Nachbarschaftsprojekten ist jedoch gering, und es bleibt schwierig, eine breitere Teilhabe zu erreichen. Obwohl sechzig Prozent der Menschen im Vereinigten Königreich sagen, dass sie sich gern an einem Nachbarschaftsprojekt beteiligen würden, sind nur drei Prozent tatsächlich in Projekte in ihrer Gegend involviert.

Warum gibt es diesen großen Unterschied?

In den sechs Projektjahren von Participatory City wurden neue Möglichkeiten erforscht und ausprobiert, wie eine breitere praktische Partizipation unterstützt werden kann. Diese Arbeit hat zur Entwicklung einer Fallstudie über das Maß an Teilhabe in einem ganzen Londoner Stadtviertel geführt – als Gesamtstudienverlauf durch Forschung, Ausführung, Evaluation und Kodifizierung soll diese Studie eine Vorlage für Veränderung schaffen. Participatory City entwirft neue Strukturen, um praktische Teilhabe auszuweiten, um Zusammenarbeit ins Gewebe der alltäglichen Tätigkeiten einzubauen und um mehr Möglichkeiten der Zusammenarbeit für eine gerechtere Gesellschaft zu schaffen.

Das Projekt Every One Every Day wurde 2017 in Barking und Dagenham, Großbritannien, gegründet und baut dort in den nächsten vier Jahren ein Netzwerk aus Anwohner*innen, Projekten und kollaborativen Unternehmen auf. Es ist ein ambitioniertes Projekt, das mit der Kreativität und Energie arbeitet, die im Viertel bereits besteht. Every One Every Day wird die Menschen dazu einladen, Projektideen und Unternehmensgründungen vorzuschlagen, die sie gern zusammen entwickeln würden. Es wird die nötige Unterstützung bieten, um Hunderte dieser Ideen schnell und unkompliziert Realität werden zu lassen. Every One Every Day wird fünf klassische, zentral gelegene Straßenläden und eine Lagerhalle eröffnen. Von diesen Kernorten aus wird das Team mit Menschen zusammenarbeiten, um Projekte zu gründen, Versicherungen – sowohl für Gesundheitsversorgung als auch zur Absicherung – abzuschließen, um den Projekten die Nutzung kleinerer funktionaler Räume zu ermöglichen, Webseiten einzurichten, Zeitungen zu produzieren, Festivals zu organisieren, Workshops abzuhalten und Existenzgründungsprogramme zu entwickeln.

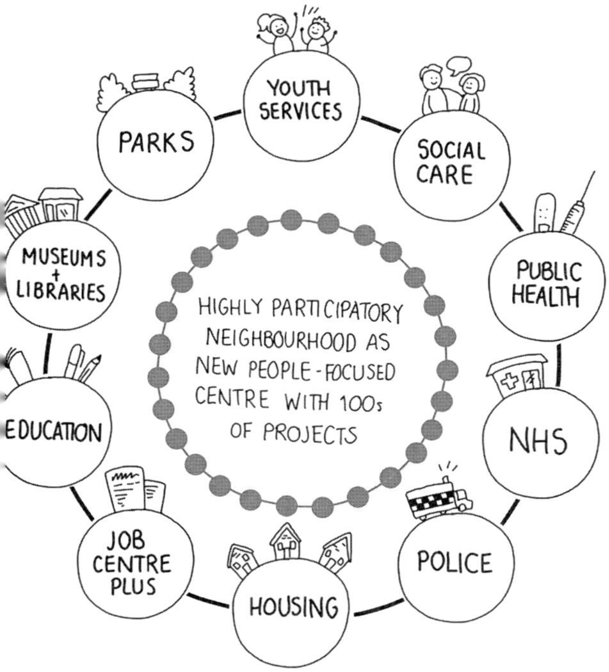

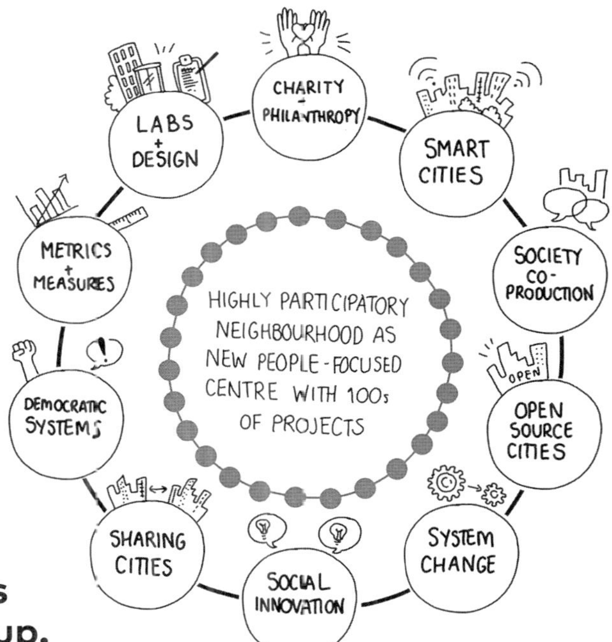

"We have thrown out ideas of top-down and bottom-up. Instead we are designing and testing new structures, new methods and new cultures – combining all of our resources for co-production."

„Wir haben die Vorstellung von Top-down und Bottom-up verworfen. Stattdessen gestalten und erproben wir neue Strukturen, neue Methoden und Kulturen der Zusammenarbeit – und kombinieren dabei all unsere Ressourcen der gemeinsamen Produktion."

Tessy Britton

working together to identify and resolve obstacles, building and strengthening networks and creating local opportunities.

The project is funded by a coalition of four funders (Esmee Fairbairn Foundation, The Big Lottery Fund, City Bridge Trust and the London Borough of Barking and Dagenham) who have agreed to pool their funding and sign up to a common set of outcome metrics and reporting schedules. The Participatory City Foundation was established as a charitable body in order to draw down this funding.

The aim is simple, but ambitious: build the structures to facilitate collaborative projects and small entreprises, thus bringing to fruition residents' ideas for improving the quality of life and services in the neighbourhoods and communities across Barking and Dagenham.

Ob Every One Every Day funktioniert, hängt von einer starken Zusammenarbeit mit den lokalen Behörden als finanzierende und kooperierende Institutionen ab, wobei Hindernisse erkannt und beseitigt, Netzwerke gebildet und gestärkt sowie lokale Chancen geschaffen werden müssen.

Das Projekt wird von einem Bündnis aus vier Institutionen finanziert (Esmée Fairbairn Foundation, Big Lottery Fund, City Bridge Trust, die Londoner Bezirke Barking und Dagenham), die zugestimmt haben, ihre Gelder zu bündeln und sich auf gemeinsame Ergebniskriterien und Berichtspflichten zu einigen. Die Participatory City Foundation wurde als gemeinnützige Einrichtung gegründet, um diese Förderung zu erhalten.

Das Ziel ist einfach, aber ambitioniert: Strukturen aufbauen, die kollaborative Projekte ermöglichen, deren Ideen Früchte tragen, um die Lebensqualität und Angebote in den Nachbarschaften und Gemeinschaften in ganz Barking und Dagenham zu verbessern.

"By combining the ideas, energies and resources of residents, local government, statutory partners and other local organisations and businesses, long-term sustainability is an achievable goal."

„Mit gemeinsamen Ideen, Energien und Ressourcen von Anwohner*innen, Kommunen und anderen lokalen Organisationen und Unternehmen wird langfristige Nachhaltigkeit ein erreichbares Ziel."

Tessy Britton

The most simple sketch for a communal and neighbourly mix belies years of negotiation and dialogue

Die einfachste Skizze für gemeinschaftlich-nachbarschaftliche Nutzungen erfordert jahrelange Dialoge und Verhandlungen

02.

Project: **Haus der Statistik**

City: Berlin
Client: N/A
Planning: BIM, WBM, Berzirksamt Berlin-Mitte (Federführung), SenSW, Genossenschaft ZUsammenKUNFT Berlin (ZKB)
Status: Concept

Taking a Stand
New Alliances for the Co-operative City

One of Berlin's best-known ruins, the Haus der Statistik (House of Statistics) at Alexanderplatz, was built between 1968 and 1970. Originally a complex of seven buildings, it was used by the German Democratic Republic's (GDR) Central Administration for Statistics, as well as by the State Security Service (Stasi). After the fall of the Berlin Wall, it served as an office for the German federal authority until 2008 and then was left empty. Today, the 40,000-square-metre property is to be transformed via an open and collaborative development process - involving a coalition between civil society and the city government - into a model project for cooperative and welfare-oriented urban development.
A further 65,000 square metres are envisaged for a potential new construction. The site includes space for art, culture, social services and education, affordable and integrated housing as well as a new town hall for the Mitte district in Berlin and administrative use.

A model for mixed use

The project has found political support: In 2017, the Berlin Senate acquired the building on Alexanderplatz for 50 million euros. At this point, a great deal of pressure was placed on the Berlin administration to renovate the complex and make it useable for Berlin residents. The Initiative Haus der Statistik, a coalition of various Berlin groups, had already started to develop concepts and ideas for the complex in 2015. The initiative aims to transform the site into affordable living and working space for social projects, education, art and culture, in an integrated and cost-effective manner. A workshop process run by the Berlin Senate for a developmental reevaluation of Alexanderplatz was decisive in this process.

A committed coalition formed in January 2018 from participating stakeholders, the municipality, the state-owned companies BIM and WBM and the ZKB Co-operative for Urban Development, which emerged from the Initiative Haus der Statistik, will announce the shared develpment: a broad spatial concept integrating diverse uses. The project sets a clear precedent, both for Berlin and beyond.

Instand(be)setzen
Neue Allianzen für eine kooperative Stadt

Es ist eine der bekanntesten Berliner Ruinen: das Haus der Statistik am Berliner Alexanderplatz, errichtet zwischen 1968 und 1970. Ursprünglich ein Komplex aus sieben Gebäuden wurde es von der Zentralverwaltung für Statistik der DDR sowie dem Staatssicherheitsdienst genutzt. Nach der Wiedervereinigung diente das Haus bis 2008 als Sitz von Bundesbehörden. Im Anschluss stand es leer. Nun sollen die 46.000 Quadratmeter Flächen im Bestand in einem offenen und kollaborativen Entwicklungsprozess von einer Koalition aus Zivilgesellschaft und Stadtregierung zu einem Modellprojekt für kooperative und gemeinwohlorientierte Stadtentwicklung werden. Weitere 65.000 Quadratmeter sind als potenzielle Flächen im Neubau vorgesehen. Auf dem Areal entstehen Raum für Kunst, Kultur, Soziales und Bildung, Wohnen sowie ein neues Rathaus für Mitte und Verwaltungsnutzungen.

Nutzungsmix mit Modellcharakter

Die Politik steht dahinter: 2017 hat der Berliner Senat das Haus am Alexanderplatz für 50 Millionen Euro erworben. Zu diesem Zeitpunkt wurde bereits lange Druck auf die Berliner Politik und Verwaltung ausgeübt, den Komplex zu sanieren und für die Bevölkerung nutzbar zu machen. Die Initiative Haus der Statistik, ein Zusammenschluss verschiedener Berliner Gruppen, hatte bereits 2015 damit begonnen, Konzepte und Ideen für den Gebäudekomplex zu entwickeln. Sie will ihn integrativ und kosteneffektiv zu bezahlbarem Wohnraum und Arbeitsfläche für Soziales, Bildung, Kunst und Kultur umwandeln. Ausschlaggebend dafür war ein Workshop-Verfahren des Berliner Senats zur städtebaulichen Neubewertung des Alexanderplatzes.

Eine im Januar 2018 geschlossene Kooperationsvereinbarung der fünf beteiligten Akteur*innen, dem Bezirksamt Berlin-Mitte, den landeseigenen Gesellschaften BIM und WBM, der SenStadtWohn sowie der ZKB Genossenschaft für Stadtentwicklung, die aus der Initiative Haus der Statistik hervorgegangen ist, soll die gemeinschaftliche Entwicklung hin zu einer breit gefächerten Raumnutzung klären. Das Vorhaben hat Modellcharakter.

Ab 2019 sind Pioniernutzungen geplant, um bereits vor Fertigstellung der Sanierungsmaßnahmen im Bestand und der Neubauten auf Raumbedarfe zu reagieren und ausgewählte Nutzungen proto-

From virtual ruin to prototype for change: the civic initiative Haus der Statistik prevents the property sale, the demolition, and shapes the mixed-use revival

Von Leerstand zu Leuchtturm: Druck der Initiative Haus der Statistik verhindert Spekulation und Abriss und formt die Koalition zur Neunutzung

Virtual obsolescence becomes a projection surface for civic demands

Von der scheinbaren Obdoleszenz zur Projektionsfläche der Stadtgesellschaft

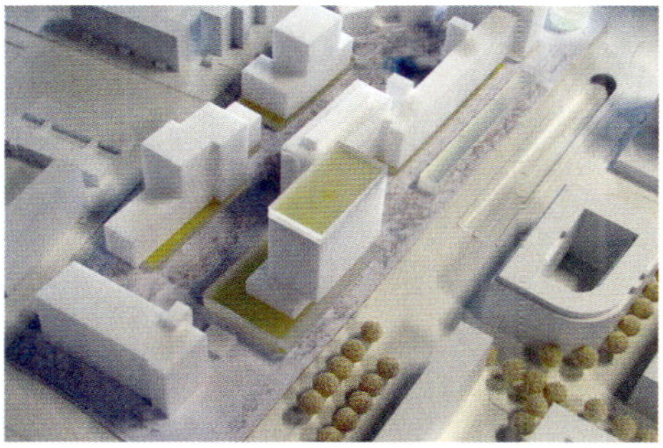

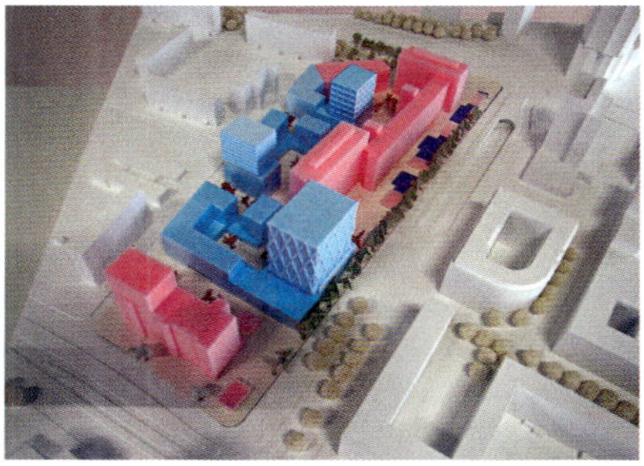

From 2019, the first pioneering projects will move in, in order to fulfil the demand for space even before the renovation of the existing and new buildings are completed and to prototype selected future uses. In an integrative workshop process that began in September 2018, three planning teams are developing a redevelopment concept for the Haus der Statistik site. Here, the Werkstatt Haus der Statistik has a key role in communicating with the urban community. Through workshops and other formats, ZKB representatives gather opinions and ideas, developing approaches for further planning together with participants and the other coalition members and, thus informing the workshop process. Over 30 concrete declarations of interest for the building's spaces have already been submitted to the ZKB - including projects requiring between 70 square metres (e.g. for a project office) to 6,000 square metres, amongst them an integrative housing co-operative or museum.

New modes of co-creation

Berlin's administration and the involved initiatives are blazing a new path towards co-creation: a complex, process-based negotiation with all involved stakeholders. The precise mix and the programming of the building must effectively be determined by five co-operation entities ranging from district to municipal level. The cooperation partners themselves are self-financed. By what means the predominantly social and cultural uses of the site will be funded is yet to be determined through the collaborative process. The Haus der Statistik has the potential to become a laboratory for plural, contemporary and concrete forms of living together. A lively point of attraction for all people in an inner-city area that is otherwise fast becoming commercialised. The following expressions of interest for Haus der Statistik have been submitted:

- Housing for refugees
- Live-in studios for artists and researchers
- Housing for the elderly and assisted-living apartments
- Spaces for vocational training
- Social initiatives
- Music production
- Cultural non-profit associations/offices for non-profit associations
- Permanent exhibitions/museums
- Art exhibitions and events
- Education (workshops, events, seminars)
- Workshops (e.g. for integration projects)
- Co-working space

typisch zu erproben. Seit September 2018 läuft das integrierte Werkstattverfahren, in dem drei Planungsteams beauftragt sind, ein städtebauliches Konzept für das Areal zu erarbeiten. Ziel des Verfahrens ist es, eine Grundlage für einen neuen Bebauungsplan für das Areal Haus der Statistik zu erarbeiten. Die Werkstatt Haus der Statistik dient als Schnittstelle zur Stadtgesellschaft. Über Workshops und andere Formate sammeln Mitarbeiter*innen der ZKB Meinungen und Impulse aus der interessierten Stadtgesellschaft und unmittelbaren Nachbarschaft. Gemeinsam mit den Teilnehmenden entwickeln die fünf Kooperationspartner*innen Ansätze zur weiteren Planung und informieren so das Werkstattverfahren. Bereits über dreißig konkrete Interessenbekundungen für die Nutzung der Flächen, die für die Initiativnutzung vorgesehen sind, liegen der ZKB vor. Sie reichen von Flächenanfragen über 70 Quadratmeter (z. B. für ein Projektbüro) bis zu 6000 Quadratmeter (z. B. für ein integriertes Wohnprojekt oder Museum).

Neuer Weg der Ko-Kreation

Berliner Verwaltung und Initiativen der Stadtgesellschaft haben mit dem Projekt zum Haus der Statistik gemeinsam einen neuen Weg der Ko-Kreation beschritten: eine komplexe und prozesshafte Verhandlung der Stakeholder. Zwischen den fünf Kooperationspartner*innen wird die genaue Nutzungsmischung und die Programmierung der Bestands- und Neubauten ausgehandelt. Alle Kooperationspartner*innen finanzieren ihren Teil selbst. Über welche Förderprogramme die vorwiegend sozialen und kulturellen Nutzungen der Initiative finanziert werden, wird im Prozess verhandelt. Das Haus der Statistik hat das Potenzial, ein Labor für plurale, zeitgemäße und kreative Formen des Zusammenlebens zu werden. Ein lebendiger Anziehungspunkt für alle Menschen und ein Gegenpol in einer kommerziell geprägten Innenstadt. Folgende Interessenbekundungen für Flächen im Haus der Statistik liegen vor:

– Wohnprojekte für Geflüchtete
– Atelierwohnen für Künstler*innen, Forscher*innen
– Alterswohngruppen und betreutes Wohnen
– Arbeits- und Ausbildungsplätze
– Sozialberatung
– Musikproduktion
– Kulturvereine/Vereinsbüros
– Dauerausstellungen/Museen
– Kunstausstellungen und -veranstaltungen
– Bildung (Workshops, Veranstaltungen, Seminare)
– Werkstätten (z. B. von Integrationsprojekten)
– Coworking-Space

Renegotiation in situ: numerous workshops with all stakeholders determine the future programme

Situatives Verhandeln: Werkstätten mit allen Stakeholdern determinieren am Ort den Nutzungsmix

03. Project: Sonnenallee

City: Berlin
Client: People
Planning: querstadtein
Status: Ongoing

Approaching Step by Step
A Perceptual Shift

The Brandenburg Gate, the Siegessäule (Victory Column) or the Bundestag (German Federal Parliament) - these are the monuments visited during traditional city tours, those that feature important historical buildings and sites. But during recent years, alternative urban tour guide concepts have been on the rise. In guided tours offered by the querstadtein initiative, locals who usually don't get a say become (urban) guides: formerly homeless people depict everyday life on the street; newly settled people who have fled from Afghanistan, Syria, or Iraq share their perspectives on their new hometown. One of these is Mohamad Khalil from Syria. Khalil, a student, became aware of querstadtein in 2017, when he met another city guide in an integration course for migrants and refugees and became curious about the initiative. Mohamad leads tours in Berlin's Neukölln district - pointing out ordinary, seemingly insignificant places along the famous Sonnenalle, vividly conveying the cultural benefit of this tour guide format in a nutshell:

Annäherungen im Schritttempo
Ein Perspektivwechsel

Brandenburger Tor, Siegessäule oder Bundestag – klassische Stadtführungen zeigen bedeutende historische Bauten und Sehenswürdigkeiten. Seit einigen Jahren haben alternative Stadtführungskonzepte und -ideen vermehrt Einzug gehalten. In den geführten Touren der Initiative querstadtein ergreifen Berliner*innen das Wort, über die sonst nur gesprochen wird: Ehemals Obdachlose berichten vom Leben auf der Straße, Neuankömmlinge, die aus Afghanistan, Syrien oder dem Irak geflüchtet sind, teilen ihre Perspektiven auf ihre neue Heimatstadt. So zum Beispiel Mohamad Khalil aus Syrien. Zu querstadtein kam der Student 2017, als er in einem Integrationskurs einen anderen Stadtführer kennenlernte und neugierig wurde. Der Student zeigt Interessierten den Berliner Stadtteil Neukölln mit seinen ganz alltäglichen, scheinbar unbedeutenden Orten entlang der Sonnenallee und bringt den gesellschaftlichen Mehrwert des Formats auf den Punkt:

"There are boundaries between people – the refugees and the inhabitants of Berlin. Many people don't dare to talk to refugees, so these tours are like a link between people to break down boundaries!"

„Es gibt Grenzen zwischen den Menschen, den Geflüchteten und den Einwohner*innen Berlins. Viele trauen sich nicht, mit Geflüchteten zu sprechen, deswegen sind diese Touren eine Verbindung zwischen den Menschen - um so Grenzen zu durchbrechen!"

Mohamad Khalil

As part of a fundamental perceptual shift, Mohamad Khalil's tours employ diverse methods to decipher the cultural diversity of the Sonnenallee

In Anspielung auf den grundsätzlichen Perspektivwechsel nutzt Mohamad Khalil in seinen Führungen diverse Methoden, die kulturelle Vielfalt der Sonnenallee zu entschlüsseln

04.

Projekt:

Begegnungshaus Poppenbüttel

City: Hamburg
Client: f&w Fördern und Wohnen Hamburg
Planning: Faculty of Urban Design at HafenCity University, Atelier Bow Wow
Status: Proposal

Fantastic Fail
A Blueprint for Collaboration

In Hamburg's city district Poppenbüttel, a unique project for a community centre brought architects, professors and teachers of the HafenCity University, local authorities and refugees together to develop a Begegnungshaus - a community centre and a space of encounter. International architects, the jazz musician Christopher Dell, students, local residents and refugees collaborated in realising its design at a scale of 1:1, living and working together on the construction site. Since the plans for the surrounding new district did not include residential accommodations with common areas, the Begegnungshaus was to serve as a place where refugees could come together.

Spatial arrangements, equipment, structure and details of the house were determined together by the newly arrived refugees and local residents. A final competition was won by the Japanese architecture studio Atelier Bow Wow with their concept of "The Bazaar X The Living Rooms" that proposed nine living rooms connected by a forum. By incorporating the surrounding environment and its modular configuration, the open format of the house would allow for diverse uses of the available rooms. The concept also included the long-term involvement of future users so that residents would continue to contribute to the construction of the building. The fact that community-driven and participatory planning processes do not always translate into reality was experienced first-hand by the community which had formed around the Begegnungshaus Poppenbüttel, when it became apparent that the project was to be discontinued. But failure opens up possibilities for future learning: the treasure chest of methodologies that emerged from the process is now available as a toolbox for empowering the newly settled migrant communities in other urban neighbourhoods. However, Poppenbüttel project is a reminder that the success of such projects is heavily reliant on political will and the social climate.

Grandios scheitern
Ein Lehrstück der Teilhabe

In Hamburgs Stadtviertel Poppenbüttel haben Architekt*innen, Lehrende und Studierende der HafenCity Universität Hamburg, Lokalverwaltung und geflüchtete Menschen gemeinsam ein Haus der Begegnung entwickelt – ein einzigartiges Projekt. Internationale Architekt*innen, der Musiker und Improvisateur Christopher Dell, Studierende, Anwohner*innen und Asylsuchende planten dazu gemeinsam im Maßstab 1:1 direkt auf der Baustelle. Da in dem neuen Quartier nur Wohnunterkünfte ohne Gemeinschaftsräume vorgesehen wurden, sollte das Begegnungshaus den Geflüchteten als Ort des Zusammenkommens dienen.

Räumliche Arrangements, Ausstattung, Struktur und Details des Hauses wurden zusammen mit geflüchteten Menschen und Anwohner*innen bestimmt. Den abschließenden Wettbewerb gewann das japanische Architekturbüro Atelier Bow Wow mit seinem Konzept „The Bazaar X The Living Rooms". Dieses sah neun Wohnzimmer vor, die über ein Forum miteinander verbunden sind. Die offene Gestaltung nach außen sollte durch den Einbezug der Umgebung und eine modulare Ausstattung eine vielfältige Nutzung der Räume ermöglichen. Das Konzept sah ebenfalls einen langfristigen Einbezug der künftigen Nutzer*innen vor; so sollten sich diese auch weiterhin am Bau mit einbringen können. Dass sich partizipative Planungsprozesse und Wunschprojektionen nicht immer in die Realität übersetzen lassen, musste leider auch das Begegnungshaus Poppenbüttel mit dem Abbruch sämtlicher Konzeptrealisierungen erfahren. Doch auch aus einem vermeintlichen Scheitern lässt sich lernen: Der aus dem Prozess hervorgegangene Methodenschatz stellt nun ein Handwerkszeug für die Stärkung von Neuankömmlingen in anderen städtischen Nachbarschaften zur Verfügung – dennoch ist der Erfolg von Projekten wie diesem vom politischen Willen und sozialen Klima abhängig.

Stages of participation from projections of desire to proposed typologies

Beteiligung in Stufen: von der Wunschprojektion zu konkreten Typologien

05.

Projekt:

Embassy for Children

City: Berlin
Client: SOS-Kinderdorf e.V.
Planning: Ludloff Ludloff Architekten
Status: Completed 2017

The Aesthetics of the Social
Designed to Resonate

Ludloff Ludloff Architects realised a new house for the association SOS-Kinderdorf Berlin: an embassy for children. In a carefully structured, heterogeneous urban landscape, the new education centre and meeting-place is intended to be a safe space. Here, young people who are experiencing difficulties and requiring support will find both the space and individualised support they need. An advisory and education centre, conference rooms, a library, 28 hotel rooms and a catering business with a kitchen for teaching home economics are made available to the children and young people on six carefully arranged storeys. Despite the challenging shape of the property and having a strict budget to work with, the architects were able to realise an atmospheric building that effortlessly creates space for both openness and privacy.

An intricate envelope made of moveable sun-protective panels creates a differentiated façade, filtering the gaze from outside. The translucent textile material of these panels give the house a veiled appearance, while also affording it visibility in its urban context. This design gives a visible locus to both the process of integration and the desire to have a societal effect.

The Embassy for Children also marks Ludloff Ludloff Architects' contribution to a fundamental debate in construction culture: for them, architecture is not a service but an ethical and moral responsibility - it cannot simply be about satisfying needs. For Make City, they therefore call for a new aesthetic: the aesthetic of the social.

Appeal

The growing disparity in our society has become an important aspect of our political discourse. However, the debate around societal participation, including access to education, work and living spaces, points towards a blindspot: a human need for aesthetic qualities. It often seems that societal participation only takes place within the framework of satisfying basic needs.

This is an astounding development. Recall, for example, the housing developments of the reform movement during the Weimar Republic. Here, it is clear that even apartments set up to accommo-

Die Ästhetik des Sozialen
Von der Resonanz der Gestaltung

Ludloff Ludloff Architekten realisierten ein neues Haus für den Verein SOS-Kinderdorf Berlin: die Botschaft für Kinder. In einer von Heterogenität und Brüchen geprägten Stadtlandschaft versteht sich das neue Bildungs- und Begegnungszentrum als Schutzraum. Junge Menschen, die in Schwierigkeiten sind und Unterstützung benötigen, finden hier ihren Platz und individuelle Unterstützung. Ein Beratungs- und Ausbildungszentrum, Tagungsräume, ein Bibliotheksraum, 28 Hotelzimmer und ein Gastronomiebetrieb mit Lehrküche stehen den Kindern und Jugendlichen auf sechs präzise arrangierten Etagen zur Verfügung. Trotz des schwierigen Grundstücks und des niedrigen Budgets ist es den Architekt*innen gelungen, ein atmosphärisches Gebäude umzusetzen, das den Spagat zwischen Offenheit und Geborgenheit mühelos schafft.

Eine schuppenartige Hülle aus verschiebbaren Sonnensegeln differenziert die Fassade und filtert Blicke. Das transluzente textile Material der Elemente gibt dem Haus etwas Schleierhaftes und lässt es in den Stadtraum strahlen. Der Entwurf gibt dem Prozess der Integration und dem Ringen nach sozialer Gestaltung einen sichtbaren Ort.

Die Botschaft für Kinder steht auch für die Forderung von Ludloff Ludloff Architekten nach einer baukulturellen Grundsatzdebatte: Architektur ist für sie keine Dienstleistung, sondern ethisch-moralische Verantwortung und darf nicht zur reinen Bedürfnisbefriedigung verkommen. Für Make City rufen sie daher zu einer neuen Ästhetik des Sozialen auf.

Appell

Die wachsende Ungleichheit in unserer Gesellschaft ist zu einem wichtigen Teil des politischen Diskurses geworden. Die Debatte um gesellschaftliche Teilhabe, die Zugänglichkeit zu Bildung, Arbeit und Wohnen weist jedoch einen blinden Fleck auf: das menschliche Bedürfnis nach einer ästhetischen Qualität. Es scheint, als dürfe über gesellschaftliche Teilhabe nur im Rahmen der reinen Bedarfsbefriedigung gesprochen werden.

Das ist erstaunlich, denkt man etwa an die Wohnsiedlungen der Reformbewegung der Weimarer Republik, so wird deutlich, dass gerade die „Wohnung für das Existenzminimum" von höchster gestalterischer Qualität geprägt war. Einfachheit verband

Textile façade with lasting charisma: the municipality maintains control over the land by acquiring the property via leasehold rights

Textile Fassade mit nachhaltiger Strahlkraft und das vorbildlich: Der Grundstückserwerb erfolgte im Erbbaurecht. Der Bezirk behält so langfristig die Handhabe über den Boden

date the bare minimum were of a high aesthetic standard. Simplicity was connected with functional, social and aesthetic qualities. Today, many of these developments have been listed as UNESCO World Heritage sites.

The economy does not produce living spaces. In the current state of spatial production, it is easy to get the impression that building according to purely economic parameters has allowed a form of decorated banal functionalism to come to the fore; but it would be wrong to believe that efficient, economically optimised construction technology and the precise satisfaction of needs are enough.

In our image-oriented world, images of the social have long been leveraged as political instruments - often without discussing or questioning their aesthetic. The discussion around societal participation, however, can only fulfil its promise if fundamental questions of design are included. An aesthetic of the essential is the precondition for communities to respect individual needs.

sich mit funktionalen, sozialen und ästhetischen Ansprüchen. Heute sind diese Siedlungen größtenteils UNESCO-Weltkulturerbe.

Ökonomie ist keine Lebensform. In der aktuellen Raumproduktion kann man den Eindruck gewinnen, dass aufgrund rein wirtschaftlicher Zielsetzungen eine Art geschmückter Banalfunktionalismus entsteht. Es ist falsch, zu glauben, dass effiziente, ökonomisch optimierte Bautechnik und präzise Nutzungserfüllung ausreichen.

In unserer bildfixierten Welt haben sich Bilder des Sozialen längst politisch gefestigt – ohne dass deren Ästhetik diskutiert oder gar hinterfragt worden wäre. Die Diskussion um gesellschaftliche Teilhabe kann jedoch nur dann glaubwürdig sein, wenn Gestaltungsfragen nicht ausgeschlossen werden. Eine Ästhetik des Wesentlichen ist die Voraussetzung für gemeinschaftliches Handeln, das individuelle Bedürfnisse respektiert.

Flowing forms and functions combine spatial experience with a social agenda: publicly accessible areas merge into training rooms and retreat zones

Fließende Formen und Funktionen vereinen Raumerlebnis mit sozialer Agenda: öffentliche Bereiche gehen über in Ausbildungsräume und Rückzugszonen

The garden city of Falkenberg (1916) and the housing estate Karl Legien (1932) by Bruno Taut: an example of the aesthetic of the essential with a social vision?

Gartenstadt Falkenberg (1916) und Wohnstadt Carl Legien (1932) von Bruno Taut: eine „Ästhetik des Wesentlichen" mit gesellschaftlicher Vision?

Purely functional or living space? Refugee shelters designed to fulfil only the most basic needs (accommodation for refugees in the former Tempelhof Airport)

Reiner Zweckbau oder Lebensraum? Flüchtlingsunterkünfte als reine Bedarfsbefriedigung (Unterkünfte für Geflüchtete im ehemaligen Flughafen Tempelhof)

06. Project: City Plaza

City: Athens
Client: N/A
Planning: N/A
Status: 2016-current

Hotel with a Difference From Refuge to Community

In the face of the ongoing refugee crisis, and as a response to the closure of the Balkan route and the consequences of the EU-Turkey deal of April 22, 2016, the "Refugee Accommodation and Solidarity at City Plaza Hotel" initiative made the political decision to take over an abandoned hotel in Athens' anarchist Exarchia neighbourhood, giving around 400 people from Syria, Afghanistan, Iran, Iraq, Palestine, Pakistan and Ghana a home. Working together, activists and refugees opened and repaired the derelict 100-room City Plaza Athens hotel in a self-organised experiment in solidarity to show that dignified cohabitation was possible within the urban fabric of the capital city.

In the 32 months of its existence, City Plaza has become an example of what a squat can do. The hotel houses a medical clinic, workshops, a cafeteria, a café and language classes. Families live in private, some have been able to find and secure employment and some maintain the hotel itself, all while building and fostering a community. The occupation received no support from municipal authorities, although it was tolerated until its owner, heiress Aliki Papachela, successfully sued for the inhabitants' eviction, despite having abandoned the hotel during Greece's financial crisis and allowing it to fall into disrepair.

Nasim Lomani, one of the community organisers recollects: "It is a counter-example to the camps. It shows an alternative to how refugees should be housed. Not in the middle of nowhere, but in the city, with access to social services. One third of the population here are children and they are able to access schools. People should live in houses and buildings, not in camps and containers far from cities. So we occupied the hotel partly as a demand to the government to house refugees properly - especially as there are so many empty houses around Athens. We also wanted to create a space to fight against EU policies of detention, deportation and general mistreatment of migrants, and to fight against the manner in which they are frquently labelled."

Today, despite the prosecutor's office of Athens ordering the refugee squat evicted, the activists and refugees of City Plaza continue their occupation. At present, however, no new refugees

Das etwas andere Hotel Aus Unterkommen wird Ankommen

Angesichts der andauernden Flüchtlingskrise und als Antwort auf die Schließung der Balkanroute und die Konsequenzen des Deals der EU mit der Türkei traf die Initiative „Refugee Accommodation and Solidarity Space City Plaza Hotel" die politische Entscheidung, ein verlassenes Hotel im anarchistischen Athener Stadtteil Exarchia zu übernehmen und etwa 400 Menschen aus Syrien, Afghanistan, Iran, Irak, Palästina, Pakistan und Ghana ein Zuhause zu geben. Gemeinsam renovierten die Aktivist*innen und Geflüchteten das baufällige Hotel City Plaza Athens mit seinen hundert Zimmern in einem selbstorganisierten Experiment der Solidarität, um zu demonstrieren, dass würdiges Zusammenleben im urbanen Geflecht der Hauptstadt möglich ist.

In den 32 Monaten seines Bestehens ist das City Plaza zum besten Beispiel dafür geworden, was ein besetztes Haus sein kann. Im Haus gibt es eine Arztpraxis, Werkstätten, eine Kantine, ein Café und Sprachkurse. Familien können für sich leben, manche haben es geschafft, Arbeit zu finden, und andere kümmern sich um das Hotel selbst, während sie zugleich eine Gemeinschaft aufbauen und stärken. Die Besetzung wurde von den örtlichen Behörden nicht unterstützt, wurde aber geduldet, bis die Besitzerin, die Erbin Aliki Papachela, erfolgreich auf Zwangsräumung klagte, obwohl sie das Hotel während der griechischen Finanzkrise aufgegeben und damit dem Verfall preisgegeben hatte.

Nasim Lomani, einer der Organisatoren und ursprünglichen Besetzer des Hotels, erinnert sich: „Es ist ein Gegenbeispiel zu den Lagern. Es zeigt uns Alternativen auf, wie Geflüchtete untergebracht werden sollten. Nicht mitten im Nichts, sondern in der Stadt, mit Zugang zu sozialen Diensten. Ein Drittel der Bewohner hier sind Kinder, die zur Schule gehen können. Menschen sollten in Häusern und Gebäuden wohnen, nicht in Lagern und Containern fernab der Städte. Wir haben das Hotel teilweise als Forderung an die Regierung besetzt, Geflüchtete anständig unterzubringen – vor allem, weil es in Athen so viele leer stehende Häuser gibt. Wir wollten auch einen Ort schaffen, der gegen die EU-Politik der Inhaftierung, Abschiebung und generell schlechten Behandlung von Migranten protestiert und gegen ihre Brandmarkung."

Trotz der Anordnung der Athener Staatsanwaltschaft, das von den Geflüchteten besetzte Haus zu

Symbol of the crisis: after years of vacancy, Athens' City Plaza Hotel is fully occupied with new guests from Syria, Iraq, Pakistan, Iran and Afghanistan

Symbol der Krise: Athens City Plaza Hotel nach jahrelangem Leerstand wieder besetzt mit neuen Gästen aus Syrien, Irak, Pakistan, Iran und Afghanistan

"Each one who resides in the building has a different perception of this endeavour. Finding a common ground is a daily goal in order to be able to function collectively in this place."

„Jeder derjenigen, die im Gebäude leben, hat eine unterschiedliche Wahrnehmung seiner Lage. Gemeinsamkeiten zu finden, ist das Ziel des täglichen Zusammenlebens, damit alle kollektiv an diesem Ort funktionieren können."

Nasim Lomani

are being admitted and the hotel is slated to be closed. City Plaza is seeking permanent housing for their inhabitants. Through this next step the initative seeks to hold the government responsible for providing adequate accommodation for all migrants.

Through these everyday encounters, City Plaza challenges, rethinks and reinterprets otherwise rigid identities between locals, strangers and refugees. The self-proclaimed "best hotel in Europe" offers us an alternative view of how to welcome and live with refugees and each other.

Facts and figures

Another measure of City Plaza Hotel are numbers recorded by organisers: a temporary home for 2,500 people, 385,000 warm meals served, 13,560 hours of shifts at the reception desk, 32,700 rolls of toilet paper, 156 van-loads of fresh produce and meat, 18 tonnes of heating oil used in boilers and radiators and innumerable hours spent cleaning the building, meeting new friends and hearing stories old and new. What is simply immeasurable, however, is the provision of safety and dignity of a home and a community.

räumen, besetzten die Aktivist*innen und Geflüchteten weiterhin das City Plaza. Aktuell werden allerdings keine neuen Geflüchteten aufgenommen, eine Schließung wird angestrebt, was allerdings keinem Eingeständnis gleichkommen soll, sondern vielmehr eine Forderung an den Staat darstellt, endlich eine angemessene Versorgung mit Wohnraum für alle Migrant*innen bereitzustellen.

Mit seinen alltäglichen Begegnungen stellt das City Plaza die starren Identitätsunterschiede zwischen Einwohner*innen, Fremden und Geflüchteten infrage und denkt und interpretiert sie neu. Das selbst ernannte „beste Hotel in Europa" bietet einen alternativen Blick darauf, wie man Geflüchtete willkommen heißen und mit ihnen zusammenleben kann.

Fakten und Zahlen

Anders kann man das City Plaza Hotel auch anhand der Zahlen beschreiben, die die Organisator*innen nennen: 2.500 Menschen erhielten ein temporäres Zuhause, 385.000 warme Mahlzeiten wurden ausgegeben, 13.560 Stunden Dienst an der Rezeption geleistet, 32.700 Rollen Toilettenpapier verbraucht, 156 Lastwagenladungen frische Lebensmittel und Fleisch geliefert, 18 Tonnen Heizöl wurden in Boilern und Heizungen verbraucht, ungezählte Stunden wurden damit verbracht, das Gebäude zu putzen, neue Freund*innen zu treffen und neue und alte Geschichten zu hören. Das Einzige, das nicht gemessen werden kann, ist ganz einfach die Sicherheit und Würde eines Zuhauses und einer Gemeinschaft.

400 Resident refugees, 185 of them children, find privacy, security and dignity here

400 Geflüchtete – darunter 185 Kinder, finden hier eine Privatsphäre, Sicherheit und Würde

"The City Plaza Hotel is a place of equality and solidarity, the lived antithesis to Fortress Europe and its borders of shame. It is a symbol of hope. Or simply: City Plaza is the best hotel in Europe."

„Das City Plaza Hotel ist ein Ort der Gleichheit und Solidarität, die gelebte Antithese der Festung Europa und ihrer Grenzen der Schande. Es ist ein Symbol der Hoffnung. Oder einfacher: City Plaza ist das beste Hotel in Europa."

City Plaza

07.

Project: **Our Skid Row**
City: Los Angeles
Client: Skid Row Los Angeles
Planning: Theresa Hwang, Skid Row Housing Trust, LOHA
Status: Ongoing/completed

Empowerment by Design
Reshaping the Margins

In cities around the world, civic labs are finding ways of engaging local communities to influence authorities and decision-makers, with many labs dealing with new approaches to urban co-existence while addressing pressing structural and cultural challenges within the city.

Alongside the glamour of Los Angeles lie invisible neighbourhoods: in downtown Los Angeles there is a 50-block district inhabited by an estimated 10,000 residents, where the median household income is just over 11,000 US dollars per year and over 3,500 people are homeless. This area is known as Skid Row, and it provides us with insight into the health and social equity of global cities.

Our Skid Row is a community-led project that collaboratively redesigned the district, with over 380 people coming together with non-profit organisations, activists and planners. The initiative stands apart in its prioritisation of marginalised and excluded residents, integrating them into planning processes. Through outreach, research and analysis, the project identified a need for interventions in supporting individual transitions out of homelessness.

The result of the project was a sourcebook, outlining how basic services can be strategically mobilised to bring vital resources to the streets: multi-functional street utilities and furniture, context-based solutions focusing on safety, places of rest and access to basic services including showers, bathrooms and drinking water. In collaboration with Theresa Hwang and the Skid Row Housing Trust, architecture firm LOHA designed guidelines to evaluate existing physical conditions alongside a set of spatial criteria. Given time, these urban interventions could be adopted and repurposed by the community, becoming an integral part of Skid Row's - and Los Angeles's - urban fabric.

Selbstermächtigung durch Design
Von den Rändern zur Stadt

In Städten rund um die Welt finden zivilgesellschaftliche Projekte Möglichkeiten, die lokale Bevölkerung einzubeziehen, um Behörden und politische Entscheidungsprozesse zu beeinflussen. Viele solcher Versuche beschäftigen sich mit neuen Ansätzen des städtischen Zusammenlebens und sprechen dringende strukturelle und kulturelle Herausforderungen der Stadt an.

Neben dem Glamour von Los Angeles gibt es auch unsichtbare Nachbarschaften: etwa ein zentraler Bezirk aus fünfzig Blocks in der Innenstadt von L. A., wo schätzungsweise 10.000 Menschen leben, das mittlere Einkommen gerade mal bei 11.000 Dollar jährlich liegt und 3.500 Menschen wohnungslos sind. Dieses Viertel ist als Skid Row bekannt. Es bietet Einsichten hinsichtlich der medizinischen und gesundheitlichen (Un-)Gerechtigkeit von Städten weltweit.

Our Skid Row ist ein selbstorganisiertes Nachbarschaftsprojekt, das den Bezirk kollektiv neu gestaltet hat: Mehr als 380 Menschen aus dem Viertel sind mit sozialen Trägern, Aktivist*innen und Stadtplaner*innen zusammengekommen. Die Initiative zeichnet sich besonders durch ihre Ausrichtung auf marginalisierte und ausgeschlossene Bewohner*innen aus, die in die Planungsprozesse einbezogen werden. Durch forschende und analytische Arbeit konnte das Projekt so den Bedarf nach Interventionen ermitteln, die persönliche Wege aus der Wohnungslosigkeit ermöglichen.

Das Projektergebnis ist eine Quellensammlung, in der skizziert wird, wie grundlegende Dienste strategisch eingesetzt werden können, um lebenswichtige Ressourcen auf die Straßen zu bringen: multifunktionale Versorgungseinrichtungen im öffentlichen Raum, Möbelweitergabe, Sicherheitslösungen, Ruheplätze und Zugang zu Grundversorgung wie Duschen, Toiletten und Trinkwasser. In Zusammenarbeit mit Theresa Hwang und dem Skid Row Housing Trust hat die Architekturfirma LOHA Richtlinien entworfen, um neben einer Reihe von räumlichen Kriterien die bestehenden physischen Bedingungen zu evaluieren. Mit der Zeit können diese städtischen Angebote von der Bevölkerung angenommen und zum integralen Bestandteil des urbanen Gewebes von Skid Row und L. A. werden.

Masterplan on the move

Masterplanung mobil

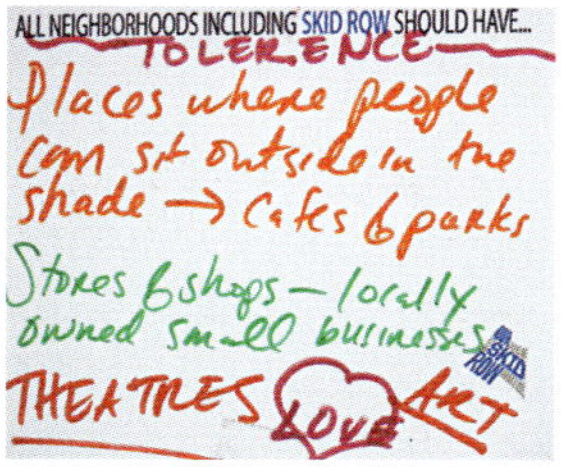

Participatory formats aimed at community and extracting desires: participatory asset mapping, resident vision card and resident-built model street

Partizipationsformate, die auf Gemeinschaft und das Extrahieren von Wünschen abzielen: Partizipatives Asset-Mapping, Visionskarte und eine von Bewohnern gebaute Modellstraße

Typologies, Third Spaces and the Porosity of Mixed Use

Typologien, dritte Räume und Mischnutzungen

3

Typologies, Third Spaces and the Porosity of Mixed Use

Typologien, dritte Räume und Mischnutzungen

Frankfurt's commercial real estate market is still in recovery after the 2008 market crash with 1.2 million square metres of office space still vacant in 2017. Since 2015, Amsterdam has converted over one million square metres of vacant offices into residential housing.

Der Gewerbeimmobilienmarkt in Frankfurt am Main hat sich seit der Wirtschaftskrise 2008 nicht mehr erholt. 2017 standen 1,2 Millionen Quadratmeter Bürofläche leer. Seit 2015 hat Amsterdam über eine Million Quadratmeter leer stehender Büros in Wohngebäude umgewandelt.

Every year in Berlin 350 artist studios are lost due to speculative development.

In Berlin gehen jährlich 350 Künstlerateliers durch spekulative Entwicklungen verloren.

Increased business activity in Berlin sees financing for start-ups up 300 percent in one year to nearly three billion euros in 2017.

Im Jahr 2017 wurde aufgrund der verstärkten Geschäftstätigkeit die Finanzierungssumme von Start-ups in Berlin auf fast drei Milliarden Euro verdreifacht.

Co-working fixed-desk average cost per month in London: 793 euros, Amsterdam: 569 euros, and in Berlin: 245 euros.

Die durchschnittlichen Kosten für einen festen Arbeitsplatz in Coworking-Büros betragen in London 793 Euro monatlich, in Amsterdam 569 Euro und in Berlin 245 Euro.

In Hamburg, over 1.8 million square metres of public space is privately managed through 25 business improvement districts (BID). Only 15 percent of retail landowners on a street are required to create a BID.

In Hamburg werden über 1,8 Millionen Quadratmeter des öffentlichen Raums in über 25 Business Improvement Districts (BID) privat verwaltet. Nur 15 Prozent der Gewerbetreibenden einer Straße sind zur Implementierung eines BID erforderlich.

Sources / Quellen:

Statista, Settle in Berlin, De Telegraaf Martin Schwegmann (Atelierbeauftragter), EY Consultancy, Statista, Zeit Magazine, STADT UND LAND Wohnbauten-Gesellschaft mbH, Boris Michel, Christian Stein, Mayor of London, One Shared House 2030, Financial Times, Knight Frank, Cushman Wakefield, PWC Emerging Trends Survey 2018, YLE Uutiset

Now 150 years old, James Hobrecht's nineteenth-century Berlin block and its ability to create liveable and efficient mixed-use urbanities continues to be an avant-garde alternative to modernist housing models.

150 Jahre alt, James Hobrechts Berliner Block aus dem 19. Jahrhundert und seine Fähigkeit, bewohnbare und effizient gemischt genutzte Urbanitäten zu schaffen, sind auch aktuell eine avantgardistische Alternative zu neueren Wohnmodellen.

The city of London – with only 13 percent of newly planned homes being affordable in 2017 – stipulates that new projects containing at least 35 percent affordable residential units will be given fast-track planning for development.

2017 galten in London nur 13 Prozent der neu geplanten Wohnungen als erschwinglich. Neue Projekte, die mindestens 35 Prozent bezahlbare Wohneinheiten enthalten, werden baubehördlich beschleunigt und bevorzugt behandelt.

Deutsche Bank signals increasing demand for co-living after backing the buyout of the world's largest co-living development in 2018. Respondents aged 25 to 39 cite co-living's socialisation and the reduction of living costs as major factors for their interest.

Die Deutsche Bank verkündete eine steigende Nachfrage nach Wohngemeinschaften, nachdem sie 2018 die Übernahme des weltweit größten Coliving-Entwicklers unterstützt hatte. Befragte im Alter von 25 bis 39 Jahren geben an, dass die sozialen Aspekte sowie die Senkung der Lebenshaltungskosten die Hauptgründe für das Zusammenwohnen sind.

The top niche real estate prospects in Europe are increasingly lucrative student housing, with an average London en-suite unit costing 892 euros per month in 2018.

Luxuswohnheime für Studierende stehen auf Platz 1 bei den europäischen Immobilienanleihen. Eine durchschnittliche Londoner Suite mit Bad kostet 2018 892 Euro pro Monat.

Within the last three years, over 100 schools have been built under the new Finnish school policy, opting for open and variable instruction spaces under a new pupil-centred curriculum.

Auf Basis der neuen finnischen Schulpolitik wurden allein in den letzten drei Jahren über hundert Schulen gebaut; im Fokus stehen offene und variable Unterrichtsräume für ein neues schüler*innenfokussiertes Lehrmodell.

Third Spaces

The Production of Communities

With the democratisation of the internet, industrial modes of production are in the process of being replaced by digital technology as the dominant mode of production. It was not long ago that architects were focused on domestic possibilities, bringing work (the so-called second space) to the home (the so-called first space) by way of the home office. Today, post-industrialisation has further reduced the working space to the sofa or the bed and it appears that the opposition between work and leisure is no longer adequate to determine the myriad of possibilities of contemporary practices. In this age of the machine, it is imperative that we seek out and define an emerging third space to qualify the technical activity that focuses on the observed need to foster communities which is not based on the economic revalorisation of an end-product, but rather on its production processes - on learning and experience.[1]

-

Third spaces: learning without a prescribed programme

Those technical activities, digital and/or cultural, propose a voluntary and continuous learning process anchored in experimentation and in the commoning of tools and methods during the realisation of a project. The spaces that allow for the development of such activities must be inclusive and open to all, without any consideration of age or social class. They must not have an imposed programme or propose any kind of evaluation. In so doing, they become ideal spaces for unexpected collaborations and experimentation. Spaces hosting such activities become the crucial link between the factory and the school, of which the main spatial typology - the classroom - is the legacy of an outdated industrial vision of learning. Such spaces, or third spaces - a term first attributed to Homi K. Bhabha, reconceptualised by

1 See Jaehee Kim's "Posthuman Labor" in e-flux's issue on Superhumanity, 15 March 2018 at http://www.e-flux.com/architecture/superhumanity/179232/posthuman-labor/. Last visited on 25.10.2018.

Dritte Räume

Die Produktion der Gemeinschaft

Mit der Demokratisierung durch das Internet lösen digitale Technologien schrittweise industrielle Produktionsformen ab. Es ist noch nicht lange her, dass Architekt*innen das Potenzial des Homeoffice entdeckten und die Erwerbsarbeit nach Hause brachten: vom sogenannten zweiten Raum in den ersten. Mittlerweile hat die Postindustrialisierung den Arbeitsraum noch weiter an Sofa und Bett gebunden. Es scheint, als sei das Gegenüber von Arbeit und Freizeit nicht länger angemessen, um die zahlreichen Möglichkeiten zu bestimmen. Wir brauchen einen dritten Raum, um Gemeinschaft wieder zu stärken: weniger um das Endprodukt wirtschaftlich aufzuwerten, sondern um dessen Herstellungsprozesse wieder mit Lernen und Erfahrungsaustausch zu verknüpfen.[1]

-

Der dritte Raum: Lernen ohne vorgeschriebenes Programm

Technische Aktivitäten legen einen freiwilligen Lernprozess nahe, der im Ausprobieren und in der gemeinsamen Nutzung von Verantwortung für Werkzeuge und Methoden in der Umsetzungsphase besteht. Räume, die die Entwicklung solcher Aktivitäten ermöglichen, müssen inklusiv und offen für alle sein – unabhängig von Alter oder gesellschaftlichem Hintergrund. Sie dürfen weder ein vorgeschriebenes Programm noch einen Bewertungsmodus beinhalten. Nur so werden sie ideale Orte für unerwartete Zusammenarbeit und Experimente. Sie verbinden Fabrik und Schule, deren zentrale räumliche Typologie – das Klassenzimmer – das Erbe einer längst überholten industriellen Vorstellung vom Lernen ist. Solche dritten Räume (der Begriff stammt ursprünglich von Homi K. Bhabha; der Geograf und Stadttheoretiker Edward Soja sowie Ray Oldenburg[2] haben ihn im Anschluss neu konzipiert und weiter

1 Siehe Jaehee Kim: „Posthuman Labor" (k. D.), in: e-flux, Superhumanity. [http://www.e-flux.com/architecture/superhumanity/179232/posthuman-labor/], letzter Zugriff am 25.10.2018.

2 Siehe „Ray Oldenburg" (31.12.2008), in: Project for Public Spaces. [https://www.pps.org/article/roldenburg], letzter Zugriff am 25.10.2018.

political geographer and urban theorist Edward Soja and later transformed by Ray Oldenburg[2] – progressively transform standardised visions of knowledge production: the goal is no longer to produce objects or subjects whose capacities are general and identical. The belief that the most desirable productivity is based on the efficient and non-critical repetition of a gesture with respect to a pre-defined problem belongs to another era.

One of the most famous examples of a historical third space – though not necessarily an inclusive one – was one of the most high profile places for interdisciplinary research and arguably the origin of hacker spaces and start-up incubators: Building 20 of the Massachusetts Institute of Technology. Built as a temporary wooden structure during the war research effort of the second world war, Building 20 stood for 55 years and was heavily used and occupied until its demolition in 1998. Despite – or because of – its temporary nature, Building 20 became a catalyst for experimentation, collaboration and design as "[i]ts temporary nature permitted its occupants to abuse it in ways that would not be tolerated in a permanent building. If you wanted to run a wire from one lab to another," according to MIT professor Paul Penfield, "you didn't ask anybody's permission – you just got out a screwdriver and poked a hole through the wall."[3] This third space benefitted from the flexibility and functionality of its empty workshop-like shell. Is the architecture of third spaces an architecture in slow-motion that successfully reinterprets that transparency healed by the glass walls of Gropius's Bauhaus?

In 2005, Google presented the interior redesign proposal by Clive Wilkinson Architects for their headquarters in Silicon Valley. Culling materials from previous buildouts, the design integrated meeting, working, learning and leisure facilities with the existing conditions of the building and its courtyards. Resting, exchanging, communicating and frequent, incidental encounters within the community were considered to be key aspects of successful creative production and, as

2 See the Ray Oldenburg entry at Project for Public Spaces at https://www.pps.org/article/roldenburg. Last visited on 25.10.2018.

3 Paul Penfield, Jr., "MIT's Building 20: The Magical Incubator 1943–1998", Archived 23 July 2008 at the Wayback Machine, MIT Department of Electrical Engineering & Computer Science, 19 December 1997, https://web.archive.org/web/20080723202157/http://www.eecs.mit.edu/building/20/. Last visited on 25.10.2018.

verändert) transformieren schrittweise standardisierte Vorstellungen der Wissensproduktion: Das Ziel ist nicht mehr, Objekte oder Subjekte zu produzieren, deren Fähigkeiten allgemein und gleich sind. Die Überzeugung, dass Produktivität auf der effizienten und unkritischen Wiederholung einer Geste in Bezug auf ein vordefiniertes Problem beruht, gehört einer vergangenen Zeit an.

Eines der berühmtesten historischen Beispiele für einen dritten Raum (wenn auch kein unbedingt inklusives) war ein Ort für interdisziplinäre Forschung und wohl einer der wichtigsten für den Ursprung von Hacker Spaces und Gründungszentren: Building 20 des Massachusetts Institute of Technology in den USA. Während der Forschungsbemühungen im Zweiten Weltkrieg als temporärer Holzbau errichtet, blieb Building 20 über 55 Jahre lang erhalten und wurde bis zum Abriss im Jahr 1998 intensiv genutzt. Trotz – oder gerade wegen – seiner provisorischen Beschaffenheit wurde es zum Katalysator von Versuchen, Zusammenarbeit und Gestaltung. Denn „seine temporäre Beschaffenheit gestattete es den Nutzenden, das Gebäude auf Weisen zu missbrauchen, die in einem langfristig angelegten Gebäude nicht toleriert würden. Wenn du ein Kabel von einem Labor ins andere legen wolltest", so MIT-Professor Paul Penfield, „dann fragtest du niemanden um Erlaubnis. Du holtest dir einfach einen Schraubenzieher und stachst ein Loch in die Wand."[3] Dieser dritte Raum profitierte von der Flexibilität und Funktionalität seiner werkstattähnlichen Hülle. Ist die Architektur dritter Räume eine, die Gropius' Glaswände-Transparenz im Bauhaus erfolgreich neu interpretiert?

2005 präsentierte Google den Innenraumentwurf von Clive Wilkinson Architects für die Firmenzentrale im Silicon Valley. Mit den Materialien vorheriger Ausbauten wurden Besprechungs-, Arbeits-, Lern- und Freizeiteinrichtungen in den Bestand des Gebäudes und seiner Höfe integriert. Pausen, Austausch, Gespräche und regelmäßige Begegnungen des Kollegiums galten als Schlüsselaspekte für die erfolgreiche kreative Produktion und wurden zum grundlegenden Bestandteil zukünftiger Arbeitspraktiken wie auch ihrer architektonischen Agenda. Das eröffnete den Weg für zahlreiche gemischt genutzte Projekte unterschiedlicher Größenordnungen, die in ihrer Glaubwürdigkeit an Beliebtheit gewannen.

3 Paul Penfield, Jr., „MIT's Building 20: The Magical Incubator 1943–1998" (19.12.1997), in: Internet Archive Wayback Machine, MIT Department of Electrical Engineering & Computer Science, archiviert am 23.07.2008. [https://web.archive.org/web/20080723202157/http://www.eecs.mit.edu/building/20/]: letzter Zugriff am 25.10.2018.

such, became a fundamental element of future working practices and their architectural agenda. High-profile projects such as these opened the way for mixed projects across a range of scales, where highly planned and designed informal spaces gained credibility and popularity.

Self-empowerment as a resource

Co-working, multi-media laboratories and other collaborative work spaces have since settled down into the contemporary landscape, enabling a re-partition of services and progressively clearing the cultural divide between first and second spaces. What is consumed and what is produced in these places is no longer clear: the promise of third spaces are another way of living and working, where voluntary commitment and self-empowerment are considered a raw material. Presumably, the end product is the community that the third space enables.

Today's third spaces often borrow their aesthetics from the iconic garage of Steve Jobs in Palo Alto, scaled up for collective use. Seemingly negating their spatial environment or developing in spite of it, these new creative laboratories hide an architectural requirement of another nature. Here, we recall Jane Jacob's urban prescriptions related to the need for temporality and unpredictability in architectural design: unlike principles of modular architecture that brought the illusion of continual movement into daily life, the design of third spaces focuses on the empowerment of their users to act and interact with and on their environment, not necessarily on the latent capacity of the space to transform itself. This is the difference between können, the ability to do, and dürfen, the permission to do - it marks a difference in architectural posturing and directs us on a path towards a resilient architecture. If the ambitions of third spaces seem to constitute an all-inclusive solution for sustainable and productive cities in the future, one of the main questions raised by their emergence and multiplication remains unanswered: if the main product of third spaces is a community itself, who is the client? Are third spaces becoming the symbol of a need to discuss global socio-economic reform towards the revalorisation of immaterial values? Or, are they enabling and reformulating excuses, thus allowing - if not encouraging outright - creative, unpaid labour?

Selbstermächtigung als Rohstoff

Gemeinsame Arbeitsräume, Multimedialabore und andere Orte der Zusammenarbeit haben sich seither in der zeitgenössischen Arbeitslandschaft etabliert. Sie ermöglichen die Neuzuweisung von Diensten und weichen die Trennung zwischen dem ersten und zweiten Raum auf. Was hier konsumiert und produziert wird, ist nicht mehr eindeutig: Es ist eine weitere Möglichkeit von Leben und Arbeiten. In dritten Räumen gelten freiwilliges Engagement und Selbstermächtigung als Rohstoff. Ihr Endprodukt ist Gemeinschaft.

Heutige dritte Räume lehnen sich ästhetisch oft an die ikonische Garage von Steve Jobs in Palo Alto an, die zur kollektiven Nutzung erweitert wurde. Diese neuen Kreativlabore scheinen ihre räumliche Umgebung zu negieren oder sich ihr zum Trotz zu entwickeln – so verbergen sie eine andere Art architektonische Notwendigkeit. Auch Jane Jacobs' Stadtrezepte betonen den Bedarf nach Temporalität und Unvorhersehbarkeit in der architektonischen Gestaltung. Anders als die Prinzipien der modularen Architektur, die die Illusion einer kontinuierlichen Bewegung ins Alltagsleben einbrachte, konzentriert sich die Gestaltung dritter Räume auf die Ermächtigung ihrer Nutzer*innen. Sie wirken auf ihre Umgebung ein und interagieren mit ihr. Das ist der Unterschied zwischen „Können" – der Fähigkeit, etwas zu tun – und „Dürfen" – dem Recht, etwas zu tun. Das ändert die architektonische Haltung und weist uns den Weg hin zu einer belastbaren Architektur. Dritte Räume scheinen also eine gesamtheitliche Lösung für zukünftige nachhaltige und produktive Städte darzustellen. Trotzdem bleibt eine der zentralen Fragen unbeantwortet: Wer gibt sie in Auftrag? Werden dritte Räume zum Symbol des Bedarfs, globale sozioökonomische Reformen zur Neubewertung immaterieller Werte zu diskutieren? Oder ermöglichen sie nur Ausreden und gestatten – oder fördern gar – unbezahlte Kreativarbeit?

NDSM Wharf Amsterdam: a large-scale scaffolding enables multiple self-organised functional adaptations for 250 enterprises

250 Unternehmen docken selbstorganisiert in der NDSM-Werft in Amsterdam an ein großmaßstäbliches Gerüst an

The City as a Shell

Stakeholders as Co-developers

If planners are to be sincere and effective in their pursuit of liveable cities, it is vital that they encourage the participation, self-organisation and entrepreneurial skills of their citizens. Today, those who live in cities are dissatisfied with the way their cities are evolving and are themselves combating the negative impacts of gentrification, mass tourism, globalisation and others forms of financially driven city development. The authority of city planners is often weak and generally not accepted by citizens, companies or other stakeholders. A new kind of urban planning is emerging: one that is not based on masterplans but on developing and offering the framework and conditions for participation. Here, Eva de Klerk, an artist and a global independent professional in participatory city development, together with Robert Marijnissen, an urban geographer and planner, share their experiences in self-organisation, community building and co-creative urban development.

A shift to participation

Real participation is achieved when user groups are equals in a horizontal, collaborative process, when they design, develop, set up and manage entire buildings, neighbourhoods, streets and squares together with municipalities and urban designers. The municipal government has an important role to play, as it can embrace such participatory initiatives and relationships through the allocation of land. Although municipalities, along with property developers and property owners, thus far have limited experience with participatory development, there exist experimental, alternative forms of urban development that are proving themselves to be a real alternative to the market-driven strategies that currently steer our urban economies. Enterprising parties, actively involved municipal governments and good governance are essential to the implementation of such models. This way, we can continue to build sustainable cities that are architecturally and socially resilient: with buildings that allow for flexible use with shared goals, collaborative

Die Stadt als Gerüst

Teileigner*innen als Mitentwickler*innen

Wenn die Stadtplanung ernsthaft und wirksam das Ziel lebensfähiger Städte verfolgen soll, dann ist entscheidend, dass sie die Beteiligung, Selbstorganisation und unternehmerischen Fähigkeiten der Stadtbevölkerung fördert. Heute sind viele Menschen unzufrieden mit der Entwicklung der Städte, in denen sie leben. Sie kämpfen gegen die negativen Auswirkungen von Gentrifizierung, Massentourismus, Globalisierung und weitere Formen der finanziell angetriebenen Stadtentwicklung. Stadtplaner*innen haben meist keine besondere Autorität inne, sie wird von der Bevölkerung, von Unternehmen und anderen Akteur*innen nicht anerkannt. Nun entsteht eine neue Art der städtischen Planung: eine, die nicht auf einem Masterplan basiert, sondern stattdessen Bedingungen für Partizipation entwickelt und einen entsprechenden Rahmen bietet. Eva de Klerk, Künstlerin und weltweit tätige Begleiterin partizipatorischer Stadtentwicklung, und Robert Marijnissen, Stadtgeograf und Planer, erzählen von ihren Erfahrungen mit Selbstorganisation, Gemeinwesenarbeit und kollektiver kreativer Stadtentwicklung.

Eine Verschiebung in Richtung Partizipation

Echte Teilhabe ist dann erreicht, wenn nutzende Gruppen in einem horizontalen Prozess der Zusammenarbeit gleichwertig beteiligt sind: wenn sie gemeinsam mit der Stadt und den Stadtplaner*innen ganze Gebäude, Nachbarschaften, Straßen und Plätze gestalten, entwickeln, errichten und verwalten. Die kommunale Regierung spielt hier eine wichtige Rolle, da sie solche partizipatorischen Initiativen und Beziehungen bei der Grundstücksvergabe aufgreifen kann. Obwohl die Kommunen, ebenso wie Baufirmen und Immobilienbesitzer*innen, bislang die Erfahrungen mit partizipatorischem Städtebau eingeschränkt haben, gibt es experimentelle, alternative Formen der Stadtplanung, die sich als reale Alternativen zu den marktgetriebenen Strategien erweisen, die derzeit die städtische Wirtschaft steuern. Unternehmen, engagierte Lokalverwaltungen und gute Führungsprinzipien sind für

development and finally shared ownership they can offer a lasting sense of belonging. If models were to start from the development costs, without profit as the primary motive, these spaces could be affordable and inclusive, with users-as-stakeholders investing over the course of time to enrich their development.

Previously one of the largest shipyards in the world, the 38-hectare NDSM Shipyard of Amsterdam is an example of a development that transcends the parameters of a building. It is now home to the largest creative incubator in the Netherlands, a monumental "Kunststad" (Art City) that houses some 250 skateboarders, artists, designers and small and medium-sized enterprises - who not only use the space but are also committed to the care of the surrounding area.

Self-organisation needs a governance code

Self-organisation is a fundamental element of participatory urban development. Participation is a process in which group members reach agreements on the legal and administrative frameworks within which they want to develop their initiative. Participation is not free of obligations: a statute, an operational plan and house rules are tools that facilitate collaboration. It is the collective that determines the development concept, respecting existing physical and social structures while making it cost effective. Of course, this process involves the investment of time, services and money. And collaboration. The collective that successfully plots its own course requires group members to participate on every level, from initiative to group dynamics, from design to construction, and from development to control. For the direct involvement of the group in developing and controlling the project, a legal entity, such as a non-profit foundation or a cooperative, is required. The choice of a legal body has consequences for the influence members can exercise on the collective. No matter which choice is ultimately made, the collective legal body must serve the shared interest of its members, carefully documenting the ownership of the initiative and the objectives of the group. Ultimately, documentation can serve to strengthen the group's position and control, while providing long-term security. Successful and innovative participation requires dedication and perseverance. Because the collective is the developing party and has to

die Implementierung solcher Modelle wesentlich. Auf diese Weise können wir weiterhin nachhaltige Städte bauen, die architektonisch und gesellschaftlich robust sind: mit Gebäuden, die mit gemeinsamen Zielen, kollaborativer Entwicklung und geteiltem Eigentum eine flexible Nutzung und ein langfristiges Gefühl der Zugehörigkeit ermöglichen. Wenn Modelle von den Baukosten ausgehen, ohne dass Profit das primäre Motiv ist, dann könnten diese Räume erschwinglich und inklusiv sein, indem Nutzer*innen als Akteur*innen über die Zeit hinweg investieren und zugleich die Planung und Weiterentwicklung bereichern.

Einst eines der größten Werftgelände der Welt, sind die 38 Hektar der Werft NDSM in Amsterdam heute ein Beispiel für eine Entwicklung, die über die Parameter eines Gebäudes hinausgeht. Die Werft beherbergt die größte kreative Brutstätte in den Niederlanden, eine monumentale „Kunststad" aus rund 250 Skateboarder*innen, Künstler*innen, Designer*innen sowie kleinen und mittelgroßen Unternehmen, die den Raum nicht nur autonom verwalten, sondern sich auch um die Pflege der Umgebung kümmern.

Selbstorganisation erfordert einen Führungskodex

Selbstorganisation ist ein grundlegendes Element von partizipatorischer Stadtplanung. Partizipation ist ein Prozess, in dem sich Gruppenmitglieder über die rechtlichen und verwalterischen Rahmenbedingungen abstimmen, innerhalb derer sie ihre Initiative entwickeln möchten. Partizipation ist nicht frei von Verpflichtungen: ein Statut, ein Durchführungsplan und Hausregeln sind Werkzeuge, die eine Zusammenarbeit dieser Art ermöglichen. Das Kollektiv bestimmt das Entwicklungskonzept; dabei werden bestehende räumliche und soziale Strukturen respektiert und zugleich Kosten eingespart. Selbstverständlich erfordert dieser Prozess den Einsatz von Zeit, Arbeit, Geld und Zusammenarbeit. Damit ein Kollektiv erfolgreich seinen eigenen Verlauf und Weg planen kann, bedarf es der Teilhabe der Gruppenmitglieder auf allen Ebenen – vom Konzept bis zur Gruppendynamik, von der Planung bis zum Bau, von der Entwicklung bis zur Steuerung. Für die direkte Einbeziehung der Gruppe in die Planung und Steuerung des Projekts bedarf es einer juristischen Person, wie etwa eines Vereins oder einer Genossenschaft. Die Entscheidung über die Rechtsform hat Auswirkungen auf die Möglich-

outsource tasks to an executive organisation and a board, the transparency of daily and financial decisions is imperative. Good governance focuses on supporting the initiator(s) of the project and on protecting the project against the pressures of the outside world.

The participation agency

The legal and financial vehicle for any development at such an XXL scale is the participation agency or company. The participation agency considers the land and buildings on it as a single unit of value. Participation companies ideally take on a legal status as co-operatives, guaranteeing that the property is collectively owned. Participation, as well as construction work and other contributions, are cost-covered and based on an objective valuation. All stakeholders - including the municipality - contribute a wide range of resources: land, buildings, time, services or money. The collective decision making within the company means that the protagonists are allocated space and a say in the development, measured in proportion to the intrinsic value they contribute to the whole. It is therefore crucial that the participation process enables small investment opportunities for users, so that their investments in time, creativity, services and small capital will also benefit their own endeavours. A percentage of each area developed is then allocated to low-earning and non-profit participants, calling for a long-term focus on social added value, healthy relationships and sustainable financial returns.

Based on the experiences of successfully self-organised buildings, the ideal or maximum number of people required to both start and maintain a project - the critical mass - seems to be around one hundred. This scale allows participants to get to know each other and to work together. At the same time, it creates a sufficient capacity for resilience to counterbalance conflicts or the departure of one or more group members while making the recruitment of new members feasible. A collaborative entity should avoid being too small, so as not to make it susceptible to individuals that might disrupt or hijack group processes. Such a critical mass also offers opportunities to organise external funding from a bank, to buy or develop a piece of land or a building. At the NDSM Shipyard, different building clusters comprised of several hundred users formed in the

keiten der Einflussnahme der Mitglieder auf das Kollektiv. Unabhängig von der schließlich getroffenen Entscheidung muss der kollektive Rechtskörper dem gemeinsamen Interesse seiner Mitglieder dienen, sorgfältig die Eigentumsverhältnisse der Initiative sowie die Ziele der Gruppe dokumentieren. Schließlich kann die Dokumentation dazu dienen, die Position und Kontrolle der Gruppe zu stärken, und sie zugleich langfristig absichern. Erfolgreiche und innovative Partizipation erfordert Hingabe und Ausdauer. Da das Kollektiv die Entwicklung leitet und Aufgaben an eine ausführende Organisation und einen Vorstand delegieren muss, ist die Transparenz der alltäglichen und finanziellen Entscheidungen zwingend. Eine gute Führung unterstützt die Initiator*innen des Projekts und schützt das Projekt gegen den Druck von außen.

Die Beteiligungsgesellschaft

Das rechtliche und finanzielle Mittel für jegliche Planung dieser Größenordnung ist die Beteiligungsgesellschaft. Die Beteiligungsgesellschaft betrachtet das Land und die Gebäude darauf als eine einzige Werteinheit. Beteiligungsgesellschaften fungieren idealerweise als Genossenschaften und gewährleisten, dass das Eigentum in Kollektivbesitz ist. Partizipation – ebenso wie Bauarbeiten und andere Beiträge – ist kostengedeckt und basiert auf einer objektiven Bewertung. Alle Akteur*innen – einschließlich der Stadtverwaltung – tragen eine Bandbreite an Ressourcen bei: Grundstücke, Gebäude, Zeit, Arbeit oder Geld. Die kollektive Entscheidungsfindung in der Firma bedeutet, dass die Protagonist*innen Raum und Stimme in der Entwicklung erhalten, die im Verhältnis zu dem intrinsischen Wert steht, den sie zu dem Ganzen beitragen. Somit ist es entscheidend, dass der Beteiligungsprozess Investitionsmöglichkeiten für die Nutzenden ermöglicht, sodass ihr Einsatz von Zeit, Kreativität, Arbeit und einem kleinen Kapital auch ihren eigenen Unternehmungen dienlich ist. Ein gewisser Prozentsatz jedes geplanten Bereichs wird dann einkommensschwachen und gemeinnützigen Beteiligten zugewiesen und erinnert an den langfristigen Fokus auf gesellschaftlichen Mehrwert, gesunde Beziehungen und nachhaltige finanzielle Renditen.

Auf der Grundlage der Erfahrungen erfolgreicher selbstorganisierter Gebäude scheint die ideale oder maximale Zahl an Personen – die kritische Masse – bei rund hundert Menschen zu liegen. Dies ermöglicht es den Beteiligten, einander kennenzulernen und zusammenzuarbeiten. Zugleich schafft diese

giant warehouse under a physical arrangement based on shared interests and wishes regarding programme, access, size, height and so on. Common to all clusters is that they have a roof over their head, a shared front door, basic facilities and public space in the form of inner streets and squares between their clusters. The common facilities are of general interest and their costs are borne by the community; this requires organisation per cluster, as well as across clusters for the common good.

The third zones

Instead of a grand master plan with a predetermined purpose, i.e., a plan that would propel the XXL development in a specific direction, user-led urban development fosters an open construction process. In addition to allowing and encouraging participatory development, we strongly advocate that local authorities include third zones in their zoning plans. Third zones are permanent experimental spaces in which an organic user-led development model is the status quo. Such zones of permanent temporality allow people to choose whether to live in areas normally excluded from development due to over-regulation, such as plots or buildings in difficult areas, along a busy railway line or in an industrial zone, or in buildings and urban areas that have lost their economic significance. Third zones allow users to choose and allocate areas for mixed-use concepts, as long as they meet basic rules of safety and hygiene. This makes it possible to see these areas in a different light.

Urban planners must dare to designate third zones within the urban fabric and incorporate flexible concepts within their planning practices. After all, user-led and collectively managed projects give the city something in return: enthusiasm, diversity, affordability, social cohesion and resilience.

Größe ausreichend Resilienz, um Konflikte oder den Ausstieg von einem oder mehreren Gruppenmitgliedern auszugleichen, und sie ermöglicht die Mobilisierung neuer Menschen in die Gruppe. Eine zu kleine Gruppengröße sollte vermieden werden, um nicht empfänglich für Einzelpersonen zu sein, die Gruppenprozesse stören oder missbrauchen. Eine kritische Masse bietet auch mehr Gelegenheiten, eine externe Finanzierung von einer Bank zu organisieren, um ein Grundstück oder Gebäude zu kaufen oder zu entwickeln. In der NDSM-Werft haben die mehreren Hundert Nutzenden auf der Grundlage von Interessen und Wünschen hinsichtlich der Nutzungsart, des Zugangs, der Größe, Höhe usw. in der riesigen Lagerhalle ein räumliches Arrangement gefunden und verschiedene Container-Cluster gebildet. Alle Cluster haben ein gemeinsames Dach über dem Kopf, teilen sich ein Haupttor, grundlegende Infrastruktur und öffentlichen Raum in Form von Innenstraßen und -plätzen in der Halle und auf dem Gelände. Die gemeinsamen Einrichtungen und Infrastrukturen sind von Gemeininteresse, und ihre Kosten werden gemeinschaftlich getragen; das erfordert Organisation für die gemeinsame Sache innerhalb und zwischen den Clustern.

Dritte Flächen

Anstelle eines Masterplans mit einem vorbestimmten Zweck, der solche besonders großen Planungen in eine bestimmte Richtung treibt, steht eine von Nutzenden angeleitete Stadtplanung für einen offenen Bauprozess ein. Zusätzlich zur Ermöglichung und Ermutigung zur beteiligenden Planung sprechen wir uns deutlich dafür aus, dass kommunale Behörden in ihren Bebauungsplänen dritte Flächen einplanen. Dritte Flächen sind dauerhafte Experimentierräume, wo eine organische, von Nutzenden geleitete Planung der Status quo ist. Diese immerwährend temporären Orte ermöglichen es Menschen, zu entscheiden, ob sie in Gebieten leben möchten, die normalerweise durch Überregulierung von Entwicklung ausgeschlossen sind. Dritte Flächen ermöglichen es Nutzenden, Bereiche für Mischnutzungskonzepte auszuwählen und sie zu gestalten, solange sie grundlegende Sicherheits- und Hygieneregeln befolgen. Das macht es möglich, diese Flächen und Gebiete in neuem Licht zu sehen. Die Stadtplanung muss es wagen, dritte Flächen zu bezeichnen und flexible Konzepte in ihre Planungspraktiken aufzunehmen. Schließlich geben kollektiv verwaltete, von Nutzenden geleitete Projekte der Stadt etwas zurück: Enthusiasmus, Vielfalt, Erschwinglichkeit, sozialen Zusammenhalt und Belastbarkeit.

Infrastructure Remixed

Creating Diversity beyond Functional Separation

When the wholesale flower market announced its departure from the Südliche Friedrichstadt – an architecturally and culturally heterogeneous area in the Kreuzberg district of Berlin – the owner of the site, together with the municipal administration, opened a call for bids. It required any potential investors to propose a concept-driven process for the development of the site, within two short weeks. This call prompted a moment in which architects, designers and other creative innovators – who themselves had been placing increasing political pressure on local government to end the practice of selling available public land to the highest bidder – were challenged to develop their own concepts of what this might look like in the city of Berlin. An ad-hoc consortium of small-scale initiatives and businesses rapidly developed and placed the first tender for one of three sites. Berlin-based Deadline Architects were the only original members of the consortium who stayed the course, driven by the potential that had emerged from neighbourhood discussions by proposing the creation of a city within a city – a unique kind of mixed commercial use development that would act as a much-needed contrast to the largely residential area.

Here, Matthew Griffin and Britta Jürgens, the co-founders of Deadline Architects, reflect on their role as architects and developers: on process, calculated risks and shaping a sense of community.

Britta Jürgens: For so long, everyone had been focusing on housing, completely ignoring the fact that people also need workspaces – small, affordable sites to start a business. We've always believed in the mixed city and in listening carefully to what is really needed on a site.

Matthew Griffin: Once the original partners in the consortium dropped out, we set about attracting as many different categories of small businesses as we could – there was no design for the building at all, merely floor plans. A naked infrastructure, with each floor valued fairly, according to market prices.

Infrastruktur neu gedacht

Heterogenität jenseits getrennter Funktionen

Als der Blumengroßmarkt ankündigte, die südliche Friedrichstadt – eine architektonisch sowie kulturell heterogene Gegend im Berliner Bezirk Kreuzberg – zu verlassen, schrieben der Grundstückseigner und die städtischen Behörden das Gelände innerhalb von zwei Wochen zur konzeptorientierten Entwicklung für potenzielle Investor*innen aus. Architekt*innen, Designer*innen und andere kreative Initiativen hatten die Politik vor Ort schon zuvor angemahnt, damit aufzuhören, öffentliche Grundstücke immer nur an Höchstbietende zu verkaufen. Ein spontaner Zusammenschluss von kleinen Initiativen und Firmen entwickelte schnell ein Angebot. Die Berliner Architekt*innen von Deadline sind die einzigen ursprünglichen Mitglieder des Konsortiums, die an Bord blieben – motiviert von dem Potenzial, das sich in Nachbarschaftsdiskussionen über das Angebot zeigte. Die Aussicht, eine Stadt in der Stadt zu schaffen, eine einzigartige Mischung verschiedener kommerzieller Nutzungen als dringend nötigen Kontrast in der hauptsächlich als Wohngebiet genutzten Gegend, spornte sie zu einem ganz besonderen Entwurf an.

Matthew Griffin und Britta Jürgens, die Gründer*innen von Deadline, reflektieren im Interview ihre Rolle als Architekt*innen und Entwickler*innen. Ein Gespräch über kalkulierte Risiken und geschärften Gemeinschaftssinn.

Britta Jürgens: Lange Zeit haben sich alle nur auf den Wohnungsbau konzentriert und dabei komplett ignoriert, dass die Menschen auch Raum zum Arbeiten brauchen: kleine, bezahlbare Räume, um von dort aus Firmen aufzubauen. Wir haben immer an die Mischung in der Stadt geglaubt und gut zugehört, um herauszufinden, was an einem Ort gebraucht wird.

Matthew Griffin: Als die ursprünglichen Partner*innen in unserem Konsortium ausgeschieden waren, versuchten wir, so viele verschiedene Arten von kleinen Firmen anzusprechen wie nur möglich. Es gab noch überhaupt keinen Plan für das Gebäude, nur Grundrisse: eine nackte Infrastruktur, bei der jedes Stockwerk grob nach Marktpreisen geschätzt wurde.

BJ: As the basic form developed, people started becoming attracted to the project, choosing their floor and scale according to their means. Our reticence as architect/developers meant we created extremely conservative estimates and a very clear cost calculation - with a prerequisite capital investment of 35 percent per stakeholder up front. We didn't have to take out a bank loan until construction started! Everyone involved was aware of their own precise needs and financial constraints.

MG: By drawing up a clear plan in terms of the social organisation of the project - the kind of community we wanted to create - we constructed the building around the community. People developed a very strong relationship to that.

BJ: We sensed a growing need for community amongst small-scale businesses, social entrepreneurs and like-minded people. They identified with the shared development of a certain kind of city: spaces where they have a say. And because the community of stakeholders is invested in the space, an added value is that the neighbourhood profits from it too, because small-scale co-operatives engage more sensitively than investment funds.

Alternative models with carefully calculated risks

MG: Of course, everyone involved is aware that the space will increase in value - possibly even twofold. That is obvious. But at the time, no one was sure and avoided being stretched beyond their means.

BJ: Effectively we've created a city within a city, with a huge variety of spaces: a jigsaw of the diverse requirements. This is small-scale commercial ownership, and there is a very different kind of architectural expression for that.

MG: The architecture does reflect the mix of enterprises - the floor plans are unique horizontally, as well as vertically. Office and studio sizes vary from 25 to 150 square metres. Some businesses extend over three floors. It's unique! It's complex!

BJ: Als sich die Grundform herauskristallisierte, interessierten sich mehr und mehr Leute für das Projekt. Sie konnten sich den Grundriss und die Größe ihren Bedürfnissen entsprechend auswählen. Als Architekt*innen und Entwickler*innen waren wir verhalten und kalkulierten die Kosten sehr konservativ und klar. Eine der Bedingungen war ein Kapitalinvestment in Höhe von 35 Prozent je Beteiligtem im Voraus. So mussten wir keinen Kredit aufnehmen, bis mit dem Bau begonnen wurde! Alle Beteiligten waren sich ihrer genauen Ansprüche und finanziellen Grenzen bewusst.

MG: Indem wir einen klaren Plan für die soziale Struktur des Projekts schufen – wir wollten eine neue Art Gemeinschaft aufbauen –, entwarfen wir das Gebäude rund um diese Gemeinschaft. Die Leute entwickelten so eine starke Beziehung zum Projekt.

BJ: Wir spürten bei den kleinen Firmen und den Leuten aus dem Sozialbereich das Bedürfnis nach Gemeinschaft und Gleichgesinnten. Sie identifizierten sich mit einem gemeinsamen Projekt, einer bestimmten Art von Stadt. Sie wollten Räume, zu denen sie etwas beitragen konnten. Und weil es sich um eine Gemeinschaft von Beteiligten handelt, die in den Ort investiert, profitiert die Nachbarschaft obendrein. Denn kleine Kooperativen engagieren sich sensibler als ein Investmentfonds.

Alternative Modelle mit sorgfältig kalkulierten Risiken

MG: Natürlich ist allen Beteiligten bewusst, dass der Ort an Wert gewinnen wird. Wahrscheinlich wird er sich sogar verdoppeln. Aber zu dem Zeitpunkt war niemand ganz sicher und wollte vermeiden, sich über seine Grenzen hinweg zu verausgaben.

BJ: Tatsächlich haben wir eine Stadt in der Stadt geschaffen, mit total unterschiedlichen Räumen; ein Puzzle unterschiedlichster Anforderungen. Das hier ist der Besitz vieler kleiner Unternehmen, und der architektonische Ausdruck davon ist etwas ganz Besonderes.

MG: Die Architektur spiegelt die Mischung wider. Die Grundrisse sind in allen Etagen unterschiedlich – auch vertikal. Die Büros und Ateliers sind zwischen 25 und 150 Quadratmetern groß. Manche Firmen haben drei Stockwerke. Das ist einzigartig und komplex!

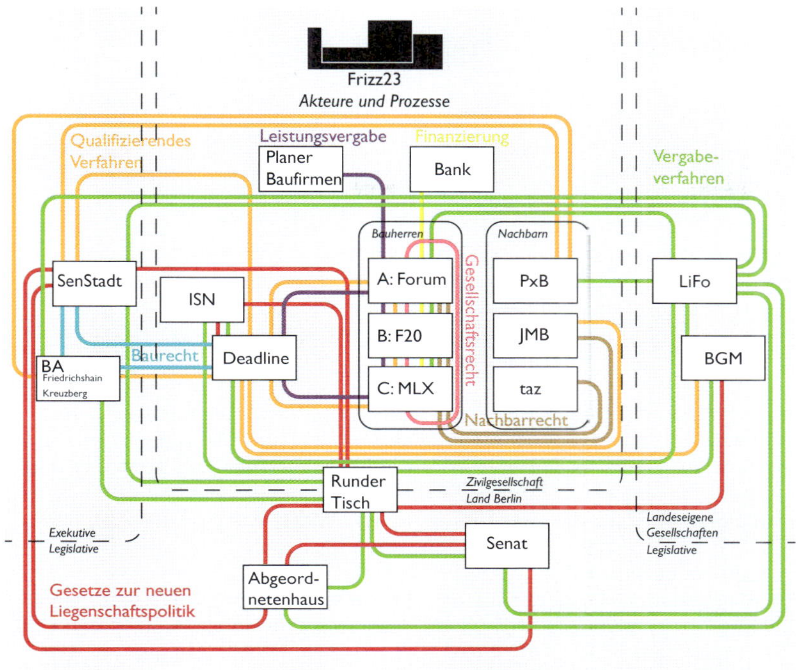

Maximum participation: negotiation processes in an unweildy network of actors

Beteiligung maximal: Verhandlungsprozesse in einem scheinbar unüberschaubaren Netz aus Akteur*innen

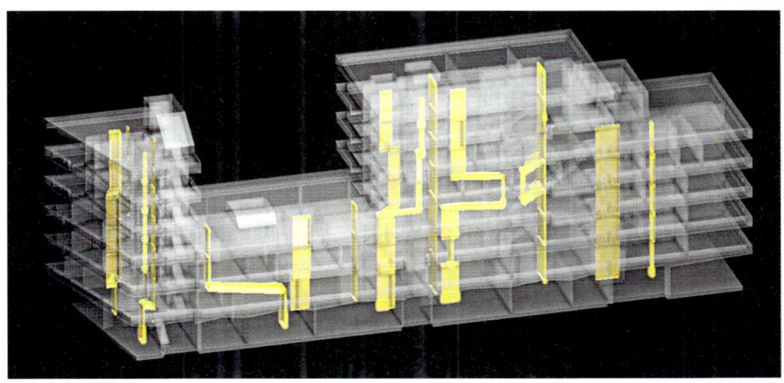

Going through the building is an adventure

BJ: Usually you walk through a commercial building and you can see the one-floor plan from the façade. Here, it's an adventure to walk through – it's full of surprises: from the way the spaces connect to the relationships from one unit to another. It's like an adventure playground.

MG: When you look at it on a structural level, we have turned the property into three different sites. Legally, there are three different buildings in one, each with its own volumes, and these are bound together by bands of charred wood that tie the building together. There are a lot of subtle references to these three volumes on the façade;

Durch das Gebäude zu gehen, ist ein Abenteuer

BJ: In der Regel betrachtet man ein Gewerbeobjekt und kann den einen Grundriss von außen erkennen. Hier ist es ein Abenteuer, durch das Gebäude zu gehen. Es ist voller Überraschungen: Wie die Räume miteinander verbunden sind, die Beziehungen einer Einheit zu einer anderen … Es ist wie ein Abenteuerspielplatz.

MG: Wir haben das Grundstück in drei verschiedene Teile gegliedert. Rechtlich gesehen, sind es drei Gebäude in einem – alle mit ihren verschiedenen Volumen. Sie sind mit Bändern aus verkohltem Holz verbunden, die das Gebäude zusammenhalten. In der Fassade sind Anspielungen auf die drei Inhalte

individual units express themselves in the variety of balconies or the different scale of windows. So the building reads as one entity, but the different layers gradually reveal themselves.

BJ: This is the way cities should be made. Not by investment funds. Not as places for multiplying your money. But as specific places - developed closely with the people who are invested in those places.

MG: The whole process of creating the city is getting decoupled from the people who actually use it. Cities like Berlin are realising that they have to defend themselves against anonymous investment funds that break the way a city should work.

BJ: By proving that this kind of cultural/commercial Baugruppe (German for co-investor model) is possible - through the coordination of conservative financial plans, dialogue to shape the development and the architecture and consideration of a diversity of vested interests - there can be a lasting resonance that spurs another kind of development in the future.

The way in which cities function economically is no longer tenable

MG: We are convinced that the way cities are economically functionally is broken. You need many examples of alternative models, like this one. Using carefully calculated risks, they are open to a variety of interests and, this is fundamentally important: they can also work financially for everyone involved.

-> Case Study 04 pp. 188 ff. Frizz23

erkennbar: eine Vielfalt an Balkons und verschieden große Fenster. Das Gebäude liest sich als eine Einheit, aber nach und nach zeigen sich die verschiedenen Schichten.

BJ: So sollten Städte gemacht sein. Nicht von Investmentfonds. Nicht als Orte, an denen Geld vermehrt wird. Sondern als besondere Orte, die in enger Zusammenarbeit mit den Menschen, die in sie investieren, entstehen.

MG: Der ganze Prozess des Städtebaus wird von den Menschen, die Stadt wirklich nutzen, entkoppelt. Städte wie Berlin merken, dass sie sich gegen anonyme Investmentfonds verteidigen müssen, weil sie die Art und Weise, wie eine Stadt funktionieren sollte, kaputt machen.

BJ: Die Umsetzung einer Art kultureller Baugruppe wird möglich, wenn solide Finanzplanung und Dialog Entwicklung und Architektur prägen – und die Einbeziehung der unglaublichen Interessenvielfalt. Dies führt zu einer dauerhaften Resonanz, die andere Entwicklungen in Zukunft anspornt.

Die Art, wie Städte ökonomisch funktionieren, ist am Ende

MG: Wir sind davon überzeugt, dass die Art, wie Städte ökonomisch funktionieren, am Ende ist. Man braucht viele Beispiele alternativer Modelle, so wie dieses hier, mit sorgfältig kalkulierten Risiken. Sie sind offen für verschiedene Interessen und funktionieren auch finanziell.

Off-the-Shelf Heterogeneity

Naked Infrastructure as a Living Model

Marc Frohn is an architect and co-founder of the architectural practice FAR frohn&rojas. A treatise on the house as naked infrastructure and on why living is an inherent part of the construction process.

When investigating architecture as so-called naked infrastructure, sooner or later - generally, sooner - Le Corbusier's Maison Dom-Ino is sure to come up. It seems that this is the source code for an infrastructural approach towards architecture, and housing in particular.

I would like to expand this narrow frame somewhat and consider Maison Dom-Ino in the context of a range of various buildings, designs and texts that, over time, has engaged the notion of naked infrastructure. In doing so, I will position the work of our architectural practice, FAR frohn&rojas, in relation to these ideas. This account does not claim to be comprehensive. However, in light of the following examples, a broad spectrum of architectural ideas and ideologies can be unearthed, all of which draw on infrastructural principles in housing.

Ein Gerüst für Vielfalt

Nackte Infrastruktur als Wohnmodell

Marc Frohn ist Architekt und Mitbegründer des Architekturbüros FAR frohn&rojas. Eine Abhandlung über das Haus als nackte Infrastruktur und warum dem Wohnen das Bauen innewohnt.

Bei der Auseinandersetzung mit Architektur als „nackter Infrastruktur" fällt der Blick früher oder später – meistens früher – auf Le Corbusiers Maison Dom-Ino. Es scheint, hier sei der Quellcode für eine infrastrukturelle Herangehensweise an die Architektur im Allgemeinen und den Wohnungsbau im Besonderen zu finden.

Ich möchte diesen verengten Blick weiten und die Maison Dom-Ino in eine Übersicht unterschiedlicher Bauten, Entwürfe und Schriften einordnen, die sich mit der „nackten Infrastruktur" im Laufe der Zeit auseinandergesetzt haben. Dabei werde ich zuletzt auch die Arbeit unseres Architekturbüros FAR frohn&rojas in Relation zu diesen Ideen setzen. Ich erhebe keinen Anspruch auf Vollständigkeit. Dennoch lässt sich anhand der folgenden Beispiele ein breites Spektrum architektonischer Ideen und Ideologien herausstellen, die allesamt Rückgriff auf infrastrukturelle Prinzipien im Wohnungsbau nehmen.

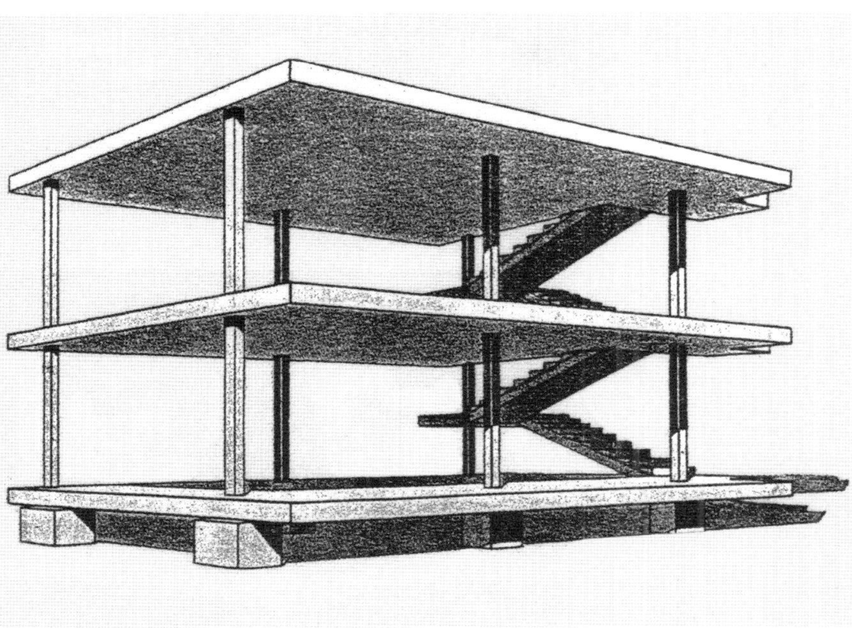

Exposed icon of modernity: Maison Dom-Ino by Le Corbusier, 1914

Entblößte Ikone der Moderne: Maison Dom-Ino von Le Corbusier, 1914

Highrise of Homes by SITE, 1981

Highrise of Homes von SITE, 1981

Maison Dom-Ino was Corbusier's answer to the large-scale destruction of Flanders in the First World War. In order to rebuild destroyed towns in a short period of time with naked infrastructure, Corbusier presented an approach that moved towards the industrialisation of construction. In his self-initiated project Plan Obus, he later put forward a plan for the radical transformation of Algiers. A significant component of this was a fourteen-storey, curved apartment complex bearing a highway on its roof. The complex was intended, in Corbusier's imagination, to provide housing for the Algerian working class. Here, too, we find one origin for the industrial approach to construction. The massive infrastructure functions as a rational frame, with which Corbusier isolated the pre-industrial households of the Medina from their complex urban and social framework.

Die Maison Dom-Ino war Corbusiers Antwort auf die großmaßstäbliche Zerstörung Flanderns im Ersten Weltkrieg. Um die zerstörten Ortschaften innerhalb kürzester Zeit wiederaufzubauen, präsentierte Corbusier mit seiner „nackten Infrastruktur" einen Ansatz zur Industrialisierung des Bauens. In seinem selbst initiierten Projekt Plan Obus schlägt er Jahre später eine radikale Umgestaltung von Algier vor. Wesentlicher Bestandteil ist ein vierzehngeschossiger geschwungener kilometerlanger Wohnriegel, auf dessen Dach eine Schnellstraße verläuft. Der Riegel sollte nach Corbusiers Vorstellungen Wohnungen für die algerische Arbeiterklasse bieten. Auch hier lässt sich jedoch primär ein Ansatz industriellen Bauens erkennen. Die massive Infrastruktur fungiert als rationales Gerüst, mit dem er die vorindustriellen häuslichen Räume der Medina aus deren komplexen urbanen und sozialen Gefügen isolierte.

Separate responsibility for "support" and "infill"

In 1961, N. J. Habraken sketched out an alternative to mass housing schemes in his book "Supports: An Alternative to Mass Housing" in response to Corbusier's approach. Habraken differentiated between support and infill and avoided static or technical definitions in doing so. Under the premise that dwelling is building, Habraken instead articulated an explicit shift of responsibility for and control over the infill to the residents themselves. The architect is responsible only for the infrastructural frame, the support. The success of this book and Habraken's ideas was also due to the fact that the work was pub-

Geteilte Verantwortung für „support" und „infill"

Im Jahr 1961 skizziert N. J. Habraken in seinem Buch „Supports: An Alternative to Mass Housing" eine Alternative zum Massenwohnungsbau, wie er aus Corbusiers Ansatz entsprang. Er unterscheidet zwischen „support" und „infill" – und es geht ihm dabei weniger um eine statische oder technische Unterscheidung. Unter der Prämisse „dwelling is building" artikuliert Habraken vielmehr eine eindeutige Verschiebung der Verantwortung und Kontrolle beim „infill" von den Architekt*innen zu den Bewohner*innen. Der/die Architekt*in zeichnet nur noch verantwortlich für den infrastrukturellen Rahmen, den „support". Der Erfolg des Buches

lished without a single drawing or visualisation: the text leaves a great deal of space for the imagination.

By contrast, the 1981 project Highrise of Homes by SITE exists as a collection of images that show an infrastructural high-rise skeleton in which each storey would house various traditional family homes. James Wines, the founder of SITE, asserted that the main value of the infrastructural skeleton lay in its polemical questioning of the architect's authorship, as well as in specific kinds of formalism.

Shelf housing: quick and individualised

Another significant reference is the housing constructed in West Berlin during the 1980s as part of the "International Building Exhibition (IBA)". The architects Stürzebecher, Nylund und Puttfarken coined the term Wohnregal, German for "shelf-housing". I do not doubt that the three planners took their cue from Habraken for their co-operative do-it-yourself project. The reinforced concrete skeleton accommodates twelve double "wooden houses", planned and realised by the residents themselves. The logic of the structure is distinguished by the material differentiation between concrete skeleton and timber structure - something absent from Habraken's designs. The grid of the façade offers a simple system of co-ordinates for synchronising all elements, in particular through the positioning of windows and other façade variations. The project took into account the abilities, means and tools required by architects and the construction company for the concrete structure, and by the residents for the wooden houses.

Our current project, the Waldenserstraße "housing shelf" in Berlin's Moabit district, demonstrates the apparent incompatibility of two new challenges. On the one hand, there is a very high demand for affordable living space in Berlin today. It is necessary to build quickly and cheaply. Standardisation and prefabrication are fast becoming necessary. On the other hand, there is an ever-broader spectrum of forms of living, each with their own spatial requirements, pressures and projections. With which speedy and individualised method could one bring these apparently contradictory conditions together in a building project?

und seiner Ideen ist sicherlich auch der Tatsache geschuldet, dass das Werk ohne eine einzige Zeichnung oder Visualisierung auskommt. Der Text lässt den Lesenden dadurch großen Spielraum zur Interpretation.

Ganz im Gegensatz dazu lässt sich das Projekt Highrise of Homes von SITE verstehen. Es existiert in erster Linie als Bildsammlung. Die Bilder zeigen ein infrastrukturelles Hochhausskelett, in das in jedem Geschoss unterschiedliche traditionelle Einfamilienhäuser eingesetzt wurden. James Wines, Gründer von SITE, argumentiert, dass der Hauptwert des infrastrukturellen Skelettes in seiner polemischen Infragestellung der Autorenschaft der Architekt*innen sowie bestimmter Formalismen liegt.

Wohnregal: Schnell und individuell

Eine weitere Referenz, die mir wichtig erscheint, ist ein im Rahmen der IBA in den 1980er Jahren in West-Berlin umgesetzter Wohnungsbau. Die Rede ist vom sogenannten „Wohnregal" der Architekten Stürzebecher, Nylund und Puttfarken. Es besteht für mich kein Zweifel, dass die drei Planer für ihr genossenschaftliches Do-it-yourself-Projekt Ansätze von Habraken aufgegriffen haben. In das Stahlbetonskelett sind zwölf doppelgeschossige „Holzhäuser" eingestellt, die die Bewohner*innen in Eigenverantwortung geplant und realisiert haben. Die Logik des Baus zeichnet die materielle Unterscheidung von Betonskelett und Holzbau aus, die wir bei Habraken so nicht finden. Das Raster der Fassade bietet ein einfaches Koordinatensystem zur Synchronisation aller Beteiligten bei der Positionierung von Fenstern und anderen Fassadendurchbrüchen. Das Projekt berücksichtigt das Können, die Mittel und Werkzeuge, die Architekt*innen und die Baufirma für die Betonstruktur und die Bewohner*innen für die „Holzhäuser" benötigen.

Unser aktuelles Projekt Wohnregal Waldenserstraße in Berlin-Moabit zeigt die scheinbare Unvereinbarkeit zweier neuer Herausforderungen auf: Zum einen ist der Bedarf an günstigem Wohnraum heute enorm hoch. Es geht also darum, günstig und schnell zu bauen. Standardisierung und Vorfabrikation liegen nahe. Zum anderen entwickelt sich ein immer breiteres Spektrum von Lebensmodellen und Wohnformen, die ihre eigenen räumlichen Bedürfnisse, Zwänge und Bilder beinhalten. Wie lassen sich diese beiden gegenläufigen Bedingungen – schnell und individuell – in einem Bauvorhaben miteinander verbinden?

The solution is to return to an infrastructural "shelf system" made from pre-fabricated, reinforced concrete units. This structure consists of standardised elements from industrial and warehouse constructions. It is inexpensive, can be put together in just a few weeks, and offers maximal range and freedom for the arrangement of interior spaces. Working with drywall construction enables highly variegated floorplans, which means that rented apartments will be able to meet many different demands. This principle can be applied to rental apartments, be inexpensively implemented in various dimensions and guarantees a short construction phase and low costs, even when the construction industry is working at full capacity.

As these partly contradictory, partly complementary examples show, naked infrastructures pose a broad range of fundamental architectural questions in relation to aesthetics, authorship, material systems and the power of images. It is this complexity and flexibility that make the concept so exciting, endowing it with far more potential than the development of an industralised construction system à la Maison Dom-Ino.

Die Lösung ist wiederum ein infrastrukturelles „Regal" aus vorfabrizierten Stahlbetonfertigteilen. Es besteht aus Standardelementen des Industrie- und Hallenbaus, ist kostengünstig, in wenigen Wochen aufzubauen und bietet mit seinen TT-Decken maximale Spannweiten und Freiheiten im Innenraum. In Trockenbauweise lassen sich die unterschiedlichsten Grundrisse verwirklichen, die den vielen Anforderungen des Mietwohnungsbaus gerecht werden. Das Prinzip lässt sich hervorragend auf günstig umsetzbare Mietwohnungen unterschiedlicher Größenordnungen anwenden und garantiert auch in Zeiten einer ausgelasteten Bauwirtschaft geringe Bauzeiten und -kosten.

„Nackte Infrastrukturen" werfen, wie die sich teilweise widersprechenden und teilweise aufeinander aufbauenden Beispiele zeigen, eine Vielzahl grundlegender architektonischer Fragen in Bezug auf Ästhetik, Autor*innenschaft, Materialsystem und die Macht von Bildern auf. Es ist diese Vielschichtigkeit und Flexibilität, die das Prinzip so spannend macht und die weit mehr Potenzial hat als die Entwicklung eines industrialisierten Bausystems à la Maison Dom-Ino.

-> Case Study 03 pp. 186 ff. Wohnregal Waldenserstraße

Model project by the architects Stürzebecher, Nylund and Puttfarken: the Residential Shelf Kreuzberg, 1984–86, challenges architectural authorship

Modellprojekt der Architekten Stürzebecher, Nylund und Puttfarken: Das Wohnregal Kreuzberg, 1984–1986, stellt auch Autor*innenschaft infrage

The Berlin Mix

On Typologies and Porosity

Die Berliner Mischung

Über Typologie und Durchlässigkeit

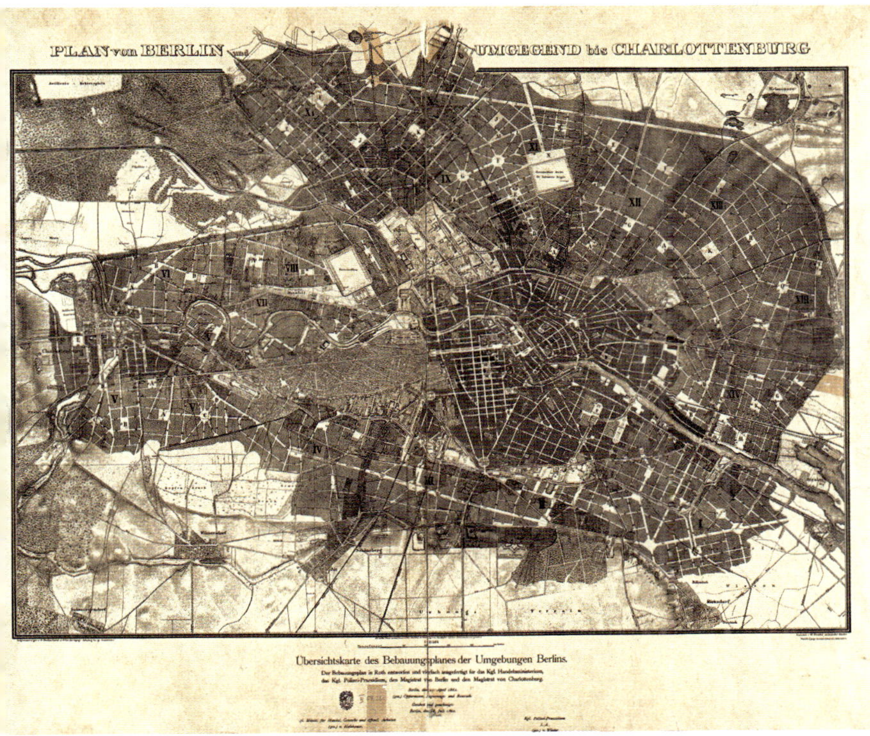

Heterogeneity and adaptability: the Hobrecht plan from 1862 as an endless carpet made of stone

Der Hobrecht-Plan aus dem Jahr 1862 als heterogen bespielbarer Endlos-Teppich aus Stein

The Berlin mix, which accommodates residential, commercial and industrial functions in the city's ubiquitous typology of the nineteenth-century Berlin apartment block, has attracted renewed attention in contemporary urban thought. This is due to its unique ability to retain industry and production in the city: not only does the Berlin mix attract creative economies, it also integrates urban living and working.

The architect and professor Katharina Borsi explores the porosity of the city block and refelcts on why its pioneer, the urban planner James Hobrecht, remains avant-garde today.

The nineteenth-century block has figured as the leitmotif for Berlin's urban development since the 1990s. The current "Master Plan Berlin Heidestraße" is but one example that draws on formal and spatial aspects of the nineteenth-century

Die Berliner Mischung, das Nebeneinander von Wohnen, Handel und Produktion in der Typologie der Berliner Mietskaserne, erhält in der zeitgenössischen urbanen Diskussion wieder neue Aufmerksamkeit. Denn: Sie hat die einzigartige Fähigkeit, Produktion und Industrie in der Stadt zu erhalten. Sie zieht kreative Ökonomien an und verbindet Wohnen und Arbeiten.

Die Architektin und Hochschulprofessorin Katharina Borsi über die Porosität des Stadtblocks und warum James Hobrecht immer noch Avantgarde ist.

Seit den 1990ern ist der Wohnblock des 19. Jahrhunderts wieder zum Leitbild der Berliner Stadtentwicklung geworden. Der aktuelle „Masterplan Berlin Heidestraße" ist nur eines der Beispiele, das sich an den formellen und räumlichen Aspekten dieser Mietskaserne orientiert: mit ihrer durchgehenden

block with its continuous street front, open courtyards, coherence and variation from block to block, and lively street level, all come together to deliver an urbanity and mix of uses that resonate with and beyond its nineteenth-century predecessor.

The block became a ubiquitous urban typology in Berlin with the publication of the city's extension plan under the guidance of James Hobrecht in 1862.[1] The urban plan was remarkable in its degree of abstraction: rolling out like an infinite carpet of stone, it carved out spaces for both movement and stillness - projecting a relatively regular, undifferentiated urban structure that extended from the pre-existing city and was regularly subdivided to achieve connectivity across the urban fabric. Its corresponding urban component, the Berlin block, follows a similar logic.

1 On the Hobrecht plan, see, for example, Felix Bentlin: "Understanding the Hobrecht Plan: Origin, Composition, and Implementation of Urban Design Elements in the Berlin Expansion Plan from 1862", Planning Perspectives 33, 4/2018: 633-655.

Straßenfront, den Hinterhöfen, ihrer Einheitlichkeit bei gleichzeitiger Variabilität und den belebten Erdgeschossen. All diese Eigenschaften ähneln in ihrer Mischung und Urbanität dem Vorgänger aus dem 19. Jahrhundert.

Die Berliner Mietskaserne wurde mit der Veröffentlichung des Bebauungsplans unter James Hobrecht im Jahr 1862 zur allgegenwärtigen urbanen Typologie.[1] Bemerkenswert ist: Hobrecht entfaltet einen „Teppich" aus Stein, schafft Räume der Bewegung und Luft für Menschen sowie eine Struktur, die sich scheinbar unendlich ausdehnen lässt. Er entwirft ein relativ einheitliches urbanes System, das sich von der existierenden Stadtmitte aus gleichmäßig unterteilt ausbreitet und Verbindungen schafft. Seine urbane Komponente, die Berliner Mietskaserne, folgt einer ähnlichen Logik. Gustav Assmanns Schrift „Grundrisse für städtische Wohngebäude"

1 Über den Hobrechtplan, siehe beispielsweise Felix Bentlin: „Understanding the Hobrecht Plan: Origin, Composition, and Implementation of Urban Design Elements in the Berlin Expansion Plan from 1862", Planning Perspectives 33, 4/2018: 633–655.

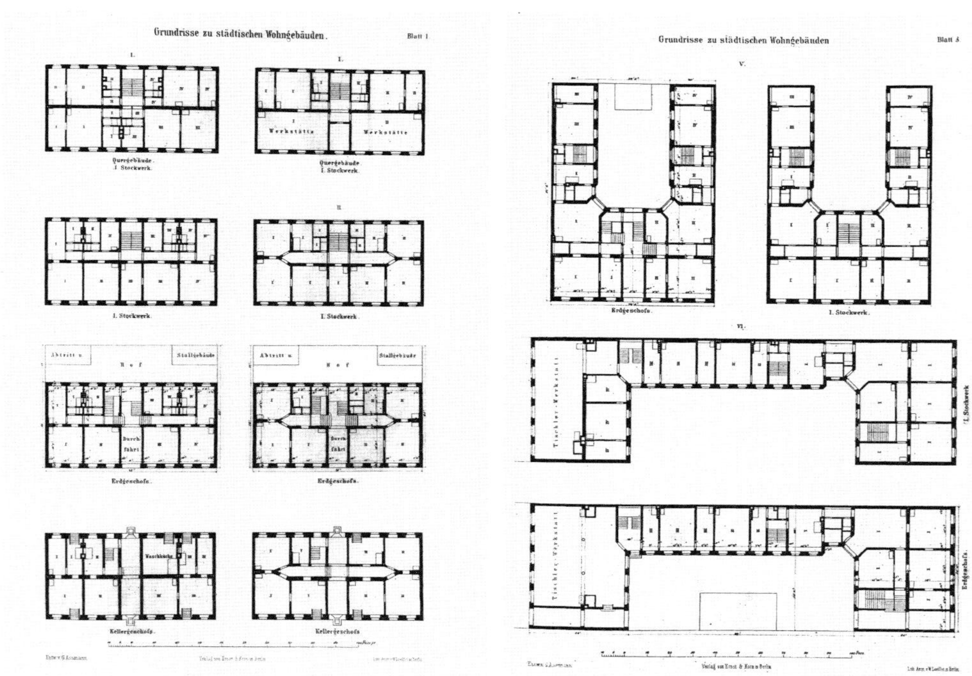

Variations of the housing block: Gustav Assmann's "Plans for Urban Residential Buildings" (1862)

Variationen der Wohnblockorganisation: Gustav Assmanns „Grundrisse für städtische Wohngebäude" (1862)

Gustav Assmann's "Plan for Urban Dwellings", also published in 1862, provided a comprehensive catalogue, rationalised the existing variations of the block's organisation, and allowed for varying sizes and shapes of plots of land.[2]

Every building is a social microcosm

Assmann proposed an urban plan that accommodates dwellings of different sizes and uses. He assumed that the population - and therefore the use of a building - is likely to change over time. Statistician Ernst Bruch provided a succinct summary of the spatial principle underlying the urban plan and the Berlin block: "The uniform subdivision of streets renders each street into a connection between all possible uses, and each house into a microcosm of the whole of human society."[3] The generic urban spaces of Hobrecht's plan, in conjunction with the series of undifferentiated spaces delineated by Assmann as its constituent prototype, asserted an infrastructural system that collected and distributed an as-yet-undifferentiated population and a multiplicity of uses throughout its territory. This system could grow and evolve according to changing requirements. It foresees our contemporary conception of housing in a diverse city. It was only over the course of the late nineteenth and early twentieth centuries that a pattern of social and functional segregation began to emerge.

The early development of Luisenstadt, coupled with the existence of trade and manufacturing, provides a particularly clear example of this urban system at work. Here, the block began to take hold as a sequence of interlinked in-between-spaces, leading to changes on both a spatial and an economic level. The resulting matrix of interconnected, adaptable spaces, in which manufacturing, production and living could evolve, grow, intensify, redistribute and

2 Gustav Assmann: "Grundrisse für städtische Wohngebäude: Mit Rücksicht auf die in Berlin geltende Bauordnung", Berlin: Ernst & Korn, 1862. See also Katharina Borsi, "Strategies of the Berlin Block". In: "Intimate Metropolis", edited by V. di Palma, D. Periton and M. Lathouri, Abingdon, Oxon: Routledge, 2009, 132-152.

3 Ernst Bruch, quoted in Dieter Hoffmann-Axthelm: "Die dritte Stadt: Bausteine eines neuen Gründungsvertrags", Frankfurt am Main: Suhrkamp, 1993, 193.

(ebenfalls 1862) bietet einen umfangreichen Katalog von Variationen der Wohnblockorganisation – je nach Grundstücksgröße.[2]

Jedes Haus ein gesellschaftlicher Mikrokosmos

Assmann empfiehlt, dass der Bebauungsplan Einheiten unterschiedlicher Größe einbeziehen und unterschiedliche Nutzungen ermöglichen soll. Er geht davon aus, dass sich die Bevölkerung und damit die Nutzung eines Gebäudes im Laufe der Zeit wandelt. Das gemeinsame urbane Konzept von Bebauungsplan und Mietskaserne brachte der Statistiker Ernst Bruch auf den Punkt: „Die einheitliche Unterteilung der Straßen macht jede Straße zu einer Verbindung zwischen allen möglichen Nutzungen und aus jedem Haus einen Mikrokosmos der ganzen Gesellschaft."[3] Die generischen urbanen Räume in Hobrechts Plan ergaben – zusammen mit der Serie einheitlicher Räume, die Assmann als Prototypen entwarf – ein infrastrukturelles System, das eine bisher undifferenzierte Bevölkerung und eine Vielzahl von Nutzungen auf seinem ganzen Gebiet zusammenbrachte und verteilte. Das System konnte – je nach Bedarf – wachsen und sich entwickeln. Es ist Vorläufer unseres modernen Konzepts des Wohnens und der durchmischten Stadt. Erst im Laufe des späten 19. und frühen 20. Jahrhunderts kamen Muster der sozialen und funktionalen Separation hinzu.

Die frühe Entwicklung der Luisenstadt stellt ein besonders gutes Beispiel dieses urbanen Systems in der Praxis dar. Hier spannte sich der Wohnblock als eine Sequenz verbundener Zwischenräume über die Häuserblöcke, was sich räumlich und ökonomisch auswirkte. Eine Matrix miteinander verbundener Freiräume ermöglicht die Anpassungsfähigkeit der Räume, in denen Produktion und Wohnen wachsen, sich entwickeln und auch umverteilt werden können. Von den Synergieeffekten profitierten die sich verändernden Herstellungs- und Produktionsketten.

2 Gustav Assmann: „Grundrisse für städtische Wohngebäude: Mit Rücksicht auf die in Berlin geltende Bauordnung", Berlin: Ernst & Korn, 1862. Siehe auch Katharina Borsi, „Strategies of the Berlin Block". In: „Intimate Metropolis", hg. von V. di Palma, D. Periton und M. Lathouri, Abingdon, Oxon: Routledge, 2009, 132–152.

3 Ernst Bruch, zitiert nach Dieter Hoffmann-Axthelm: „Die dritte Stadt: Bausteine eines neuen Gründungsvertrags", Frankfurt am Main: Suhrkamp, 1993, 193.

benefit from the synergistic effects of location and proximity, supporting the then-changing nature of manufacturing and production chains.

Free spaces, responsive to what the city might become

The strategic value of the Berlin block was twofold: first, its flexibility and adaptability meant that entire urban areas could evolve over time as required. Second, the block typology came to constitute the urban area as a matrix of interconnected free spaces, responsive to what the city might become.

Today, some 160 years later, we are beginning to see the effects of dramatic demographic changes on patterns of work, mobility and globalisation. The modern domestic family is reconfiguring itself, single households are on the rise and an increasingly ageing population means that it is again necessary to reconsider urban housing. Employment trends have seen the rise of serviced, shared and flexible workspaces, while changes in technology and work patterns are increasingly blurring the boundaries between living and working - the bedroom, the café, the co-working office and the new open-plan learning and working spaces can be both intimate and productive. Although the growth of the service and knowledge economy allows for a return to city living, it also brings with it the threat of polarisation: who can afford to live in a city where distribution of access to work and other resources is increasingly unequal?

While we cannot simply return to the open, adaptable urban matrix as constituted by the early Berlin block, its flexible spaces operating across scales continue to offer a valid contribution to a culture of sharing, learning and knowledge exchange. This is not a call for the reinstatement of the block's formal principles, but instead, a reflection on the capacity of architecture to constitute shared urban spaces, interlinking landscapes of work, civic and residential life.

Freiräume, die darauf warteten, was aus der Stadt werden würde

Der Berliner Häuserblock hatte einen doppelten strategischen Wert: Einerseits konnten sich städtische Räume im Laufe der Zeit nach den Bedürfnissen entwickeln. Andererseits konstituierte die Mietskaserne den städtischen Raum als Matrix verbundener Freiräume, die darauf warteten, was aus der Stadt werden würde.

Heute, etwa 160 Jahre später, betrachten wir die Auswirkungen des dramatischen demografischen Wandels auf Arbeit, Mobilität und Globalisierung. Die moderne Kleinfamilie löst sich auf, Singlehaushalte nehmen zu, und eine immer älter werdende Bevölkerung erfordert neue Auseinandersetzungen mit städtischem Wohnen. In der Arbeitswelt geht der Trend zu geteilten und flexiblen Räumen für Dienstleistungen, während gleichzeitig technologische Veränderungen die Grenzen zwischen Leben und Arbeiten auflösen: Man arbeitet im Schlafzimmer, im Café, im Coworking-Büro. Die neuen Großraumlern- und -arbeitsräume können sowohl intim als auch produktiv sein. Obwohl das Wachstum der Dienstleistungs- und Wissensökonomie eine Rückkehr in das Stadtleben ermöglicht, verstärkt es gleichzeitig auch eine zunehmende Polarisierung: Wer kann sich das Leben in einer Stadt leisten, in der die Verteilung von Arbeit und anderen Ressourcen immer ungerechter wird?

Obwohl wir nicht einfach zu der offenen Matrix, die der frühe Berliner Wohnblock schuf, zurückkehren können, bieten sich seine flexibel nutzbaren Räume verschiedener Größenordnungen noch immer für eine Kultur des Teilens, Lernens und Wissensaustauschs an. Dies ist kein Aufruf, die formellen Prinzipien des Wohnblocks wieder einzuführen, sondern vielmehr eine Reflexion über das Vermögen der Architektur, Stadt als ein Netzwerk gemeinsamer Räume zu entwerfen, das Arbeit, öffentliches und privates Leben miteinander verbindet.

Even today, Hobrecht's sequential courtyards have the potential as sites for cultural, economic and social exchange

Hobrechts Hofsequenzen haben auch heutzutage das Potenzial für Orte des kulturellen, ökonomischen und sozialen Austausches

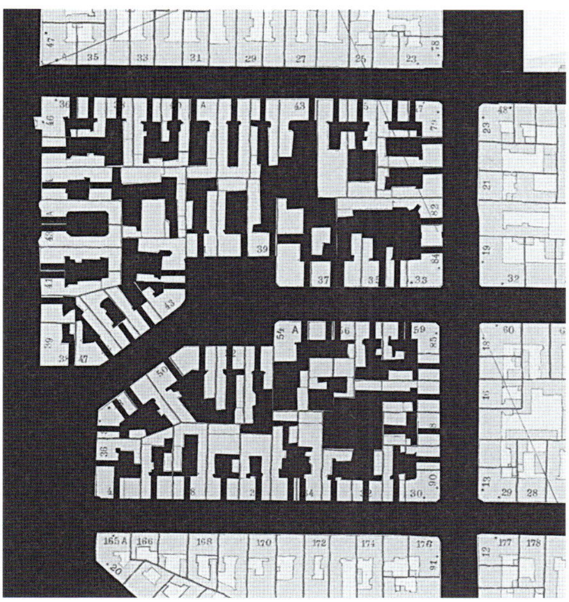

The ground-level permeability in Luisenstadt around 1910: a matrix of interconnectedness enabled multiple appropriations – from market stalls, butchers and outhouses to workshops and playgrounds

Permeabilität in der Luisenstadt um 1910: Eine Matrix der Vernetzung ermöglichte vielfältige Nutzungen, von Marktständen über Metzgereien und Lagerräumen bis hin zu Werkstätten und Spielplätzen

Condensed groundfloor: the Berliner block is a spatial system for an innovative mix of urban production types and social spaces

Erdgeschoss verdichtet: Der Berliner Block als ausdauerndes räumliches System für den innovativen Mix urbaner Produktion und Gemeinschaftsfläche

Not undisputed but still relevant: Jane Jacobs fought for mixed neighbourhoods

Nicht unumstritten, aber immer noch aktuell: Jane Jacobs' Kampf für durchmischte Nachbarschaften

Open City?

The Ground Floor as Socio-urban Resource

With the Metropolenhaus at the Jewish Museum, bfstudio-architects realised inner-city space that connects living and working with programmatic concepts of use. The principle of cross-financing within buildings removes the added value of the ground floor and enables open cultural uses. This stimulates not only the household but the entire neighbourhood. The architect Benita Braun-Feldweg writes on the responsibility of urban planning and the socio-political and economic significance of the ground floor area.

Residential and traffic areas of cities make up just 13.8 percent of the 357,580 square kilometres of the total area of Germany. Increasingly, this land has become an investment object of the global financial market. In the last ten years, land prices in Berlin have risen by 1,100 percent and construction costs by approximately 20 to 30 percent – while average net income has remained static. The consequences of selling off land are fatal. If, with the lifting of rent controls, a city state like Berlin were to continue relinquishing its "family silver" (for example, the IBA buildings) to the mercy of real estate speculators, it would demonstrate the lack of prospects for urban planning policy. The land and housing crises have long been a social crises. Rising rents affect social housing as much as the middle class.

The city and its residents are at their limit

Berlin's greatest social resource is an urban space designed for everyday needs. A socially, culturally and functionally mixed city – with the human being at its centre – is a prerequisite for successful co-existence. This, however, is increasingly being destabilised due to online trading and tourism: the city centre is being homogenised into a transit zone by a pattern of DHL pick-up points and ground-floor Starbucks that meet only the needs of arriving and departing tourists. The domination of the street level by elite-friendly cafés and wellness companies prevents the

Offene Stadt?

Das Erdgeschoss als sozialräumliche Ressource

Mit dem Metropolenhaus am Jüdischen Museum in Berlin realisierten bfstudio-architekten innerstädtischen Raum, der Wohnen und Arbeiten mit programmatischen Nutzungskonzepten in Beziehung setzt. Das Prinzip der gebäudeinternen Querfinanzierung entzieht das Erdgeschoss dem Wertschöpfungsdruck und ermöglicht offene kulturelle Nutzungen. Das stimuliert nicht nur die Hausgemeinschaft, sondern die gesamte Nachbarschaft. Die Architektin Benita Braun-Feldweg über die Verantwortung von Stadtplanung und die sozialpolitische und ökonomische Bedeutung des urbanen Sockelgeschosses.

Der Boden der Stadt, die Siedlungs- und Verkehrsfläche, entspricht lediglich 13,8 Prozent der 357.580 Quadratkilometer Boden der Bundesrepublik. Dieser Boden ist immer mehr zur Anlagekategorie des globalen Finanzmarktes geworden. In den letzten zehn Jahren ist in Berlin eine Steigerung der Bodenpreise um 1.100 Prozent sowie ein Anstieg der Baupreise um etwa zwanzig bis dreißig Prozent bei einem annähernd gleichbleibenden Nettoeinkommen zu verzeichnen. Die Folgen der Ausverkaufspolitik von öffentlichem Vermögen sind fatal. Wenn das Land Berlin selbst sein „Tafelsilber", wie beispielsweise die IBA-Bauten, einhergehend mit dem Auslaufen der Mietpreisbindung sogenannten Heuschrecken überlässt, zeigt sich die Perspektivlosigkeit städtischer Planungspolitik. Aus der Boden- und Wohnungskrise ist längst eine soziale Krise geworden. Immer teurer werdende Mieten im sozialen sowie im gehobenen Wohnungsbau sind ein Phänomen, das untere Einkommen ebenso betrifft wie die Mittelschicht. Die Stadt und ihre Bewohner*innen sind am Limit.

Soziale Ressource innerstädtischer Raum und seine Akteur*innen

Berlins größte soziale Ressource ist eine auf die vielfältigen Abläufe des alltäglichen Lebens ausgerichtete Gestaltung des innerstädtischen Raums, der in Europa in einer langen Tradition gesellschaftlicher Nutzung steht. Eine sozial, kulturell und funktio-

Cross-financing for busy urban spaces: the Metropolenhaus am Blumengroßmarkt

Querfinanzierung für belebte Stadträume: Das Metropolenhaus am Blumengroßmarkt

feldfünf in Metropolenhaus: ground floor use with a curated cultural neighbourhood programme

feldfünf im Metropolenhaus: Nachbarschaftliche Erdgeschossnutzung mit kuratiertem Kultur- und Workshop-Programm

emergence of social zones where residents of the city can interact. "Understanding urban territory as a common resource" is a prerequisite for active neighbourhoods, sustainable communities and social growth.[1] Planners and builders can no longer avoid the social responsibility that comes with construction. Only efficient processes of urban design in cooperation with authorities, builders and residents - which go beyond bureaucratic, procedural participation - will make the city as a social space possible once again.

-

Vision for an active street level

In 1963, American activist Jane Jacobs described streets and sidewalks as "the main public places of a city ... its most vital organs."[2] The ground floor is an indispensable element for the maintenance of diversity in central urban neighbourhoods. Taking this into account, the architecture office East 2012 developed a complex concept of ground floor use and design for high streets in London. After the London Riots in 2011, public funds were used to economically and socially strengthen those areas that were hit hardest by the uprising. In close co-operation with residents and shop owners, East 2012 paid particular attention to the revival of the intercultural ground floor zone, making a significant contribution to the improvement of the social climate.

The Garden City Atlantic is a housing estate in the Berlin district of Gesundbrunnen that has experienced a similar degree of precarity but for different reasons. Built between 1925 and 1929 according to the designs of architect Rudolf Fränkel, the demolition of the Lichtburg cinema, arguably the heart of the estate, the construction of the Berlin Wall in the early 1960s, as well as the construction of the Gesundbrunnen Centre in 1997 led to the significant deterioration of the site, both materially and economically. Its redevelopment centralised the role of the ground floor area, which had been a "microcosm of a memorial city". In the private-private partnership, learning workshops for children and adolescents were created which ended up contributing great-

nal gemischte Stadt, in der der Mensch im Fokus steht, ist Voraussetzung für die langfristige Sicherung des positiven Zusammenlebens einer offenen Gesellschaft, die durch Onlinehandel und Tourismus immer mehr ins Wanken gerät. Die zunehmende Aneinanderreihung von DHL-Annahmestellen oder Starbucks-Cafés in den Erdgeschosszonen der Stadt, die die Bedürfnisse an- und abfahrender Tourist*innen erfüllen, führen zu einer Innenstadt als Transitzone. Eine elitäre Enclosure-Erdgeschossnutzung mit Kantinen und Wellness für Mitarbeiter*innen durch Unternehmen, die ihren Sitz innerstädtisch in Neubauten erweitern, verhindert die Entstehung von Sozialzonen, in denen es Austausch zwischen Bewohner*innen der Stadt gibt. Wo können Bewohner*innen im innerstädtischen Raum noch verweilen? Das „städtische Territorium als Gemeinressource zu begreifen", ist Voraussetzung für das Aktivieren von Nachbarschaft und das Wirken ins Umfeld im Sinne eines nachhaltigen Gemeinschaffens mit sozialem Wachstum. Dieses sollte anstelle von kapitalorientierter Rendite das Ziel sein.[1] Planer*innen und Macher*innen kommen nicht mehr umhin, Bauen als gesellschaftliche Verantwortung zu verstehen. Effiziente Prozesse der Stadtgestaltung im Vertrauen und Miteinander zwischen Behörden, Bauherr*innen und Bewohner*innen, die über bürokratische Partizipationsverfahren hinausgehen, machen Stadt als Sozialraum möglich.

-

Vision aktives Erdgeschoss

Die amerikanische Aktivistin Jane Jacobs beschreibt 1963 Straßen und Bürgersteige als die „wichtigsten öffentlichen Orte einer Stadt, [...] ihre lebenskräftigsten Organe".[2] Das Erdgeschoss ist dabei unerlässlicher Baustein für die Erhaltung von Vielfalt in den Quartieren in zentraler Lage und schafft Raum für innerstädtisches Leben mit gewerblichen sowie sozialen und kulturellen Nutzungen. Dies berücksichtigend entwickelte das Architekturbüro East 2012 ein komplexes Konzept der Erdgeschossnutzung und -gestaltung der High Streets in London. Nach den London Riots 2011 sollten mithilfe öffentlicher Gelder konkret jene Gebiete wirtschaftlich und sozial gestärkt werden, die von den Aufständen am schlimmsten betroffen waren. In enger

1 Tom Avermaete: "Die Konstruktion von Gemeingütern". In: Arch+: "An Atlas of Commoning/Orte des Gemeinschaffens", 232/2018, 32-43, here 34.

2 Jane Jacobs: "Tod und Leben großer amerikanischer Städte". Berlin: Ullstein, 1969, 27.

1 Tom Avermaete: „Die Konstruktion von Gemeingütern". In: Arch+: „An Atlas of Commoning/Orte des Gemeinschaffens", 232/2018, 32–43, hier 34.

2 Jane Jacobs: „Tod und Leben großer amerikanischer Städte". Berlin: Ullstein, 1969, 27.

Atelier Fanelsa activates the street level of a building by Werner Duttmann

Atelier Fanelsa aktiviert das Sockelgeschoss eines Werner-Duttmann-Baus

ly to the sustainable development of the neighbourhood.

The cultural and commercial concept of the street level's rejuvenation was also integral to the construction of the Metropolenhaus at the Jewish Museum, completed in 2018. One thousand square metres of street level space were cross-financed through the sale of apartments and office units on the upper floors. A curated business management firm now directs the programme, including small-scale shops: a barber shop, vintage clothing, a photo studio and a restaurant. At street level, 40 percent of the area is dedicated to non-commercial spaces, 5 percent of which is utilised for neighbourhood projects in-

Zusammenarbeit mit Bewohner*innen und Shop-Besitzer*innen legte East das Augenmerk besonders auf die Wiederbelebung der interkulturell geprägten Erdgeschosszone, für die das Architekturbüro ein spezielles Gestaltungskonzept entwickelte und so maßgeblich zu einer Verbesserung des sozialen Klimas beitrug.

In einem prekären Zustand befand sich auch die 1925 bis 1929 nach den Plänen des Architekten Rudolf Fränkel erbaute Gartenstadt Atlantic Anfang 2000 in Berlin-Gesundbrunnen. Der Abriss der Lichtburg und der Bau der Berliner Mauer Anfang der 1960er Jahre sowie die Errichtung der Mall „Gesundbrunnen Center" 1997 stuften die Anlage inhaltlich sowie wirtschaftlich drastisch herab. Bei

Bar Babette on Karl-Marx-Allee was a cultural site which succumbed to eviction

Die Bar Babette an der Karl-Marx-Allee war Ort kultureller Vermittlung und steht im Schatten der Verdrängung

The Alte Münze, a laboratory and working space for NGOs with a contested future

Die Alte Münze als Versuchslabor und Arbeitsraum für NGOs diskutiert die Zukunft des Areals und die Einbindung in den Stadtraum

FabLab Berlin: an open workshop makes public the modes of production

FabLab Berlin: Offene Werkstatt mit Produktionsmitteln

The Industriesalon Schöneweide: new forms of co-operative production, in an industrial heritage site?

Industriesalon Schöneweide: Neue Formen der kooperativen Produktion in einem Industriekulturerbe?

cluding local and international projects from the fields of art, culture and design.

Getting things done and letting things happen

When land is allocated for construction, concepts should be called for that do not focus solely on housing and transport but also take into account the entire spectrum of a city's quality of life. In comparison to other European metropolises, Berlin still has ample space for inner-city densification. Here, the "sensitive zone of the ground floor ... becomes a strategic component of urban development".[3] The maximisation of profit as the sole measure in the awards procedure is no guarantee of sustainable urban development. By aiming for the maximum return on the smallest possible area, faceless, uninhabited units for temporary living are created and with them the end of the neighbourhood?

"Property entails responsibility"! Germany's Basic Law legally enshrines this social responsibility: property owners must give something back to the inner city in order to secure it as a common space. The street level, with its bakeries, dry cleaners, tailors, small businesses and craft shops, is a space for meeting and exchange. If "the public hand lacks money and the investor lacks interest ... then (these) spaces for integrating housing into the city are at risk. Their use cannot be packed into a spreadsheet or used to generate

3 Stefan Rettich: "Public on Demand: Das Erdgeschoss als verlängertes Wohnzimmer der Stadt", Stadt Bauwelt 36, 13/2013, 52–54, here 53.

der Modernisierung war daher das Entwickeln eines Konzepts für die Erdgeschosszone, eines „Mikrokosmos im Denkmal Gartenstadt", wesentlicher Bestandteil der Reurbanisierung. Die klassischen Gewerbenutzungen im Erdgeschoss waren aufgrund des Staubsaugereffektes der Shoppingmall hinfällig, sodass vor allem soziokulturelle Partnerschaften mit Fokus auf Lernwerkstätten für Kinder und Jugendliche in Form einer Private-private-Partnership Initialzündungen für das Umfeld und eine nachhaltige Entwicklung des Quartiers wurden.

Mit einem Fokus auf interkulturellen Mehrwert wird bei dem 2018 fertiggestellten Neubau des Metropolenhauses am Jüdischen Museum das Erdgeschoss zum Programm. Unter der Prämisse „Konzept überbietet Preis" überzeugte das Kultur- und Gewerbekonzept des aktiven Erdgeschosses: Über den Verkauf von Wohnungen und Büroeinheiten in den Obergeschossen konnten 1.000 Quadratmeter Erdgeschoss querfinanziert werden. Ein kuratorisches Gewerbemanagement steuert das Programm: kleinteilige Läden für Barber-Shop, Vintage-Kleidung, Fotostudio, orientalisches Restaurant. Auf vierzig Prozent der Erdgeschossfläche ermöglichen es die nicht kommerziellen Projekträume feldfünf lokalen und internationalen Akteur*innen aus Kunst, Kultur und Design, Nachbarschaft zu gestalten.

Zulassen und Machen

Es braucht innovative Konzepte in der Vergabe von Baugrund. Konzepte, die sich nicht allein auf Wohnungsbau und Verkehr konzentrieren, sondern die das gesamte funktionale und soziale Spektrum der Lebensqualität einer Stadt berücksichtigen. Im Vergleich zu anderen europäischen Metropolen hat Berlin noch immer ausreichend Platz für innerstädtische Nachverdichtung, bei der die „sensible Zone

profit."[4] A land use policy that puts concepts, incentives and procedures to use to stimulate investors and contractors to conceive of the street level as a community-building social resource for their own projects might be capable of counteracting the selling-off of the contemporary city.

Copy: Anne-Marie Sanders

Definition of "urban area"

An urban area is a building area in German building planning law, which, according to Section 6a of the Building Use Regulation (Baunutzungsverordnung, or BauNVO) serves the housing and accommodation of commercial enterprises and social, cultural and other facilities that do not significantly impact the residential use.

4 Kaye Geipel: "Zwischen ‚terasses communes' und Kampfzone Erdgeschoss", Stadt Bauwelt 36, 13/2013, 12–15, here 12.

des Erdgeschosses [...] zu einem strategischen Baustein der Stadtentwicklung wird".[3]

Der Höchstpreis als alleiniges Maß im Vergabeverfahren ist kein Garant für eine nachhaltige städtebauliche Entwicklung. Im Pokerspiel um die maximale Rendite auf kleinster Fläche entstehen gesichtslose, unbewohnte Units zum Temporär-Wohnen. Das Ende der Nachbarschaft?

„Eigentum verpflichtet"! Die im Grundgesetz verankerte Sozialverpflichtung, der Stadt etwas zurückzugeben, muss Innenstädte als Gemeinschaftsorte sichern. Die Erdgeschosse der Stadt mit Läden wie Bäckereien, Reinigungen und Schneidereien, Kleingewerbe und Handwerksbetrieben initiieren Begegnung. Fehlt „der öffentlichen Hand das Geld und dem Investor das Interesse [...], stehen [diese] Vermittlungszonen von Wohnen und Stadt auf dem Spiel. Ihr Nutzen passt nicht in Tabellenform; sie fallen durchs Raster der Renditekalkulation."[4]

Sind das Zusammentreffen und Gsemeinschaffen von unterschiedlichen Menschen, Kulturen und sozialen Schichten aber ein Anliegen von Politik und Gesellschaft, können aktives Erdgeschoss und Stadt entstehen. Eine Bodenpolitik, die durch Vorgaben, Anreize, Konzepte und Verfahren so stimuliert, dass Investor*innen und Bauherr*innen die Nutzung des Erdgeschosses für gesellschaftsrelevante Zwecke als Ressource für das eigene Projekt definieren, ist notwendige Voraussetzung dafür.

Redaktionelle Ausarbeitung: Anne-Marie Sanders

Definition „Urbane Gebiete"

Urbanes Gebiet ist im deutschen Bauplanungsrecht ein Baugebiet, welches nach § 6 a der Baunutzungsverordnung (BauNVO) dem Wohnen sowie der Unterbringung von Gewerbebetrieben und sozialen, kulturellen und anderen Einrichtungen dient, die die Wohnnutzung nicht wesentlich stören.

3 Stefan Rettich: „Public on Demand: Das Erdgeschoss als verlängertes Wohnzimmer der Stadt", Stadt Bauwelt 36, 13/2013, 52–54, hier 53.

4 Kaye Geipel: „Zwischen ‚terasses communes' und Kampfzone Erdgeschoss", Stadt Bauwelt 36, 13/2013, 12–15, hier 12.

Remix!

Urban Entrepreneurial Responsibility

Nicole Srock.Stanley, CEO & Founder of dan pearlman Group, Berlin, outlines the need to renegotiate urban corporate social responsibilities with developers and investors in order to keep the notion of a resilient urban mix of life/work/production alive – and to strengthen it.

As architects and experts for destination development, we are regularly entrusted with inner city zone project development in Germany, as well as internationally. We advocate for the responsible planning and use of urban and public spaces: this is especially the case when investors, project developers or corporations are involved.

Value-oriented processes of give-and-take

Every form of investment needs a balanced, value-oriented process of give-and-take. The perfect mix is by definition not monocultural but diverse, both in architectural form and conceptual use. Those who leave a footprint in the city should ensure that public spaces arise through a diverse range of concepts for urban life and space and open urban cultures. An urban quarter, a neighbourhood, a whole city – these are complex systems comprised of competing needs and demands: industry and trade, co-working and co-living, manufacturing and maker labs, urban gardening and urban farming: the right balance is required in order to attract local diversity.

Developers who come to us are highly future-oriented. They seek to innovate by devising lively neighbourhoods – the perfect balance between culture, retail, housing, life and work. Integration and social aspects play an increasingly central role. Space is consciously structured in order to promote culture, but also in order to create better places for children, integrating them into the urban fabric. Increasingly, it has become imperative to plan diverse neighbourhoods together with retail concepts. This is because the old methods – the homogeneous shopping strip, for example – are no longer effective. Alongside classical developers who want to extract the maximum from every square centi-

Neu mischen!

Unternehmerische Verantwortung Stadtraum

Nicole Srock.Stanley ist Geschäftsführerin und Gründerin der dan pearlman Group in Berlin. Sie skizziert, wie die unternehmerische Verantwortung für Städte mit Projektentwickler*innen und Investor*innen neu verhandelt werden muss, um einen resilienten urbanen Mix aus Leben, Arbeit und Produktion zu fördern und zu erhalten.

Als Architekt*innen und Expert*innen für Destinationsentwicklung sind wir oftmals bereits im frühen Stadium mit zentralen innerstädtischen Projektentwicklungen in Deutschland und auch international betraut. Wir plädieren für eine verantwortungsvolle Planung und Nutzung städtischer Räume und öffentlicher Orte. Dies schließt ganz besonders einen verantwortungsbewussten Umgang mit der Nutzung der Stadt durch Investor*innen, Projektentwickler*innen oder auch Konzerne ein.

Werteorientiertes Geben und Nehmen

Entscheidend für jede Art von Investition ist ein ausgeglichenes und werteorientiertes Geben und Nehmen. Die perfekte Mischung bedeutet nicht Monokultur, sondern Diversität in der Architektur und in der konzeptionellen Nutzung. Wer in der Stadt seinen Fußabdruck hinterlässt, sollte dafür sorgen, dass öffentliche Orte sowie eine Vielfalt an städtischen Lebens- und Raumkonzepten und eine mitgestaltbare, urbane Kultur entstehen. Ein Quartier, ein Kiez oder eine ganze Stadt sind dabei ein komplexes System aus Bedürfnissen und Wünschen: Gewerbe und Handwerk, Coworking und Coliving, Manufakturen und Maker-Labs, Urban Gardening und Urban Farming: Attraktivität braucht Durchmischung.

Entwickler*innen, die zu uns kommen, sind sehr der Zukunft zugewandt. Sie wollen lebendige Quartiere, die eine schöne Durchmischung von Kultur, Retail, Wohnen, Leben und Arbeiten bieten. Integration und soziale Aspekte nehmen dabei eine immer zentralere Rolle ein. Es wird bewusst Platz eingeräumt, um Kultur zu fördern, oder aber auch, um für Kinder einen schönen Ort zu gestalten und sie zu integrieren. Immer häufiger gilt es, lebenswerte

metre, a new Zeitgeist is taking hold. The next generation is all about thinking responsibly. Increasingly, it is about creating high quality - with quarters that have a long lifetime, that age well, that are thought through from the outset and well integrated into their wider surroundings and the city itself.

All that is local creates identity

Trade has always been an essential part of urban society. Cities arose from trade centres and around marketplaces. If we are to reach an optimal mix within a city or a quarter, the criticism of the retail trade will dissolve. Often, this criticism is above all directed at the homogeneous international chains, which result in every high street becoming generic. Here, urban planners and retail developers have the challenging task of strengthening the local in particular - meaning local traders, local gastronomy and local inner-city structures. Everything that is local creates quality, uniqueness and identity.

Two defining future-oriented projects have already been realised in Barcelona and Vienna. Over a number of years, the city of Barcelona listened to its people, avoided selling out to corporations and investors, developed its neighbourhoods for the people who live there and introduced a legal instrument to slow rental increases. For the developers, it was clear that a healthy city improves the overall quality of life while deflecting stress, vandalism and criminality. A city's main task is to bring people together to live in the same space, without dealing with constant conflict. Another example is Seestadt Aspern on the outskirts of Vienna. The wonderful - and above all thoughtful - aspect of this project is the fact that the developers were able to develop a large green area, and were able to take the time to do so. To begin with, a first construction site is realised, then analysed, so that lessons can be learned. The knowledge and experience that is gained then flows into the development of the next construction site. Plans for retail are developing slowly, as this activity is dependent on the population's size and needs. At Seestadt, through cooperation between developers, the city and retail experts SES Spar European Shopping Centres, the first managed shopping strip will be developed. First, the foundation will be set up: a grocery, a chemist. Then perhaps a small bookshop pops up that is run as a local

Quartiere und Retail-Angebote zu schaffen, weil die alte Methodik der beispielsweise immer gleich wirkenden Einkaufsstraßen nicht mehr greift. Neben ganz klassischen Entwickler*innen, die aus jedem Quadratzentimeter etwas herausholen wollen, hält ein neuer Zeitgeist Einzug. Eine jüngere Generation ist in der Verantwortung. Es geht zunehmend darum, eine hohe Qualität zu schaffen, die lange Bestand hat, die gut altert, die im Vorfeld gut durchdacht und stark mit dem Umfeld und der Stadt vernetzt ist.

Alles Lokale schafft Identität

Der Handel war schon immer ein essenzieller Teil der städtischen Gemeinschaft. Städte sind erst aus Handelszentren und rund um Marktplätze gewachsen. Wenn wir diesen optimalen Mix innerhalb einer Stadt oder eines Quartiers erreichen, wird auch die Kritik am Handel schwinden. Oftmals richtet sich die Kritik vor allem gegen die immer gleichen internationalen Handelsketten, die jede High Street gleich erscheinen lassen. Hier haben Stadtplaner*innen und Retail-Entwickler*innen die herausfordernde Aufgabe, insbesondere das Lokale zu stärken, also lokale Händler*innen, lokale Gastronomie und lokale innerstädtische Strukturen. Alles Lokale schafft Qualität und Einzigartigkeit.

Zwei tolle und sehr zukunftsorientierte Projekte werden bereits in Barcelona und in Wien umgesetzt. Die Stadt Barcelona hat über Jahre hinweg ihre Bewohner*innen befragt, um den Ausverkauf an die Corporates und Investor*innen dieser Welt zu vermeiden und für ihre Bevölkerung Quartiere ganz behutsam weiterzuentwickeln. Es wurde auch eine Mietbremse mit betrachtet. Für die Entwickler*innen ist ganz klar, dass eine gesunde Stadt, eine gesunde Mischung und ein gesundes Umfeld eine höhere Lebensqualität bedingen und viel Stress, Vandalismus und Kriminalität aus einer Stadt heraushalten. Es ist ihre fundamentale Aufgabe, die Menschen zusammenzuführen und sie zusammenleben zu lassen, ohne dass ständig überall Konflikte entstehen. Ein weiteres Beispiel ist die Seestadt Aspern am Stadtrand Wiens: Das Schöne und vor allem sehr Umsichtige an diesem Projekt ist, dass die Entwickler*innen ein sehr großes Areal auf der grünen Wiese entwickeln dürfen und sich dafür viel Zeit nehmen. Zu Beginn wird ein Baufeld realisiert, danach wird es analysiert und daraus gelernt. Die gewonnenen Erkenntnisse und Erfahrungen fließen im Anschluss in die Entwicklung des nächsten Baufeldes ein. Auch der Retail entwickelt

cultural co-op. Once the fundamental needs are met, new themes rise beyond the horizon, such as small shops or boutiques. The planners feel responsible for retail tenants. In Aspern, the overall concept remains central to planning decisions, in order to avoid a constant turnover in renters and to establish a feeling of stability and security.

Mixing up the world with exciting formats

If the city and municipality itself carry out urban development, this can create a fantastic foundation that is extremely contemporary. A municipality should not only plan projects for the next five years, but it should plan for the long term; for example, in Aspern, the masterplan is set to a course of 30 years. This builds a healthy foundation that encourages planners to avoid short-term, profit-oriented solutions when they are addressing architectural and planning concerns. I am convinced that this is a development to be welcomed and encouraged.

We need a stronger, integrative approach that involves all stakeholders. We should invite all citizens to participate: both adults and children. With ownership comes responsibility - property brings with it not only economic responsibilities but also the inclusion of social and cultural compatibility within urban development. A city must be able to unfold in line with sustainable development and a heterogeneous mix in order to remain liveable. We need to define the rules of the game, and we can do this through politics. Our task is to introduce strategic change for project developers and companies, and to mix up their world with new, enticing, alternative formats.

sich langsam und ist auf die Zahl der Bevölkerung und ihre Bedürfnisse zugeschnitten. In der Seestadt wird die erste gemanagte Einkaufsstraße dieser Art entwickelt, in einer Kooperation zwischen Entwickler*innen, Stadt und dem Retail-Experten SES Spar European Shopping Centers. Zuerst schafft man die Grundstruktur, zum Beispiel für Lebensmittel und Drogerie. Dann entsteht etwa ein kleiner Bücherladen, der wie ein Kiezkulturladen funktioniert. Erst wenn diese Grundbedürfnisse erfüllt sind, kommen Themen dazu, die außerhalb der Grundbedürfnisse liegen, wie zum Beispiel kleine Läden oder Boutiquen. Die Planung fühlt sich verantwortlich für die Retail-Mieter*innen. In Aspern wird sehr partnerschaftlich am Gesamtkonzept gearbeitet, um einen ständigen Mieter*innenwechsel zu vermeiden.

Die Welt mit spannenden Formaten aufmischen

Wenn die Stadt beziehungsweise die Kommune die Stadtentwicklung selbst trägt, dann ist das eine fantastische Grundlage und extrem zeitgemäß. Eine Kommune muss Projekte nicht nur fünf Jahre im Portfolio halten, sondern langfristig planen. In Aspern, zum Beispiel, ist der Masterplan auf zirka dreißig Jahre angelegt. Das ist einfach extrem gesund und führt dazu, sich nicht von kurzfristigen Schachzügen verführen zu lassen, die eben nur renditeoptimiert sind – in der Architektur, der Planung, der Nutzung von Flächen. Ich finde, das ist eine wünschenswerte Entwicklung.

Wir brauchen einen stärkeren integrativen Ansatz unter Einbeziehung aller Stakeholder. Wir müssen nicht nur die erwachsenen Bürger*innen der Stadt zur Teilhabe einladen, sondern auch ihre Kinder. Eigentum verpflichtet und braucht sowohl eine Übernahme der wirtschaftlichen Verantwortung als auch einen Einbezug der sozialen und kulturellen Verträglichkeit innerhalb der städtischen Entwicklung. Eine Stadt muss im Sinne einer nachhaltigen Entwicklung und einer guten Durchmischung agieren, um lebenswert zu sein und zu bleiben. Das ist der Punkt, in dem die Politik gefordert ist, Spielregeln zu definieren. Unsere Aufgabe ist es, einen strategischen Wandel bei Projektentwickler*innen und Unternehmen selbst herbeizuführen und deren Welt mit spannenden Formaten „aufzumischen".

-> Case Study 03 pp. 200 ff. Seestadt Aspern

The Baupiloten's Visions-for-the-School game is an enabling tool for fluid concepts of education

Das Schul-Visionen-Spiel von die Baupiloten: Ein Ermöglichungsformat für wandelbare Schulkonzepte

Architecture as Teacher?

Learning from the Berlin School Offensive

In the coming years, Berlin will need over 60 new schools, for which 5.5 billion euros have been allocated. A specialised working group – consisting of educators, planners and representatives from parent groups, schools, municipalities and associations – is currently consolidating their recommendations in a final report for the Senate's administration for schools. Susanne Hofmann, a member of the group Baupiloten, is involved as an architecture specialist together with president of the Berlin Chamber of Architects, Christine Edmaier. Aside from new pedagogical concepts, an emphasis is being placed on broadening participation and situating schools in urban space. These two experts reflect on what the schools of tomorrow can achieve, and on whether the current expansion plan in Berlin will provide the conceptual freedom necessary for the new schools.

Susanne Hofmann: I'm convinced that one needs conceptual planning space in order for unexpected urban landscapes, innovative school models and building typologies to form. The question that occupies us at the moment, not just socially, but also long term with respect to primary schools, the secondary and final school years, is how the learning landscapes of tomorrow might develop. The Hellerup School by Arkitema Architects in Denmark offers an exemplary model: an open school with no need for classrooms. Those classrooms that were deemed necessary were built only after the school opened. Working together with a primary school, we also established that the first grade still needs its own, sheltered space, but that having reached the fourth grade, students are better at independent learning when they are placed in an open school environment. Our working group developed a pedagogically valuable model. However, it's only appropriate for one type of learning, mediation and teaching. An inflexible model offers neither the pedagogical nor the physically free spaces that constitute a good school. This needs an urgent rethink!

Christine Edmaier: I couldn't agree more. No matter how ambitious the specialist working group was, it was clear from the very beginning what was going to come out of the pro-

Architektur als Pädagogin?

Von der Berliner Schulbauoffensive lernen

Berlin benötigt in den nächsten Jahren über sechzig neue Schulen, für die 5,5 Milliarden Euro bereitstehen. Eine Facharbeitsgruppe aus Pädagog*innen, Planer*innen, Eltern- und Schüler*innenvertretungen, Bezirken und Verbänden formulierte im Auftrag der Schulverwaltung ihre Empfehlungen in einem Abschlussbericht. Als Expertinnen für Architektur waren Susanne Hofmann von den Baupiloten und Christine Edmaier, Präsidentin der Architektenkammer Berlin, eingebunden. Neben neuen pädagogischen Konzepten ging es ihnen um mehr Partizipation und Öffnung in den Stadtraum. Was die Schule von morgen leisten muss und ob die laufende Schulbauoffensive ihr dazu den nötigen Freiraum gibt, reflektieren die beiden in einem Gespräch. Eine Positionierung.

Susanne Hofmann: Ich bin überzeugt davon, dass innovative Schulmodelle oder auch Schulbautypologien planerische Freiräume brauchen, damit sich auch unerwartete Lernlandschaften herausbilden. Die Frage, mit der wir uns gerade sehr beschäftigen, ist, wie sich die Lernlandschaften jetzt nicht nur gesellschaftlich, sondern auch langfristig entwickeln – von der Grundschule über die Sekundarschule bis hin zum Gymnasium. Die Schule in Hellerup in Dänemark von Arkitema Architects ist beispielgebend: eine offene Schule, die ganz ohne Schulräume auskommt. Klassenräume, die fehlten, wurden erst ergänzt, nachdem die Schule in Betrieb ging. Wir haben in einem Partizipationsprozess mit einer Grundschule herausgearbeitet, dass die erste Klasse noch geschützte Räume braucht, zur vierten hin bereiten offene Lernlandschaften Schülerinnen und Schüler schon besser auf eigenständiges Lernen vor. In unserer Facharbeitsgruppe wurde zwar ein pädagogisch wertvolles Modell entwickelt, das sich aber nur für eine einzige Art des Lernens, des Vermittelns und des Lehrens eignet. Ein solches starres Modell bietet weder die notwendigen pädagogischen noch planerischen Freiräume, die eine gute Schule braucht. Das muss zwingend überdacht werden!

Christine Edmaier: Da kann ich nur zustimmen. So ambitioniert die Facharbeitsgruppe auch war, stand doch von Anfang an fest, was herauskommen würde: das sogenannte Berliner Teamhaus, in dem sich um ein zentrales „Forum" die Räume für allgemeine

High-quality modularity: European School Frankfurt am Main by NKBAK Architects

Modulbau geht auch anders: Europäische Schule in Frankfurt am Main von NKBAK Architekten

ject: the so-called Berlin team house model, in which spaces for general learning and teaching areas are arranged around a central forum-type space. Again and again, we said that experimental school formats should be possible and that schools should be able to decide for themselves what model they would like to work with. The Hamburg model is, in my opinion, far more flexible. A square metre value per child is fixed, but the school itself decides how exactly this area is to be deployed and used. In the Berlin approach, this flexibility is not really taken into account. Schools defined around corridor spaces are outdated, and instead we have the forum-type school. How this looks is already pre-determined by the Senate, right through to the smallest detail: the size and dimensions of each and every room. In this case, it was also particularly important to pay attention to modular schools as a potential model. I venture to question whether this was really the aim of the working group – instead, a new model was simply imposed on the old one. Now there are fixed standards for school-build-

Lern- und Unterrichtsbereiche anordnen. Wir haben immer gesagt, dass Experimente und verschiedene Schulformen möglich sein sollten und Schulen selbst entscheiden können müssen, nach welchem Modell sie bauen. Die Hamburger Vorgangsweise ist meines Erachtens hier flexibler: Pro Schulkind wird ein bestimmter Quadratmetersatz vorgesehen, und die Schule entscheidet selbst, wie sie diese Fläche nutzt. Das ist im Berliner Ansatz überhaupt nicht berücksichtigt! Die Flurschule hat ausgedient, stattdessen haben wir jetzt die Forumschule. Und wie diese auszusehen hat, ist von der Senatsverwaltung bis ins kleinste Detail festgelegt worden: alle Standards, alle Raumgrößen. In diesem Fall ist es tatsächlich sehr naheliegend, Modulschulen als Baumöglichkeit in Betracht zu ziehen. Ob das jedoch wirklich das Ziel der Facharbeitsgruppe war, das wage ich zu bezweifeln. Es wurde einfach nur ein neues Modell an das alte gesetzt. Jetzt gibt es diese festgelegten Schulbaustandards, die sich wie die Baubeschreibung für einen Generalunternehmer lesen. Das führt dazu, dass die Hauptarbeit der Architekt*innen darin besteht, Begründungen für

ing that read like building instructions for a contractor. That means the main work for architects will be in justifying the exceptions to these predetermined standards. In order to generate some extent of architectural diversity, every exception will have to be substantiated. Where is the experimentation in that?

SH: The other aspect that has been completely overlooked is the degree to which a school is open to socio-spatial processes. Today's schools are taking on completely new societal responsibilities. If we want to talk of life-long learning, we should work together to find synergies between schools and neighbourhoods: for example, homes for the elderly that can work together with schools to offer extra tuition or reading. Everyone profits from that! An intensive exchange with the local neighbourhood could generate new site-specific situations. Berlin is different from Munich. It's possible to generate other synergies. I'm convinced that such hybrids would also help to cut costs.

CE: The examples that you mention could also be realised in a modular school. But both urban development and the significance of schools in building and architecture circles cannot be left out of the picture. Schools shouldn't be mono-functional points in the city, buildings that are desolate and empty in the evenings. What we need are hybrids that are integrated into neighbourhoods. I would even go further and suggest combining school buildings with housing. Unfortunately, the current planning of new schools in Berlin prevents these new typologies. As soon as a school is built on a fenced-off property as an isolated implant, it becomes difficult to integrate it into urban space at a later stage.

SH: This is incredibly important: the school of the future must be a cultural and social meeting-place that facilitates differentiated learning processes, brings together diverse groups of people and encourages community.

CE: This requires good school management, not just good facility management. That is, people who feel responsible for the school as an entire organism. Not everything can be solved with architecture. New typologies are just the beginning. An interesting example is Campus Rütli in Neukölln. A school, a kindergarten, a youth centre, a health service centre and a new neighbourhood centre have been brought together – spatially and managerially. The school realised a number of our recommendations. Its special

die Ausnahmen von diesen Standards durchzusetzen. Um ansatzweise architektonische Vielfalt zu ermöglichen, braucht es überall Begründungen. Wo ist da das Experiment geblieben?

SH: Total übersehen wurde auch die sozialräumliche Öffnung einer Schule. Die Schule übernimmt heutzutage ganz neue Formen der gesellschaftlichen Verantwortung. Wir sprechen von lebenslangem Lernen und sollten gemeinsam Synergien finden, wie sich Schule und Quartier gegenseitig ergänzen können: zum Beispiel Altenheime, die mit Schulen zusammenarbeiten und Lesepaten oder Nachhilfe stellen. Davon profitieren alle! Bei einer intensiveren Auseinandersetzung mit dem Quartier können ortsspezifische Szenarien entstehen. Berlin funktioniert anders als München, es lassen sich andere Synergien entwickeln. Ich bin überzeugt, dass solche Hybride sogar Einsparpotenzial bergen.

CE: Die Beispiele, die du nennst, ließen sich auch in einer Modulschule umsetzen. Aber sowohl der Städtebau als auch die baukulturelle Bedeutung der Schule dürfen nicht außer Acht gelassen werden. Schulen sollten nicht diese monofunktionalen Punkte in der Stadt sein, wo abends keiner vorbeigehen will, weil alles leer und zu ist. Was wir brauchen, sind Hybride, die ins Quartier integriert sind. Ich würde sogar weitergehen und vorschlagen, Wohnungsbau mit Schulbau zu kombinieren. Leider verhindert die aktuelle Schulbauoffensive in Berlin solche neuen Typologien, und wenn eine Schule erst einmal auf einem eingezäunten Grundstück als isoliertes Implantat gebaut ist, ist es schwierig, sie später in den Stadtraum zu integrieren.

SH: Das ist enorm wichtig: Die Schule der Zukunft muss ein kultureller und sozialer Treffpunkt werden, der differenziertes Lernen ermöglicht, unterschiedlichste Leute zusammenbringt und die Gemeinschaft fördert.

CE: Dafür braucht es ein gutes Schulmanagement, nicht nur gute Hausmeister*innen. Personen, die sich für die Schule als Gesamtkonglomerat verantwortlich fühlen. Nicht alles ist über Architektur lösbar. Neue Typologien sind nur der Anfang. Ein interessantes Beispiel ist der Campus Rütli in Neukölln. Auf unvorhergesehene Weise sind hier Schule, Kitas, Jugendfreizeitheim, Gesundheitsdienst, eine Berufswerkstatt und ein neues Stadtteilzentrum miteinander räumlich und organisatorisch zusammengekommen. Die Schule hat viele unserer Forderungen umgesetzt. Die besondere Situation als ehemalige „Problemschule" hat dieses neue Konzept möglich gemacht. Leider braucht es immer erst einen Anlass, um bürokratische Stereotype zu überwinden. Des-

situation as a former so-called problem school made it possible for us to try out new concepts. Unfortunately, it always seems a crisis situation is necessary before bureaucratic stereotypes can be overcome. That's why it is my hope that we can free ourselves from this bureaucratic monster to which we, as part of the working group, have also contributed. We have to be open to exceptions! That could also include modular building typologies. Basic facilities can be expanded upon by the school itself according to its individual needs. In this way, every location can develop its particular qualities and identity.

SH: Modular building typologies offer a great deal of potential. This has been proven, for example, by NKBAK Architects in their modular timber construction design for a preschool and primary school in Frankfurt am Main. I foresee the possibility that flexible modules for classrooms, sanitary facilities and differentiated spaces can be combined according to the wishes of the school community. In this way, the school becomes a special place with open zones, and firmly embedded in the urban environment. Pupils, parents and the teaching body are happy when they can identify with their school. This is an appeal to society: be accountable to the environment! The population should be able to formulate its own wishes and visions, providing a basis upon which architecture can work. A great example of this is C.F. Møller Architects from Denmark: they carefully consider how the school is likely to develop and how it might be skilfully integrated into the local context.
We need more participation in order to develop our shared dreams and visions together. Schools cannot be led as if they were bureaucratic companies. A school as an organism can solve countless questions for the city. This must be recognised - on an administrative and a political level!

CE: Precisely. For that reason, I call for leaving space for exceptions and experimentation in tenders for new school buildings! And, an appeal to architects - that they continue to find ways to bypass meaningless construction specifications.

This conversation was led by Lukas Staudinger.

halb hoffe ich, dass wir uns von diesem bürokratischen Monster, das wir in der Facharbeitsgruppe auch selbst mit geschaffen haben, wieder befreien. Wir müssen Ausnahmen zulassen! Das können grundsätzlich auch Typenbauten in Modulbauweise leisten. Eine auf ein Minimum reduzierte Basisausstattung könnten die Schulen nach eigenem Bedarf ausbauen. Dadurch bekommt jeder Standort ein eigenes Gesicht und seine Identität.

SH: Dass Modulbau großes Potenzial birgt, haben zum Beispiel NKBAK Architekten in ihrem modularen Holzbauentwurf für eine Vor- und Primarschule in Frankfurt am Main bewiesen. Ich sehe auch folgende Chance: Flexible Module für Klassenräume, Sanitäreinheiten und Differenzierungsräume können nach den Vorstellungen der Schulgemeinschaft miteinander kombiniert werden. So entsteht ein besonderer Ort mit Freiraum und Bezug zum Stadtraum. Schulkinder, Eltern und der Lehrkörper sind froh, wenn sie sich mit ihrer Schule identifizieren können. Ich appelliere an die Gesellschaft, Umweltgerechtigkeit herzustellen! Die Bevölkerung sollte ihre Wunschvorstellungen und Visionen formulieren können, auf deren Basis die Architektur dann gestalten kann. Ein gutes Vorbild sind C.F. Møller Architects aus Dänemark: Sie überlegen sich genau, wie sich die Schule entwickeln wird und wie sie sich geschickt in einen Ort integrieren lässt.
Wir benötigen mehr Partizipation, um gemeinsam Träume und Visionen zu entwickeln. Schule darf nicht als bürokratisches Unternehmen geführt werden. Der Organismus Schule kann ganz viele Probleme für die Stadt lösen. Das müssen unsere Verwaltungen wie auch die Politik endlich verinnerlichen!

CE: Das sehe ich genauso. Daher meine Forderung: Ausnahme- und Experimentierklauseln in Wettbewerbsausschreibungen für Schulbauten! Und ein Appell an die Architekturschaffenden, sich über sinnentleerte Vorgaben hinwegzusetzen.

Das Gespräch führte Lukas Staudinger.

Façade structure and insect hotel: Tiunda School by C.F. Møller Architects, Sweden

Fassadenstruktur und Insektenhotel: Schule in Tiunda von C.F. Møller Architects, Schweden

Fluid spaces for fluid curricula make the classroom redundant: Hellerup School by Arkitema Architects

Fließende Unterrichtsräume für sich wandelnde Lehrmethoden: Schule in Hellerup von Arkitema Architects

Extended learning rooms: Arndt-Gymnasium in Berlin-Dahlem, with access zones as squares and alleys

Erweiterte Lernräume: Arndt-Gymnasium in Berlin-Dahlem mit Erschließungszonen als Plätze und Gassen

Harbour, Playground, Zoo

The School as City Space

Anja Fröhlich is an architect and professor of architecture and planning in Lausanne. Together with Martin Fröhlich, she heads up the Atelier EAST (Laboratory of Elementary Architecture and Studies of Types). In her working practice at AFF Architekten, she calls for a more playful mode of dealing with the school building typology. Instead of imposing standardised classroom modules for pre-existing schools in rapidly growing cities, their work proposes the development of hybrids in urban contexts, which connect to a different understanding of learning and teaching. Schools in the zoo, on the water, in a public bus ... Even Jean-Jacques Rousseau wrote, in his pedagogical treatise, of the importance of the role of play in teaching. Connecting hybrids: a call to architects and municipalities.

The school's role in education consists of teaching and supervising, conveying knowledge and passing on societal values - such as environmentalism or a sense of responsibility for future generations. In his pedagogical treatise of 1762, Émile ou de l'éducation, educator and philosopher Jean-Jacques Rousseau proposed that we are formed by three teachers: (1) nature: which allows us to develop skills and strengths; (2) people: who teach us how to apply skills and strengths; and (3) things: which teach us insofar as they facilitate experiences and opinions. Nature is a scarce resource in the city, and we need to be attentive to its urban qualities and in particular to the capacity of its complex structure - composed of various spatially dense or even overlapping fragments - to enrich us by teaching us. Urban textures facilitate social interactions and at the same time enable the expansion of spaces for teaching and learning. The city has the potential to become a laboratory through which new typologies might be developed, recombining the resources at hand and opening the possibility of a different understanding of learning in - and with - the urban environment.

A decisive element in every school design is the questioning of linkages between uses. Classic corridors become spaces for communication, whilst shared sanitary facilities can lead to a questioning of gender neutrality. We aim to provoke

Hafen, Spielplatz, Zoo

Die Schule als Stadtraum

Anja Fröhlich ist Architektin und Professorin für Architektur und Entwurf in Lausanne. Dort leitet sie gemeinsam mit Martin Fröhlich das Atelier EAST am Institut für Architektur und Stadt. Die Brücke zur praktischen Tätigkeit schlägt sie im Team von AFF Architekten und fordert einen lustvolleren Umgang mit der Typologie Schule. Statt in den wachsenden Städten Klassenraummodule monoton vor bestehende Schulen zu stapeln, wäre es sinnvoller, im städtischen Kontext Hybride zu schaffen, die eine andere Auffassung von Lernen und Lehren anstoßen. Schule im Zoo, auf dem Wasser, im Bus. Schon Jean-Jacques Rousseau hat in seinem pädagogischen Hauptwerk den umgebenden Dingen eine lehrende Rolle zugesprochen. Hybride verbinden. Ein Aufruf an Architekturschaffende und Verwaltungen.

Der Bildungsauftrag der Schule besteht weitestgehend im Lehren und Betreuen, also in der Vermittlung von Wissen und der Weitergabe gesellschaftlicher Werte wie Umweltschutz oder Verantwortung für zukünftige Generationen. Der Pädagoge und Schriftsteller Jean-Jacques Rousseau legte 1762 in seinem pädagogischen Hauptwerk „Émile ou De l'éducation" dar, dass wir von drei Lehrenden geprägt werden: 1. der Natur: Sie entwickelt Fähigkeiten und Kräfte, 2. den Menschen: Sie lehren den Gebrauch der Fähigkeiten und Kräfte, und 3. den Dingen: Sie lehren uns, indem sie Erfahrung und Anschauung ermöglichen. Da die Natur in der Stadt eine knappe Ressource darstellt, müssten wir ihre urbanen Qualitäten in den Blick nehmen und die komplexe Struktur aus unterschiedlichen, räumlich unmittelbar benachbarten oder sogar räumlich überlagerten Fragmenten nach ihrem lehrenden Reichtum befragen. Städtische Texturen ermöglichen soziale Interaktionen und zugleich die funktionale Ergänzung von Lern- und Lehrräumen. Die Stadt hat das Potenzial zum Labor, um neue Typologien zu entwickeln, vorhandene Ressourcen neu zu kombinieren und damit eine andere Auffassung vom Lernen in und mit dem urbanen Umfeld anzustoßen.

Entwurfsbestimmendes Element jedes unserer Schulaufträge ist das Hinterfragen von Nutzungsverknüpfungen. So öffnen sich klassische Flure zu Kommunikationsräumen, und Sanitärbereiche lo-

a way of thinking that considers the school not as an introverted space but as a site that might be rethought and meaningfully integrated into an urban context and vice versa. The urban is a field in which the school can rediscover itself.

Schools as hybrids: welcome to a period of reorientation

In today's age, dominated by norms and policies, the investigation of new school construction methods needs to become more radical. That is why we ask: why are schools never constructed together with other public buildings, as hybrids? The library as a reservoir of knowledge, or the museum as the site where history is maintained and presented, or recycling centres, where waste and resources are processed - all of these could be places to make a useful contribution to existing teaching content. A symbiosis with a zoo or wildlife park and its green spaces is also possible, connecting schools with nature. A school in a zoo would not require an additional canteen; restaurants in zoos experience peak use on the weekend and holidays, meaning that they could easily feed students during the week. Classic laboratories for cooking, biology, physics, craft and chemistry could be connected to animal nutrition, research and care - and also be offered to weekend visitors. A school's thematic focus could help create a local identity that, in a period of reorientation, would be more than welcome.

School barges and travelling specialist spaces

Neighbourhoods are always subject to fluctuations in diverging demographics. How might an open, lively city address this problematic? Berlin consists of up to 6.7 percent water. Why aren't there any school boats moving through the city? Space and mooring docks are available, and projects such as the Badeschiff and the Floating University have revealed new possibilities in Berlin.[1]

1 The Badeschiff is a floating swimming pool at the banks of the Spree River; the Floating University was a temporary school in an inner city rainwater basin in the Kreuzberg district of Berlin. Constructed by raumlabor in collaboration with students, it was a laboratory for experimental building.

ten die Genderneutralität aus. Wir wollen jedoch anregen, das Thema Schule nicht ausschließlich introvertiert zu betrachten, sondern im städtischen Kontext neu zu denken und das Außen sinnvoll einzubinden. Die Stadt ist ein Feld, auf dem sich Schule neu erfinden lässt.

Schule als Hybrid: In einer Zeit der Orientierungssuche mehr als willkommen

Das Ausloten neuer Wege für den Schulbau kann in dieser von Normen und Richtlinien dominierten Zeit nicht radikal genug ansetzen. Deshalb fragen wir uns: Warum werden Schulen nicht in Verbindung mit anderen öffentlichen Gebäuden als Hybride gebaut? Die Bibliothek beispielsweise als Wissensspeicher oder das Museum als Ort der Aufbewahrung und Präsentation von Zeugnissen oder die Wertstoffhöfe als Umschlagplatz für Abfall und Ressourcen scheinen eine durchaus sinnvolle Ergänzung zu den bestehenden Lehrinhalten zu sein. Auch eine Symbiose mit dem Zoo oder Tierpark und ihren Grünräumen wäre denkbar, um Schule mit Natur zu verbinden. Eine Schule im Zoo würde auch keine zusätzliche Mensa benötigen. Weil die Gastronomie eines Tierparks ihre Nutzungsspitzen vorwiegend am Wochenende und in den Ferien hat, könnte sie die Essensversorgung an Wochentagen problemlos übernehmen. Klassische Labore für Kochen, Biologie, Physik, Handwerk, Chemie ließen sich mit Tierhaltung, Tierforschung und Tierpflege verbinden und den Wochenendbesuchern als zusätzliches Angebot zur Verfügung stellen. Die gezielte thematische Ausrichtung der Schule würde Identität stiften, die in einer Zeit der Orientierungssuche mehr als willkommen ist.

Schulkähne und fahrende Fachräume

Städtische Quartiere unterliegen immer einem Wandel divergenter Alterspyramiden. Wie könnte eine aufgeschlossene und lebendige Stadt auf diese Problematik reagieren? Berlin besteht zu 6,7 Prozent aus Wasserfläche. Warum existieren keine Schulschiffe, die sich durch die Stadt bewegen? Flächen und Anlegepunkte gibt es hinreichend und Projekte wie das Badeschiff und die Floating Univer-

Even Le Corbusier was able to prove this in 1929, when rebuilding a coal barge into accommodation for asylum seekers. We should also ask ourselves why the potential of the one hundred Citaro buses, which the Berlin transport infrastructure is phasing out in the near future, shouldn't be used to build mobile specialist spaces? Already in 1925, the first Migros shopping trucks arrived in Zurich, becoming a part of the identity of the Swiss region. This wouldn't just be a homage to the good old mobile library: in densifying urban contexts, the buses could convey rotating content to various places. Both approaches challenge us to unify the concepts of school and mobility together – turning ships and buses into a pedagogical advantage.

Emergency building programme? Classrooms and imposed standardisation

The Berlin Senate is searching for solutions in the face of growing demand for space in the educational sector. So far, their answers include a ten-year building and renovation plan for schools and an emergency building programme for dozens of modular buildings to expand facilities. In the past three years, approximately 380 standardised classrooms were imposed on existing schools. It remains to be seen whether an overly regulated corset of norms and guidelines is capable of answering these urgent questions related to value compatibility, sustainability and societal participation. However, it is clear that this approach does not question the way we deal with growing population structures. Nor does it consider the relevance of the school as the cornerstone of the urban fabric. But this is exactly what should be done!

sity[1] haben auch eigene Berliner Wege aufgezeigt. Dass diese Art von Lösung sinnvoll ist, hat schließlich schon Le Corbusier 1929 mit dem Umbau eines Kohlekahns als Asylunterkunft für die Heilsarmee bewiesen. Außerdem fragen wir uns, warum eigentlich das Potenzial der hundert Citaro-Busse, die von den Berliner Verkehrsbetrieben (BVG) in nächster Zeit ausgemustert werden sollen, nicht in Betracht gezogen wird, um mobile Fachräume zu bauen. Bereits 1925 trafen die ersten Verkaufslastwagen der Migros in Zürich den Zeitgeist und zählten mit ihren bewährten Haltepunkten kurzerhand zum Ortsbild in den Schweizer Regionen. Es wäre nicht nur eine Hommage an die gute alte Fahrbibliothek. Die Busse könnten im dichten städtischen Kontext an unterschiedlichen Orten wechselnde Inhalte vermitteln. Beide Ansätze fordern uns auf, Schule und Mobilität zusammenzudenken und aus Schiffen und Bussen einen pädagogischen Gewinn zu ziehen.

Notbauprogramm? Klassenräume monoton gestapelt

Der Berliner Senat sucht nach Lösungen gegen die Raumnot im Bildungsbereich. Antworten sind eine auf zehn Jahre angelegte Schulbau- und Sanierungsoffensive sowie ein Notbauprogramm für Dutzende modulare Ergänzungsbauten. In den letzten drei Jahren wurden etwa 380 Klassenräume monoton neben vorhandene Schulen gestapelt. Ob mit einem überregulierten Korsett aus Normen und Richtlinien die dringenden Fragen nach Wertestabilität, Nachhaltigkeit und gemeinschaftlicher Partizipation beantwortet werden, wird sich sicher erst nach Abschluss herausstellen. Eines ist jedoch jetzt schon klar: Es geht dabei nicht um das Hinterfragen des Umgangs mit wachsenden Bevölkerungsstrukturen und schon gar nicht um die Relevanz der Schule als Baustein im städtischen Gefüge. Aber genau das sollte es!

1 Das Badeschiff ist eine schwimmende Badekonstruktion am Ufer der Spree; die Floating University ist ein temporärer Bau in einem innerstädtischen Regenrückhaltebecken – ein Labor für kollektives, experimentelles Lernen.

Architecture creates identity: Ludwig Hoffman School in Berlin-Friedrichshain

Die Architektur schafft Identität: Ludwig-Hoffmann-Grundschule in Berlin-Friedrichshain

"Family, friends and schools are important identifiers in the development of a young person. Architecture should also make a rich contribution to this. It should create nuanced opportunities for spatial occupation by the teachers and the pupils."

„Familie, Freunde und Schule sind wichtige Identifikationspunkte im Prozess des Heranwachsens eines jungen Menschen. Auch die Architektur sollte dazu einen vielfältigen Beitrag leisten. Sie sollte in ihrer räumlichen Organisation differenzierte Angebote zur Inbesitznahme durch die Lehrer*innen und Schüler*innen anbieten."

AFF Architekten

Norms at the limit: common washrooms for pupils and teachers as places of communication and social negotiation

Normen ausgereizt: Gemeinsame Waschräume für Schüler*innen und Lehrpersonal als Orte der Kommunikation und sozialen Verhandlung

VIELE GRÜSSE AUS MEINER NEUEN SCHULE
Mir
gefalen die Grosen Waschbecken
Max
23.02.2012

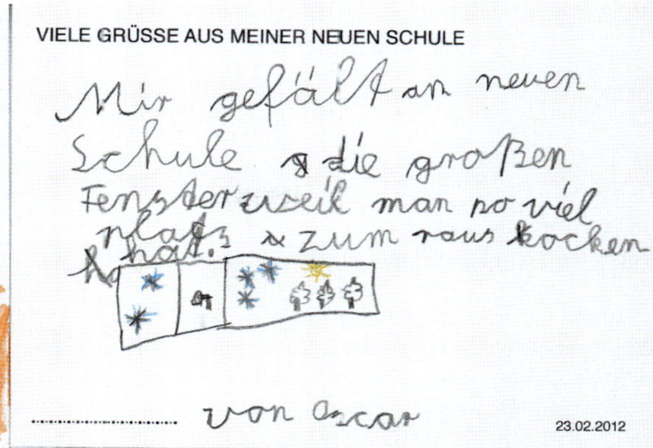
VIELE GRÜSSE AUS MEINER NEUEN SCHULE
Mir gefält an neuen Schule die großen Fenster weil man so viel platz hat. zum raus kocken
von Oscar
23.02.2012

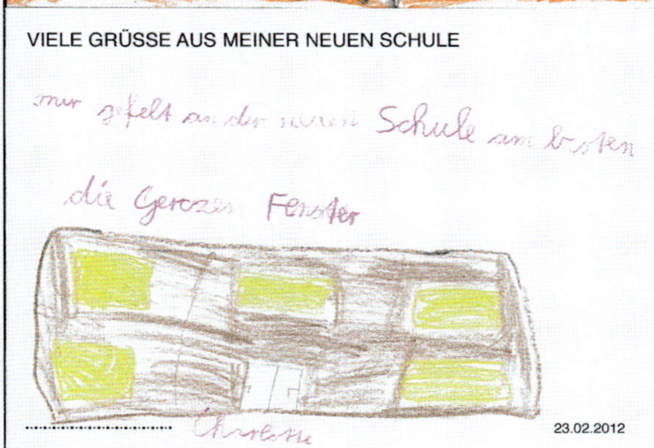
VIELE GRÜSSE AUS MEINER NEUEN SCHULE
mir gefelt an der neuen Schule am besten die Gerozen Fenster
Christie
23.02.2012

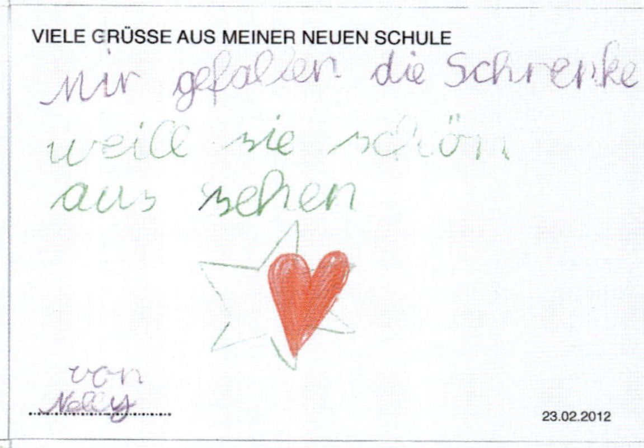
VIELE GRÜSSE AUS MEINER NEUEN SCHULE
Mir gefallen die Schrenke weille sie schön aus sehen
von Nelly
23.02.2012

VIELE GRÜSSE AUS MEINER NEUEN SCHULE
Mir gefällt der Klassenraum weil er so schön weisist.
Lyn
23.02.2012

VIELE GRÜSSE AUS MEINER NEUEN SCHULE
Meine Schule gefät mir weil wir so schöne große Waschbäcken haben.
Lea
23.02.2012

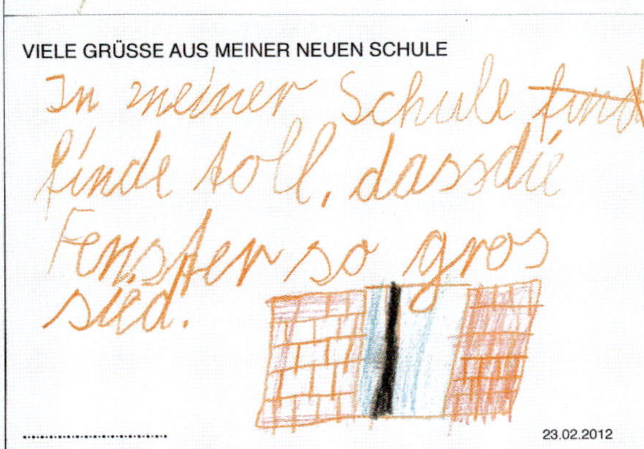
VIELE GRÜSSE AUS MEINER NEUEN SCHULE
In meiner Schule finde toll, dassdie Fenster so gros sied.
23.02.2012

VIELE GRÜSSE AUS MEINER NEUEN SCHULE
Meine Schule Gefällt mir das die Fenster so groß sind.
Annelie
23.02.2012

01. Nordic Schools

Project: Syvälahti Education Centre / New Sauland School
City: Turku, Finnland / Hjartdal, Norway
Client: City of Turku, Finland / Hjartdal commune, Norway
Planning: Verstas Arkkitehdit / Helen & Hard with PPAG
Status: Both completed August 2018

Planning Learning
School Typologies in Scandinavia

The Nordic education system has garnered international interest for its unparalleled success in staying atop European school rankings for almost two decades. Two new schools - one in Turku, Finland, and one in Hjartdal, Norway - show us that the Nordic system is not content to rely upon proven pedagogical methods alone and is, in addition, using design to foster active learning. Two examples show the capacity of innovative school typologies to adapt to changing societal conditions.

In August 2018, Verstas' Syvälahti education centre opened. A multipurpose building, it combines the functions of a school and a day-care centre, a public library and a home for young people. The organisation of learning spaces follows Finland's curriculum guidelines, with spaces designed as flexible, open clusters around central learning squares. Spaces are used in different ways, depending on the subject and the size of the group of students. All squares are closely connected to the more public areas, which can also be used as learning spaces if needed.

Similarly, the Norwegian community of Sauland built a new school building with Helen & Hard / PPAG. Together with an existing administration building and elementary school, the new school surrounds the schoolyard and playground, with each educational space having a visual relationship to the central learning space and the exterior landscape. The Norwegian approach means that here, too, work and free learning are possible. And like Syvälahti, room areas can be expanded or contracted. These permanently impermanent spaces create amplified zones of learning, design, communication and social exchange. The uninterrupted spatial concept for modern education clusters creates a pattern of educational spaces arrayed around a shared learning landscape without boundaries.

Lernen planen
Schultypen in Skandinavien

Das skandinavische Bildungssystem erregt internationales Interesse, da es seit beinahe zwei Jahrzehnten an der Spitze europäischer Schulvergleiche steht. Zwei neue Schulen – eine in Turku, Finnland, und eine in Hjartdal, Norwegen – zeigen, dass sich das nordische System nicht mit erprobten pädagogischen Methoden zufrieden gibt, sondern räumliche Gestaltung nutzt, um aktives Lernen zu fördern. Die beiden Beispiele zeigen die Fähigkeit innovativer Schultypologien, sich an veränderliche gesellschaftliche Bedingungen anzupassen.

Im August 2018 wurde das Bildungszentrum Syvälahti des Architekturbüros Verstas eröffnet. Das Mehrzweckgebäude verbindet die Funktionen einer Schule und eines Tagesbetreuungszentrums, einer öffentlichen Bibliothek und eines Jugendhauses. Die Organisation von Lernräumen folgt Finnlands Lehrplan-Richtlinien: Mehrere flexible und offene Gruppenräume sind um zentrale Großräume angeordnet und bilden ein Cluster. Die Räume werden je nach Lernfach und Gruppengröße auf verschiedene Weisen genutzt. Alle Cluster sind eng mit den öffentlicheren Gebäudebereichen verbunden, die bei Bedarf auch als Lernräume genutzt werden können.

Die norwegische Gemeinde Sauland hat mit dem Büro Helen & Hard/PPAG ein ähnliches Schulgebäude errichtet. Gemeinsam mit einem bestehenden Verwaltungsgebäude und einer Grundschule umschließt das neue Schulgebäude den Schulhof und Spielplatz. Jeder Lehr- und Lernraum hat eine visuelle Beziehung zum zentralen Lernraum und zur umgebenden Landschaft. Der norwegische Ansatz hat zur Folge, dass auch hier Arbeiten und freies Lernen möglich sind. Wie beim Syvälahti-Zentrum können Räume erweitert oder zusammengezogen werden. Das räumliche Konzept für moderne Bildungscluster schafft ein Geflecht aus Lernräumen, die ohne Begrenzungen um eine gemeinsame Lernlandschaft angeordnet sind.

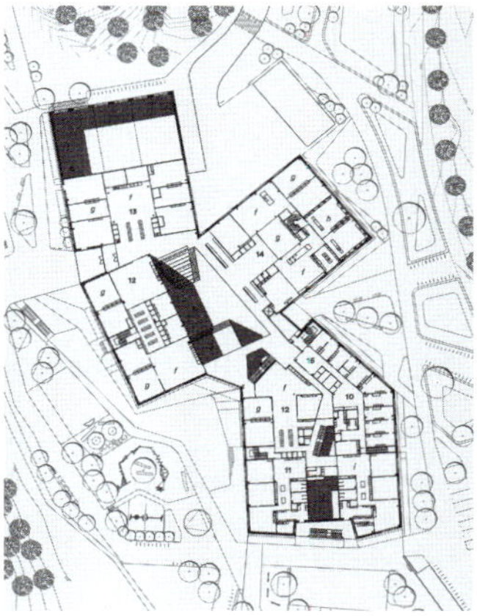

The school as a community centre: Syvälahti school by Verstas Arkkitehdit

Stadtteilzentrum Schule: Syvälahti-Schule von Verstas Arkkitehdit

"Crystalline Rotational Spatial Structure": permanently impermanent spaces create amplified zones of learning, design, communication and social exchange; New Sauland school, Helen & Hard / PPAG

„Kristalline Struktur der Abwechslung": Beständig unbeständige Räume schaffen Bereiche zum intensivierten Lernen und Gestalten, für Kommunikation und Austausch. New Sauland Schule, Helen & Hard/ PPAG

02. Project: Ausbauhaus Neukölln

City: Berlin
Client: Ausbauhaus Neukölln GbR Baugruppe
Planning: Praeger Richter Architekten
Status: Completed in 2014

Self-Build for Less! Socially Affordable Housing Schemes?

The principle of self-made homes opens up all sorts of possibilities: a building project led by Praeger Richter Architects in Berlin-Neukölln trail-blazes the possibilities of cheap living space with individual designs. The users can choose at which stage of completion they would like to take on their flats - depending on their construction skills and financial means. Various stages of completion are available - from "standard loft" or "standard flat" to "structure only for self-builders". Those taking the self-build option can even install their own heating. This makes for prices upwards of 1,020 euros/m^2 (excluding furnishings) - a figure usually only achieved by public housing projects.

The guiding principle of the planning process was as follows: less involvement of the developers in the structure and exterior shell balanced with flexibility in determining fittings and further development. This division was also incorporated in the implementation, both contractually and onsite during construction. Constraints in the construction process, fundamental legal requirements and responsibilities were arranged through a development agreement between the self-builders and the developers. Modifications and reconstructions were also possible: the structure was based around a simple shelving system. By freeing the floor plan from the support structure and the flexible punctuated façade, a wide variety of floor plan variations can be implemented as needed in the 24 units for living and working so that the structure can be adapted to future uses.

Such low production costs speak for themselves: could self-building also become a new strategy for social housing?

Individualität ausbauen Wohnen zu sozial verträglichen Preisen?

Das Ausbauhaus Neukölln von Praeger Richter Architekten zeigt, wie Wohnraum günstig entstehen und individuell gestaltet werden kann: Das Prinzip des Selbstausbaus macht es möglich. Die Nutzer*innen können wählen, in welcher Ausbaustufe sie ihre Wohnungen übernehmen möchten – je nach handwerklichen Kenntnissen und finanziellen Möglichkeiten. Verschiedene Ausbaustandards stehen zur Verfügung – von „Standard Loft" über „Standard Wohnung" bis hin zu „Übernahme als Rohbau zum Selbstausbau". Selbst die Heizung konnte von den Selbstbauer*innen eingebaut werden. Das ermöglicht abhängig vom Ausbaustandard Quadratmeterpreise ab 1.020 Euro – Werte die man sonst nur aus dem sozialen Wohnungsbau kennt.

Das Credo im Planungsprozess lautete: wenig Mitbestimmung der Baugruppe am Rohbau und an der Außenhülle, dafür viel Spielraum beim Ausbau. Dieses Konzept wurde auch organisatorisch, rechtlich und praktisch in der Werkplanung, in den Verträgen und auf der Baustelle umgesetzt. Bauliche Zwänge, gesetzliche Grundanforderungen und rechtliche Verantwortungen wurden über eine „Ausbauvereinbarung" zwischen den Selbstbauer*innen und der Baugruppe klar geregelt. Umbau jederzeit möglich: Konstruktiv gleicht der als Baugruppe realisierte Wohnungsbau einem einfachen Regalsystem. Durch die Befreiung des Grundrisses von der Tragstruktur und die flexible Lochfassade sind in den insgesamt 24 Wohn- und Gewerbeeinheiten vielfältigste Grundrissvarianten je nach Bedarf möglich und für zukünftige Anforderungen anpassbar.

Die niedrigen Herstellungskosten sprechen dafür: Selbstausbau auch als Strategie für den sozialen Wohnungsbau?

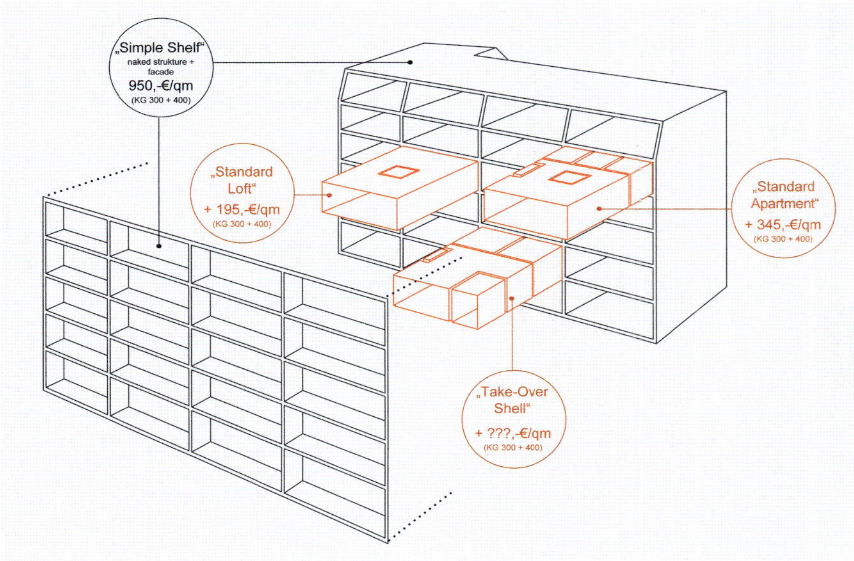

Spatial adaptablility: each unit filled and adapted according to the owners' individual means

Schubladenprinzip: Jede Einheit wird individuell von den Eigentümer*innen ausgebaut – je nach finanziellen und handwerklichen Möglichkeiten

03.

Project: **Wohnregal Waldenserstraße**

City: Berlin
Client: N/A
Planning: FAR frohn&rojas
Status: Under construction

Living in the Shelf
An On-Site Inspection

A model for social housing and self-building? The shelf-style living system on Berlin-Moabit's Waldenserstraße is growing: the building costs of the entire process are, in terms of gross floor area, approximately 1,500 euros/m². In order to make such figures possible, the architects FAR frohn & rojas developed a stringent building concept capable of achieving architectural diversity.

Made in Saxony-Anhalt, assembled in Berlin – prefabricated concrete parts can save up to 50 percent of costs compared with cast-in-situ concrete (1).

Fabricating concrete parts in advance reduces the construction period by many months, allowing one storey to be built per week (2 and 3).

Maximum spatial variance despite minimum building costs: throughout the entire internal span and depth of the building, each storey is free of columns and can be freely designed, including two units containing building services that can be flexibly installed (4 to 8). Metallic gauze curtains cloak the building, providing a constantly shifting façade and and allowing for individual configurations while creating privacy (9).

Wohnen im Regal
Eine Baustellenbegehung

Vorbild für den sozialen Wohnungsbau und Selbstausbaumodelle? Das Wohnregal Waldenserstraße in Berlin-Moabit wächst: Die Baukosten des gesamten Vorhabens liegen bei ca. 1.500 Euro/m² Bruttogrundfläche. Um solche Kennzahlen zu erreichen, haben die Architekten FAR frohn&rojas ein stringentes, jedoch zur architektonischen Vielfalt fähiges Gebäudekonzept entwickelt.

Hergestellt in Sachsen-Anhalt, zusammengebaut in Berlin, ermöglichen Fertigteile aus Beton eine Kostenersparnis gegenüber Ortbeton um bis zu 50 Prozent (1).

Die Verwendung von Betonfertigteilen wirkt sich signifikant auf die Bauzeit aus und bedeutet mehrere Monate Zeitersparnis – pro Woche wächst das Haus um ein Rohbaugeschoss (2–3).

Die günstigen Herstellungskosten schließen maximale räumliche Varianz nicht aus: Durch die Spannweite über die gesamte Gebäudetiefe und zwei Haustechnikkerne, an die flexibel angedockt werden kann, sind die Ebenen stützenfrei und dadurch frei gestaltbar. Aus statischer Hinsicht sind auch nachträgliche Umbaumaßnahmen problemlos möglich (4–8). Vorhänge aus metallisierter Gaze hüllen das Gebäude in ein sich ständig wechselndes Gewand. Das schafft Privatsphäre und ermöglicht individuelle Anpassung der Belichtung (9).

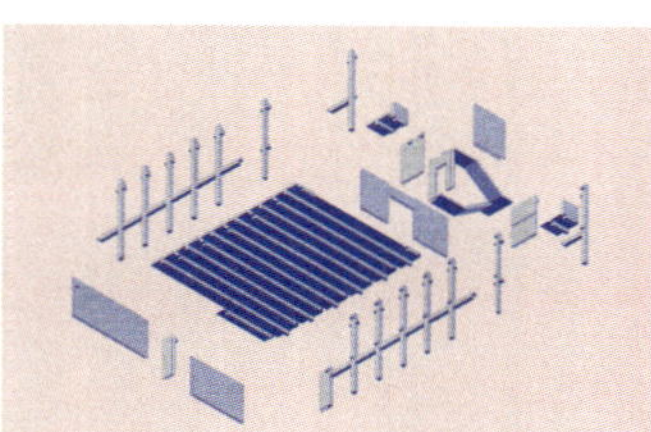
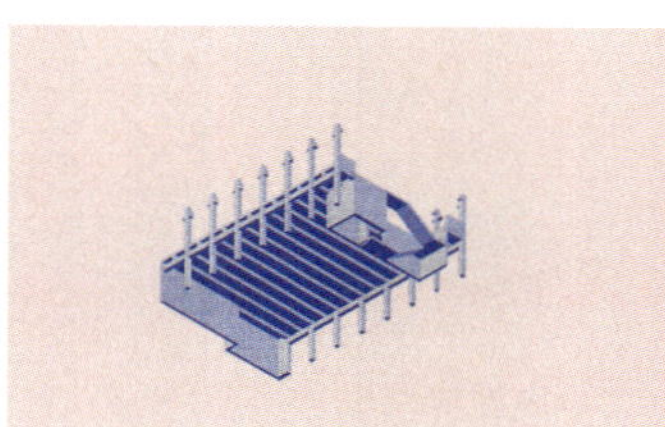
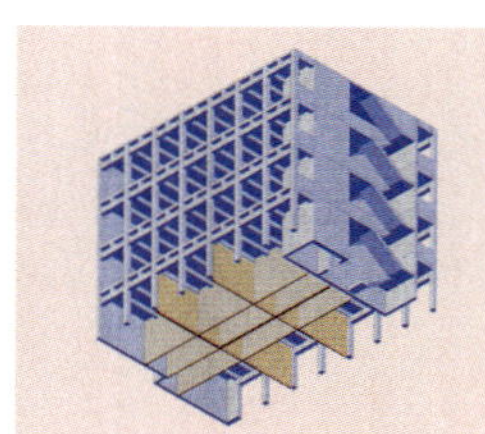
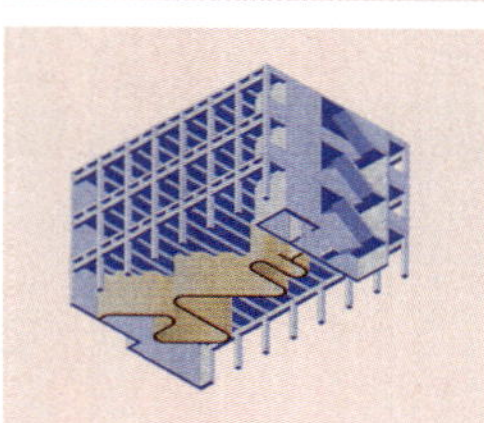
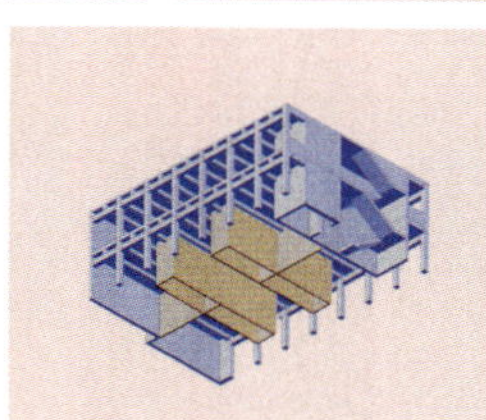
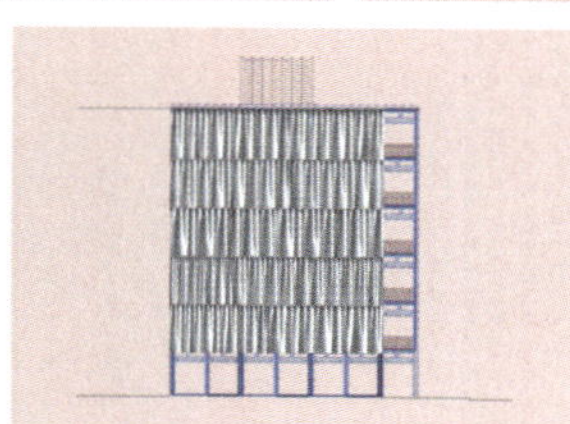

A small but generous kit of parts: flexible floor plans allow for spatial complexity and variable residential forms

Kleinteilig und doch großzügig: Flexible Grundrissplanungen erlauben räumliche Komplexität und einen Mix an Wohnformen

(4-9)

-> Essay pp. 151 ff. Off-the-Shelf Heterogeneity

(3)

(1)

(2)

Optimisation on the construction site - faster and cheaper assembly

Optimierung auf der Baustelle – schneller und günstiger in der Zusammenstellung

04.

Project: **Frizz23**
Blumengroßmarkt Berlin
City: Berlin
Client: Forum Berufsbildung e.V, FrizzZwanzig GbR. Miniloft Kreuzberg GbR
Planning: Deadline Architekten
Status: Completed 2018

The City in the Building
A Co-operative for Enterprises

"First the dialogue, then the design": according to this motto, the Berlin based architecture firm Deadline has implemented the first building co-operative for enterprises in the former Haus am Blumengroßmarkt (house of the wholesale flower market) as part of a Konzeptverfahren (concept procedure) and in so doing, united a wide spectrum of entrepreneurs and social providers. All units were individually planned in an extensive negotiation processes, taking into account the needs and possibilities of users - all of whom are co-investors in the project.

The differentiated elevations do not suggest that there are three separate building volumes behind the façade. With its horizontal bands of charred wood elements, the building presents itself to the outside as a unit and offers a robust framework to the heterogeneous mix of art, small business, creative industries, education, gastronomy, retail and residential units to be found inside.

Modules and intensive participation in the planning process are not new - but the programmatic mix à la Frizz23 and its associated complexity are trend-setting, a verifiable contribution in terms of Baukultur (culture of building) and the upgrading of inner-city commercial and residential culture.

Over 5,648 square metres of floor space, the Haus am Blumengroßmarkt unites:

46 commercial units for

- Workshops for bicycles and upcycling bags
- Seminar rooms for professional development
- Studios for creatives from literature, scenography, music and the comedy scene
- Co-working spaces
- Offices for architecture firms
- Online Services
- Communication agencies
- Café and project space
- Community Gallery

21 residential units

14 minilofts (short-term apartments)
3 apartments
4 residential/commercial units

Die Stadt im Haus
Innovation Gewerbebaugruppe

„Erst der Dialog, dann das Design": Nach diesem Motto hat das Architekturbüro Deadline im Rahmen eines Konzeptverfahrens die erste Baugemeinschaft für Gewerbe in Berlin umgesetzt und vereint unterschiedlichste Unternehmer*innen und soziale Träger*innen unter einem Dach. Alle Einheiten wurden in umfangreichen Verhandlungsprozessen gemäß den Bedürfnissen und Möglichkeiten der Nutzer*innen – allesamt auch Ko-Investor*innen des Projekts – individuell geplant.

Die entsprechend den Nutzungen differenzierten Ansichten lassen nicht direkt erahnen, dass sich hinter der Fassade drei separate Gebäude verbergen. Mit seinen horizontalen Bändern aus angekohlten Holzelementen präsentiert sich das Gebäude nach außen als Einheit und bietet dem heterogenen Mix aus Kunst, Kleinunternehmer*innen, Kreativwirtschaft, Bildung, Gastronomie, Einzelhandel und Wohnen einen robusten Rahmen.

Baugruppen und Partizipation im Planungsprozess sind nicht neu – die programmatische Mischung à la Frizz23 und die damit verbundene Komplexität der Kommunikation ist jedoch richtungsweisend und ein veritabler baukultureller Beitrag zur Aufwertung innerstädtischer Gewerbe- und Wohnkultur.

Auf 5.648 Quadratmetern Nutzfläche vereint das Haus am Blumengroßmarkt:

46 Gewerbeeinheiten für

- Werkstattläden für Fahrräder und Upcycling-Taschen
- Seminarräume für die berufliche Weiterbildung
- Studios für Kreative aus Literatur, Szenografie, Musik und Comicszene
- Coworking-Räume
- Büros für Architektur
- Online-Dienstleistungen
- Kommunikationsagenturen
- Café und Projekthalle
- Gemeinschaftsgalerie

21 Wohneinheiten

14 Minilofts (Kurzzeitapartments)
3 Wohnungen
4 Wohn-/Gewerbeeinheiten

-> Interview pp. 147 ff. Infrastructure Remixed

Scattered balconies reflect the heterogeneity of the floorplans and "bands" of charred wood tie the building segments into one whole

Die Positionierung der Balkone spiegelt die Heterogenität der Grundrisse wider, angekohlte Holzbänder verbinden die Gebäudeeinheiten zu einem Ganzen

A house with several faces: three buildings united in one volume orient themselves towards park and square

Ein Haus mit mehreren Gesichtern: Drei Gebäude vereint in einem Volumen orientieren sich zu Park und Platz und bespielen sie

Mix, small-scale, responsibility: all project participants are users and investors at the same time

Mischung, Kleinteiligkeit, Verantwortung: Alle Projektbeteiligten sind Nutzende und Investierende zugleich

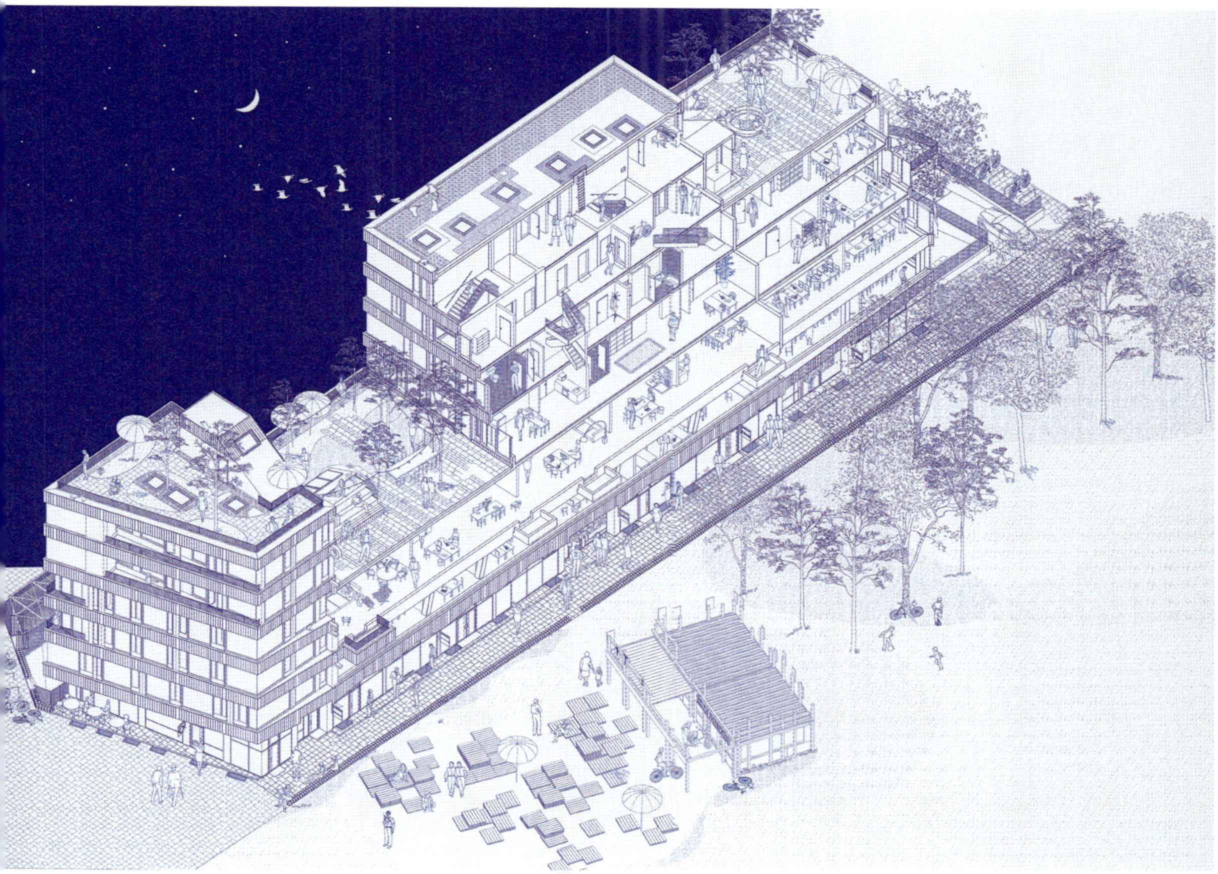

The structure frames diversity: a city within the city

Vision Stadt in der Stadt: Schlichte Struktur umfasst die Vielfalt

05. Dong Xuan Center

Project: Lichtenberg
City: Berlin
Client: N/A
Planning: Various
Status: Ongoing

Market Power
Discover the Periphery

The largest market of Vietnam's capital has an offshoot in the east of Berlin: the Lichtenberg Dong Xuan Center. Since 2003, foods and goods imported from Southeast Asia have been available for purchase in several lightweight halls on an industrial site of around 200 hectares. About 300 vendors from Vietnam, as well as India, Pakistan and China sell everything from plastic flowers to nail dryers, fans to rice noodles, training pants to Vietnamese mangoes alongside Asian food staples. Additional services, including German tax advice, are also available. The centre's clientele use it for shopping and as a meeting place. The restaurants offer authentic Vietnamese cuisine and are a destination listed on international food blogs and in Berlin travel guides.

The centre's influence on local urban development is undisputed: politicians and business people are aware of the relevance and growth potential of the market - both from an economic and social perspective. The expansion into a Southeast Asian neighbourhood and enclave has already begun: in 2017, a hotel opened on site, and by 2020 a cultural centre is to be created as a multifunctional event space. A wholesaler turning into a cultural and district centre: an unusual mix that may also exert influence on its surrounding neighbourhood of prefabricated buildings, car repair workshops and scrap dealers. This existing potential for space has been met with increasing interest from those in the art and cultural scene, who are being priced out of Berlin's inner city. But this, too, is complicated: the district and Senate offices express concern for the existing and established industrial and commercial enterprises, fearing the danger of gentrification that might be attracted by such new artistic and cultural uses. What is less complicated is that the financially and culturally strong Dong Xuan Center will continue to be an anchor for the area, and an open negotiation on the part of market operators and politicians is necessary; only in this way can a heterogeneous urban area develop that reflects - and extends - the diversity of the Dong Xuan market.

Die Macht des Marktes
Peripherie entdecken

Der größte Markt der vietnamesischen Hauptstadt hat einen Ableger im Osten Berlins: das Lichtenberger Dong Xuan Center. Auf einem Industrieareal von rund 200 Hektar können seit 2003 in mehreren Leichtbauhallen fernöstliche Lebensmittel und Waren erworben werden. Etwa 300 Händler*innen aus Vietnam, aber auch Indien, Pakistan und China vertreiben alles, von Plastikblumen, Nageltrocknern und Ventilatoren über Reisnudeln und Trainingshosen bis hin zu vietnamesischen Mangos. Auch Dienstleistungen wie Steuerberatung stehen zur Verfügung. Die Kundschaft nutzt das Center sowohl zum Einkauf als auch als Treffpunkt. Die Restaurants gelten mittlerweile als authentischer Geheimtipp der vietnamesischen Küche und werden bereits in internationalen Food-Blogs und Berlin-Reiseführern genannt.

Der Einfluss des Centers auf die lokale Stadtentwicklung ist unbestritten: Die Politik sowie Wirtschaftstreibende sind sich der Relevanz und des Wachstumspotenzials des Marktes bewusst – sowohl aus ökonomischer als auch sozialer Perspektive. Der Ausbau zu einer modernen „Asiatown" hat demnach bereits begonnen: 2017 eröffnete ein Hotel auf dem Gelände, bis 2020 soll ein Kulturhaus als multifunktionales Veranstaltungsgebäude entstehen. Ein Großhandel, der sich zum Kultur- und Stadtteilzentrum wandelt – ein ungewöhnlicher Mix, der auch die von Plattenbauten, Autowerkstätten und Schrotthändlern geprägte Nachbarschaft beeinflusst. Das dort vorhandene Flächenpotenzial stößt zunehmend auch auf Interesse in einer Kunst- und Kulturszene, die sich die Berliner Innenstadt nicht mehr leisten kann. Ein komplizierter Wandel: Die Bezirks- und Senatsämter fürchten um die noch angesiedelten Industrie- und Gewerbebetriebe und wittern in den neuen Kunstnutzungen die Gefahr der Gentrifizierung. Klar ist, dass sich das finanzstarke Dong Xuan Center weiter in der Umgebung verankern wird. Starke Konzepte und eine offene Verhandlung vonseiten der Marktbetreiber*innen und der Politik sind daher gefordert. Nur so kann sich ein lebendiges urbanes Gebiet entwickeln, das die Vielfalt des Dong-Xuan-Marktes widerspiegelt und diese in die Umgebung trägt.

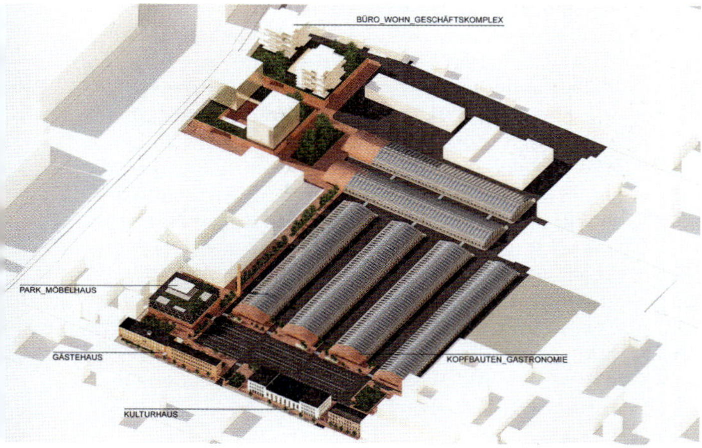

An economic engine between GDR-housing estates and car repair shops: stimulating the neighbourhood

Wirtschaftsmotor zwischen Plattenbau und Autowerkstätten: Stimulierung der Nachbarschaft?

Small-scale wholesale in the halls of the Dong Xuan market

Kleinteiligkeit trotz Großhandel in den Hallen des Dong-Xuan-Marktes

A cultural-economic hybrid and contemporary spatial resources mingle with the market

Peripherie erlaubt Wachstum: kulturökonomischer Hybrid und zeitgemäße Raumressource im Dunstkreis des Marktes

06. Die Gerichtshöfe

Project: Die Gerichtshöfe
City: Berlin
Client: N/A
Planning: N/A
Status: In negotiation

Culture Caught in the Act of Urban Development
Spaces of Creative Production in Danger

In Berlin, the question of available space is reaching a crisis point that affects not only housing but also artistic trades and sites of production, all of which are increasingly threatened. The negotiation of opposing interests is demonstrated by the example of Berlin's Gerichtshöfe in the district of Wedding. This 1912 ensemble of six heritage-listed trade complexes and courtyards - and connects Berlin's Wiesenstraße with Gerichtsstraße; it has offered space for living, art and production since the 1980s. The creative quarter brings together around 70 studios, a joinery, a violin-maker, tool production, literary magazines and other trades, with residential buildings facing the street.

The ensemble is rented out by the city's housing association Gesobau, which plans to modernise the buildings and build 150 flats for students in the central courtyard. Gesobau is under pressure: as a housing association, its remit is to create housing as quickly and effectively as possible - including those for students. This conflict means that the artists and tradespeople based here face an uncertain future. The city is making an effort to reach a solution but is itself in a jam: how can questions regarding planning politics take into account social and cultural responsibility, which the city also bears for shared creative spaces?

Artists and tradespeople have joined together to form a non-profit association in order to salvage their studios and working spaces. The mediation process is unfolding between several parties: Gesobau, the municipal council, Berlin's artists' studio commissioner Martin Schwegmann and the current tenants. All participants are of the opinion that the area should remain a cultural site for the long-term. An additional opening for social projects and extended use - through and for the local neighbourhood - is on the table. Gesobau and the municipality are still assessing whether the new housing structure might be adapted to the site with a house for the homeless or a vocational training kitchen for refugees also being considered. Would the establishment of a non-profit foundation be an option for the complicated situation in the Gerichtshöfe?

Kultur im Spannungsfeld der Stadtentwicklung
Kreativräume in Gefahr

Die sich zuspitzende Raumfrage in Berlin betrifft nicht nur das Wohnen, auch künstlerische Gewerke und Produktionsstätten haben zunehmend existenzbedrohende Schwierigkeiten. Die Verhandlung konträrer Interessen zeigt das Beispiel der Berliner Gerichtshöfe. Das Ensemble aus sechs denkmalgeschützten Gewerbekomplexen und Hinterhöfen, erbaut 1912, das die Berliner Wiesenstraße mit der Gerichtsstraße verbindet, bietet seit den 1980er Jahren Raum für Wohnen, Kunst und Produktion. Das Kreativquartier vereint rund siebzig Ateliers, eine Schreinerei, einen Geigenbauer, Werkzeughersteller*innen und andere Gewerke. Zu den Straßen hin wird gewohnt.

Als Vermieterin fungiert die städtische Wohnungsbaugesellschaft Gesobau. Diese möchte die Gebäude sanieren und plant im Hof einen Neubau mit 150 Wohnungen für Studierende. Der Druck auf die Gesobau ist hoch: Als Landesunternehmen soll sie möglichst schnell und umfangreich Wohnraum schaffen – ausdrücklich auch studentisches Wohnen. Dieser Konflikt konfrontiert die ansässigen Kunst- und Gewerbetreibenden mit einer ungewissen Zukunft. Die Stadt ist bemüht, einen Kompromiss herbeizuführen, und ist dabei selbst in der Bredouille: Wie können Fragen der Wohnraumpolitik mit der sozialen und kulturellen Verantwortung der Stadt gegenüber kreativen Gemeinschaftsräumen in Einklang gebracht werden?

Künstler*innen und Gewerbetreibende haben sich in einem Verein mobilisiert und versuchen, ihre Räume zu sichern. Das Verfahren befindet sich derzeit in Vermittlung zwischen den verschiedenen Parteien: Gesobau, Bezirksamt, dem Beauftragten für Atelierflächen Martin Schwegmann wie auch den derzeitigen Mieter*innen. Alle Beteiligten sind sich einig, dass das Gebiet langfristig ein Kulturbezirk bleiben sollte. Eine zusätzliche Öffnung für soziale Projekte und damit eine erweiterte Nutzung durch und für die ortsansässige Nachbarschaft wird in Betracht gezogen. Gesobau und Bezirksamt prüfen noch, ob das neue Wohnhaus an den Ort angepasst werden kann. Ein Wohnhaus für Obdachlose oder eine Ausbildungsküche für Geflüchtete sind ebenso im Gespräch. Würde eine Stiftungsgründung durch die Kunst- und Gewerbetreibenden eine Option für die vertrackte Situation in den Gerichtshöfen darstellen?

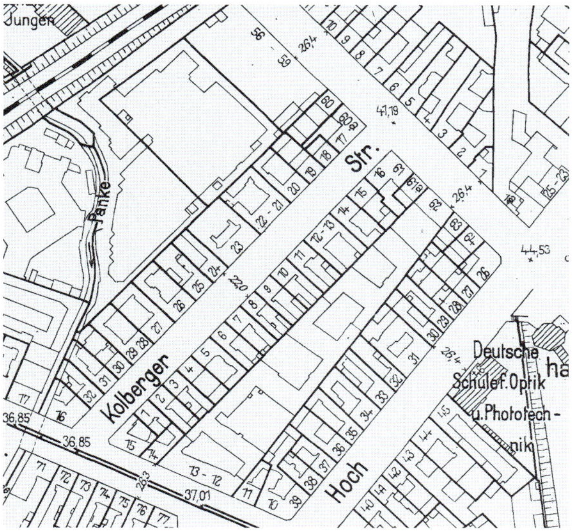

Heterogenous mix: six courtyards combine culture, workshops and small businesses

Heterogene Mischung im Wedding: Sechs Innenhöfe verbinden Kultur, Werkstätten und Kleingewerbe

"Given that Berlin is currently experiencing a crisis in businesses, and that the emigration of artists is already a clear reality, the diversity of the Gerichtshöfe makes it a very important place for Berlin."

„Vor dem Hintergrund, dass Berlin auf eine Gewerberaumkrise zusteuert und die Abwanderung von Künstler*innen bereits harte Realität wird, sind die Gerichtshöfe in ihrer Vielfalt ein sehr wichtiger Ort für Berlin."

Martin Schwegmann

Demand for affordable studios in Berlin is high and space is scarce - and the Gerichtshöfe is not an isolated case. Examples such as Wiesenburg, Bar Babette, the RAW Gelände and Dragoner Areal demonstrate that the Berlin mix is under pressure, and that both politics and the independent scene will have to devise alternatives on a case by case basis. This will require new constellations of stakeholders working together with formats and concepts that will bring together housing, cultural use, retail and social responsibility.

Die Nachfrage nach bezahlbaren Ateliers in Berlin ist so hoch wie der Raum knapp – und die Gerichtshöfe sind kein Einzelfall. Auch Beispiele wie die Wiesenburg, die ehemalige australische Botschaft in Pankow, die Bar Babette, das RAW-Gelände oder das Dragoner-Areal zeigen, dass die Berliner Mischung zunehmend unter Druck gerät und die Politik mit der Szene gemeinsame Lösungen finden muss. Neue Akteurskonstellationen, die ein Zusammenspiel zwischen Wohnen, Kunst, Gewerbe und sozialer Trägerschaft ermöglichen, könnten dabei eine Lösung sein.

The case of interim use at the former Australian Embassy in Pankow: can 30 artists stay in their studios?

Fall temporäre Nutzung der ehemaligen australischen Botschaft Pankow: Können die dreißig Künstler*innen in ihren Ateliers bleiben?

The Wiesenburg case: Who can stay and who must go? The Wedding institution has been a place for art and culture since the 1960s. In 2015, the Berlin housing construction company Degewo took over the 12,000 squaremetre site: living vs. art and business? In two workshops attended by about 30 participants from city administration, politics and representatives of the Wiesenburg, possible solutions were discussed and determined. A general consensus on fundamental conditions was found: the need for 102 residential units with studio apartments on the ground floor

Fall Wiesenburg: Wer darf bleiben, wer muss gehen? Die Weddinger Institution ist seit den 1960ern Ort für Kunst und Kultur. 2015 hat die Berliner Wohnungsbaugesellschaft Degewo das 12.000 Quadratmeter große Gelände übernommen: Wohnen vs. Kunst und Gewerbe? In zwei Werkstattverfahren mit rund dreißig Beteiligten aus Stadtverwaltung, Politik und Vertreter*innen der Wiesenburg wurden mögliche Lösungen erarbeitet. Auf wesentliche Rahmenbedingungen konnte man sich einigen: 102 Wohneinheiten mit Atelierwohnungen im Erdgeschoss

07.

Project: The Livesey Exchange, Old Kent Road
City: London
Client: Livesey Exchange Ltd
Planning: what if: projects (Ulrike Steven) in collaboration with Pempeople (Nicholas Okwulu), the London Borough of Southwark, the Greater London Authority (GLA)
Status: 2015–current

what if: projects

Open Workshops
Rendering Local Expertise Visible

The Livesey Exchange is a grassroots initiative that aims to bring new life, skills and jobs to the culturally diverse Old Kent Road in Southwark, London. One of the city's oldest roads, the Old Kent Road has long been a central industrial area producing hats, costumes, trays and household goods menders, fabricators and much more.

Today, this neglected corner of South East London is among the 10 percent most deprived areas in the country, with high levels of youth unemployment and low levels of educational attainment. As part of the new London Plan that highlights industry as a part of the city, Old Kent Road was identified as an opportunity area with potential for growth in homes (20,000 new homes) and job creation (5,000 new jobs). In 2015 what if: projects, a London-based architecture practice that works with communities on public space projects, was asked how the 60 unused garages on the social housing tower complex Ledbury Estate could be activated. In collaboration with Pempeople, what if: projects organised discussions, talks, hands-on workshops and walks. Together, they offered a window into the ways Old Kent Road's history could inspire new forms of development, proposing that the garages could be filled with different types of artisans, creating opportunities for training of young people linked to the existing network of manufacturers. It was proposed that the garages include workshops, studios and a kitchen while a multi-functional space and a friendly café would welcome people as they entered the site from Old Kent Road. Although the plan attracted funding from the Mayor's Regeneration Fund, Southwark Council, Southwark Tenant Fund, Airbnb and additional crowdfunding, the Grenfell tower fire of 2017 triggered fire assessments of housing estates. In their examination, Arup engineers found serious structural issues in the tower blocks. As a result, the Livesey Exchange had to be put on hold and an alternative site on Old Kent Road was offered for the development of the project by Southwark Council. A new building will now be constructed, housing a similar programme of workshops and communal space. It is anticipated that the construction will be completed in 2020.

Offene Werkstätten
Lokale Expertise sichtbar machen

Die Livesey Exchange ist eine Graswurzelinitiative, die neues Leben, neue Kompetenzen und neue Jobs in das kulturell vielfältige Quartier um die Old Kent Road im Londoner Bezirk Southwark bringt. Die Straße ist eine der ältesten der Stadt und ist immer noch eine industriell dominierte Gegend, in der Hutmode, Kostüme und Tabletts produziert wurden. Außerdem befanden sich hier Reparaturwerkstätten, verarbeitendes Gewerbe und Kurierdienste.

Heute gehört diese vernachlässigte Ecke von Südostlondon zu den zehn Prozent der am stärksten benachteiligten Gegenden des Landes; dies geht einher mit einer hohen Jugendarbeitslosigkeit und einem niedrigen Bildungsgrad. Als Teil des „New London Plan", der Industrie als Teil der Stadt begreift, wurde die Old Kent Road als Gegend identifiziert, in der potenziell 20.000 neue Wohnungen und 5.000 neue Jobs entstehen können. Im Jahr 2015 wurde what if: projects, ein Londoner Architekturbüro, beauftragt, ein Konzept zu entwickeln, wie man sechzig ungenutzte Garagen im Gebäudekomplex beleben könnte. Zusammen mit Pempeople organisierte what if: Diskussionen, Gespräche und Spaziergänge. Gemeinsam schufen sie einen Ausblick auf die Möglichkeiten, wie die Geschichte der Old Kent Road als Inspiration für neue Formen der Entwicklung genutzt werden könnte. Sie schlugen vor, in den Garagen Macher*innen anzusiedeln und neue Möglichkeiten für die Bildung und Stärkung des existierenden Gewerbenetzwerks zu schaffen. Die Garagen sollen Werkstätten, Ateliers und eine Quartiersküche beheimaten. Für Passant*innen der Old Kent Road soll es einen Mehrzweckraum mit Café geben. Das Projekt bekam ein Budget aus dem Erneuerungsfonds des Bürgermeisters, der Verwaltung von Southwark, der Mieter*innenvereinigung von Southwark, Airbnb und darüber hinaus Mittel aus Crowdfunding. Mit dem Feuer im Grenfell Tower im Jahr 2017 wurde der Brandschutz von Wohnanlagen neu geprüft. Das Ingenieursbüro Arup entdeckte ernsthafte Probleme in den Häuserblöcken, als Ergebnis wurde das Projekt auf Eis gelegt: Der Southwark Council bot einen alternativen Standort in der Old Kent Road an. Dort wird nun ein neues Gebäude errichtet, in dem das gleiche Programm von Werkstätten und Gemeinschaftsräumen untergebracht sein wird. Fertigstellung voraussichtlich im Jahr 2020.

Visualising craftsmanship and hidden know-how for resilient communities

Sichtbarmachen von Handwerk und verstecktem Know-how für widerstandsfähige Communitys

08. Project: Seestadt Aspern

City: Vienna
Client: City of Vienna
Planning: Multiple
Status: Partially complete/ongoing

Targeting the Urban Mix On Solid Grounds

Vienna is building a new city on a lake: Aspern. Amongst the green fields between the Austrian capital and Bratislava, new living and working spaces for 40,000 people will be developed. Although the plan is unique in Europe, the attempt to pre-plan heterogeneity from the drawing-board is relevant to many cities and urban areas. The master-planners in Aspern are developing simple yet direct measures for basic urban infrastructures with planning guidelines developed by Gehl Architects that focus on the diversity of spaces at the street level. For example, the ground levels of the new living quarters are consistently 4 metres high, meaning they are predestined for use as local shops or offices for small businesses. Curated shopping strips instead of shopping malls: in order to avoid empty buildings on the future boulevards, the developers of the lake city formed a co-operation retail expert Dan Pearlman. Their newly established Aspern Seestadt Einkaufsstraßen GmbH strategically rents out retail space to ensure a mix that secures a range of products and services nearby. In this way, banal and homogeneous shopping malls can be avoided and street areas kept lively - and locally specific.

Highly densified and permeable

"One hundred years ago, the mantra of urban planning was the division of functions. Now, functions are coming back together!" proclaims architect Anna Popelka, creator of the living quarter Slim City. The co-founder of the Viennese office PPAG is an advocate of new building typologies that support a heterogeneous and complex society. Her blueprint for Seestadt Aspern is based on permeability and positive density, weaving together various uses: thirteen variegated building types define the publicly accessible space outside and reinterpret the urban quarter. "We wanted to build a site of negotiation - a test field - in which fences and borders are not necessary, even though the sense is created that one is 'inside'."

Everyone profits from an urban mix!

"There is no room for excuses: developers and the authorities can generate a good urban mix, so long as the necessary political will can be

Urbaner Mix vom Reißbrett? Das Potenzial Erdgeschoss

Wien baut eine neue Stadt: die Seestadt Aspern. Zwischen der österreichischen Hauptstadt und Bratislava entsteht auf der grünen Wiese neuer Wohn- und Arbeitsraum für 40.000 Menschen. Diese Größenordnung ist einzigartig in Europa. Heterogenität auf dem Reißbrett zu planen, ist eine Herausforderung, der sich die Masterplaner*innen stellten, indem sie Anreize für die Ansiedlung urbaner Basisinfrastruktur schafften. Das Planungshandbuch stammte von Gehl Architects und fokussiert auf belebte Straßenräume. So sind zum Beispiel die Sockelzonen der neuen Wohnbauten durchgehend vier Meter hoch und damit prädestiniert für die Nutzung als Geschäftslokal oder Büros von Kleinunternehmen. Kuratierte Einkaufsstraßen statt Shoppingzentren: Um Leerstände an den künftigen Boulevards zu vermeiden, ging die Entwicklungsgesellschaft der Seestadt mit einem Retail-Experten eine Kooperation ein. Die neu gegründete aspern Seestadt Einkaufsstraßen GmbH mietet Flächen an und stellt eine Mischung zusammen, die ein gutes Nahversorgungsangebot sicherstellen und dabei Shoppingzentren verhindern soll.

Hochverdichtet und durchlässig

„Vor hundert Jahren lautete das Mantra Funktionstrennung, jetzt kommen die Funktionen wieder zusammen!", proklamiert die Architektin Anna Popelka, die in der Seestadt das Wohnprojekt Slim City realisiert hat. Die Mitbegründerin des Wiener Büros PPAG fordert neue Gebäudetypologien, die der heterogenen und komplexen Gesellschaft gerecht werden. Ihr Entwurf für die Seestadt Aspern setzt auf Permeabilität und positive Dichte: 13 unterschiedlich orientierte Baukörper definieren den öffentlich zugänglichen Außenraum und interpretieren den Stadtblock neu. „Wir wollten einen Ort der Verhandlung – ein Testfeld –, wo keine Zäune und Abgrenzungen nötig sind, aber trotzdem das Gefühl entsteht, ‚drinnen' zu sein."

Alle profitieren vom urbanen Mix!

„Es gibt keine Entschuldigung: Entwickler*innen und Behörden können einen guten urbanen Mix erzeugen, vorausgesetzt, der nötige politische Wille ist vorhanden!", so Friedrich Passler von AllesWirdGut Architekten. Sein Büro zeichnete für einen sozialen Wohnungsbau in der Retortenstadt verantwortlich. Er konstatiert dem Masterplan eine

Surrounded by garden allotments and fields, a new city is being built on 240 hectares just outside Vienna

Umgeben von Kleingärten und Feldern entsteht auf 240 Hektar vor den Toren Wiens eine Großstadt

Organic development: phased programming of the shopping streets

Organischer Entstehungsprozess: Schrittweise Programmierung der Einkaufsstraßen

found!" according to Friedrich Passler from AllesWirdGut Architects. His office is responsible for a public housing complex in the Retortenstadt area. The master plan rests on the successful, strategic design of the ground floor, where it is likely that developers will be forced to open the ground levels of the building for non-living-related uses, and in some cases, the second floor as well. Although this may not be lucrative in the short term, it is in the public interest and will, over time, have a positive effect on the development of the area overall. This is in everybody's interests in the long term – including the developers themselves. According to Passler, certain negotiation processes are necessary: "Open ground levels from up to two storeys can be rented for 5 euros/m² if the investor is able to build three storeys on top of this. That way, everybody is happy."

gelungene Erdgeschossstrategie. Entwickler*innen wurden über Dichteanforderungen dazu gezwungen, die Sockelzonen teilweise bis zum zweiten Stockwerk für Nicht-Wohnnutzungen zu öffnen. Das sei kurzfristig zwar nicht lukrativ, dafür aber im öffentlichen Interesse und wirke sich langfristig positiv auf die Entwicklung des Gebietes aus. Laut Passler seien gewisse Verhandlungsprozesse nötig: „Offene Sockelgeschosse über zwei Etagen können für 5 Euro/m² vermietet werden, wenn der Investor dafür drei Geschosse zusätzlich bauen darf. So sind alle glücklich."

Permeability in PPAG'S Slim City: a tight mix of 178 apartments, community areas, commercial spaces, office units and gastronomy

Permeabilität in PPAGs Slim City: Eine dichte Packung aus 178 Wohnungen gemischt mit Gemeinschaftlichem, Geschäftsflächen, Büros und Gastronomie

Social, green and urban: in the residential and commercial area of AllesWirdGut, the "home-of-life" concept envisages 100 residents – demographically balanced – around a common stairwell

Nachbarschaft, grüne und urbane Straßenräume: Im Wohn- und Geschäftsareal von AllesWirdGut sieht das „Haus des Lebens"-Konzept einhundert Bewohner*innen – demografisch ausbalanciert – an einem gemeinsamen Treppenhaus vor

Hybrid Infrastructures, Climate Change, Land- and Foodscapes

Hybride Infrastrukturen, Klimawandel, Stadt- und Ernährungslandschaften

4

Between 2008 and 2018, over 22 million people were displaced by climate change or weather-related events.

Seit 2008 sind mehr als 22 Millionen Menschen infolge des Klimawandels oder wetterbedingter Entwicklungen auf der Flucht.

By 2100, sea levels are estimated to rise over 1.2 metres as ice sheets continue to melt rapidly with an annual loss of 413 gigatonnes of ice.

Bis 2100 wird der Meeresspiegel um schätzungsweise 1,2 Meter ansteigen, wenn die Eisschilde mit einem Jahresverlust von 413 Gigatonnen weiterhin rapide schmelzen.

Sources / Quellen:

World Meteorological Organization, New York Times, John Rueter, Portland State University, Blue Green Cities Research Project, Public Space, British Design Council, Land8, Radbahn Berlin, SSPA Sweden, Baunetz, Grand Lyon, Berliner Morgenpost, Leibniz Center for Agricultural Landscape Research, Ernährungsrat Berlin

Between 1998 and 2004, over 100 major flooding incidents in Europe killed 700 people and destroyed 250,000 homes at an estimated loss of 25 billion euros.

Zwischen 1998 und 2004 führten mehr als hundert europäische Hochwasservorfälle zu 700 Todesfällen und 250.000 zerstörten Haushalten mit einem Schaden von 25 Milliarden Euro.

Hybrid (blue-green) infrastructure is a combination of grey and blue-green infrastructures that merge concrete and steel construction with natural ecosystem processes and is woven into existing (urban) landscapes. Hybrid landscape planning and design has been proven to be more resilient to extreme weather.

Eine hybride Infrastruktur ist eine Verbindung aus grauer und grüner Infrastruktur, die Beton- und Stahlbau mit Pflanzen und Ökosystemleistungen mischt und in die bestehende (Stadt-)Landschaft intergiert ist. Hybride Landschaftsplanung ist widerstandsfähiger gegenüber Extremwetterereignissen.

Cloudbursts create extreme flooding conditions by producing large quantities of precipitation in a short period of time. In 2013, Rotterdam developed 9,500 square metres of civic space that doubles as a site for rainwater storage.

2013 ließ Rotterdam eine Fläche von 9.500 Quadratmetern zu öffentlichem Raum mit Regenwasserspeicherfunktion umgestalten, nachdem Wolkenbrüche mit großen Niederschlagsmengen extreme Hochwasserbedingungen verursachten.

Blue-green cities "aim to reintroduce the natural water cycle into urban environments and provide effective measures to manage river, coastal and urban runoff/surface flooding."

Blau-grüne Städte „streben die Reintegration des natürlichen Wasserkreislaufs in die städtische Umwelt an und bieten effiziente Maßnahmen zur Steuerung von Fluss-, Küsten- und städtischen Abfluss- und Oberflächenüberflutungen."

In Berlin, nine kilometres of disused space under the U1 subway viaduct has been proposed as a bicycle highway, the Radbahn. In Xiamen, China, a seven-kilometre elevated bicycle highway was completed in 2017 with a capacity for 2000 bicycles.

Aus der ungenutzten Fläche unter dem U-Bahn-Viadukt der U1 in Berlin könnte eine neun Kilometer lange Fahrradautobahn werden. So lautet ein aktueller Vorschlag. Xiamen stellte im Jahr 2017 eine sieben Kilometer lange, aufgeständerte Fahrradautobahn für bis zu 2.000 Fahrräder fertig.

In Madrid, between 2006 and 2011, 43 kilometres of tunnels were dug to submerge highways, allowing for the connection of the Manzanares River to the city centre by developing 150 hectares of continuous public park.

In Madrid wurden 43 Kilometer Autobahn in Tunnel verlegt, um den Fluss Manzanares mit dem Stadtzentrum zu verbinden und 150 Hektar durchgehenden öffentlichen Park zu entwickeln.

Over 15 years, the city of Lyon has redeveloped over 20 kilometres of inner-city waterways with public walkways and protected natural spaces.

Seit 2003 hat Lyon über zwanzig Kilometer innerstädtische Wasserstraßen mit öffentlichen Wegen und geschützten Naturräumen saniert.

Berlin has 197 kilometres of inner-city waterways managed by the German Federal Ministry of Transport and Digital Infrastructure, whose use is highly restricted.

Berlin verfügt über 197 Kilometer innerstädtische Wasserstraßen, die vom Bundesministerium für Verkehr und digitale Infrastruktur verwaltet werden und deren Nutzung stark eingeschränkt ist.

In 2017, 0.7 percent of Sweden's domestic goods were transported through inland waterways. In 2017, 18 percent of the Netherland's domestic goods were transported through inland waterways.

Im Jahr 2017 wurden 0,7 Prozent der schwedischen Inlandsgüter auf Binnenwasserstraßen transportiert. Im Jahr 2017 wurden 18 Prozent der niederländischen Inlandsgüter auf Binnenwasserstraßen transportiert.

In a study of four major European cities in 2017, only Berlin was deemed capable of supplying itself with regional meat and produce. In 2017, only 7 percent of meat and produce consumed in Berlin was regionally sourced.

Eine Studie über vier europäische Großstädte aus dem Jahr 2017 kommt zu dem Schluss, dass nur Berlin in der Lage ist, sich vollständig aus regionalen Fleisch- und Lebensmittelvorkommen zu versorgen. Im Jahr 2017 wurden allerdings nur sieben Prozent der in Berlin konsumierten Nahrungsmittel aus der Region bezogen.

Greenery and built urban fabric connect rather than separate: WOHA's Kampung Admiralty Singapore

Grün und Grau verbunden statt getrennt: WOHAs Kampung Admiralty, Singapur

Industrial sublime at Parco Dora, Turin, by Latz + Partner: a merging of nature, urbanity and the past

Erhabene Industrie im Parco Dora, Turin, von Latz + Partner: Natur, Urbanität und Vergangenheit verwoben

Truth, Beauty, Goodness

Nature or City?

The relationship between green and grey infrastructure in our cities is something I think about often. The notion of "nature vs. urban" seems to be marked by an inherent, age-old divide that presupposes an "us" and an "other", which in turn defines people - the "us" - as something separate from nature and the animal kingdom. But, in reality, we're clever apes. Does this duality - green and grey infrastructure - need to exist? Instead, shouldn't we focus on how to evoke or distil the essence of sensory experiences we have in the natural world, so that we can develop sensual spaces that appeal to our appetite for visual, auditory and tactile experiences? At all times, rather than as an exceptional case? Interconnected rather than separate?

I think that the notion of ourselves as an "us" - as something in a separate category - is no longer relevant: I suggest that we think beyond this dichotomy and (re)consider the possibility of a coherent whole. It offers greater opportunities to engage with future questions that will arise when we blur the boundaries between nature and city, between green and grey.

Perhaps our efforts to articulate differences and create dualities are unnecessary, since what we are really looking for is a place that brings together sensory experiences within a unified world. I don't want to sit in an office all day and then go out into nature in the evening. I want to be able, at all times, to pass through spaces that appeal to my senses while connecting me to my humanity - through materials, greenery and actions. Spaces that not only lift our spirits but also establish a link to our corporeal nature, strengthening our connection to it. Cultural development is a product of human nature! Interweaving (our) nature with (our) culture, enmeshing spaces constructively - that is the goal.

The term "landscape" is helpful for describing spaces nestled between nature and the city. Landscape is multidimensional and offers a broad spectrum of typologies of nature and human nature, instead of an overarching dichotomy. Public space, parks, gardens and local recreation areas are all part of landscape. They offer a differentiated perspective on nature, urbanity and

Dem Wahren, Schönen, Guten

Natur oder Stadt?

Das Verhältnis von grüner und grauer Infrastruktur in unseren Städten ist etwas, worüber ich oft nachdenke. Dem Thema „Natur versus Stadt" scheint eine uralte Spaltung innezuwohnen, die ein „Wir" und ein „Die anderen" postuliert und damit den Menschen – das „Wir" – als etwas anderes definiert als das Natur- und Tierreich. Dabei sind wir in der Realität nur kluge Affen. Muss es die Dualität – grüne und graue Infrastruktur – überhaupt geben? Geht es nicht vielmehr darum, den natürlichen Zusammenhängen sinnliche Erfahrbarkeit zu entlocken, letztlich Lustorte zu entwickeln, die Sehen, Hören, Fühlen ermöglichen? Jederzeit und nicht ausnahmsweise? Verbunden statt getrennt?

Ich glaube, dass die Wahrnehmung unserer selbst als „wir" – als etwas anderes – nicht mehr zeitgemäß ist. Stattdessen schlage ich vor, die Dichotomie zu ignorieren und dadurch die Perspektive einer Einheit (wieder) zu eröffnen. Sie bietet mehr Möglichkeiten, sich mit zukünftigen Fragen auseinanderzusetzen, die sich stellen werden, sobald die Grenzen zwischen Natur und Stadt, zwischen Grün und Grau, verschwimmen.

Vielleicht ist unser Bemühen, Unterschiede zu definieren und Dualität zu schaffen, unnötig, da das, was wir eigentlich suchen, ein Ort der vereinten sinnlichen Erfahrungen dieser einen Welt ist. Ich will eben nicht den ganzen Tag in einem Büro sitzen und abends in die Natur gehen. Ich will mich jederzeit in Räumen bewegen, die mich auf sinnliche Weise beherbergen und mich an mein Menschsein anbinden – durch Materialien, Begrünung, Aktion. Räume, die nicht nur unseren Geist befriedigen, sondern auch eine Verbindung zu unserer körperlichen Natur herstellen und sie stärken. Unsere kulturelle Entwicklung entspricht ja unserer menschlichen Natur! Die Natürlichkeit mit der Kulturtechnik zu verweben und ein konstruktives Verschmelzen der Räume zu ermöglichen, darum geht es.

Der Begriff Landschaft ist hilfreich, um verdeckte Räume zwischen Natur und Stadt zu beschreiben. Landschaft ist vielschichtig und bietet ein ganzes Spektrum an Typologien von „Natur" und „menschlicher Natur" statt pauschaler Zweiteilung. Öffentlicher Raum, Parks, Gärten und Naherholungsgebiete sind Teilbereiche von Landschaft. Sie bieten eine differenzierte Perspektive auf Natur und Urbanität

their potential for interaction. To develop this potential, it is helpful to redefine what we mean by nature and natural experience; these terms tend to conjure a narrow set of Romantic associations, though they can be applied to a much broader range of experience. In her 1978 book "The Life of the Mind", Hannah Arendt speaks of the "heart of time" - those overwhelming moments in which breath and time stand still. Of course, such moments are not restricted to a walk through the woods or a park but can be found in the sensory experience of music or dance; when witnessing an expansive, open vista; in the sensual qualities of space and material; through yoga; and so on. What I'm imagining is the large-scale cultivation of a "heart of time" that is integrated into everyday routine; this would intermingle these special moments with the less important moments of our daily environment.

Give up dichotomies: A plea for creative misappropriation

From Baroque to Bauhaus, architectural movements have tended to separate, organise and sort experiences into typologies and distinct categories. Even if concerns relating to today's growing urban populations - climate change, flooding, sustainable food supply - force us to think more deeply about green architecture, this alliance between green and grey is the result of external pressures: industrial park and green façades, residential areas and local recreation, highway and accompanying green spaces. I believe in the alternatives: refined chaos, dense experience, aesthetic and perceptible frictions. I believe in cultivated accidents. Isolationism and sameness are bland: nature here, city there - elderly people here, babies there. Office here, green space there. It is the spaces that challenge dichotomies and typological designations - spaces that resist classification and, indeed, revel in their ambiguities - that are intriguing.

At Topotek 1, creative misappropriations are a pervasive theme in our design work. We take inspiration from Jorge Louis Borges' playful approach to translation, where Borges saw translation errors and fragmentary translations as opportunities to introduce displacements and localised shifts - situations that enrich the original, deepening rather than limiting its meaning. This contains a huge potential for an open-ended,

und auf deren Potenzial zur Interaktion. Um es zu entfalten, halte ich es für hilfreich, das, was wir unter Natur und Naturerlebnissen verstehen, neu zu definieren und zu erweitern. Denn oft wird die Natur mit Gras und Bäumen verwechselt – eine romantische und oft eingeschränkte Sichtweise. Sie erfüllt aber ein viel größeres Erfahrungsspektrum. Hannah Arendt spricht in „The Life of the Mind" (1978) vom „Herz der Zeit" und meint damit jene überwältigenden Momente, in denen der Atem und die Zeit stehen bleiben. Diese Momente sind natürlich nicht auf einen Spaziergang durch den Wald oder den Park beschränkt, sie lassen sich in der sinnlichen Erfahrung von Musik oder Tanz, in einer weiten, offenen Aussicht, in der Sinnlichkeit von Raum und Material oder beim Yoga finden – und so weiter. Was ich mir vorstelle, ist die größere Kultivierung eines „Herzens der Zeit" und seine Integration in den Alltag. So vermischen sich diese besonderen Momente mit den weniger wichtigen Momenten unserer täglichen Umgebung.

Dichotomie aufgeben: Ein Plädoyer für die kreative Veruntreuung

Ob Barock oder Bauhaus, architektonische Bewegungen haben stattdessen oft Erfahrungen und Typologien fest eingeteilt, organisiert und sortiert. Und auch wenn wir uns heute aufgrund von Klimawandel, Hochwasser oder Fragen der Ernährung einer wachsenden Stadtbevölkerung wieder intensiver mit grüner Infrastruktur befassen müssen, bleibt es ein Zweckbündnis aus Grün und Grau: aus Gewerbepark und Fassadenbegrünung, aus Wohnsiedlung und Naherholung, aus Schnellstraße und Begleitgrün. Alternativ glaube ich an das raffinierte Chaos, die Dichte der Erfahrung und an ästhetische und erfahrbare Konflikte. Ich glaube an kultivierte Unfälle. Isolationismus und Gleichheit sind fade: Natur hier, Stadt dort, alte Menschen hier, Babys dort. Büro hier, Grünanlage dort. Meiner Meinung nach sind Räume interessant, die die Vorstellungen von Dichotomie und typologischen Bezeichnungen infrage stellen, Räume, welche die Unannehmlichkeiten der fehlenden Klassifizierung genießen.

Kreative Veruntreuungen sind ein durchgehendes Motiv in der gestalterischen Arbeit von Topotek 1. Damit nehmen wir Bezug auf Jorge Luis Borges' Spiel mit Übersetzungen. Denn Borges versteht Übersetzungsfehler und bruchstückhafte Übersetzungen als eine Chance, Verschiebungen und lokale Umsetzungen vorzunehmen: eine Situation, die

liberating approach to green and grey infrastructure in our cities.

Moments of desire: rooting people in their environment

Interwoven spaces provide multidimensional potential that goes beyond conventional, anticipatory conceptions of recreational spaces as cultivated natural areas with clear borders. A constructive melding of typologies and occupancies is made possible through the acceptance - or tolerance - of annexations within a dense space, opening up a spectrum of experiences that can root people in their environment at different levels of sensory perception. The progression of climate change must be seen as an integral factor in designing urban spaces in order to accommodate the resulting natural events through sustainable solutions. Innovative interventions and a deeper interlocking of infrastructure and landscape must be found at all levels and dimensions in future design plans.

The cultivated landscape - especially for foodstuffs - must be intelligently designed using modern technology as intelligently as possible, and infrastructures must be optimised so that existing natural resources are used as efficiently as possible. At the same time, a dramatic re-think of urban spaces and landscapes is required in order to design hybrid landscapes that capture new forms of nature's sensuality. As such, embodied (sensory) experiences remain possible - or perhaps become possible once again.

das Original bereichert und nicht beschränkt. Hierin liegt großes Potenzial für einen offenen und befreienden Umgang mit grüner und grauer Infrastruktur in unseren Städten.

Lustmomente: Den Menschen in seiner Umwelt verwurzeln

Verwobene Räume bieten damit vielschichtige Potenziale, die über konventionelle, antizipatorische Vorstellungen von Naherholung im Sinne abgegrenzter kultivierter Naturflächen hinausgehen. Ein konstruktives Verschmelzen von Typologien und Belegungen wird über die Akzeptanz/Toleranz von Aneignungen auf dichtem Raum möglich und eröffnet ein Spektrum an Erfahrungen, die den Menschen auf verschiedensten Ebenen der Sinneswahrnehmung in seiner Umwelt verwurzeln können. Auch der fortschreitende Klimawandel muss als integraler Faktor hinsichtlich der Gestaltung urbaner Räume verstanden werden, um resultierenden Naturereignissen mit nachhaltigen Lösungen zu begegnen. Innovative infrastrukturelle Interventionen und eine stärkere Verzahnung von Infrastruktur und Landschaft müssen bei zukünftigen Planungen auf allen Maßstabsebenen Berücksichtigung finden.

Kultivierte Landschaft muss auf Basis modernster Technologien so intelligent gestaltet, Prozesse der Produktion – insbesondere von Nahrungsmitteln – und Infrastrukturen müssen so extensiv optimiert werden, dass vorhandene Naturressourcen so effizient wie möglich zum Einsatz kommen können. Dabei hybride Landschaften gleichzeitig so zu gestalten, dass die Sinnlichkeit unserer Natur neue Formen findet, sodass körperverbundene (sinnliche) Erlebnisse wieder und weiterhin möglich sind, erfordert ein Neudenken urbaner Räume und Landschaften.

Hamburg-Veddel: hybrid use of the dyke by Topotek 1

Hamburg-Veddel: hybride Nutzung des Deichs von Topotek 1

Before: Kallang River at Bishan-Ang Mo Kio Park, Singapore

Vorher: Kallang-Fluss im Park Bishan-Ang Mo Kio, Singapur

After: Ramboll Studio Dreiseitl and CH2M engineering of a functional canal into a naturalised landscape

Nachher: Ramboll Studio Dreiseitl und CH2M transformierten den trostlosen Kanal in eine renaturierte Flusslandschaft, die Oberflächenwasser filtert

Tomorrow's Cities Today

Urban Waterscapes

The increasing effects of climate change are presenting cities around the world with major infrastructure challenges - often unprecedented in their scope and complexity. Here, Dieter Grau - landscape architect and executive partner at Ramboll Studio Dreiseitl - shares how cities can learn from and live with their environmental conditions through integrated urban design approaches that help cities and their residents achieve resilience through blue-green (hybrid) infrastructure solutions.

Many cities across the globe are experiencing the increasing effects of climate change, including extreme rainfall and flooding events, drought and drinking water scarcity. Visible or hidden, too much or too little, water plays an essential role in the vitality of urban life. In the face of such complicated and often intertwined challenges, the design and implementation of blue-green infrastructure that is purposefully integrated into a network of public spaces are critical to enhancing the safety and health of cities. Now, more than ever, integrated approaches to city planning and design are needed.

The core problem of contemporary urban developments can be found in the disconnect between the functional solutions of water engineering and the multi-faceted, aesthetic approach to urban and landscape design. Although the traditional silo method of planning and designing cities is slowly changing, planners and designers are being outpaced by the very challenges they must address, including but not limited to stormwater management, flooding and poor air quality. The multiplicity of these urban challenges, however, can be resolved when the planning and design professions work together; projects can no longer take the traditional approach of being prepared under the aegis of one discipline, with the other disciplines to be brought in later. It is crucial that all disciplines be involved throughout the process - throughout the planning, design, construction and maintenance of projects at all scales, especially when it comes to fundamental conceptual planning decisions.

Städte für morgen von heute

Urbane Wasserlandschaften

Die zunehmenden Auswirkungen des Klimawandels stellen Städte und ihre Infrastruktur auf der ganzen Welt vor große Herausforderungen – oft beispiellos in ihrem Umfang und ihrer Komplexität. Dieter Grau, Landschaftsarchitekt und geschäftsführender Gesellschafter von Ramboll Studio Dreiseitl, berichtet, wie Städte von ihren Umweltbedingungen lernen und mit ihnen leben können. Das Verfolgen von integrierten städtebaulichen Ansätzen kann Städten und ihren Bewohner*innen helfen, durch blau-grüne (hybride) Infrastrukturlösungen Resilienz zu erlangen.

Weltweit erleben Städte die wachsenden Auswirkungen des Klimawandels, mit extremen Niederschlägen, Überflutungen, Dürre und Trinkwasserknappheit. Wasser – sichtbar oder versteckt, zu viel oder zu wenig – spielt für städtisches Leben eine enorme Rolle. Angesichts der komplizierten und häufig miteinander verwobenen Herausforderungen ist die Gestaltung und Einführung einer blau-grünen Infrastruktur entscheidend, die so einsatzfähig in den öffentlichen Raum integriert ist, dass sie die Sicherheit und Gesundheit von Städten verbessert. Mehr denn je brauchen wir integrierte Ansätze.

Das Kernproblem gegenwärtiger städtischer Entwicklungen liegt in der Entkopplung funktionaler wassertechnischer Lösungen von den ästhetischen Ansätzen urbaner Gestaltung und Landschaftsarchitektur. Obwohl sich das traditionelle Silo-Denken in der Stadtplanung und -gestaltung langsam ändert, werden Planer*innen und Architekt*innen von denselben Herausforderungen überholt, die sie angehen müssen – einschließlich (aber nicht ausschließlich) Sturmwassermanagement, Überflutung und schlechter Luftqualität. Nur wenn die planenden und ausführenden Berufe zusammenarbeiten, können sie diesen multiplen städtischen Herausforderungen wirkungsvoll begegnen. Projekte können nicht länger – dem traditionellen Ansatz folgend – unter Federführung eines einzelnen Berufsstandes stehen und die übrigen Disziplinen erst später hinzuziehen. Entscheidend ist, dass alle Disziplinen während des gesamten Prozesses beteiligt sind: an der Planung, Gestaltung, dem Bau und der Instandhaltung von Projekten jeder Größenordnung. Das gilt insbesondere für die grundlegenden konzeptuellen Planungsentscheidungen.

How beautiful, functional, ecological and safe cities are created

The design of blue-green infrastructure represents the next generation of water infrastructure, where natural, urban and recreational spaces are combined to form integrated solutions. That creates beautiful, functional, ecological and safe cities that are fit for the future. By developing - and fostering - a sustainable, interdisciplinary planning and design culture, we will be able to re-establish the ability of our urban rivers and waterways to create powerful urban spaces for the benefit of livability in our cities while, crucially, responding to the changing rhythms and dynamic forces of water, in all of its forms.

A recent example of this type of blue-green infrastructure is Singapore's flagship Kallang River at Bishan-Ang Mo Kio Park. A joint venture between the Ministry of the Environment and Water Resources (PUB) and the National Parks Board (NParks), Ramboll Studio Dreiseitl and CH2M transformed a concrete canal through a process of coordinated design and engineering into a naturalised, picturesque river. Under the auspices of the city-state's Active, Beautiful, Clean (ABC) Waters Programme, the formerly hard edges of the grey infrastructure were removed, and the designers and planners - in tandem with civil engineers - softened the edges of the soon-to-be-river by replacing the concrete with natural materials including rocks, soil and plants. Rainwater, slowed down with the material and topographical changes made to the site, now has the opportunity to infiltrate the soil, irrigating the ground - and it is filtered and cleaned through the site's new hydrogeology, for use onsite or as drinking water. Based on a flood plain concept, the river channel's course is linked to the city's storm drain network, increasing the flood capacity of the catchment area by an estimated 300 percent. During dry and temperate weather, the water moving through the site is contained as a stream in the river bed. In the event of a storm, the softened edges alternate between slowing and holding the water, allowing it to take its time, moving down through the park, into the river and downstream.

The dynamic nature of the park has not only attracted human visitors, but wildlife too - increasing biodiversity with new types of birds and in-

So entstehen schöne, funktionale, ökologische und sichere Städte

Die nächste Generation der Wasserinfrastruktur ist eine blau-grüne Infrastruktur, in der natürliche, urbane Räume und Erholungsräume zu integrierten Lösungen zusammengeführt sind. So entstehen schöne, funktionale, ökologische und sichere Städte, die für die Zukunft gewappnet sind. Die Stärkung einer nachhaltigen, interdisziplinären Planungs- und Baukultur ermöglicht es uns, die Fähigkeit unserer städtischen Flüsse und Wasserwege wieder zu entfalten und urbane Räume voller Kraft für mehr Lebensqualität in unseren Städten zu schaffen; denen es zugleich gelingt – und das ist entscheidend –, mit dem wechselhaften Rhythmus und den dynamischen Kräften des Wassers in all seinen Formen umzugehen.

Ein jüngeres Beispiel dieser Art der blau-grünen Infrastruktur ist Singapurs Vorzeigeprojekt, der Kallang-Fluss im Park Bishan-Ang Mo Kio. Dieses Gemeinschaftsprojekt des Ministeriums für Umwelt und Wasser (PUB), der Nationalen Parkverwaltung (NParks), von Ramboll Studio Dreiseitl sowie CH2M hat in einem Prozess der koordinierten Planung und Ausführung den vorherigen Betonkanal in eine naturnahe, malerische Flusslandschaft verwandelt. Unter der Schirmherrschaft des Wasserprogramms Active, Beautiful, Clean (ABC) des Stadtstaats wurden die harten Kanten der grauen Infrastruktur entfernt. Die Architekt*innen und Planer*innen schufen in Zusammenarbeit mit Bauingenieur*innen weiche Ufer für den entstehenden Fluss. Durch natürliche Materialien wie Felsen, Erde und Pflanzen ersetzten sie den Beton. Das Material und die topografischen Veränderungen des Ortes bremsen nun das Regenwasser, das in den Boden einsickern kann und so die Erde bewässert. Durch die neue Hydrogeologie des Geländes wird das Wasser gefiltert und gereinigt und ist vor Ort als Trinkwasser nutzbar. Der Wasserkanal ist auf Basis eines Überschwemmungskonzepts mit dem Regenwasserkanalisationsnetz verbunden, was die Wasseraufnahmekapazität der Fläche um schätzungsweise 300 Prozent erhöht. Bei trockenem und gemäßigtem Wetter wird das Wasser, das sich durch das Gelände bewegt, im Flussbett gehalten. Bei Sturm übernehmen die weichen Kanten gleich zwei Funktionen: Sie entschleunigen das Wasser und speichern es. Gemächlich läuft es durch den Park in den Fluss und schließlich flussabwärts ins Meer.

A trans-sectoral cooperation with the Parks and Environment Ministries results in the evolution of a new hydrogeology – filtering the water, storing it, and, through this eco-infrastructure, transforming the landscape

Eine transsektorale Zusammenarbeit im Stadtstaat führt zu einer neuen Hydrogeologie: Wasser wird gefiltert, gehalten und – aufgrund der Eco-Infrastruktur – entsteht eine neue Landschaft

sects while encouraging residents to get close to water and nature in ways that were not possible before. This significant new city park – this blue-green infrastructure – addresses the dual needs of water supply and flood protection, while creating space for people, flora, fauna and water in the city. Today, even as it provides protection from flooding events, Bishan Park is one of the most actively used open spaces in Singapore, a hub for community interaction, culture and recreation.

Living and learning from the environment

Resilient urban ecological waterscapes such as these are the foundation for establishing vibrant public spaces that are culturally and socially significant, contribute to the economic well-being of cities and sustain the longevity of liveable cities in the future. The result of a well-planned and strategic integration of resources, people, elements and systems create strengthened communities where people are in direct contact with nature; where the environment is a source of learning, pleasure, health and wellness; and where interdisciplinary collaboration, hands-on public participation and cross-agency coordination are understood as the critical first step in arriving at inspirational solutions that generate pride in our civic spaces and places.

Die lebhafte Natur des Parks zieht nicht nur Menschen, sondern auch Wildtiere an. Neue Vogel- und Insektenarten erhöhen die Biodiversität. Zugleich werden Anwohner*innen motiviert, dem Wasser und der Natur so nah zu kommen, wie es zuvor nicht möglich war. Der neue Stadtpark – diese blau-grüne Infrastruktur – erfüllt zweierlei Bedürfnisse: Er versorgt mit Wasser und schützt vor Überschwemmungen, schafft aber zugleich auch Raum für Menschen, Flora und Fauna in der Stadt. Obgleich er dem Überschwemmungsschutz dient, ist der Bishan-Park heute eine der am meisten genutzten öffentlichen Flächen Singapurs, ein Knotenpunkt für nachbarschaftliche Interaktion, Kultur und Erholung.

Umwelt als Lebens- und Lernquelle

Robuste städtisch-ökologische Wasserlandschaften wie diese sind die Grundlage für die Schaffung lebendiger öffentlicher Räume, die sowohl kulturell als auch gesellschaftlich bedeutsam sind. Sie fördern das ökonomische Wohlergehen der Städte und erhalten ihre Lebensqualität für die Zukunft. Eine gut geplante, strategische Integration von Ressourcen stärkt im Ergebnis Nachbarschaften, in denen die Menschen in direktem Kontakt mit der Natur leben; wo Umwelt eine Quelle des Lernens, der Freude, Gesundheit und Erholung ist; und wo interdisziplinäre Zusammenarbeit, praktische öffentliche Teilhabe und behördenübergreifende Koordination als entscheidende erste Schritte verstanden werden, um inspirierende Lösungen zu verwirklichen, die uns stolz auf unsere öffentlichen Flächen und Plätze machen.

Ancient construct methods rediscovered in the urgent era of climate change:
left: Adaptation of natural rock and terrain in a rain-scarce region to hold water for humans and cattle: the water cistern at Nahargarh Fort 1734.AD, near Jaipur, Rajasthan India
right: Peripheral movement space screened by stone and lime-plastered exterior walls shield the core from heat, while allowing air circulation: the interior space – Jehangir Mahal Orchha 17th c. AD, central India

Ursprüngliche Konstruktionsmethoden werden durch die Dringlichkeit des Klimawandels neu entdeckt:
links: Anpassung von Naturstein und Boden in einer regenarmen Region zur Wasserspeicherung für Mensch und Tier: Die Wasserzisterne am Nahargarh Fort 1734.AD, nahe Jaipur, Rajasthan Indien
rechts: Peripherer Bewegungsraum, abgeschirmt durch Stein- und Kalkputzaußenwände, die den Kern vor Hitze schützen und gleichzeitig eine Luftzirkulation ermöglichen: Der Innenbereich – Jehangir Mahal Orchha 17. c.A.D. Zentralindien

The New Normal

Resilient Buildings that Breathe and Adapt

Over the last two decades, Indigo Architects, founded by Mausumi and Uday Andhare, has worked to develop technically appropriate and ecologically sensitive approaches that weave together threads of traditional - and often local - wisdom into design. Four aspects are found at the core of their practice: the site and its context, programme, water and thermal comfort. In the discussion that follows, the team, which is based in Ahmedabad, India, discuss their studio practice via email with Berlin-based editor Elise Hunchuck ("Scapegoat Journal") and architect Lukas Staudinger.

Elise Hunchuck: In recent years, we have seen a dramatic rise in the frequency of temperature and weather anomalies in all climate zones; abnormal is becoming the new normal. For designers and planners, there is a clear and urgent need to develop designs that respond to the localised circumstances of each project and location, while addressing the global need to minimise ecological impact. Your work has been, for the most part, focused on developing ecological building strategies in hot climates. Can you tell us more about this and how you would describe the possibilities of transferring this expertise elsewhere?

Indigo Architects: To understand the particularities of context, both geo-physical and social forces must be understood. Locally established practices that have been responding to context for some time often embed local, specialised knowledge that must be learned and understood before they can be converted into appropriate opportunities for design.
The thought processes and methods are, of course, humanly possible to transfer and put into effect. The trick is to synergise that which currently exists with that which has always been around. It is always wonderful to create a pool of people, from various disciplines, to work together and bring new perspectives to an existing problem.

EH: We are particularly interested in how you have learned - and how you continue to learn - the methods and design techniques that respond to the localised circumstances and locations of

Das neue Normal

Widerstandsfähige Häuser, die atmen und sich anpassen

Seit den vergangenen zwei Jahrzehnten arbeiten Indigo Architects, gegründet von Mausumi und Uday Andhare, an der Entwicklung technisch adäquater und umweltbewusster Ansätze, die die Fäden traditionellen – oftmals lokalen – Wissens in Designprojekte zusammenwebt. Vier Aspekte bilden die Grundlage ihres Handelns: Kontext, Programm, Wasser und Temperatur. Das Team, das in Ahmedabad in Indien arbeitet, erläutert seine Arbeit im E-Mail-Gespräch mit der Berliner Redakteurin Elise Hunchuck („Scapegoat Journal") und dem Architekten Lukas Staudinger.

Elise Hunchuck: In den vergangenen Jahren haben die Temperatur- und Wetteranomalien in allen Klimazonen dramatisch zugenommen. Unnormal wird das neue Normal. Designer*innen und Planer*innen wächst die Aufgabe zu, Designs zu entwickeln, die die ortsspezifischen Umstände jedes Projekts mitdenken und zugleich dem Klimawandel entgegenwirken. Ihre Arbeit konzentriert sich darauf, ökologische Strategien für das Bauen in den warmen Klimazonen zu entwickeln. Welche Möglichkeiten gibt es, diese Expertise auch auf andere Orte zu übertragen?

Indigo Architects: Um den Kontext eines Bauprojekts zu verstehen, muss man zuerst seine geophysischen und sozialen Kräfte erkennen. Bestehende lokale Praktiken reagieren seit Langem auf die Umgebung und enthalten oft genau das Wissen, das man für die Übertragung auf Designstrategien braucht. Der Trick ist, aus dem, was aktuell entsteht, und dem, was schon da war, eine Synergie zu erzeugen. Es ist immer toll, eine Gruppe von Menschen aus verschiedenen Disziplinen zusammenzubringen, damit sie zusammenarbeiten und neue Perspektiven auf ein bestehendes Problem eröffnen.

EH: Uns interessiert besonders, wie Sie herausgefunden haben – und weiterhin herausfinden –, welche Methoden und Entwurfstechniken den spezifischen Umständen vor Ort entsprechen und gleichzeitig gut für die ökologische Nachhaltigkeit eines Projekts sind.

IA: Grob gesagt sind Studien lokaler Wohngebäude, historischer Strukturen und traditioneller Siedlungen verschiedener Kulturen und Epochen traditio-

your projects, while simultaneously addressing the very terrestrial need to minimise ecological impact.

IA: Broadly speaking, studies of vernacular habitats, formal historic structures and traditional settlements from across cultures and histories have traditionally been a part of early learning in architectural design education. This exposure is the foundation for sensitising designers even today and must be looked at more clearly.
Our design methods are driven by absorbing local sensibilities and available technologies to interpret, adapt and act upon depending on the time, place and space of engagement. We also work to synergise learning across disciplines as we seek out (often) frugal solutions. This has helped us, as designers, make informed choices and sometimes offers us a counter-measure against oppressive and expensive technological compulsions.
This is an early stage of building design in which principles of passive design must be fundamental and not mere technological toppings! All of this can be achieved under the codes and regulations that govern the building industry with just a little effort from all participants and policymakers. Globally, design practices must become laboratories or bridges for connecting deeper structures, while both adopting and adapting. This is possible only if we bring design to the forefront of our endeavour, not just as a visual objective, but as something more meaningful. No matter their situation or site - buildings must breathe - and material choices must support this need.

Lukas Staudinger: You mentioned vernacular habitats, and I would like to return to that: what is your take on housing typologies in the context of localised conditions; and what do you see as the needs for contemporary housing in terms of spatiality, ecology, economy, socially and, of course, in terms of materiality?

IA: Globally we have seen housing typologies shift from the traditional, low-rise, high-density, socio-climatic-concern-driven model to an aspirational consumptive one that almost always leads to a monoculture of urban living. This is particularly true in the developing world. However, we still believe that within the realities of a purely economically-driven global housing stock, there is room to rethink and infuse contemporary housing with fundamental parameters: namely, that access to human comfort and the improvement of building resilience across geographic and climatic diversities are mandatory.

nell Teil der frühen Architekturausbildung. Diese Auseinandersetzung ist auch heute noch die Grundlage, um Architekt*innen zu sensibilisieren. Unsere Entwurfsmethoden werden davon beeinflusst, was wir vor Ort vorfinden und welche Technologien sich als geeignet herausstellen. Wir handeln zeit-, orts- und raumspezifisch. Wir arbeiten interdisziplinär und suchen (oft) einfache Lösungen. Das hilft uns als Planer*innen, Entwurfsentscheidungen auf einer guten Informationsgrundlage zu treffen. Die Methode hat viele Vorzüge und ermöglicht uns, gegen teure und bevormundende technologische Zwänge zu planen.
Das ist ein essenzieller Teil der Planung und Konzeption von Entwürfen: Klimagerechtes passives Design muss Grundlage sein und nicht einfach nur ein technologisches Extra darstellen! Mit dem Bemühen von Planer*innen und Politik lässt sich das auch auf Basis bestehender Verordnungen und Regulierungen des Baugewerbes erreichen. Das schaffen wir, wenn wir das Design in den Mittelpunkt unserer Anstrengungen stellen und es nicht nur als formale Herausforderung betrachten, sondern ihm mehr Bedeutung geben.
Aus Entwurfsprozessen müssen Forschungsprojekte werden. Sie bilden Brücken, die teilweise verstecktes, lokales Know-how, welches im Entwurfsprojekt eingesetzt werden kann, sichtbar machen. Gebäude müssen atmen: Wo und wie auch immer sie gebaut werden – danach muss sich die Materialauswahl richten.

Lukas Staudinger: Sie erwähnten den Aspekt des Lokalen, und ich möchte darauf zurückkommen: Wie können Gebäudetypologien auf ihren Kontext reagieren? Und was sind Ihrer Meinung nach die räumlichen, ökologischen, ökonomischen und sozialen Anforderungen an zeitgenössischen Wohnungsbau? Welche Auswirkungen haben diese Aspekte auf die Materialbeschaffenheit von Gebäuden?

IA: Weltweit beobachten wir einen Wechsel der Wohntypologien weg vom traditionellen niedrigen, dichten und sozioklimatischen Bauen hin zu einem ressourcenverschwendenden, das urbane Monokulturen hervorbringt. Dies gilt insbesondere für Länder des globalen Südens. Trotzdem glauben wir, dass selbst innerhalb eines rein ökonomisch gesteuerten Wohnungsmarktes Raum für Alternativen ist und dass es möglich ist, zeitgenössische Wohnformen mit den elementaren Bedürfnissen menschlichen Wohlbefindens auszustatten.
Gesunder Menschenverstand zusammen mit computergestützten Methoden muss dazu führen, dass thermischer Komfort sommers wie winters garantiert ist und dabei nur minimal Ressourcen verbraucht werden. Wohngebäude müssen technisch

Design must involve the use of common sense in tandem with detailed computational models in order to ensure thermal comfort in summer and winter, using minimal resources. Housing must be low-tech in construction when possible, low on maintenance over time, and it must engage advanced technologies to ensure equity in the distribution of resources like water and energy. Thermal comfort and water-centric design approaches must be at the core, through a concerted effort from all stakeholders challenging the norm. Each geographic context sets and poses specific challenges, which must be negotiated. The spatial, ecological, economic, social and technological aspects of housing are intertwined. The ecologically relevant approach is one that remains to be tested and has the ability to inform the spatial and social. The economic potential of simple meaningful interventions has not always been understood.

EH: The fundamental tenets of your design practice could, in some ways, be described as "a practice of listening". How, then, does your practice share its information with others and communicate the localised knowledge and skills that you yourselves have learned, onwards, to future generations?

IA: Dissemination of knowledge is best done through the sharing of practices and methods at the professional and institutional levels. Here, where we work and teach in India, it has become common for practising professionals, city government officials and students to engage with each other through professional development programmes.
Construction skills that are otherwise vanishing quickly are being brought into practice through personal initiatives on private projects and, whenever possible, on those projects that involve government funding, especially in areas of conservation when traditional materials - such as lime - are used in construction. We have also found government-initiated skill development programmes to be effective.
Interestingly, institutional programmes at universities have been developing craft-based approaches to disseminate knowledge and are compiling a national atlas of building skills and crafts for design professionals to use when needed. This repository is invaluable for any country, as it makes its master crafts persons available to any industry, as resources. This ensures the survival of persons and their crafts against economic forces and time.

so einfach wie möglich sein, wenig Wartung benötigen und ausgefeilte Technologien einbeziehen, damit die Verteilung von Ressourcen wie Wasser und Energie gerechter wird. Thermische Qualitäten und Wasser müssen Bestandteil der Planung werden; alle Beteiligten müssen hier spezifische Leistung erbringen, um die Norm zu verbessern. Jeder geografische Kontext gibt seine besonderen Herausforderungen vor, die es auszuloten gilt. Die räumlichen, ökologischen, ökonomischen, sozialen und technologischen Aspekte des Wohnens sind miteinander verwoben. Ökologisch nachhaltige Ansätze müssen weiter ausgebaut werden: Noch immer wird das wirtschaftliche Potenzial einfacher, aber effizienter Lösungen nicht verstanden.

EH Die Prinzipien Ihrer Entwurfspraxis könnten in gewisser Weise als eine „Praxis des Zuhörens" beschrieben werden. Wie könnten Sie Ihre Arbeit demnach mit anderen teilen und ortsspezifisches Wissen und Fähigkeiten, die Sie selbst erworben haben, an zukünftige Generationen weitergeben?

IA: Vermittlung von Wissen geschieht am besten, indem man Praxis und Methodik auf professioneller und institutioneller Ebene teilt. Hier in Indien, wo wir arbeiten und lehren, ist es für praktizierende Spezialist*innen mittlerweile üblich, mit Stadtverwaltungen und Studierenden über professionelle Entwicklungsprogramme zu kommunizieren und sich zu vernetzen.
Baukenntnisse, die sonst schnell in Vergessenheit geraten, bleiben einerseits durch persönliche Initiativen und private Projekte erhalten. Andererseits können auch staatlich finanzierte Projekte den Einsatz traditioneller Materialien wie Kalk im Bau fördern. Außerdem haben wir festgestellt, dass die von der Regierung initiierten Weiterbildungsmaßnahmen sehr effektiv sind.
Interessanterweise haben einige Universitäten Formate entwickelt, um handwerkliche Fähigkeiten und lokales Wissen zu sammeln. Sie arbeiten an einem nationalen Atlas der Bau- und Handwerkskenntnisse für Planer*innen. Eine solche Sammlung ist für jedes Land von unschätzbarem Wert. Es macht Expert*innen und ihre Fähigkeiten für die Bauindustrie sichtbar. Dies sichert das Überleben der Menschen und ihres Könnens gegen ökonomische Kräfte.

A spatial resource unlocked: Toronto's annual Ride for the Heart transforms the urban highway landscape, making it available for a fundraising bike ride

Eine räumliche Ressource wird freigeschaltet: Torontos jährliche Veranstaltung „Ride for the Heart" verändert die städtische Straßenlandschaft und sammelt dabei gleichzeitig Spenden für karitative Zwecke

The End of Traffic

Forward-Thinking Mobility Concepts

Cars: our cities are full of them. For decades, almost all states around the world have encouraged the use of motor vehicles, and the resulting rearrangement of the city for cars, with its highways, ring roads and endless car parks, has allowed the volume of traffic to explode. This has been compounded by tax breaks for car-owners and the privilege of the company car. The car stands for the promise of freedom and comfort – and with it, the use of a lot of space. At the same time, however, urbanisation has meant that cities are densifying: every parked-in centimetre is costly.

What to do about this dwindling space and congestion? Make City talked to Professor Andreas Knie, managing director of the Innovation Centre for Mobility and Social Change (InnoZ) GmbH, on forward-thinking traffic concepts. How might urban areas be used differently, we wonder, if streets and parking lots were freed up?

"In Germany, we have traffic regulations that permanently prioritise the car over all other means of transport under the umbrella term Gemeingebrauch (common use). That worked just fine – up until the point where our public space was completely filled up and over-burdened. A broad-sweeping change to this situation, given the pre-existing structures, is difficult to imagine." For Andreas Knie, a radical rethink of current mobility concepts is required: "Today in Germany we have nearly 45 million cars – and 81 million inhabitants. The continued focus on the private car means that we have reached the limit in terms of traffic infrastructure. As a result, we now need to bring about a turnaround by flexibilising mobility and interconnecting different forms of transport."

"It is up to politicians to create the conditions for a change in transport policy. They conjured up the car, and now it's time for them to conjure it away – at least as a means of mass transportation. It simply cannot be that public areas are claimed by private vehicles that stand around uselessly." In Berlin, only 8 percent of the available urban surface is subject to parking space management. Almost everywhere else, car owners can park for free. Higher prices would be an immediate solution.

Das Ende des Verkehrs

Mobilität vorausgedacht

Unsere Städte sind voll von ihnen. Nahezu alle Staaten der Welt haben den Einsatz von Kraftfahrzeugen jahrzehntelang gefördert: Der Umbau zur autogerechten Stadt mit ihren vielspurigen Schnellstraßen, Ringautobahnen, endlosen Parkplätzen ließ das Verkehrsaufkommen explodieren. Hinzu kamen Steuervergünstigungen für Autobesitzer*innen und das Dienstwagenprivileg. Das Auto gilt als Freiheits- und Wohlstandsversprechen – mit hohem Platzbedarf. Durch die Urbanisierung werden Städte jedoch immer dichter. Jeder zugeparkte Zentimeter wird kostbar.

Was hilft gegen schwindenden Platz und den Staualltag? Make City sprach mit Andreas Knie, Geschäftsführer des Innovationszentrums für Mobilität und gesellschaftlichen Wandel (InnoZ) GmbH, über zukunftsweisende Verkehrskonzepte. Wie lassen sich städtische Flächen nutzen, wenn Straßen und Parkplätze frei werden?

„Wir haben eine Straßenverkehrsordnung definiert, die unter dem Begriff Gemeingebrauch dem Auto einen dauerhaften Vorrang gegenüber allen anderen Verkehrsmitteln einräumt. Das hat wunderbar funktioniert – bis unser öffentlicher Raum ausgelastet – und überlastet – war. Aus den gegebenen Strukturen heraus ist ein abrupter Wechsel schwer vorstellbar." Für Andreas Knie bedarf es eines radikalen Umdenkens bezüglich aktueller Mobilitätskonzepte: „Zurzeit haben wir in Deutschland fast 45 Millionen Personenkraftwagen – bei 81 Millionen Einwohner*innen. Mit der bisherigen Konzentration auf das private Auto haben wir die verkehrstechnische Grenze erreicht. Demzufolge muss nun über flexible Mobilität und die Verknüpfung der Verkehrsmittel eine Trendwende herbeigeführt werden."

„Es ist an der Politik, Rahmenbedingungen für einen verkehrspolitischen Wandel zu schaffen: Sie hat uns das Auto herbeigezaubert, jetzt muss sie es wieder wegzaubern – jedenfalls als Massenverkehrsmittel. Es kann nicht sein, dass öffentliche Flächen von Privatfahrzeugen beansprucht werden, die nutzlos herumstehen." In Berlin unterliegen nur acht Prozent des Stadtgebietes der Parkraumbewirtschaftung. Nahezu überall sonst können Autobesitzer*innen ihre Wagen kostenlos abstellen. Höhere Preise für privates Parken wären demnach eine Lösung.

Taking a walk on the highway: utopia or realistic scenario for the post-fossil city?

Spaziergang auf der Autobahn: Utopie oder realistisches Szenario in der postfossilen Stadt?

Vehicles used for car-sharing should be exempted, Knie comments. Additionally, it is necessary to adapt the Personenbeförderungsgesetz (Public Transport Act) that will facilitate door-to-door mobility, as well as trains, buses and trams: "You can't just tell people: 'walk, or ride your bike!' These gaps in local public transport must be closed. Of course, different solutions should be considered for peripheral and metropolitan areas, which are often not included in car-pooling options on offer." One suggestion by InnoZ, is the digitisation of commuter traffic. Following prior registration, commuters could make use of citizen services to and from train stations. The rail network is extensive enough. However, it is important to utilise and modernise existing infrastructure.

Traffic turnaround to save space

Andreas Knie underscores the fact that support for such a change in transport policy exists throughout the population: "This is particularly true of large cities, which - as in Berlin - have suffered from crowded traffic routes for at least the last decade." Berlin in particular, with its well-developed public transport network and bike and car-sharing infrastructure, would provide the best conditions for a shift in mobility towards a city with fewer cars. Waterways could also play a significant role, as demonstrated by Rotterdam or Amsterdam. Further expansion of road infrastructure, however, is problematic: "The construction of the A100 must be stopped. Every day in Germany, an area equivalent to 70 football fields is destroyed for traffic. And the erosion of space continues." Although the car will continue to play a role in the future urban mix: "Our aim, however, is to reduce the number of cars on the roads of Berlin from 1.2 million to 350,000. The space

Sharing-Fahrzeuge müssten davon ausgenommen sein, empfiehlt Knie. Weiterhin sei ein angepasstes Personenbeförderungsgesetz notwendig, das neben U-Bahnen, Bussen, Straßenbahnen auch eine Door-to-door Mobility ermögliche: „Man kann den Leuten nicht einfach sagen: Geht doch zu Fuß oder nehmt das Rad! Lücken im öffentlichen Nahverkehr muss man schließen. Natürlich müssen auch Lösungen für den Stadtrand und Ballungsgebiete mitgedacht werden, die meist gar nicht in Sharing-Angebote einbezogen sind." Ein Vorschlag des InnoZ ist deshalb die Digitalisierung des Pendlerverkehrs. Nach vorheriger Anmeldung könnten Pendler*innen Bürger*innenfahrdienste von und zu Bahnhöfen nutzen. Das Schienennetz sei groß genug. Wichtig sei allerdings eine bessere Auslastung der Schienen wie auch die Modernisierung der Bahnen.

Verkehrswende gegen den Flächenfraß

Andreas Knie macht deutlich, dass es durch alle Bevölkerungsschichten hindurch Unterstützung für einen solchen verkehrspolitischen Wandel gäbe: „Dies ist besonders in Großstädten – wie etwa in Berlin –, die unter überfüllten Verkehrswegen leiden, seit mindestens zehn Jahren spürbar." Gerade Berlin mit seinem gut ausgebauten öffentlichen Nahverkehrsnetz und der Möglichkeit Car- oder Bike-Sharingsysteme zu nutzen, böte beste Voraussetzungen für eine Mobilitätswende hin zur autoärmeren Stadt. Auch Wasserwege könnten eine wichtige Rolle spielen, wie es Rotterdam oder Amsterdam zeigten. Den weiteren Ausbau der Straßeninfrastruktur bewertet der Experte als Problem: „Der Bau der A100 muss gestoppt werden. Jeden Tag wird in Deutschland eine Fläche von siebzig Fußballfeldern für den Verkehr vernichtet. Und der Flächenfraß geht weiter." Nichtsdestotrotz wird

saved can be put to uses that could see roads transformed into collective meeting places. In cities that are increasingly densifying, we need street life instead of street noise pollution: this means more space for efficient public transport and on-demand mobility concepts; more space for green areas, children's play areas and street football. The goal of convincing 20 to 30 percent of car drivers to ride a bicycle can only be achieved if we offer more spacious and safer bike paths - and for that, we need space."

Berlin: blueprint for other cities?

Berlin could become a testing ground for new forms of mobility, setting a global example: "In the perception of the world, Berlin is set apart from other cities because of its past and the fall of the Wall. This attention can and must be used to reverse the tide of traffic and transform this into a fluid, diverse and socially-just city that can serve as a blueprint for other major cities. Oslo, Copenhagen and Helsinki are testing out similar trends and developments for a traffic turnaround, but these cities do not yet have the same global appeal as Berlin. Metropolises such as London, Paris, Sao Paolo or Tokyo are so complex that a turnaround would be difficult to implement. That is why Berlin is the ideal city for a turnaround in traffic, which could set a new geopolitical standard."

This conversation was held with Simikka Hansen.

das Auto auch im zukünftigen Verkehrsmix gebraucht: „Unser Ziel ist es aber, die momentane Anzahl von 1,2 Millionen Autos auf Berlins Straßen auf 350.000 zu senken. Die eingesparten Flächen können für Nutzungen verwendet werden, die den Straßenraum als Kollektivfläche und Begegnungsort aufwerten. In immer dichter werdenden Städten benötigen wir Straßenleben statt Straßenlärm: das heißt mehr Platz für effizienten öffentlichen Verkehr und On-Demand-Mobilitätskonzepte; mehr Platz für Grünflächen, spielende Kinder und Straßenfußball! Auch das Ziel, zwanzig bis dreißig Prozent der Verkehrsteilnehmer*innen vom Fahrrad zu überzeugen, kann nur dann erreicht werden, wenn wir großzügigere und sicherere Fahrradwege anbieten – und dafür brauchen wir Platz.

Berlin: Blaupause für andere Metropolen?

Berlin könnte ein Erprobungsraum für neue Formen der Mobilität werden und ein weltweites Vorbild setzen: „In der Wahrnehmung der Welt setzt sich Berlin aufgrund seiner Vergangenheit – und den Fall der Mauer – von anderen Städten ab. Diese Energie können und müssen wir nutzen, um durch eine Verkehrswende hin zu einem flüssigen, vielfältigen und sozial gerechten Verkehr zu kommen, der als Blaupause für andere Metropolen dient. Andere Städte wie Oslo, Kopenhagen oder Helsinki, die ähnliche Strömungen und Entwicklungen einer Verkehrswende versuchen, haben eine solche globale Strahlkraft noch nicht. Metropolen wie London, Paris, São Paulo oder Tokio sind wiederum so komplex, dass eine Wende nicht einfach umsetzbar ist. Deshalb ist Berlin die ideale Stadt für eine Verkehrswende, die geopolitisch neue Maßstäbe setzt.

Das Gespräch führte Simikka Hansen.

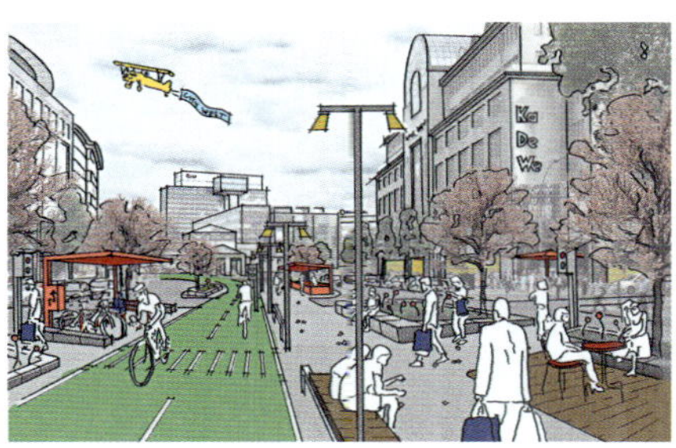

The Berlin initiative Radbahn: 9 kilometres of potential space under a metro viaduct

Die Berliner Initiative Radbahn: Neun Kilometer potenzielle Fläche unter der U-Bahn

From the parking lot to the so-called parklet: Bergmannstraße in Berlin

Vom Parkplatz zum sogenannten Parklet: Bergmannstraße in Berlin

Next to the Pavement, the Beach

Hybrid Streets for the 21st Century

Today, as global cities face increasing pressures on public and shared spaces, the monofunctionality of thoroughfares and carparks in cities are being questioned and critiqued and the streets are being reclaimed. Here, Steffan Robel, co-founder and managing director of A24 Landscape Architecture takes up the current "utopian turn in mobility" to explore temporary interventions and the reclamation of the street as a living space of the city in order to develop and propose hybrid street typologies for a new city.

We have rediscovered the potential of the city street as a space for everyday life. Our mobility has shifted and become multi-modular. Simultaneously, urbanisation and digitisation have led to increased use of public space and to the increased significance of physical, local areas. Globally, monofunctional thoroughfares are increasingly becoming problematised and carparks are being condemned.

How do we take up the current utopian turn in mobility to formulate new narratives for urban space which correspond to the contemporary urban mode of living? How should urban spaces be transformed? Where can we integrate public life into streets, creating an improved quality of living? Which new typologies support today's - and tomorrow's - city life?

Reclaiming the street as a space to live in

There are many arguments and approaches for rendering visible shifts in mobility and reclaiming the urban qualities of the streets: if automated driving is to improve the utilisation of private cars - which, according to mobility researcher Sina Nordhoff, decreases the need for parking - then newly freed-up parking areas will then be made available to urban citizens through the radical restructuring of street space.

Today, Gehl Architects from Copenhagen think that a different city is possible: "In almost every city, streets dominate public space." According

Neben dem Pflaster liegt der Strand

Hybride Straßen für das 21. Jahrhundert

Seit Städte weltweit einem zunehmenden Druck auf den öffentlichen und gemeinsamen Raum ausgesetzt sind, wird die Monofunktionalität von Straßen und Parkplätzen im urbanen Raum infrage gestellt und kritisiert. Die Straßen werden zurückgefordert. Steffan Robel, Mitbegründer und Geschäftsführer von A24 Landschaftsarchitektur, greift hier die aktuelle „utopische Wendung in der Mobilität" auf, um temporäre Interventionen und die Rekultivierung der Straße als Lebensraum der Stadt zu untersuchen. Dabei schlägt er hybride Straßentypologien für eine neue Stadt vor.

Wir entdecken das Potenzial der Stadtstraße als Lebens- und Alltagsraum neu. Unser Mobilitätsverhalten verändert sich und wird multimodaler. Parallel führen Urbanisierung und Digitalisierung zur stärkeren Nutzung des öffentlichen Raums, und das physische, kleinräumliche Lebensumfeld gewinnt an Bedeutung. Global werden monofunktionale Durchgangsstraßen zunehmend problematisiert und Parkplätze abgebaut. Dieses utopische Moment der Mobilitätswende können wir aufgreifen, um neue Narrative für den Straßenraum zu formulieren, die der gegenwärtigen urbanen Lebenswelt entsprechen.

Wie sollten sich Straßenräume verwandeln? Wo können wir das öffentliche Leben in den Straßen integrieren und Aufenthaltsqualität schaffen? Welche neuen Typologien unterstützen das heutige Stadtleben?

Rückeroberung der Straße als urbaner Lebensraum

Argumente und Ansätze, um den Mobilitätswandel sichtbar zu machen und die urbanen Qualitäten der Straßen zurückzugewinnen, gibt es viele: Das voll automatisierte Fahren wird die Auslastung privater Pkws verbessern und den Parkverkehr verringern, prognostiziert die Mobilitätsforscherin Sina Nordhoff. Die Parkflächen, die dann frei werden, können den Bürger*innen der Stadt durch eine radikale Umgestaltung des Straßenraums zurückgegeben werden.

to Kristian Villadsen from Gehl, "they could become the social, economic and ecological backbone of the city." Socially, because all groups of society meet on the street. Economically, because start-ups are linked to local economies and neighbourhood facilities that use the streets. Ecologically, because people walk, ride their bikes and use local public transport - all on the streets.

The living room of the city

Traffic planner Burkhard Horn has researched the potential for redevelopment: many new dimensions may open up: from broader spatial urban repair to improved quality in attention to detail. "Urban street spaces are the 'outdoor living room' of people in the city. Structuring them as integrated spaces - where one would want to linger - must reflect adjacent uses such as living, eating and working, as well as the mobility demands of people and goods," says Horn. In this sense, spaces currently reserved for cars could be reclaimed and redesigned into urban living spaces.

In Berlin, new examples for the redesign of hybrid urban spaces offer a possible way forward. The concept of such spaces for meeting is being applied by the Senate Department for Urban Development and Environment in rebuilding streets for people. In 2015, Maaßenstrasse in Schöneberg was restructured along these lines, and after widespread public criticism of its technical results, the landscape of the A24 highway has led to the suggestion of alternative spatial solutions that on the one hand, take the street into account as a mobility corridor, while on the other, transforming streets into a space for meeting and acquiring groceries in the urban quarter. These suggestions involves taking apart carparks, narrowing space for cars and encouraging a mix between local residents, pedestrians, bikes and cars. A clear focus is placed on landscape-based architecture, clear spatial order, secure traffic crossings, versatile meeting places, space for movement and creating zones for people that exist outside of traffic chaos.

Temporary interventions are useful in order to avoid negative experiences. For example, the meeting-zone in Bergmannstraße in Berlin-Kreuzberg is to be redesigned so that the process is reversible. In order to make the advantages of deceleration and accessibility visible,

Schon heute halten Gehl Architekten aus Kopenhagen eine andere Straße für machbar: „Straßen dominieren den öffentlichen Raum in fast allen Städten und könnten das soziale, ökonomische und ökologische Rückgrat der Stadt werden", meint Kristian Villadsen von Gehl. Sozial, weil hier alle Gruppen der Gesellschaft aufeinanderstoßen; ökonomisch, weil Start-ups, die lokale Ökonomie und Nachbarschaftseinrichtungen hier angesiedelt sind; und ökologisch, weil die Menschen hier laufen, Fahrrad fahren und zum öffentlichen Nahverkehr anschließen.

Das Wohnzimmer der Stadt

Auch der Verkehrsplaner Burkhard Horn untersucht die Umgestaltungsmöglichkeiten. Dabei geht es ihm um mehrere Dimensionen: von der großräumlichen städtebaulichen Reparatur bis zur Schaffung von Qualität im Detail. „Urbane Straßenräume sind das ‚Außenwohnzimmer' der Menschen in der Stadt. Ihre Gestaltung als integrierte Räume mit Aufenthaltscharakter muss die angrenzenden Nutzungen wie Wohnen, Versorgung, Gastronomie und Arbeit genauso wie die Anforderungen für die Mobilität von Menschen und Gütern widerspiegeln", sagt Horn. So lassen sich Fahrbahnflächen für eine Vielzahl von Nutzungen und Nutzern zurückerobern und zum urbanen Lebensraum umgestalten.

In Berlin zeigen neue Beispiele hybrider Straßenraumgestaltung einen möglichen Weg in die Zukunft. Mit dem Konzept der „Begegnungszonen" baut die Senatsverwaltung für Stadtentwicklung und Umwelt Straßen für Menschen um. Schon 2015 wurde die Maaßenstraße in Schöneberg verkehrsplanerisch umgestaltet. Nach breiter öffentlicher Kritik am eher technischen Resultat hat A24 Landschaft alternative räumliche Lösungsansätze vorgeschlagen. Sie berücksichtigen einerseits die Straße als Mobilitätskorridor, andererseits machen sie den Straßen- zum Aufenthaltsraum und Lebensmittelpunkt im Quartier. Der Vorschlag beinhaltet den Rückbau von Parkstreifen, verengte Fahrspuren und die Förderung des Miteinanders von Anwohner*innen, Fußgänger*innen, Rad- und Autofahrer*innen. Mit einem deutlichen Fokus auf Landschaftsarchitektur, die eine klare Ordnung des Raums, sichere Querungsstellen, vielseitige Aufenthaltsorte und Raum für Bewegung schafft, wird aus Verkehrschaos Begegnungszone.

Temporäre Interventionen eignen sich, um negative Erfahrungen zu vermeiden. Die Begegnungs-

temporary and small-scale interventions reclaim the street through designed parklets with urban greenery and public seating. The success of such pilot projects is necessary in the process of actively reappropriating parking spaces in order to convince people that less traffic leads to more free space. The interventions should invite passersby to take the street into their own hands, opening up new potential for co-production and shared use. The city of tomorrow thus gains space for experimentation and, in this way, the wish for accessible and useable streetscape can be realised.

Hybrid street typologies for a new city

Examples such as these demonstrate that the reduction of parking spaces leads to the opportunity to transform monofunctional cities into multifunctional urban spaces. Adaptive and flexible urban design can inform the beginnings of new urban structures with new types of streetscapes offering complex physical spaces for variegated forms of movement and use. Hybrid streets provide an open urban stage for a better quality of life, where functions of mobility, meeting, consumption, political manifestation and ecology can overlap.

zone Bergmannstraße in Berlin-Kreuzberg beispielsweise wird deshalb zunächst reversibel umgestaltet. Damit die Vorteile von Entschleunigung und Fußläufigkeit ersichtlich werden, kommen temporäre „reclaiming the street"-Eingriffe im kleinen Maßstab zum Einsatz, unter anderem durch vielfältig gestaltete „Parklets" bespielt mit Stadtgrün und Sitzgelegenheiten. Für das Gelingen eines solchen Pilotprojekts ist es entscheidend, den Parkraum entsprechend positiv zu besetzen und die Menschen davon zu überzeugen, dass weniger Autoverkehr mehr Freiraum bringt. Die Interventionen sollen sie dazu einladen, die Straße einzunehmen und neue Potenziale der Nutzung und Mit-Produktion herausstellen. So lassen sich die Wünsche nach einer betret- und nutzbaren Straße verwirklichen. Die Stadt von morgen gewinnt Raum für Experimente.

Hybride Straßen-typologien für eine neue Stadt

Die Beispiele zeigen, dass mit dem Abbau von Parkplätzen die Chance entsteht, monofunktionale Straßen in mehrfachkodierte urbane Räume umzuwandeln. Adaptive, flexible Gestaltungen können den Beginn einer anderen Stadtstruktur bilden. Hybride Straßen bieten eine offene urbane Bühne für mehr Lebensqualität. Neue multifunktionale Straßenräume bieten einen komplexen physischen Rahmen für viele verschiedene Arten der Fortbewegung und Nutzung. Hier überlagern sich sowohl Funktionen der Mobilität, des Aufenthalts, des Konsums, der politischen Manifestation als auch ökologische Themen.

Brussels' Ferme Abattoir combines a 2000 square-metre high-tech greenhouse, a fish farm, a rooftop garden and the only remaining slaughterhouse in Europe in the centre of a city

Ferme Abattoir, Brüssel: ein 2000 Quadratmeter großes High-tech-Gewächshaus, eine Fischzucht, und Dachgarten über der einzig noch vorhandenen handwerklichen Schlachthofaktivität eines Europäischen Stadtzentrums

Nourishing Our Cities

Urban Foodscapes

Leading global cities such as Toronto and Copenhagen have been working to integrate nutrition into urban planning, engaging with food and foodscapes with the same rigour that they bring to issues such as infrastructure and education. Here, Renate Künast, the former German Minister of Consumer Protection, Food and Agriculture, advocates for the inclusion and integration of foodscapes in urban planning, in Berlin and elsewhere.

We need a holistic approach to the topic of nutrition. A change in nutrition requires a change in urban planning.

Toronto and Copenhagen have paved the way: they have integrated nutrition into urban planning and they are engaging with nutrition just as intensively as they are with the issues of energy, roads and schools.

Copenhagen is a model city: all 900 community kitchens in the city are switching to organic food, with 90 percent already there. This has a direct influence on consumer decisions, creating opportunities for farmers, benefitting local ecologies and increasing biodiversity. Change is possible.

The shift is also happening in Berlin: local organisations are developing concepts for how the city might feed itself and how nutrition can become an integral part of urban development.

Consumers, too, have a stake in this development. They are highly conscious of topics around nutrition, sustainable lifestyles and ecological and fair trade products. In many global cities, nutrition movements are unfolding: people want to know where their food comes from and what ingredients it contains.

"Foodscape" is the new word to describe the state of nutrition in cities. Not surprisingly, urban landscapes play a key role as this includes the use of land, gardens, farmland, trade, gastronomy and communal catering.

This means that we need to carefully plan how the city feeds itself. This means taking into

Lebensmittel für unsere Städte

Urbane Ernährungslandschaften

Führende globale Städte wie Toronto und Kopenhagen arbeiten daran, die Ernährung in die Stadtplanung zu integrieren, indem sie sich mit der gleichen Strenge mit Lebensmitteln und Lebensmittellandschaften befassen wie mit Themen wie Infrastruktur und Bildung. Renate Künast, ehemalige Bundesministerin für Verbraucherschutz, Ernährung und Landwirtschaft, setzt sich für die Einbeziehung und Integration von Lebensmittellandschaften in die Stadtplanung ein.

Wir brauchen einen ganzheitlichen Ansatz beim Thema Ernährung. Zu einer Ernährungswende gehört deshalb auch die Stadtplanung.

Toronto und Kopenhagen haben es vorgemacht. Sie erklären die Ernährung zum Teil der Stadtplanung. Sie beschäftigen sich mit Ernährung genauso konzeptionell wie mit den Themen Energie, Straßen oder Schulen und Kindergärten.

Vorzeigestadt ist Kopenhagen: Alle 900 Gemeinschaftsküchen der Stadt werden auf „Bio" umgestellt. In neunzig Prozent der Fälle ist dies bereits gelungen. Das hat Einfluss auf die Einkaufsentscheidungen der Verbraucher*innen, ist eine Absatzchance für die Landwirtschaft und tut dem Klima und der Biodiversität gut. Es geht also.

Auch bei uns tut sich etwas: In den Städten gründen sich Ernährungsräte, die Konzepte entwickeln, wie sich Städte ernähren können und wie Ernährung zum Bestandteil von Stadtentwicklung wird.

Auch die Verbraucher*innen haben an dieser Entwicklung Interesse. Sie haben ein großes Bewusstsein für die Themen Ernährung, nachhaltiger Lebensstil, ökologische und faire Produkte. In vielen großen Städten gibt es eine regelrechte Ernährungsbewegung. Die Menschen wollen wissen, wo ihre Lebensmittel herkommen und welche Inhaltsstoffe sie enthalten.

„Foodscape" ist das neue Wort für die Ernährungssituation der Städte. Abgeleitet ist es vom englischen „landscape" (Landschaft). Die Stadtlandschaft gestaltet Landschaft. Dazu gehört auch der Umgang mit Böden, Gärten, Äcker, Handel, Gastronomie und Gemeinschaftsverpflegung.

account not only biodiversity but also the maintenance and sustainability of regional, seasonal and organic products - a process of education around nutrition. In this way it is possible to explain to children - and each other - why certain vegetables are available at certain times of the year.

A holistic approach, in which nutrition becomes an integrated component of urban planning, offers new perspectives for agriculture in the areas surrounding cities, connecting the city with the countryside and bringing new possibilities for places to gather, share and buy food.

Wir müssen also gezielt planen, wie sich eine Stadt ernährt. Dabei geht es um Biodiversität ebenso wie um die Pflege von regionalen, saisonalen und biologischen Produkten. Und das gehört bereits zur Ernährungsbildung. Denn so kann man auch Kindern erklären, warum es nicht zu jeder Jahreszeit dasselbe Gemüse geben kann.

Ein ganzheitlicher Ansatz, bei dem die Ernährung endlich Bestandteil der Stadtplanung wird, bietet der Landwirtschaft im Umland neue Perspektiven, verbindet Stadt und Land und beschert neue Absatzmöglichkeiten.

Appetite for the City

Why We Need a Nutrition Revolution

Making by doing: how can this be accomplished in cities that are currently growing? By 2050, three quarters of the world's population will be urban. This question preoccupies Markthalle Neun, which was built around 1900 as part of the historic food supply network that was meant to secure nutrition for the industrial metropolis of Berlin. Today, Markthalle Neun is part of an urban network declaring regional organic products from small agricultural producers to be part of a creative culture. What is "good food for everybody"? In 2015, 150 cities from around the world with more than 450 million inhabitants signed the Milan Urban Food Policy Pact, with each needing new trading centres to raise awareness and enthusiasm for food in an ongoing effort to work against the prevailing trend of monocultures and mass production.

Berlin's Nutrition Revolution

How to provide for the cities of the future? This question is increasingly urgent in light of global transformations and their accelerating velocity. Since the middle of the twentieth century, more people live in large cities and urban agglomerations than in rural areas. In 2050, this will increase to three quarters of the global population, which is predicted to increase to ten billion, doubling within less than 75 years! And Berlin? In 2030, Berlin will be home to over four million people: people who need to eat to live. As a site of densified living, the existence of any city has always been dependent on the provision of food. The contemporary city has been formed by the organisation of food production and consumption, as well as the increasing application of technology within these processes. This can be seen in the first Parisian arrondissement, where an entire quarter known as Les Halles is still named after the nineteenth-century market halls, which were destroyed in the energetic urban renewal of the 1970s. Or in the historic Meatpacking District in south-west Manhattan, which, from around 1900, was home to more than 250 slaughterhouses and meatpacking plants.

Hunger auf die Stadt

Warum wir eine Ernährungswende brauchen

Stadt satt machen. Wie kann das in den wachsenden Städten funktionieren? Bereits 2050 werden drei Viertel der Weltbevölkerung dort leben. Diese Fragen beschäftigt die Markthalle Neun. Sie stammt selbst aus einem historischen „Versorgungsgeflecht", das die Ernährung der Industriemetropole Berlin um 1900 sicherstellen sollte. Heute ist sie Teil eines urbanen Geflechts der Zeichen und Positionen, die regionale Bioprodukte aus kleinteilig-bäuerlicher Produktion zum Teil der Kreativkultur erklärt. Was ist „Gutes Essen für alle"? Viele Metropolen der Welt haben 2015 den Milan Urban Food Policy Pact unterzeichnet. Sie brauchen neue Umschlagplätze für Lebensmittelbegeisterung, gegen Monokultur und Massenproduktion.

Die Berliner Ernährungswende

Wie wird die Stadt künftig satt? Diese Frage ist virulent angesichts der globalen gesellschaftlichen Transformationsprozesse und ihrer zunehmenden Geschwindigkeit. Gerade einmal seit der Mitte des vergangenen Jahrhunderts leben mehr Menschen in Großstädten und urbanen Agglomerationen als im ländlichen Raum. Bereits im Jahr 2050 werden es aber drei Viertel der Weltbevölkerung sein. Sie wird auf zehn Milliarden Menschen anwachsen – eine Verdopplung innerhalb von nicht einmal 75 Jahren! Und Berlin? Berlin wird bereits 2030 mehr als vier Millionen Einwohner*innen zählen: Menschen, die wohnen müssen. Menschen, die Hunger haben. Die Existenz jeder Stadt, das verdichtete Miteinander, ist seit jeher abhängig von der Versorgung mit Lebensmitteln. Die Organisation der Lebensmittelproduktion und -konsumption sowie ihre Technologisierung und Rationalisierung haben die moderne Stadt geformt. Das ist im ersten Pariser Arrondissement noch heute zu besichtigen, wo ein ganzes Viertel (das Quartier Les Halles) nach den in der Erneuerungswut der 1970er Jahre abgerissenen Markthallen aus dem 19. Jahrhundert benannt ist. Tatsächlich war das Areal bereits seit dem zwölften Jahrhundert der zentrale Marktplatz von Paris. Oder im historischen Meat Packing District im Südwesten Manhattans: Hier hatten sich um

And on that note: slaughterhouses

It was the conveyer belts of slaughterhouses that inspired Henry Ford and the invention of industrial car production. In these things, sociologist Michel Foucault found a form of powerful, radically optimised architecture which he compared to prison architecture. The slaughterhouse with its conveyor belts stands in for the optimised organism of the city and the power relationships written into the urban fabric. On the other hand, cooking and eating can also be part of a subversive urban praxis and have been part of subversive appropriations of urban space. The French philosopher Michel de Certeau calls this "the practice of everyday life", writing of the "metaphorisation of the ruling order". We could think, here, of the burgeoning food truck culture in Los Angeles or San Diego, or of the improvised roadside market stands of large East European cities, where vegetables and salami, smoked and home-baked goods are sold. Or, of the cooking stalls of South-East Asia, which have also found a home in Berlin's Thai-Wiese (Thai Park) found during the summers in Preußenpark.

Clear position in the urban nutrition network

Markthalle Neun positions itself within an urban network of signs, positions and locations. In 1891, Berlin's Director of Urban Development, Hermann Blankenstein, had the Markthalle built as one of 14 market halls in response to similar conditions: Berlin had become a rapidly growing industrial metropolis and so a well-thought out network of market halls with modern cooling cellars and a hygiene control system was to provide the population with healthy - or at least unspoiled - foodstuffs. This is the point taken up by Markthalle Neun, formed in 2011 from a neighbourhood initiative in response to the question of whether today's cheap food provision has hidden costs, such as the development of monocultures, agricultural mass production and industrialised, standardised and increasingly artificial food. The city has enough - this, at least, has been achieved by the food industry. At all costs, however, we should take steps to deflect the consequences of an industrialised food culture, whose hidden

1900 mehr als 250 Schlacht- und Zerlegebetriebe angesiedelt.

Überhaupt: Die Schlachthöfe

Von ihnen hat sich der Automobilindustrielle Henry Ford die Fließbandproduktion abgeschaut. Der Soziologe Michel Foucault fand in ihnen jene Form einer machtvollen, radikal optimierten Architektur, wie er sie für seine Gefängnisbauten so pointiert beschrieb. Der Schlachthof mit seinen Transportbändern steht paradigmatisch für den optimierten Organismus der Stadt und für die in ihr eingeschriebenen Machtverhältnisse. Andererseits taugen Kochen und Essen auch zur subversiven urbanen Praxis, zur devianten Aneignung des Stadtraums. Der französische Philosoph Michel de Certeau nannte sie eine „Kunst des Handelns" und sprach von der „Metaphorisierung der herrschenden Ordnung". Man denke an die Food Trucks in Los Angeles oder San Diego, an die improvisierten Marktstände an den Einfallstraßen osteuropäischer Großstädte, wo Gemüse und Würste, Selbstgebranntes und -gebackenes verkauft werden. Oder an die Garküchen Südostasiens, die mit der „Thai-Wiese" im Wilmersdorfer Preußenpark ja auch zu einer Berliner Interpretation gefunden haben.

Klare Position im urbanen Geflecht der Ernährungszeichen

Die Markthalle Neun positioniert sich in diesem urbanen Geflecht der Zeichen, Positionen und Verortungen. Stadtbaurat Hermann Blankenstein ließ sie 1891 als eine von 14 Markthallen erbauen. Und es ging genau darum: Berlin war zu einer rasant wachsenden Industriemetropole geworden. Ein Netz aus überdachten Markthallen mit modernen Kühlkellern und einer Hygiene-Aufsicht sollte die Ernährung der Bevölkerung mit gesunden – zumindest unverdorbenen – Lebensmitteln sicherstellen. An diesen Punkt knüpft die 2011 aus einer Nachbarschaftsinitiative heraus entstandene Markthalle Neun an. Und stellt die Frage, ob die heutzutage garantiert günstige Versorgung einer Supermarkt- und Discounterkultur der Gesellschaft nicht andererseits allzu teuer kommt. Sie befördert Monokulturen, die landwirtschaftliche Massenproduktion und industrialisierte, standardisierte, zunehmend künstliche Lebensmittel. Die Stadt wird

costs are becoming increasingly visible: precarious working conditions, rising health tolls, environmental exploitation and the depletion of rural agricultural spaces and their resources. Cultural food technologies, recipes and their ingredients are disappearing. Knowledge of natural, edible growth is being forgotten.

Hungry for discovery: new forms of appropriation

In 2015, Berlin, together with other global cities, signed the Milan Urban Food Policy Pact. In doing so, it committed to making urban nutrition a central focus and building-block of every form of urban development. People must be able to live under fair conditions; they must have fair and equal access to participation in education and culture; and they must have fair and equal access to good nutrition. In 2018, the SPD-Left-Green political coalition committed to a reorientation of urban nutrition, making 700,000 euros available for a "House of Food". Following Copenhagen's example, an organisational structure and knowledge base should be founded in order to reorganise, for example, communal catering, with food for kindergartens and schools, the administration, hospitals, or business canteens being produced from regional and seasonal food - provided by small-scale local agriculture. What does Copenhagen show us? In the Danish capital, 90 percent of the 80,000 such meals served daily are prepared using regional, organic products.

Creating value instead of exhausting it

Food handiwork is part of a creative culture and a fundamental part of feeding the city. The new esteem that our food has in many circles - no longer just in the "organic Bohemian" circles - adds weight to this movement. Many cities have the potential to create value, instead of exhausting it. The food revolution is coming, but it needs space, networks and support. The new sites of enthusiasm for and production of food stand for a new appropriation process, hungry to be discovered. They also stand for a nutrition system that functions - with and because of - the city.

satt. Jedenfalls in unseren Gefilden. Das hat die Industrie schon irgendwie eingerichtet. Nicht einrichten sollten wir uns mit den Folgekosten einer industrialisierten Ernährungskultur, die zunehmend die hohen Gemeinkosten offenbart, auf denen sie gründet: prekäre Arbeitsverhältnisse, steigende Gesundheitskosten, Umweltausbeutung, ein Raubbau am ländlichen, landwirtschaftlichen Raum und seinen Ressourcen. Kulturtechniken, Rezepte und ihre Zutaten verschwinden. Wissen über die essbare Natur geht verloren.

Die neue entdeckungshungrige Aneignung

2015 hat Berlin, wie inzwischen weltweit mehr als 160 weitere Metropolen, den Milan Urban Food Policy Pact unterzeichnet. Und damit festgelegt, dass die Stadternährung künftig eine zentrale Fragestellung, ein Baustein jedweder Stadtentwicklung sein muss. Die Menschen müssen fair wohnen. Sie müssen faire Chancen auf Partizipation an Bildung und Kultur haben. Und sie müssen sich fair ernähren können. Immerhin: 2018 hat sich der rot-rot-grüne Senat zu einer Neuorientierung der Stadternährung bekannt und 700.000 Euro für ein sogenanntes House of Food bereitgestellt. Nach dem Vorbild Kopenhagens sollen damit die Strukturen und das Wissen geschaffen werden, um beispielweise die Gemeinschaftsverpflegung umzustellen. Das Essen für Kitas und Schulen, Behörden, Krankenhäuser oder Betriebskantinen soll mit Erzeugnissen aus regional-saisonaler und kleinteilig-bäuerlicher Landwirtschaft hergestellt werden. Vorbild Kopenhagen? In der dänischen Hauptstadt sind inzwischen neunzig Prozent der 80.000 täglich ausgegebenen kommunalen Essen aus regionalen Bioprodukten zubereitet.

Aus der Wertschätzung eine Wertschöpfung machen

Lebensmittelhandwerk ist eine Kreativkultur und ein Grundnahrungsmittel der Stadt. Die neue Wertschätzung, die unserem Essen in vielen Milieus – und längst nicht mehr nur in der oft verschrienen Bio-Boheme – entgegengebracht wird, ist ein Kapital. Viele Städte haben das Potenzial, aus dieser Wertschätzung auch eine Wertschöpfung zu machen. Die Ernährungswende liegt in der Luft.

Indes sie braucht Raum und Räume. Sie braucht Netzwerke, und sie braucht das Miteinander. Stadt machen. Stadt satt machen. Die neuen Orte der Lebensmittelproduktion und -begeisterung stehen für eine entdeckungshungrige Aneignung. Sie stehen aber auch für ein Ernährungssystem, das nicht trotz der Stadt funktioniert – sondern mit, wegen und in ihr.

-> Case Study 01 pp. 236 ff. Großmarkt 9.0
-> Case Study 02 pp. 240 ff. Thai Park

Roof Water-Farm, Berlin-Kreuzberg: fresh fish and vegetables directly from the roof; aquaphonic farming using treated grey water on site

Frischer Fisch und frisches Gemüse direkt vom Dach, hergestellt mit aufbereitetem Abwasser aus dem Haushalt

01. Project: Großmarkt 9.0

City: Berlin
Planning: Markthalle Neun
Client: N/A
Status: Concept

The Belly of the City
Refining Food Cycles

The stomach of Paris. That is how the writer Émile Zola described the extensive market halls of the Les Halles quarter. For a long time, the stomach of Berlin was located in Beusselstraße. In the future, according to Markthalle Neun, it could again become the centrepiece of the city's nutrition infrastructure. The vision for Großmarkt 9.0 has at least three facets - as a place of production for new, creative foodcraft: brewing and baking, sausage making and tofu-manufacture; a logistical hub for the regional, small-scale agricultural industry of Brandenburg; and, not least, a place of learning, where knowledge and how to prepare healthy, regional, seasonal and economical food might be passed on and shared. Similar projects, such as the House of Food in Copenhagen, have demonstrated just how important the role of education and training of canteen employees can be. Last but not least, parts of the wholesale market should - at least temporarily - be open to the city's population with the wholesale market once again becoming part of the sensory experience of the appetite of Berlin!

Der Bauch der Stadt
Ernährungskreisläufe erschließen

Der Bauch von Paris. So hat der Schriftsteller Émile Zola die raumgreifenden Markthallen im nach ihnen benannten Quartier Les Halles genannt. Der Bauch von Berlin lag lange in der Beusselstraße. Künftig, so die Vision der Markthalle Neun, könnte das Großmarktgelände wieder zu einem Herzstück der Stadternährung werden. Die Vision des Großmarktes 9.0 hat dabei mindestens diese drei Facetten: ein Produktionsort für junges, kreatives Lebensmittelhandwerk, Brauer*innen und Bäcker*innen, Wurstwerkstätten und Tofu-Manufakturen. Ein logistischer Knotenpunkt für die regionalen, kleinteilig-bäuerlichen Landwirtschaften Brandenburgs. Und nicht zuletzt ein Lernort, an dem das Wissen und die Zubereitung von gesundem, regional-saisonalem und nicht zuletzt auch wirtschaftlich darstellbarem Essen vermittelt werden. Haben doch die Erfahrungen des House of Food in Kopenhagen gezeigt, wie wichtig gerade die Sensibilisierung und Schulung von (Kantinen-)Mitarbeiter*innen ist. Nicht zuletzt sollen Teile des Großmarktes temporär der Stadtbevölkerung geöffnet werden, der Großmarkt wird wieder zum (sinnlich) erfahrbaren Bauch Berlins.

The Großmarkt Beusselstraße dominates the logistics of urban food supply

Der Großmarkt Beusselstraße dominiert die Logistik der städtischen Lebensmittelversorgung in Berlin

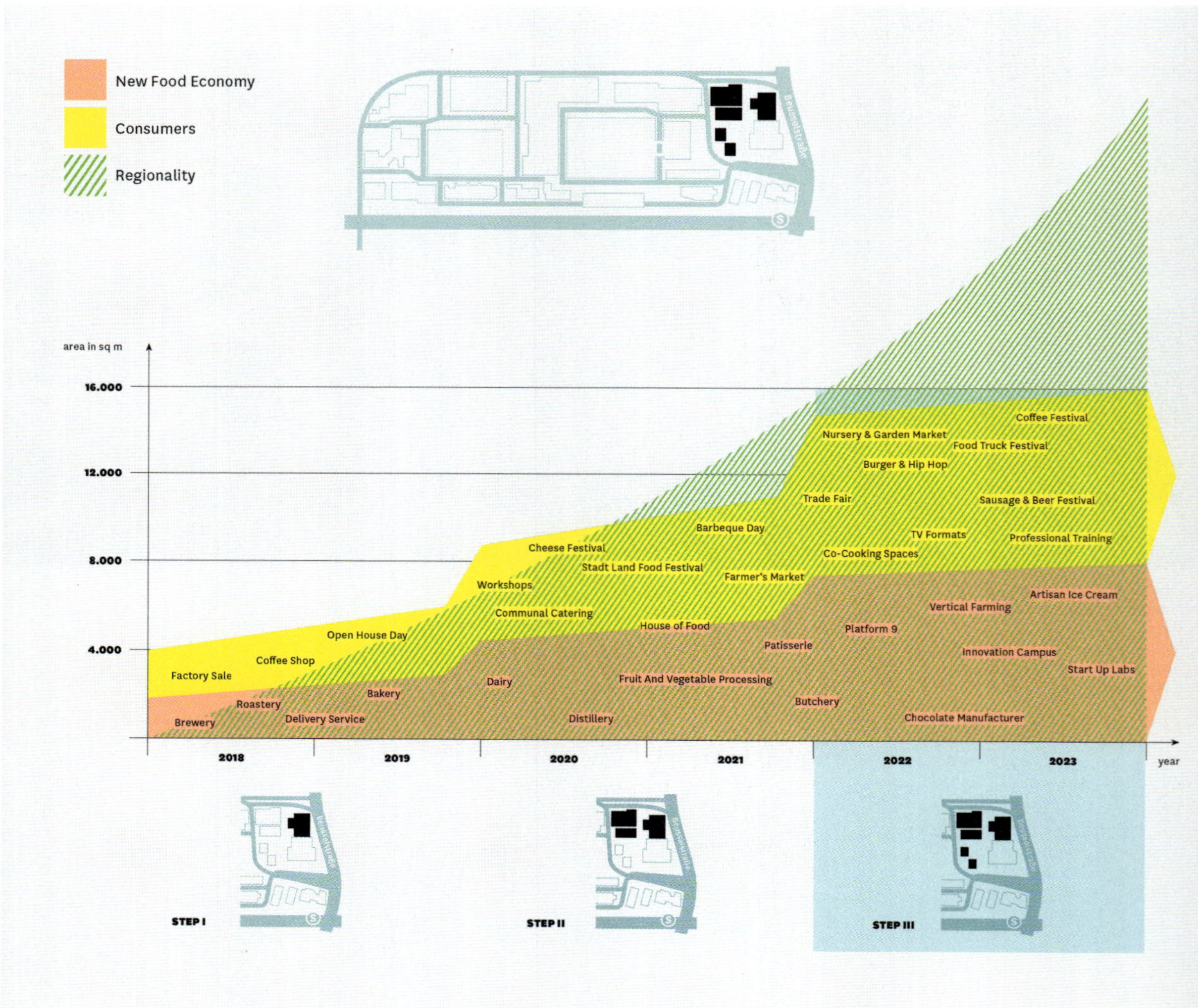

Progress in steps: coordination phases of development include an influx of food stalls and education programmes

Entwicklung in Stufen: Die unterschiedlichen Entwicklungsphasen berücksichtigen einen Zustrom von Essensständen und Bildungsprogrammen

Communication is crucial: the mission of Markthalle Neun includes cheese trade fairs, international food festivals and diverse workshop programmes that communicate the cultural value of food

Kommunikation ist essenziell: Die Mission der Markthalle Neun umfasst Käsemessen, internationale Food-Festivals und verschiedene Workshop-Programme, die den kulturellen Wert von Lebensmitteln vermitteln

02. Thai Park

Project: Thai Park
City: Berlin
Client: N/A
Planning: N/A
Status: Ongoing

Thai-Picnic
A Microeconomic Foodscape

Some 20 years ago, on the grass of Preußenpark in western Berlin, groups of Thais and other South East Asians began to gather, cook and eat together. Shortly thereafter, park visitors asked to try and buy the food being prepared. The community saw an opportunity and began to sell their food. Over the years this unauthorised food market has come to be known as Thai Park, and on summer weekends visitors - an estimated 60,000 per year - descend on the open-air market, taking in the sights, smells and tastes on offer.

The struggle for the vendors to remain on the lawn is as old as Thai Park itself. Although its popularity has established it as a favourite among Berliners, tourists and food bloggers, it has also drawn unwanted attention, from neighbours to the Ordnungsamt - the bureaucratic body charged with overseeing municipal codes and regulations. For those who use the park, thousands of feet on the grass result in heavily compacted soil and a lawn of dead grass. For the Ordnungsamt, the concern is that food cooked on portable grills does not follow hygiene preparation regulations. For now, Thai Park continues to thrive in Berlin; but its existence is precarious.

To understand the survival of Thai Park is to understand how a migrant community leveraged their informal micro-economy into a tourist attraction while forging strategic alliances to continue producing space and community. On the ground, this means vendors have developed supporting infrastructure including waste collection. Throughout the city, this means that supporters advocate for a community and a place that has become an intrinsic part of Berlin's foodscape. This contested space has evolved into self-managed, informal community by way of constant adaptation, claiming its status within the urban fabric of Berlin.

Esskultur im Park
Eine Ernährungslandschaft als Mikroökonomie

Vor ungefähr zwanzig Jahren begannen Gruppen von Berliner*innen mit thailändischen und anderen südostasiatischen Wurzeln, sich auf der Wiese des kleinen Preußenparks im Westen der Stadt zu treffen, zu kochen und gemeinsam zu essen. Es dauerte nicht lange, bis andere Parkbesucher*innen darum baten, die zubereiteten Gerichte probieren oder kaufen zu dürfen. Die Community sah eine Geschäftsgelegenheit und verkaufte von nun an ihr Essen im Park. Über die Jahre ist dieser inoffizielle Freiluftmarkt als Thai-Wiese (oder Thai-Park) bekannt geworden, und über die Sommerwochenenden besuchen bis zu 60.000 Menschen den Markt mit seinen Gerüchen und Geschmäckern.

Der Kampf der Verkäufer*innen, auf dem Rasen bleiben zu dürfen, ist so alt wie ihr Markt selbst. Obwohl die Stände bei Berliner*innen, Tourist*innen und Food-Blogs sehr beliebt sind, haben sie auch ungewollte Aufmerksamkeit auf sich gezogen – von der Nachbarschaft bis zum Ordnungsamt. Für Parknutzer*innen bedeuten die Tausenden Füße auf der Wiese einen festgetrampelten Boden und eine tote Rasenfläche. Für das Ordnungsamt steht die Essenszubereitung auf mobilen Grills nicht im Einklang mit den amtlichen Richtlinien. Die Thai-Wiese in Berlin blüht weiterhin – doch ihr Bestehen bleibt in einem Schwebezustand.

Um das Überleben dieses Marktes zu verstehen, muss man verstehen, wie eine migrantische Community ihre informelle Mikroökonomie zu einer touristischen Attraktion ausgebaut hat. Zugleich ist sie strategische Bündnisse eingegangen, um einen gemeinschaftlichen Raum zu erhalten. Vor Ort bedeutet das konkret, dass die Verkäufer*innen eine unterstützende Infrastruktur entwickelt haben, die auch die Abfallentsorgung umfasst. Unterstützer*innen in der ganzen Stadt sprechen sich für diese Gemeinschaft und ihren Ort aus, der ein fester Bestandteil der Berliner Esslandschaft geworden ist. Dieser umstrittene Raum hat sich kontinuierlich angepasst und einen Platz im urbanen Gewebe Berlins beansprucht – und hat sich so zu einer selbstverwalteten, informellen Gemeinschaft entwickelt.

These desire trails trace the footsteps of the thousands of visitors who descend on Thai Park every summer

Trampelpfade zeugen von den Schritten Tausender Besucher*innen, die jeden Sommer den Thai Park besuchen

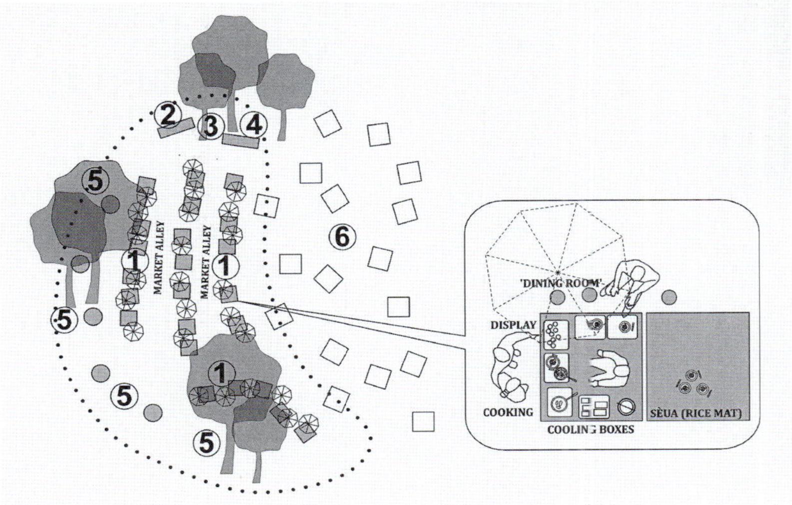

A summer weekend at Thai Park: food market (1), nailbars (2), massage (3), haircutting (4), gambling (5) and numerous visitors (6)

Der Thai Park an einem Wochenende im Sommer: Marktstände (1), Nagelstudios (2), Massage (3), Frisör*innen (4), Glücksspiel (5) und zahlreiche Besucher*innen (6)

03.

Project: **Common Archipelagos**

City: global
Planning: Imke Woelk
Client: N/A
Status: Concept

Moss, Leaves, Stone
Interchanging Habitats

What if the city was designed in a symbiotic co-existence of urbanity and natural space? Could natural habitats cultivate urban habitats to nurture diverse human activities that are mutually beneficial?

The project Common Archipelagos by Imke Woelk responds to the contemporary re-negotiation of city and nature and dares a futuristic view into possibilities of the city of tomorrow. Starting from the yearning for more closeness to nature in urban space, alternative hybrid spaces are offered in adaptable large-scale structures between landscapes and densification - embedded in landscapes in analogous geological formations with urban density.

Emerging from an extensive analysis on the subject of Berlin as a city of stone, Werner Hegemann's analysis of the "largest tenement city in the world", coupled with alternative generations of density and agglomeration, a counterproposal to current city models is being formulated. Contrary to the polarised, less sustainable development of the contemporary city with its sprawling, low-density, carpet-like urban structures and extremely densely populated city centres, the project formulates a third way for a new resourceful urbanism in closer harmony with nature. With decidedly decentralised infrastructure networks and hybrid large structures of great variability, Common Archipelagos deliberately disengages from all conventional city models.

Moos, Blätter, Steine
Lebensräume verbinden

Was wäre, wenn die Stadt in symbiotischer Koexistenz von Urbanität und Naturraum gestaltet werden könnte? Könnten in naturnahe Landschaftsräume urbane Habitate vielfältiger menschlicher Aktivitäten implantiert werden, wovon beide Lebensräume profitierten?

Das Projekt Common Archipelagos von Imke Woelk antwortet auf die zeitgenössische Neuaushandlung von Stadt und Natur und wagt einen futuristischen Ausblick auf die Stadt von morgen. Von der Sehnsucht nach mehr Naturnähe im urbanen Raum ausgehend, werden alternative Hybridräume in adaptierbaren Großstrukturen zwischen Verlandschaftlichung und Verdichtung angeboten, die in analogen geologischen Formationen mit urbaner Dichte in der Landschaft eingebettet sein sollen.

Hervorgegangen aus einer umfangreichen Analyse zum Thema des steinernen Berlins – Werner Hegemanns Analyse zur „größten Mietskaserne der Welt" – und alternativen Generierungen von Dichte und Agglomeration, wird ein Gegenvorschlag zu den überkommenen Stadtmodellen formuliert. Entgegen der polaren, wenig nachhaltigen Entwicklung der zeitgenössischen Stadt mit ausufernden Teppich-Strukturen niedriger Dichte und extrem verdichteten Stadtzentren formuliert das Projekt einen dritten Weg für einen neuen ressourcenschonenden Urbanismus im stärkeren Einklang mit der Natur. Mit dezidiert dezentralen Infrastrukturnetzwerken und hybriden Großstrukturen maximaler Variabilität löst sich Common Archipelagos dazu bewusst von allen konventionellen Stadtmodellen.

Large, hybrid mega-structures weave urban habitats through the landscape

Große, hybride Megastrukturen verweben städtische Wohnflächen durch die Landschaft

04.

Project: **Lime House 3**

City: Ahmedabad, Gujarat, India
Client: N/A
Planning: Indigo Architects in collaboration with Ami Engineers
Status: Completed 2015

From Hot to Cold
What Can Architecture Do?

In the 1990s, before climate change was a widespread topic of discussion in the design community, a small architecture practice was beginning to develop what would become the fundamentals of their practice. With most of their projects located in the hot-dry/humid zone in and around the desert city of Ahmedabad in India, Indigo Architects learned that the first order of business was to prevent buildings from heating up. Over the years, they have learned to use durable materials, like lime mortar and plaster, that do not become too hot or too cold; to design passive systems to drain heat from surfaces; to store thermal masses, using them to passively cool or warm; to use the cool night-time air to dissipate heat; to harvest rainwater to satisfy drinking water needs; and, by circulating stored water within the structure, that they could cool and warm the building as needed.

The deployment of their passive material and design strategies can be seen in Lime House 3. With a mandate to design a dwelling connected to the outdoors, the main challenge was to provide thermal comfort. The home was built on a raised plinth, as the area is prone to flooding, and is aligned north to south on its longer axis, not only owing to the site's dimensions but also to keep the sun at bay and to allow natural breezes to flow through the home. A bamboo trellis extrudes from the east and west façades, encouraging creepers, vegetables and other vine plants to provide a shaded area. Service spaces, washrooms, utilities and staircases are located on the south and west sides to insulate the living areas. A courtyard is formed through the manipulation of the massing, creating a thermal barrier between the dining block and the open garden; a verandah on the west and a patio, pond and deck on the east provide useful spaces in the mornings and evenings. On sunny, hot days, large doors with wooden louvers that lead in and out of the house control sunlight and glare. Breezes are drawn into the home through a shaft over the puja space. The material strategy was to use lime and surkhi bricks, lime mortar and lime plaster on the exteriors and dolomite plaster inside - materials that are naturally emissive. This extended to the flooring, with brown kotah on the outside and marble inside. The roof was insulated using nodules of lightweight expanded

Von Wüste bis Dschungel
Was Architektur leisten kann

In den 1990ern, also bevor der Klimawandel ein allgemeines Gesprächsthema in der Architektur wurde, begann das Architekturbüro Indigo Architects, die Grundlagen seiner Arbeit zu entwickeln. Die meisten seiner Projekte waren in der heiß-kalten/schwülen Zone in und um die Wüstenstadt Ahmedabad in Indien angesiedelt, und so lernten die im Team Mitarbeitenden, dass ihr wichtigstes Augenmerk darauf gerichtet sein müsse, Häuser vor der Überhitzung zu bewahren. Über die Jahre lernten sie, langlebige Materialien wie Kalkmörtel und Gips einzusetzen, die nicht zu heiß oder zu kalt werden. Sie lernten, passive Systeme zu entwerfen, Hitze von Flächen abzuleiten und Wärmemasse zu speichern, um sie passiv zum Kühlen oder Heizen zu verwenden. Sie lernten, wie man die kühle Nachtluft nutzen kann, um Hitze zu zerwirbeln, und wie man Regenwasser sammelt, um Trinkwasser zu gewinnen. Und sie lernten, wie man in den Gebäuden gespeichertes Wasser zirkulieren lässt, um sie je nach Bedürfnis zu temperieren.

Der Einsatz ihrer Strategien mit passivem Baumaterial und ihr Designansatz können am Beispiel des Lime House 3 betrachtet werden. Der Auftrag bestand darin, ein Wohngebäude zu bauen, das mit dem Außen verbunden ist. Als größte Herausforderung stellte sich heraus, Wärmekomfort zu gewährleisten. Das Haus in einer hochwassergefährdeten Gegend wurde auf einem Sockel errichtet und ist an seiner Längsachse von Nord nach Süd ausgerichtet, nicht nur wegen des Baufeldes, sondern auch, um die Sonne in Schach zu halten und den natürlichen Luftzug durch das Gebäude zu ermöglichen. Ein Bambusgitter rankt an der östlichen und der westlichen Fassade und bietet mit Kletterpflanzen, Gemüse und anderen rankenden Pflanzen Verschattung. Wirtschafträume, Badezimmer, Versorgungsräume und Treppenhäuser befinden sich an der südlichen und westlichen Seite, um die Wohnräume vor Hitze zu dämmen. Ein Innenhof schafft eine thermische Barriere zwischen dem Essenstrakt und dem offenen Garten. Eine Veranda an der Westseite sowie eine Terrasse und ein Teich auf der Ostseite bieten Aufenthaltsorte. An sonnigen, heißen Tagen kontrollieren luftige Holztüren mit Schlitzen das Sonnenlicht. Ein Schacht über dem Puja-Zeremonieraum sorgt für Luftzüge durch das Gebäude. An Material wurden Kalk- und Surkhi-Ziegel verwendet, außen Kalkmörtel und Kalkputz und innen Dolomitputz, also Materialien, die ein natürliches

Architectural expression is the direct result of sustainable and climate-friendly building methods

Der architektonische Ausdruck ist das Ergebnis nachhaltiger und klimafreundlicher Baumethoden

clay aggregate mixed with aerated cement, its surface finished with white china mosaic for thermal reflectivity. After completion of the house, interior surface temperature readings gave a consistent reduction in temperature by 10°C during summer months.

By honing a practice that re-integrates traditional wisdom in construction paired with a respect for the qualities of natural resources, Indigo Architects responds directly to today's challenges, generating an architecture that unambiguously belongs to its time and is, crucially, transposable elsewhere as the earth's climate and weather patterns continue to shift.

Emissionsverhalten haben. Diese Strategie wurde beim Boden fortgeführt: braunes Kotah außen und Marmor innen. Das Dach wurde mit Modulen aus Blähton und Porenbeton isoliert und die Oberfläche mit weißem Porzellanmosaik überzogen, um die thermische Reflexion zu fördern. Nach Fertigstellung des Hauses ergaben Messungen an Innenflächen in den Sommermonaten eine konsistente Reduktion um zehn Grad.

Indem sie ein Verfahren verbessern, das traditionelles Bauwissen mit einbezieht und die Eigenschaften natürlicher Ressourcen respektiert, reagieren Indigo Architects direkt auf die Herausforderungen von heute und schaffen eindeutig zeitgemäße Architektur. Wenn die Klima- und Wettermuster sich weiterhin verändern, könnten diese Methoden überallhin auf der Erde übertragen werden.

A building that breathes: the home is oriented in such a way to encourage regular circulation inside and flush the interior with cool night-time air

Ein Gebäude, das atmet: Ein natürlicher Luftzug versorgt den Innenraum mit kühler Nachtluft

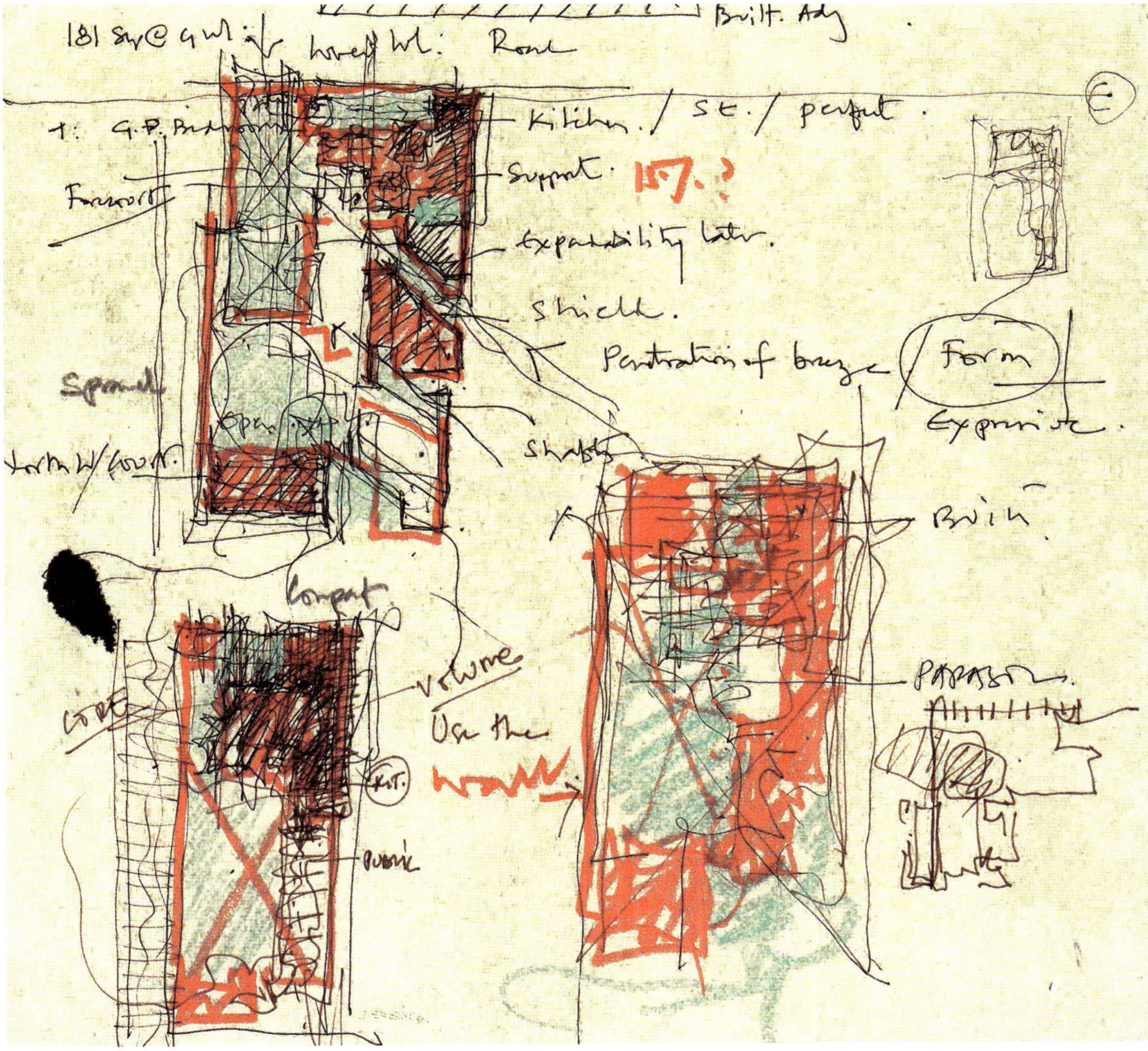

The integration of traditional wisdom in construction and materials responds directly to each site and today's challenges

Die Integration von traditionellem Wissen über Konstruktion und Materialien ist eine direkte Antwort auf den jeweiligen Standort und seine akuten Herausforderungen

05. Cloudburst Masterplan

Project: Cloudburst Masterplan
City: Copenhagen
Client: Municipality of Copenhagen, Municipality of Frederiksberg, Greater Copenhagen Utilities (HOFOR)
Planning: Ramboll Group, Studio Dreiseitl
Status: Completed 2013

Cloudburst Boulevards
Building with the Rain

The effects of climate change are increasingly apparent, with escalating effects affecting coastal cities in particular. In recent years, Copenhagen has experienced flooding due to cloudbursts, a weather event that results in an extreme amount of rain in a short period of time. On three occasions between August 2010 and 2011, large areas of the city were flooded by a cloudburst; the damage to the city was extensive.

In response, the city sought out an integrated, citywide masterplan that divided the city into catchments based on how water falls and gathers. Ramboll, an engineering and design firm and landscape architect Studio Dreiseitl worked with the city to develop a blue-green approach. Blue-green infrastructure refers to a network designed to work with natural systems, with blue referring to water and green to parks, green spaces and urban landscapes. For Copenhagen, this meant that instead of quickly funnelling storm-water through underground pipes, which often leads to flooding, water was slowed down at the street level using a network of parks, cloudburst boulevards and retention zones. The network functions as an absorption mechanism while providing desirable social services such as community gardens or sports fields, all of which can function as ponds when needed. This slow and hold approach is important for two reasons. First, it takes the pressure off older infrastructure that can only hold so much during severe storms. Second, it makes visible the extent to which urban landscapes can offset the effects of extreme weather.

By moving blue-green infrastructure through a city-wide implementation of integrated planning and design, Copenhagen has positively affected the socio-cultural life of the city while increasing its long-term resiliency.

Wolkenbruch-Boulevards
Bauen mit dem Regen

Die Auswirkungen des Klimawandels zeichnen sich immer deutlicher ab. Küstenstädte sind von den ausufernden Folgen besonders betroffen. In den vergangenen Jahren gab es in Kopenhagen mehrere Überflutungen durch Wolkenbrüche – bei einem derartigen Wetterereignis fällt in einem sehr kurzen Zeitraum eine enorme Niederschlagsmenge. Bereits drei Mal zwischen August 2010 und 2011 wurden große Stadtgebiete auf diese Weise überflutet – mit umfassenden Schäden.

Als Reaktion hat die Kommunalverwaltung einen integrierten, stadtweiten Masterplan aufgestellt, der das Stadtgebiet auf der Grundlage von Wassermengen und Wasserspeichermöglichkeiten in Auffangflächen einteilt. Die Landschaftsarchitekturbüros Ramboll und Dreiseitl arbeiteten gemeinsam mit der Stadtverwaltung an einem Entwurf für einen blau-grünen Lösungsansatz. Blau-grüne Infrastruktur bezeichnet ein Netzwerk, das mit natürlichen Systemen zusammenwirken soll – „blau" bezieht sich auf Wasser, „grün" auf Parks, Grünflächen und städtische Landschaften. Anstatt Sturmniederschläge schnell durch unterirdische Leitungen zu kanalisieren, was oft zu Überflutungen führt, kann die Nutzung von Parks, sogenannten Wolkenbruch-Boulevards und Auffangbecken das Wasser in Kopenhagen nun auf Straßenebene bremsen. Dieses Netzwerk funktioniert als Absorptionsmechanismus und umfasst zugleich ohnehin wünschenswerte gesellschaftliche Angebote wie Gemeinschaftsgärten oder Sportplätze, die bei Bedarf als Teiche fungieren. Dieser Ansatz, das Wasser zu verlangsamen und zurückzuhalten, ist aus zwei Gründen wichtig. Erstens wird so Druck aus älteren Infrastrukturen genommen, die bei schweren Stürmen nur begrenzt aufnahmefähig sind. Zweitens macht er sichtbar, inwiefern städtische Landschaften die Folgen extremer Klimasituationen ausgleichen können.

Durch die stadtweit implementierte integrierte Planung und Gestaltung blau-grüner Infrastrukturen hat Kopenhagen das soziokulturelle Leben der Stadt gefördert und zugleich ihre langfristige Resilienz gestärkt.

In 2011, a cloud burst inundated Copenhagen with just over six inches of rain in less than three hours, causing six billion Danish kroner in damage

Im Jahr 2011 wurde Kopenhagen in knapp drei Stunden durch etwas mehr als 15 cm Regen überschwemmt, was einen Schaden von sechs Milliarden dänischen Kronen verursachte

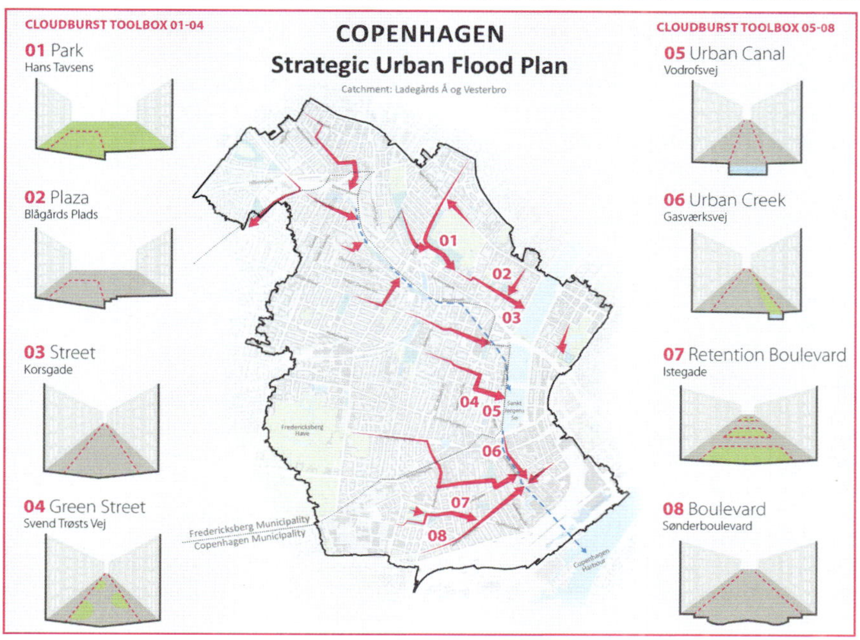

Designed in cross-section: Copenhagen's streets act as canals that slow down and retain water in extreme weather. Ramboll Studio Dreiseitl developed a network of parks, downpour boulevards and retention zones

Im Schnitt konzipiert: Die Straßen Kopenhagens fungieren als Kanäle, die bei Extremwetterereignissen Wasser verlangsamen und zurückhalten. Ramboll Studio Dreiseitl entwickelten ein Netzwerk aus Parks, Wolkenbruch-Boulevards und Retentionszonen

06. Project:

Water Square Benthemplein

City: Rotterdam
Client: Rotterdam Climate Initiative, City of Rotterdam supported by the Waterboard Schieland & Krimpenerwaard
Planning: De Urbanisten
Status: Completed

The City as a Sponge Meteorological Streetscapes

For more than 1000 years, the Netherlands has been designing ways to live with water. Today, due to climate change, the country is facing rising seas and increasing rainfall. Rotterdam, the second largest city in the country, has the distinction of being mostly below sea level in addition to the majority of the city having an impervious surface; the water comes into Rotterdam from the sea, the river, the ground and the sky.

In 2005, Rotterdam-based De Urbanisten developed "The Flood", a new typology of water square. Why hide expensive rain water storage and infrastructure underground, they asked; is there a way to develop a water-sensitive systems approach, linking infrastructure planning, waste management and landscape design?

Invited by the city to develop a design, De Urbanisten began by holding workshops with students, teachers and neighbours to bring together ideas about what the square could be; they wanted dynamic space, space for play and lingering and space for the water to run through. Construction was financed by the City of Rotterdam, the Schieland and Krimpenerwaard District Water Board, the Dutch Ministry of Infrastructure and the Environment and the European Commission's European Regional Development Fund, with 80 percent coming from the city's sewage budget. The resulting design has been adopted - alongside green roofs and underground water storage - as part of "Waterplan 2", Rotterdam's policy to become 100 percent climate proof by 2025.

The Benthemplein water square retains water from the square's pavement and rainwater from rooftops of surrounding buildings in three basins painted blue - two shallow and one deep - able to hold 1.7 million litres of water during rainfall. When they are dry, these basins are basketball courts, skate parks and a theatre. After the rain, the water from the two shallow basins flows into an underground infiltration device from which it is infiltrated into the soil beneath the pavement or pumped out, into canals elsewhere in the city. As a result, the ground water balance is kept relatively steady and can be managed to help cope with dry periods. This also keeps trees and plants healthy while reducing urban heat island effect. After 36 hours, the water from the deep

Die Stadt als Schwamm Klimagerechte Straßentypologien

Seit mehr als tausend Jahren finden die Niederlande Möglichkeiten, mit dem Wasser zu leben. Angesichts des Klimawandels kommen nun steigende Meeresspiegel und zunehmender Niederschlag auf das Flachland zu. Rotterdam, die zweitgrößte Stadt der Niederlande, zeichnet sich besonders dadurch aus, dass sie weitgehend unterhalb des Meeresspiegels liegt und ihre Flächen großteils versiegelt sind. Nach Rotterdam kommt das Wasser vom Meer, vom Fluss aus, aus dem Boden und vom Himmel.

Das Rotterdamer Büro für Landschaftsarchitektur De Urbanisten entwickelte 2005 einen neuen Typ des städtischen Wasserplatzes. „Warum die teuren Regenwasserspeicher und -infrastrukturen unterirdisch verstecken?", fragten sie sich. Gibt es nicht eine Möglichkeit, einen wasserorientierten Systemansatz zu entwickeln, der Infrastruktur, Stadtplanung, Abwassersysteme und Landschaftsgestaltung miteinander verknüpft?

Die Stadt lud sie ein, einen Entwurf vorzulegen, und De Urbanisten begannen das Projekt, indem sie Workshops mit Studierenden, Lehrenden und Nachbar*innen durchführten, um Vorstellungen des zukünftigen Platzes zusammenzubringen. Sie wollten einen dynamischen Raum schaffen, einen Ort zum Spielen und Verweilen, einen Platz, durch den das Wasser hindurchfließen kann. Der Bau wurde von der Stadt Rotterdam, vom Bezirkswasserverband Schieland und Krimpenerwaard, vom niederländischen Ministerium für Infrastruktur und Umwelt sowie vom Europäischen Fonds für Regionale Entwicklung finanziert, wobei achtzig Prozent aus dem Abwasserbudget der Stadt kamen. Die entstandene Architektur wurde – neben Dachbegrünungen und Unterwasserspeichern – als Teil des „Waterplan 2" umgesetzt, Rotterdams Richtlinie, um bis 2025 hundert Prozent klimasicher zu werden.

Der Benthemplein-Wasserplatz fängt in drei blau gestrichenen Becken Wasser von der Asphaltierung des Platzes sowie Regenwasser von den Dächern der umliegenden Gebäude auf. Zwei flache und ein tiefes Becken können bei Niederschlag bis zu 1,7 Millionen Liter Wasser auffangen. Wenn sie trocken sind, sind sie als Basketballplatz, Skatepark und Theaterbühne nutzbar. Nach dem Regen fließt das Wasser aus den zwei flacheren Becken in ein unterirdisches Filtersystem, von wo aus es in den Boden

The Benthemplein water square retains water from streets, the square's pavement and surrounding rooftops - the basins can hold up to 1.7 million litres of rain water

Der Wasserplatz Benthemplein speichert das Oberflächenwasser der Straßen, Gehwege und der umliegenden Dächer; die Becken fassen 1,7 Millionen Liter Regenwasser

basin is allowed to flow back into the open water system. Slowing storm water prevents the inundation of the mixed sewage system and lowers the frequency of sewage flowing into the open water.

By retaining water during rainfall, this dynamic water square eases stress on the city's sewage system, prevents urban floods and separates storm water from the black water system. In so doing, the entire system moves towards an improvement of the overall quality of the open water in the city while mitigating the increasing effects of climate change.

unter dem Asphalt gefiltert oder in Kanäle aus der Stadt hinausgepumpt wird. So wird das Gleichgewicht des Grundwassers stabil gehalten und kann in Trockenzeiten genutzt werden.

Auch die Bäume und Pflanzen profitieren davon und dämmen das Phänomen der städtischen Hitzeinseln ein. Das Wasser aus dem tiefen Becken fließt erst nach 36 Stunden wieder in den offenen Wasserkreislauf ein. Diese Verlangsamung von Sturmniederschlag verhindert die Überlastung der Mischwasserkanalisation und verringert den Überlauf von Abwasser in offene Gewässer.

Indem er das Wasser während des Regenfalls zurückhält, entlastet dieser dynamische Wasserplatz das Abwassersystem, verhindert Überflutungen und trennt Sturmwasser vom Schmutzwassersystem. Dadurch wird die allgemeine Wasserqualität in der Stadt schrittweise verbessert, und zugleich werden die zunehmenden Auswirkungen des Klimawandels gelindert.

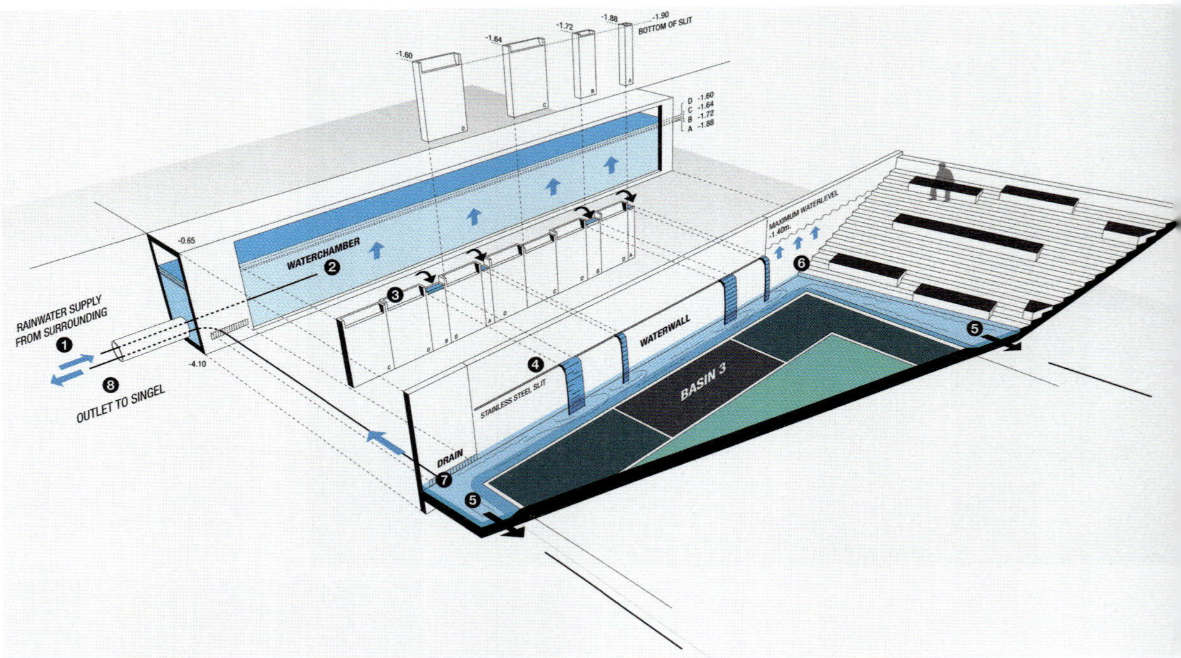

After the rain, the water of the two shallow basins flows into an underground filtration device

Nach dem Regen fließt das Wasser der beiden Becken in eine unterirdische Filteranlage

"An overreliance on technical problem solving merely leads to bigger and bigger dikes, pumps and pipes. ... Make the city move with the water."

„Ein übertriebener Verlass auf technische Problemlösungen führt bloß zu immer größeren Deichen, Pumpen und Rohren ... Die Stadt sollte sich lieber mit dem Wasser bewegen."

De Urbanisten

Planters, pavers and drains slow storm water, preventing the inundation of the mixed sewage system

Pflanzgefäße, Pflastersteine und Drainagen für langsames Regenwasser verhindern das Überschwemmen der Mischkanalisation

07.

Project: **Pool is cool**

City: Brussels
Client: N/A
Planning: Pool is cool
Status: Concept

Urban Bathing Campaign
On Negotiating Urban Water Landscapes I

Kids splash and scream, teens hang out trying to impress each other, adults do laps and seniors paddle through the water: this is a scenario that can't be found in Brussels today. Unlike most major European cities, the city has no outdoor swimming facilities - no public pools, no lakes and no clean rivers.

Outdoor swimming can provide contact with the environment and promote social interaction. It is an activity that is often found at the crossroads of social differences, allowing for meetings and fostering the development of mutual understanding; public pools are places of pleasure and social cohesion. Convinced of the impact of outdoor swimming on a city's overall quality of life, Pool is cool strives to re-introduce this lost leisure activity to the European capital.

Canals in the city, lakes on the outskirts, redevelopment sites and leftover spaces along train tracks: through in-depth research conducted across the city, the initiative has identified potential sites and urban landscapes that could become swimming locations. In a series of debates, actions and temporary pool projects, Pool is cool brought citizens and municipal authorities together in an effort to demonstrate the need for such spaces. For a city infamous for its institutional fragmentation, spatial diversity and cultural differences, Pool is cool provides a lively but serious proposal for Brussels that fosters identity, creates cohesion and ultimately unites people in realising a shared dream for their city.

Stadtbadeoffensive
Vom Verhandeln städtischer Wasserlandschaften I

Kinder planschen und kreischen, Jugendliche hängen ab und versuchen, einander zu beeindrucken, Erwachsene schwimmen ihre Bahnen, und Senior*innen paddeln durch das Wasser: Diese Szenerie kann man in Brüssel heute nirgends finden. Anders als die meisten anderen großen europäischen Städte hat die Stadt keine Freibäder – keine öffentlichen Bäder, keine Seen und keine sauberen Flüsse.

Das Schwimmen im Freien stellt einen Kontakt zur Umwelt her und fördert die soziale Interaktion. Es ist eine Freizeitaktivität, die häufig an den Schnittstellen sozialer Differenzen anzutreffen ist, die Begegnungen ermöglicht und eine Entwicklung gegenseitigen Verständnisses fördert. Öffentliche Freibäder sind Orte des Vergnügens und des Zusammenhalts. Überzeugt von den Auswirkungen auf die allgemeine Lebensqualität möchte Pool is cool dieses verlorene Vergnügen in die europäische Hauptstadt zurückbringen.

Kanäle in der Innenstadt, Seen am Stadtrand, neue Wohnquartiere und Brachen entlang von Schienen: In intensiven Suchen quer durch die Stadt hat die Initiative potenzielle Orte und städtische Landschaften ausgemacht, die als Orte zum Baden infrage kommen. Mit einer Reihe von Debatten, Aktionen und temporären Schwimmbadprojekten hat Pool is cool Bürger*innen und städtische Behörden zusammengebracht, um den Bedarf solcher Orte aufzuzeigen. Für eine Stadt, die für ihre institutionelle Fragmentierung, ihre räumliche Diversität und ihre kulturellen Differenzen bekannt ist, bietet Pool is cool ein lebendiges und zugleich ernsthaftes Angebot für Brüsseler*innen, das Identität schaffen kann, Zusammenhalt fördert und schließlich in der Realisierung eines gemeinsamen Traums für ihre Stadt die Menschen zusammenbringt.

A campaign of appropriations and actions reinstated outdoor swimming facilities in Brussels

Eine Kampagne aus Aneignungen und Aktionen reintegriert Schwimmen im Freien in Brüssel

08. Flussbad Berlin

Project: Flussbad Berlin
City: Berlin
Client: N/A
Planning: realities:united
Status: Concept

Streaming the City
On Negotiating Urban Water Landscapes II

At the end of the nineteenth century, swimming in the river was part of Berlin's cityscape. Over 30 bathing spots existed along the Spree River. In the wake of industrialisation, the Spree became so polluted that it was no longer suitable for swimming. Since 1998, Flussbad, a Berlin initiative, has been working on changing this, with the dream of a clean, swimmable river in the middle of the city. The idea is that a 1.8 kilometre stretch of the largely unused Spree Canal, running through the heart of historic Berlin, will be reactivated in three phases each with a different use, atmosphere and function. Upstream ecological regeneration and filtration zones are intended not only to make the canal suitable for swimming, but also to allow the adjacent public and open spaces to be reconnected.

Flussbad is simultaneously working to ensure the realisation of the project through mediation work and permanent exchanges with the direct and indirect environment and events such as the Flussbad Cup, thereby testing the potential for swimming. Water purification concepts using test filters have been developed together with international and local experts. This effort is happening in the context of a number of successful examples from across Europe to clean city water, such as in Copenhagen, where until a few years ago the port area was heavily polluted, but where it is now possible to again jump into the cool Baltic water. When citizens and/or municipal administrators voice concerns, the initiative counters these with facts and figures, while remaining sensitive to the requirements of historic conservation codes. Swimming in the river is just one aspect: Flussbad Berlin sees itself as part of a social movement aiming to open up and enrich urban space.

From 2019, the Flussbad will have its own allocation in the state budget - a strong political commitment and a sign that with perseverance and the willingness to negotiate, utopia can become a reality. In an age in which clean rivers are being restored worldwide in cities like Chicago, London, New York, Paris and Sydney, a natural swimming pool in the river in Berlin is also conceivable.

Stadt im Fluss
Vom Verhandeln städtischer Wasserlandschaften II

Das Schwimmen im Fluss gehörte Ende des 19. Jahrhunderts in Berlin zum Stadtbild. Über dreißig Flussbadeanstalten waren an der Spree angesiedelt. Im Zuge der Industrialisierung verschmutzte die Spree derart, dass sie nicht mehr zum Baden geeignet war. An einem Wandel arbeitet eine Berliner Initiative seit 1998. Ihr Traum: Eine saubere Spree inmitten des Zentrums. Die 1,8 Kilometer des weitgehend ungenutzten Spreekanals im Herzen des historischen Berlins sollen in drei Abschnitten mit unterschiedlicher Nutzung, Atmosphäre und Funktion aktiviert werden. Vorgeschaltete ökologische Regenerations- und Filterzonen sollen den Kanal nicht nur zum Schwimmen tauglich machen, sondern die angrenzenden Räume und Freiflächen neu miteinander in Beziehung setzen.

Der Verein Flussbad Berlin zieht zeitgleich an mehreren Strängen, um das Projekt zu realisieren: Vermittlungsarbeit, permanenter Austausch mit dem direkten und indirekten Umfeld sowie Veranstaltungen, wie zum Beispiel der Flussbad-Pokal mit Probeschwimmen im Kupfergraben. Konkrete Konzepte zur Wasserreinigung des Flusses werden mit internationalen und lokalen Expert*innen in einem Testfilter entwickelt. Bedenken aus der Bevölkerung und der Verwaltung kann der Verein durch fundiertes Fachwissen aus dem Weg räumen. Den Anforderungen des Denkmalschutzes versucht er gerecht zu werden. Das Schwimmen im Fluss möglich zu machen, ist aber nur ein Aspekt: Flussbad Berlin versteht sich als Teil einer gesellschaftlichen Bewegung, die städtischen Raum öffnen und bereichern will.

Ab 2019 hat das Flussbad Berlin einen eigenen Titel im Landeshaushalt – ein starkes politisches Bekenntnis und Zeichen, dass mit Durchhaltevermögen und der Bereitschaft zu Verhandlungen utopische Ideen Wirklichkeit werden können. In einer Zeit, in der weltweit die Rückgewinnung sauberer Flüsse in den Städten wie Chicago, London, New York, Paris oder Sidney selbstverständlich wird, ist ein Berliner Flussbad also auch vorstellbar.

Swimming in the Spree has long been part of Berlin's cityscape

Das Schwimmen in der Spree ist seit Langem Teil des Berliner Stadtbildes

Communication is key: Flussbad Berlin's communication strategy works on multiple fronts

Kommunikation ist der Schlüssel: Die Kommunikationsstrategie von Flussbad Berlin arbeitet an mehreren Fronten

09. Project: Die Schlange

City: Berlin
Planning: Poligonal Office for Urban Communication
Client: N/A
Status: Ongoing

Learning from the Everyday

The Berlin-based agency Poligonal has set itself the goal of bringing some of the more forgotten aspects of urban development and planning to the attention of urban society - on foot and with an interdisciplinary focus: "Alternative views of the city - unexpected observations and unforeseeable encounters constitute a political and democratic act for us!"

And not only are urban phenomena and neglected architectures pointed out, but also architectural-historical experiments and utopias, such as the infamous motorway construction Schlangenbader Straße in Berlin. Experts and residents share their opinions and stories, give insights into their everyday lives and deal with prejudices: the previously uninteresting becomes a source of inspiration and new ideas.

The Swiss sociologist and self-proclaimed pedestrian-scientist Lucius Burckhardt considers breaking down barriers of everyday perception and their associated stigmas to be an essential prerequisite for a meaningful co-creation of the urban environment. The founders of Poligonal also emphasise the educational aspect of their work: "City expeditions help in gaining a new understanding of unknown life worlds, bringing different actors together in conversation and opening up new perspectives. Such experiences are the essential foundation for an informed participation in the production of the city!"

Vom Alltäglichen lernen

Die Berliner Agentur Poligonal hat sich zum Ziel gesetzt, unterrepräsentierte Themen der Stadtentwicklung und -planung ins Bewusstsein der Stadtgesellschaft zu bringen – zu Fuß und mit interdisziplinärer Ausrichtung: „Der alternative Blick auf die Stadt, das Zulassen von unerwarteten Beobachtungen und unvorhersehbare Begegnungen stellen für uns einen politischen und demokratischen Akt dar!"

Ergangen werden nicht nur urbane Phänomene und unbeachtete Architekturen, sondern auch baugeschichtliche Experimente und Utopien, wie zum Beispiel die verhasste Autobahnüberbauung Schlangenbader Straße. Expert*innen und Bewohner*innen kommen zu Wort, geben Einblicke in ihren persönlichen Alltag und rücken dabei festgefahrene Vorurteile zurecht: Scheinbar Uninteressantes wird so zur Quelle für Inspiration und neue Ideen.

Die Alltagswahrnehmung aus ihren Schranken zu befreien, betrachtete schon der Schweizer Soziologe und selbst ernannte Spaziergangswissenschaftler Lucius Burckhardt als wesentliche Grundvoraussetzung für eine sinnhafte Mitgestaltung der Umwelt. Auch die Organisatoren von Poligonal betonen den edukativen Aspekt ihrer Arbeit: „Stadtexpeditionen helfen, unbekannte Lebenswelten besser kennenzulernen, bringen unterschiedliche Akteur*innen ins Gespräch und eröffnen neue Sichtweisen. Solche Erfahrungen sind für uns ein essenzielles Fundament für eine informierte Teilhabe an der Produktion von Stadt!"

Living on top of the highway: built Utopia? For many residents, the housing complex from the 80s decried as bad planning is an oasis above the roaring traffic

Wohnen über der Autobahn: gebaute Utopie? Für viele Bewohner*innen stellt die als Fehlplanung verschriene Wohnungsbauanlage aus den 80ern eine Oase über dem tosenden Verkehr dar

Variety despite repetition: the building structure of "the snake" creates heterogeneous apartment layouts and customisable outdoor spaces – a green landscape

Vielfalt trotz Repetition: die Gebäudestruktur der Schlange erzeugt heterogene Wohnungsgrundrisse und individualisierbare Außenräume – eine grüne Landschaft

A radical architectural monument – the expert's perspective: Poligonal asks architect Wolf Bertelsmann for a field report on the history of the building

Ein radikales Baudenkmal aus Alltags- und Expertensicht: Der Schlange-Architekt Wolf Bertelsmann und Poligonal beim Erfahrungsbericht zur Entstehungsgeschichte

10. The Ruin Academy

Project: The Ruin Academy
City: Taitung, Taiwan
Client: Casagrande Laboratory and Taiwanese JUT Foundation for Arts & Architecture
Planning: Casagrande Laboratory
Status: 2010-current

Industrial Nature
What Ruins Teach

In central Taipei city, a building is occupied by the Finland-based Casagrande Laboratory and the Taiwanese JUT Foundation for Arts and Architecture. Since 2010, The Ruin Academy has been operating as an independent multi-disciplinary biourbanism research centre. In conjunction with projects throughout Taiwan, the Ruin Academy and its architects have been selectively combining elements of environmentalism and design, developing methods of punctual manipulation and urban acupuncture to manipulate urban energy flows in an effort to find the ecologically sustainable urban development known as the third-generation city.

The academy began in an abandoned Japanese-Taiwanese sugar factory in Taitung, Taiwan, its core located in the factory's evaporator tanks area and from where it was able to grow to occupy the entire factory. It offered multifunctional research and educational spaces for workshops and studios, supported by extensive community gardening and spontaneous flora inside the factory.

Now located in an abandoned apartment building, the structure was pulled back to its basic construction. Interior walls and windows were removed. Six-inch holes were punctured through walls throughout the building. It now rains inside the building, watering the plants found there. Raw mahogany planks and columns are used in a changing interior that provides shelter for professors and students. There is a public sauna on the fifth floor.

The students/operators are not volunteers; they are constructor-gardeners. "We want to farm the city, treating it with the urban acupuncture methods we have learned through shared local knowledge."

-> Essay 5 pp. 295 ff. Designing Ruins

Industrienatur
Was Ruinen lehren

Das finnische Casagrande Laboratory und die taiwanesische JUT-Stiftung für Kunst und Architektur haben ein Gebäude in der Innenstadt von Taipeh besetzt. Seit 2010 arbeitet die Ruin Academy als unabhängiges multidisziplinäres Forschungszentrum zu Biourbanismus. Im Rahmen von Projekten in ganz Taiwan haben die Ruin Academy und ihre Architekt*innen ausgewählte Elemente aus Ökologie und Gestaltung miteinander kombiniert und Methoden der punktuellen Manipulation städtischer Verbindungen – urbane Akupunktur – entwickelt. Sie bemühen sich um eine ökologisch nachhaltige Entwicklung, die sie als Stadt der dritten Generation bezeichnen.

Die Akademie nahm ihren Anfang neben den Verdampferkesseln einer verlassenen japanisch-taiwanesischen Zuckerfabrik in Taitung, Taiwan, von wo aus sie wachsen und das ganze Fabrikgelände übernehmen konnte. Hier boten sich multifunktionale Forschungs- und Bildungsräume für Workshops und Studios, eingerahmt von umfassenden Gemeinschaftsgärten und spontanem Pflanzenwuchs innerhalb der Fabrik.

Jetzt befindet sich die Akademie in einem verlassenen Wohngebäude, dessen Struktur auf die Grundkonstruktion zurückgebaut wurde: Wände und Fenster wurden entfernt; im ganzen Gebäude wurde Mauerwerk mit 15 Zentimeter großen Löchern punktiert. Es regnet nun in das Gebäude hinein, sodass die im Inneren wachsenden Pflanzen gewässert werden. Im Innenraum ist zum Witterungsschutz der dort lebenden Lehrenden und Lernenden rohes Mahagoniholz zu Böden, Stützen und Zwischenwänden verbaut. In der fünften Etage gibt es eine öffentliche Sauna.

Die hier Lernenden sind nicht bloß Freiwillige, sie studieren und betreiben, errichten und pflanzen ein Modell der Stadt der dritten Generation. Sie möchten die Stadt bewirtschaften und behandeln sie mit den Methoden der urbanen Akupunktur, die sie durch geteiltes lokales Wissen erlernt haben.

Urban acupuncture: in the evaporator tanks of an abandoned sugar factory in Taitung, Taiwan, specifically placed interventions open spaces for a jungle, a gathering space and a walkway – each a point that can grow to occupy the entire factory

Städtische Akupunktur: In den Verdampfertanks einer aufgegebenen Zuckerfabrik in Taitung, Taiwan, schaffen punktuelle Manipulationen Freiräume für einen Dschungel, einen Gemeinschaftsraum und einen Spazierpfad

11.

Humboldt Volcano

Project: Humboldt Volcano
City: Berlin
Client: N/A
Planning: Hybrid Space Lab (Elizabeth Sikiaridi, Frans Vogelaar)
Status: Concept, unrealised

Jungle Replaces Concrete
An Alternative to the Stadtschloss Berlin

In Berlin, across from the Museuminsel (Museum Island), one finds the newly rebuilt Humboldt Forum, housed in a replica of the Berlin Schloss, a fixture of the German and Prussian imperial past that was bombed during the Second World War and then replaced by the government of the German Democratic Republic (GDR), the former East Germany with the Palast der Republik in 1976. After the Palast der Republic was torn down in 2003, the ongoing reconstruction of the palace façade has been fraught with controversy, with a public discussion centring around the international role of Berlin, national and historical symbols and how to confront Germany's colonial history.

The polemical, arresting image of the Humboldt Volcano is a spatial-conceptual insertion into this conversation from Berlin-based Hybrid Space Lab studio as they work to open discursive and positive visions for the Forum and the city. With the slogan "Jungle instead of concrete!", a radical greening of the façade is proposed, a not-so-subtle reference to the geographer and naturalist Alexander von Humboldt. The project and its vibrant imagery were developed in 2015, when the financing for the Forum's façade had not yet been secured - meaning that the possibility of consultation for alternative proposals was still open. Proposing a crystalline architecture, the volcano refers to German traditions that have opposed the palace and its power structures. And standing in for a pluralistic multiculturalism, it enables the appropriation of the building, forcing it open towards the city, the international public and its own history.

Hybrid Space Lab unleashed and subsequently curated a heated discourse around this utopian proposition. The combination of tabloid-friendly imagery with international expertise on greening cities and climate change proved to be a highly effective strategy.

Dschungel statt Beton
Eine Alternative zum Stadtschloss Berlin

Gegenüber der Museumsinsel in Berlin befindet sich das neu errichtete Humboldt Forum in einer Replika des Berliner Schlosses, das auch für die deutsche und preußische imperiale Vergangenheit steht. Es wurde im Zweiten Weltkrieg zerbombt und 1976 von der DDR-Regierung durch den Palast der Republik ersetzt, der 2003 abgerissen wurde. Die noch laufende Rekonstruktion ist von Kontroversen begleitet. Die öffentliche Diskussion dreht sich um die internationale Rolle Berlins, um nationale und historische Symbole und um den Umgang mit der eigenen (Kolonial-)Geschichte.

Das polemische, eindrückliche Bild des Humboldt-Vulkans ist ein räumlich-konzeptueller Beitrag des Berliner Büros Hybrid Space Lab zu dieser Debatte. Sie soll diskursive und positive Visionen für das Forum und die Stadt eröffnen. Nach dem Motto „Dschungel statt Beton!" wird eine radikale Begrünung der Fassade vorgeschlagen und so wenig subtil auf den Geografen und Naturforscher Alexander von Humboldt Bezug genommen. Das Projekt und seine lebendige Bilderwelt wurde 2015 entwickelt, als die Finanzierung für die Fassade des Forums noch nicht stand – was bedeutete, dass noch offen über Alternativvorschläge beraten wurde. Mit dem Entwurf einer kristallinen Architektur verweist der Vulkan auf deutsche Traditionen, die dem Palast und seinen Machtstrukturen entgegen- und für einen pluralistischen Multikulturalismus einstanden. Er ermöglicht die Aneignung des Gebäudes, erzwingt dessen Öffnung – in die Stadt, in die internationale Öffentlichkeit und in seine eigene Geschichte.

Hybrid Space Lab hat eine hitzige Debatte rund um diesen utopischen Vorschlag entzündet und dann kuratiert. Die Kombination aus boulevardpressefreundlichen Bildern und internationaler Expertise zur Begrünung von Städten und zum Klimawandel erwies sich als überaus wirksame Strategie.

Berlin neu denken

Das Architektur-Festival „MakeCity 2018“ mit 250 Veranstaltungen in 18 Tagen will Baukunst in der Hauptstadt transparenter machen und lädt zum Mitreden und Mitentwickeln ein

Architektur ist eine Kunst. Aber wie kann man diese Kunst einem Nicht-Fachpublikum gut vermitteln?“, fragt Matthew Griffin, 48, Architekt in Berlin. „Es geht darum, dass Bürger die Architektur verstehen und motiviert sind, Teil daran zu haben: Mitreden, mitgestalten, mitentwickeln.“

Baukunst zum Anfassen: Zum zweiten Mal findet „das größte Festival für Architektur und Andersmachen in Deutschland“ statt. „MakeCity 2018, Stadt Neu Gemischt“ möchte mit 250 Stadt- und Kiezrundgängen, Fahrradtouren, Vorträgen, Diskussionen und Ausstellungen an 103 Orten in 18 Tagen die Bürger dazu einladen, bestehende Stadtentwicklungen kennenzulernen und sich an künftigen Projekten auch selbst zu beteiligen.

„Sollten wir nicht alle Stadtentwickler sein?“, heißt ein Workshop. „Wie kann man Projekte entwickeln und gleichzeitig mehr Leute darin einbinden? Das war die Grundidee des Festivals“, sagt Griffin. Der Kanadier lebt seit 26 Jahren in Berlin und betreibt mit seiner Partnerin Britta Jürgens das Architekturbüro Deadline.

Zusammen mit der Initiatorin und künstlerischen Leiterin Francesca Ferguson riefen sie das Festival ins Leben. So stellen sie dem Publikum auch ein eigenes Projekt als ein Beispiel für mehr Bürgerbeteiligung vor: „Frizz23“, der ehemalige Blumengroßmarkt in der Friedrichstraße 23. „Bürger wurden befragt, erst dann wurde das Objekt, drei Grundstücke, über ein Konzeptverfahren vergeben.“

Auch das Bauherrenmodell ist ein anderes: Eine Baugemeinschaft aus über 30 Leuten hat Frizz23 gemeinsam gestaltet. Heraus kam ein Gebäude für Kunst, Kultur und Kreativwirtschaft mit vielen kleinteiligen Ateliers. Ein Bildungsträger, eine Taschenmanufaktur, ein Fahrradladen, eine Werbeagentur, Künstler und Schriftsteller werden dort arbeiten.

„Im Idealfall sollten Bürger und Anwohner bereits in die Planung einbezogen werden“, sagt Griffin. Ein anderes Beispiel zumindest bürgernaher Architektur sei die kooperative Entwicklung des Holzmarkt-Village, wo ein ganzes Viertel mit Mischgewerbe, Wohnungen oder Ateliers mit dörflichem Charakter und Märchenpark an der Spree entsteht. Fachkundige leiten eine Führung durch das Gelände.

Im Studio Talk „Flussbad Berlin: Idee, Vision, Protagonisten“ stellen Verantwortliche das Projekt eines Freibades an einem stillen Arm der Spree am Bode-Museum vor sowie die nächsten Schritte der Umsetzung. Eine Führung gibt es noch dazu: „Ich weiß nicht, ob das Flussbad vor oder nach dem Flughafen fertig sein wird – aber das Projekt ist sehr realistisch“, so Griffin.

Von der schlafenden Industriestadt Oberschöneweide bis zum modernen Wissenschaftsstandort Adlershof, vom wilden Südkreuz über Tempelhof, Kreuzberg bis zum Dong-Xuan-Center erstrecken sich die vielfältigen und angeleiteten Exkursionen durch Berlins Vorzeigeprojekte und vielversprechende Brachen.

„Hütten & Paläste“, „A100. Der Klang der Berliner Stadtautobahn“ oder „die nachwachsende Stadt“ sind die Themen. Auch für Kinder gibt es viel zu tun. Praktische Architektur-Workshops, unter- und überirdische Stadterkundungen, Entwerfen und Bauen in Bäumen. „Architektur ist etwas, das man fühlen und erleben muss, das Festival ist eine gute Gelegenheit mit Leuten zu sprechen, die diese Projekte umsetzen.“

Auf lange Sicht aber sollte die Mitgestaltung noch viel weiter gehen. „Ziel ist es, ein Bewusstsein in die Öffentlichkeit zu tragen: Das ist unsere Stadt! Wir können mitmachen!“

„MakeCity 2018, Stadt Neu Gemischt“, Architektur-Festival, 250 Veranstaltungen, Programm unter www.makecity.berlin

Ein kühnes Gedankenspiel: Das neue Humboldt Forum wird Teil eines Urwaldes. Thema des Studiogesprächs „Alexander von Humboldt und der Humboldt-Vulkan“

Der Architekt Matthew Griffin (48) erklärt, wie die Stadt neu gebaut wird.

Kuhns Kulturstück

Helmut Kuhn schaut, liest und hört für den KURIER

Rethinking Berlin, article in Berliner Zeitung: the arresting image of the Humboldt Volcano served as a spatial-conceptual polemic by Berlin-based Hybrid Space Lab, firing up the discussion on the construction of the Humboldt Forum

„Berlin neu denken“, Artikel in der Berliner Zeitung: Das fesselnde Bild des Humboldt Vulkans diente als raumkonzeptionelle Polemik des Berliner Hybrid Space Lab, das die Diskussion über den Bau des Humboldt Forums befeuerte

Utopia in Berlin, reality in Singapore: Gardens by the Bay conservatory complex in Singapore

Utopie in Berlin, Realität in Singapur: Gewächshaus im künstlich angelegten Parkgelände Gardens by the Bay in Singapur

Resources, Materiality and the Circular City

Ressourcen, Materialität und Kreislaufwirtschaft

5

Earth Overshoot Day is an ecological measuring point that marks the date when humanity's annual demands on nature exceed what the planet's ecosystems can renew in that year.

Der Earth Overshoot Day markiert jenes Datum im Jahresverlauf, an dem sämtliche Ressourcen, die der Menschheit pro Jahr zur Verfügung stehen, verbraucht sind.

In 2018, Earth Overshoot Day fell on August 1, the earliest date measured since the 1970s, when humans started to consume more than the planet could produce.

Im Jahr 2018 verbrauchten die Menschen bereits bis zum 1. August mehr natürliche Ressourcen, als die Erde im gesamten Jahr erzeugen kann. Im Jahr 2000 war dieser Stichtag noch am 23. September.

Sources / Quellen:

Global Footprint Network, World Economic Forum, NYC CoolRoofs, GreenFacts, Foreign Policy, World Bank, T. Saleh, A. Chin, Journal of Sustainable Forestry, Construction Canada UCAR SciEd, Berlin Senate Department for Urban Development and Housing, LWARB

Between 1900 and 2050, worldwide resource extraction will have increased by 2400 percent.

Zwischen 1900 und 2050 wird die weltweite Rohstoffförderung um 2.400 Prozent zunehmen.

In 2016, the world produced 45 million metric tonnes of electrical waste, equivalent to 4,500 Eiffel Towers.

Im Jahr 2016 produzierte die Welt 45 Millionen Tonnen Elektroschrott. Das entspricht 4.500 Eiffeltürmen.

By 2030, Singapore plans to increase its urban area by 30 percent, making it one of the world's largest and most consistent sand importers.

Bis 2030 plant Singapur, sein Stadtgebiet um dreißig Prozent zu vergrößern, und ist damit einer der größten Sandimporteure der Welt.

Since 2005, 24 Indonesian islands have disappeared due to sand extraction.

Seit 2005 sind durch die Sandgewinnung 24 indonesische Inseln verschwunden.

A Circular Economy is "an economic system based on business models that replace the 'end-of-life' concept by reducing, reusing, recycling and recovering materials in production, distribution and consumptive processes."

Zirkuläre Wirtschaft meint „ein Wirtschaftssystem, das auf Geschäftsmodellen basiert, die das End-of-Life-Konzept ersetzen, indem sie Materialien in Produktions-, Vertriebs- und Konsumprozessen reduzieren, alternativ wiederverwenden, recyceln und verwerten."

In 2015, only 20 percent of plastics were recycled. New plastic asphalt alternatives can reuse up to 70,000 single-use plastic bags and 20,000 bottles in every ton.

Im Jahr 2015 wurden nur zwanzig Prozent der Kunststoffe recycelt. In einer Tonne Kunststoffasphalt könnten künftig bis zu 70.000 Einwegplastiktüten und 20.000 Einwegflaschen wiederverwendet werden.

By 2036, London's Waste & Recycling Board estimates that the city could save seven billion pounds annually if textiles, electricals, plastics and the built environment were directed towards a circular economy.

Das Londoner Waste & Recycling Board schätzt, dass die Stadt bis 2036 jährlich sieben Milliarden Pfund einsparen könnte, wenn die gebaute Umwelt sowie Textilien, Elektrogeräte und Kunststoffe auf Kreislaufwirtschaft ausgerichtet würden.

50 percent of global solid waste is the result of the construction industry. Significant cost savings of up to 80 percent can be achieved by adaptively reusing existing buildings.

Fünfzig Prozent der weltweiten Feststoffabfälle stammen aus der Bauindustrie. Durch die adaptive Umnutzung bestehender Gebäude könnten erhebliche Kosteneinsparungen von bis zu achtzig Prozent erzielt werden.

Building with wood consumes 600 percent less embodied energy than steel and 350 percent less embodied energy than concrete when tested in comparable wood structures.

Vergleichstests zeigen, dass das Bauen mit Holz 600 Prozent weniger Bauenergie als Stahl und 350 Prozent weniger als Beton verbraucht.

Wood building products meet and surpass fire safety and protection codes worldwide due to their ability to char their outer layers first, burning slowly and preventing inner layers from burning.

Holzbauteile erfüllen und übertreffen weltweit die Brandschutz- und Sicherheitsvorschriften, da sie eine verlangsamte Brenndauer besitzen. Die äußeren Schichten verkohlen und verhindern das Verbrennen der inneren Schichten.

Urban Heat Islands are urban areas that are significantly warmer than their surroundings due to the absorption rather than reflection of heat by buildings and energy produced by human activity.

„Urban heat islands" sind städtische versiegelte Flächen, die aufgrund fehlender Verdunstung die Sonneneinstrahlung und menschlich produzierte Abwärme speichern. Sie werden dadurch deutlich heißer als ihre Umgebung.

Since 2009, more than 450,000 square metres of rooftops in New York have been painted white to reduce the urban heat island effect.

Seit 2009 wurden in New York mehr als 450.000 Quadratmeter Dächer weiß gestrichen, um den Energieverbrauch zu verringern.

In 2017, 3.9 percent of Berlin's roofed areas were green. In 2017, 23 percent of Basel's roofed areas were green – the highest percentage of greened roofs in Europe.

Im Jahr 2017 waren 3,9 Prozent der überdachten Flächen Berlins grün. Mit 23 Prozent weist Basel (Schweiz) den höchsten Anteil an begrünten Dächern in Europa auf.

The use of ferrocement technology is environmentally and economically affordable, with steel bars replaced by steel mesh, 25 mm thick wall elements being used instead of 125 mm and no need for aggregates, as the superior ductile properties of steel also protect against seismic forces at work in many areas around the world

Der Einsatz der Ferrozementtechnologie ist ökologisch und ökonomisch sinnvoll; Stahlstäbe werden durch Stahlgewebe ersetzt; ohne weitere Zuschläge sind statt 125 mm dicken Wandelementen 25 mm dicke möglich. Die hervorragende Formbarkeit hat sich auch bei Erdbeben bewährt

Rethinking Materiality

Constructing under Climate Change

As the world continues to undergo rapid urbanisation, natural resources are under enormous strain. Globally, development is occurring at the cost of the environment. Urbanisation in general – and buildings in particular – are considered one of the single largest consumers of energy, in all of its forms. The so-called green buildings of today remain an elitist fiction; affordable by a select few, the resource consumption involved is often higher than that for traditional buildings. The standard of these green buildings needs to be reset with the global situation in mind – before it becomes the norm. The materiality of our built environments needs radical rethinking in anticipation – and in the midst – of emerging concerns in the age of climate change.

Whenever materials are chosen, a series of choices are made, some consciously and some not. Natural materials such as stone, wood, soil and so on tend to require less energy consumption in order to be transformed into standardised, manufactured materials. Further, selecting locally sourced building materials significantly reduces transportation energy costs. The energy savings of selecting locally extracted natural materials may attempt to balance the environmental impact on territories which the extraction of those very same materials caused; for example, rather than the normal situation where material is extracted, it is transformed into manufactured materials and then shipped to a far-away destination.

In the case of several widely used manufactured materials, there are health concerns, as they exude compounds harmful to humans and impact our well-being. Then there are the pollution concerns, which are present throughout the extraction and supply chain. In cases where natural materials are unable to meet spatial needs, facts such as these must be considered. The importance of building material choices cannot be overstated. These choices may be the result of habitual practice, personal convenience or ignorance, and they come at costs that register across multiple scales. These range from the scale of the body, for those who inhabit the buildings, to the scale of the territory, for the environment. Unfortunately, as it stands, the selection of materials

Baustoffe überdenken

Materialentscheidungen im Zeitalter des Klimawandels

Die zunehmende Urbanisierung verstärkt den Druck auf die natürlichen Ressourcen der Erde enorm. Die weltweiten Entwicklungen gehen zulasten der Umwelt. Urbanisierung im Allgemeinen und Gebäude im Besonderen gehören zu den größten Energieverbrauchern – in allen ihren Formen. Sogenannte grüne Gebäude, die gerade angesagt sind, bleiben eine elitäre Fiktion. Erschwinglich sind sie nur für wenige Auserwählte. Ihr Ressourcenverbrauch ist häufig höher als der von traditionellen Gebäuden. Bevor sie zur Norm werden, muss der Standard solcher grüner Gebäude in Bezug auf die globale Situation erst neu durchdacht werden. Die materielle Beschaffenheit unserer gebauten Umwelt erfordert radikales Umdenken angesichts der zu erwartenden – und bereits vorhandenen – Auswirkungen des Klimawandels.

Bei der Auswahl von Materialien werden gleich eine Reihe von Entscheidungen getroffen: manche bewusst, andere unbewusst. Natürliche Materialien wie Stein, Holz, Lehm und dergleichen verbrauchen weniger Energie als Standardmaterialien. Vor Ort vorhandene Baumaterialien verringern die Energiekosten zusätzlich, weil der Transport entfällt. Die Energie, die die Auswahl lokal gewonnener natürlicher Materialien einspart, kann die ökologischen Auswirkungen ihrer Gewinnung auf die Umwelt ausgleichen. Anders im Normalfall, wo Material abgebaut, in Baumaterial verarbeitet und an weit entfernte Orte transportiert wird.

Im Fall vieler der eingesetzten, vorproduzierten Materialien gibt es auch häufig Gesundheitsbedenken, weil sie Stoffe ausdünsten, die für Menschen schädlich sind und unser Wohlbefinden beeinträchtigen. Außerdem führen sowohl die Gewinnung wie auch die Lieferkette solcher Materialien zu Luftverschmutzung. Wenn natürliche Materialien den Bedarf vor Ort nicht erfüllen können, müssen diese Faktoren also mit bedacht und abgewogen werden. Die Bedeutung der Materialwahl ist ausgesprochen groß. Sie kann aufgrund gängiger Praxis getroffen werden, von persönlicher Bequemlichkeit oder Ignoranz beeinflusst sein – immer geht sie auf Kosten verschiedenster Beteiligter: auf Kosten des Körpers derjenigen, die das Gebäude bewohnen, auf Kosten der Umgebung, auf Kosten der Umwelt. Leider ist es eine Tatsache, dass bei der Wahl des Materials im Fall moderner Gebäude

for contemporary buildings is often an act that fails to consider these larger implications.

all diese wichtigen Überlegungen kaum einbezogen werden.

Contemporary architecture consumes more resources than ever before

Despite every technological advance - or perhaps because of them - contemporary architecture consumes more resources today than ever before. The standards of design efficiency and intelligence have already demonstrated the ability to perform at high levels, where materials and know-how can achieve a lot with very little. New technologies - and the designers who wield them - must seize upon and extend these achievements and their benefits to the many, rather than serving the whimsical and frivolous expressions of the few. The purposeful acknowledgement of the environment and the ecological, social and economic concerns connected to it should not be seen as a limitation on creative endeavours or expressions. Instead, it should be viewed as a provocation towards even more imaginative solutions and scenarios.

There is a tendency to consider higher consumption standards as a benchmark of progress. However, it is evident that the consumption standards of urban life in developed countries cannot merely be extended to the rest of the world: there are simply not enough resources. And although we aspire towards a more equal society, technology often comes with a high cost and is restricted to the few who can afford it. It has led to social segregation and developmental disparity in many global cities. If we are seeking to build a more equitable society, then technology should serve the bulk of the population, rather than widening existing - or creating new - social gaps. The need of the hour is to redefine development so that it does not come at the cost of environmental destruction, social imbalance or economic crisis.

Affordability is a major factor and a significant contributor to social and spatial exclusion in rapidly urbanising societies. Current building technologies are not affordable for the majority of the population and perpetuate the growing trend of urban poverty where there is a substantial mismatch between salaries and housing costs, and even people with full-time jobs are not always able to afford shelter.

Zeitgenössische Architektur verbraucht mehr Ressourcen als je zuvor

Trotz aller technologischer Fortschritte – oder vielleicht sogar deswegen – verbraucht zeitgenössische Architektur heute mehr Ressourcen als je zuvor. Die Standards der Designeffizienz und -intelligenz haben gezeigt, dass es möglich ist, auf hohem Niveau zu handeln. Mit Materialien und Know-how kann aus wenig sehr viel entstehen. Neue Technologien – und Designer*innen, die sie einsetzen – müssen diese Errungenschaften aufgreifen und sie zum Nutzen aller ausbauen, anstatt den kapriziösen und leichtfertigen Bedürfnissen einiger weniger zu dienen. Der Respekt vor dem Umfeld – vor seinen ökologischen, sozialen und ökonomischen Belangen – sollte weniger als Einschränkung kreativen Ausdrucksvermögens gesehen werden denn als Herausforderung für fantasievollere Lösungen und Szenarien.

Es gibt die Tendenz, höhere Konsumstandards als Zeichen des Fortschritts zu betrachten. Offensichtlich ist jedoch, dass die Konsumstandards des urbanen Lebens in den „entwickelten" Ländern wohl kaum auf den Rest der Welt übertragbar sind: Es gibt einfach nicht genügend Ressourcen dafür. Und obwohl wir eine gleichberechtigtere Gesellschaft anstreben, ist Technologie häufig mit höheren Kosten verbunden und den Wenigen vorbehalten, die sie sich leisten können. Das hat zu sozialer Segregation und Entwicklungsunterschieden in vielen Städten weltweit geführt. Wenn wir eine gerechtere Gesellschaft aufbauen wollen, dann sollte die Technologie der Masse der Bevölkerung dienen, anstatt bestehende soziale Unterschiede zu vergrößern oder neue zu schaffen. Das Gebot der Stunde lautet, „Entwicklung" neu zu definieren, damit sie Umweltzerstörung, soziale Ungerechtigkeit und Wirtschaftskrisen verhindert.

Erschwinglichkeit ist ein Hauptfaktor und ein wichtiger Motor sozialer und räumlicher Verdrängung in den sich rapide urbanisierenden Gesellschaften. Moderne Bautechnologien sind für die Mehrheit der Bevölkerung unbezahlbar und unterstützen damit den wachsenden Trend zu urbaner Armut, der eine grundlegende Diskrepanz zwischen Einkommen und Wohnkosten mit sich bringt. Sogar Men-

Inclusive solutions are the key

Continued research, innovation and experimentation are required to expand our options when it comes to developing and incorporating environmentally sound, socio-economically beneficial approaches into building. Strategies are urgently required to make building and housing technology more inclusive, specifically building economic strategies contrary to traditional and exclusionary debt financing.

Globally, there is huge - and unacceptable - disparity in access to basic services and quality of life. Technological advances have their advantages but cannot be expected to solve everything; other areas of development are necessary in order to bring everyone along. In the context of disparity, digital technologies continue to empower the already privileged. At the same time as our gadgets are being designed and programmed to regulate our buildings and our lives, we are growing more passive and less knowledgeable; we have no idea about first principles as we rely more and more on devices that we learn how to operate. In only learning how to operate these devices, we forget how to resolve problems and improve our lives directly - a dangerous trend. Alongside smart cities and intelligent buildings we should be concerned with wise and intelligent citizens, in a wise and intelligent, humane society.

The only way forward is through knowledge

Architecture is a complex profession that requires the capacity to actively synthesise multiple kinds of information and knowledge. The path to simplicity is a complex one, and the solutions to our complicated times cannot be too simple or naïve.

If we choose to devote time to listening to and reflecting upon the collected wisdom from across geographies and histories, we can improve upon current practice. Overdesign is often due to a lack of knowledge and expertise, and it is an area where significant savings in resources - both financial and material - can be achieved. Academia, industry and practice must collaborate towards understanding the emerging global picture. Only collectively can we initiate change.

schen mit Vollzeitjobs sind dann nicht mehr in der Lage, eine Wohnung zu bezahlen.

Inklusive Lösungen sind der Schlüssel

Weiterführende Studien, Innovationen und Experimente sind nötig, um unsere Möglichkeiten zu erweitern, um ökologisch solide und sozioökonomisch vorteilhafte Ansätze im Bauen zu entwickeln. Strategien, mit deren Hilfe wir die Bautechnologie inklusiver machen können, werden dringend benötigt – insbesondere ökonomische Strategien, die gegenläufig zur üblichen Schuldenfinanzierung funktionieren.

Weltweit gibt es riesige – und inakzeptable – Unterschiede beim Zugang zu elementaren Leistungen und Lebensqualität. Technologische Fortschritte haben ihre Vorteile, aber es ist nicht zu erwarten, dass sie alles lösen; andere Bereiche der Entwicklung sind nötig, um alle ins Boot zu holen. Ungleichheit führt dazu, dass auch digitale Technologie die bereits vorhandenen Privilegierten weiter stärkt. Und während Geräte entworfen und programmiert werden, um unsere Gebäude und unser Leben immer weiter zu regulieren, werden wir selbst immer passiver und unwissender. Wir haben keine Ahnung mehr von Grundprinzipien, da wir uns mehr und mehr auf Geräte verlassen, die wir zu bedienen lernen. Und weil wir nur noch lernen, Geräte zu bedienen, vergessen wir, wie man Probleme direkt löst und damit das Leben direkt verbessert – ein gefährlicher Trend. Deshalb sollten wir uns, außer über intelligente Städte und Smart Homes, Gedanken über intelligente Bürger*innen und eine intelligente, menschliche Gesellschaft machen.

Nur durch Wissen kommt man vorwärts

Architektur ist ein komplexer Beruf, der erfordert, verschiedene Informationen und Wissen aktiv zu synthetisieren. Der Weg zum Einfachen ist komplex, und die Lösungen für unsere komplizierten Zeiten dürfen nicht zu einfach und naiv sein.

Wenn wir uns dafür entscheiden, dem Zuhören und Reflektieren des gesammelten Wissens von überall auf der Welt und durch die Geschichte hinweg Zeit zu widmen, dann können wir die heutige Praxis verbessern. „Überdesigntes" ist häufig ein Zeichen von mangelndem Wissen und Expertise

The stark contrast that exists in global cities between informal settlements without basic infrastructure and high-end centrally air-conditioned skyscrapers should be a thing of the past. The architecture of the future needs to be more efficient, combining the benefits of technological advances with traditional knowledge in order to deliver a higher quality of life for all, while using fewer resources. Such a future architecture could include climatic comfort through passive techniques to reduce energy demands, new ways to use familiar natural materials, and larger budgets for people's involvement to benefit the local economy.

Throughout the architectural process, the materials we choose to use - and how we choose to use them - are not only reflective of our current social and economic context; they will also serve to determine the future context for buildings, cities and the people who will inhabit them.

und ein Bereich, in dem erhebliche Einsparungen sowohl finanzieller als auch materieller Natur gemacht werden können. Wissenschaft, Industrie und Praxis müssen für ein Verständnis der weltweiten Situation zusammenarbeiten. Nur in Gemeinschaft gelingt es, den Wandel zu gestalten.

Der krasse Kontrast, der in der globalen Stadt zwischen informellen Siedlungen ohne Basisinfrastruktur einerseits und den luxuriösen klimatisierten Wolkenkratzern andererseits besteht, sollte der Vergangenheit angehören. Die Architektur der Zukunft muss effizienter sein und die Vorteile des technologischen Fortschritts mit traditionellem Wissen verknüpfen, um eine bessere Lebensqualität für alle zu schaffen und weniger Ressourcen zu verbrauchen. Eine solche Architektur der Zukunft könnte vieles beinhalten: klimatischen Komfort durch Passivtechniken, um den Energieverbrauch zu verringern, neue Arten, bekannte Materialien zu verwenden, und höhere Budgets für das Engagement der Bürger*innen in der örtlichen Wirtschaft.

Im gesamten architektonischen Prozess sind die Materialien, die wir aussuchen und nutzen, und die Art, wie wir sie nutzen, nicht nur eine Reflexion des aktuellen sozialen und ökonomischen Kontexts. Sie bilden den Grundstein für den zukünftigen Kontext von Gebäuden, Städten und den Menschen, die darin wohnen werden.

Modular prefabricated ferrocement hollow block units can be assembled on site in less than six days, including the foundations – a design suitable for all, including disaster relief efforts

Modulare vorgefertigte Ferrozement-Hohlblockeinheiten können vor Ort in weniger als sechs Tagen inklusive Fundament montiert werden; die Konstruktion ist für alle geeignet, auch bei Katastropheneinsätzen

How Urban Is Wood?

Why Timber Resonates

Half of solid waste produced globally is the result of the construction industry. The continued production and disposal of concrete and steel are only possible through enormous energy and transportation costs, with timber continuing to be an underutilised and underestimated alternative. Here, architects Eike Roswag-Klinge, founder of the Natural Building Lab at the Technische Universität (TU) Berlin and Hermann Kaufmann, a specialist in timber construction and professor at TU Munich, talk about how wood combines high and low tech, getting rid of ventilation systems and why using wood can reduce chaos on construction sites.

Eike Roswag-Klinge: Timber constructions are now a part of the metropolises of the future and have long lost their rural associations. The wood-building cluster TUM:wood at TU Munich is the leading research institute in Germany and you yourself are involved in a number of pilot projects. What potential does building with wood offer for the future?

Hermann Kaufmann: First, the potential lies in the growing need for ecological sustainability. The question of energy has long been a focal point, but we now want to know where our materials come from. Second, it is also about the building process. Timber constructions require prefabrication and, as such, production processes can be carried out in a workshop, rather than onsite. This brings with it a new and orderly quality: the chaos on building sites will disappear. You co-founded the network DieNachwachsendeStadt (The Regenerative City). What is your vision?

ER: Natural building substances such as timber, straw or hemp have a great number of advantages, both in terms of energy optimisation and urban densification building projects. That is why regenerative resources will increasingly attract attention as preferred building materials. What do you think of the current competition to build the tallest high-rise out of timber?

HK: With the wooden high-rise, civil engineering has discovered a new field. Naturally, partic-

Wie urban ist Holz?

Warum der nachwachsende Rohstoff überzeugt

Fünfzig Prozent der globalen Abfallproduktion stammen aus der Baubranche. Die Herstellung und die Entsorgung von Beton und Stahl sind nur mit enormem Energie- und Transportaufwand möglich. Holzbau ist immer noch eine unterschätzte Alternative. Wie der nachwachsende Rohstoff Hightech und Lowtech verbindet, weshalb man gänzlich auf Lüftungsanlagen verzichten könnte und warum Holz für weniger Chaos auf der Baustelle sorgt, darüber sprechen der Architekt Eike Roswag-Klinge, Gründer des „Natural Building Lab" an der TU Berlin, und der Holzbauexperte Hermann Kaufmann, Architekt und Professor an der TU München.

Eike Roswag-Klinge: Der Holzbau hat schon lange sein ländliches Image abgelegt und baut mit an den Metropolen der Zukunft. Du bist an vielen Pionierprojekten beteiligt. In Deutschland ist das Holzbaucluster TUM.wood an der TU München die führende Forschungseinrichtung. Wo liegt das Potenzial des Holzbaus für die Zukunft?

Hermann Kaufmann: Einerseits im wachsenden gesellschaftlichen Bedürfnis nach Ökologie und Nachhaltigkeit. Nachdem lange die Frage der Energie im Fokus stand, wollen wir nun wissen, woher unsere Materialien kommen. Es geht andererseits aber auch um das Thema des Bauprozesses. Denn Holzbau bedeutet Vorfertigung. Die Produktion wandert von der Baustelle in die Werkstatt. Das bringt eine neue Qualität: Das Chaos auf dem Bau wird verschwinden. Ihr habt das Netzwerk DieNachwachsendeStadt gegründet. Welche Vision habt ihr vor Augen?

ER: Naturbaustoffe wie Holz, Stroh oder Hanf haben sowohl für die energetische Optimierung wie für Nachverdichtung sehr viele Vorteile. Deshalb werden nachwachsende und regenerative Rohstoffe in Zukunft als Baumaterial zunehmend Beachtung finden. Was hältst du vom aktuellen Wettlauf um das höchste Holzhaus?

HK: Mit den Hochhäusern aus Holz hat das Bauwesen ein neues Feld entdeckt, das es bislang noch nicht gab. Natürlich positioniert man sich mit der Jagd nach Rekorden im Wettbewerb. Auf der anderen Seite macht sie aber auch die Potenziale des

ipating in a competition for a record means you position yourself within the field; it also makes the potentials of timber construction known. Outside of these competitions, timber construction has generally been used for buildings up to three storeys high. In that sense, this competition is certainly a driver for technological innovation. Timber still has to prove how economical it is when it is applied to higher buildings. At the Büro ZRS and the Natural Building Lab, you are looking at clay and climate-sensitive structures. What role do you see timber playing in low-tech buildings?

ER: Today, timber constructions are implemented mainly as constructions that are vapour-permeable. When we use natural moisture-active insulation materials and surfaces made out of clay, for example, the building's envelope controls the humidity inside. In this way, we can dispose of ventilation systems and meet even the highest insulation standards, so long as the building is aired out twice a day. As summer insulation, clay's moisture absorption and release have also been highly rated. We therefore advocate climate-adapted building envelopes made from natural materials, recommending that ventilation technology be avoided when it can be applied only sparingly. This principle can be applied to buildings for administration or production, as well as schools. Despite this obvious trend, there are often technical concerns. Which gaps still need to be filled in by research?

HK: Fire protection is certainly still an issue, particularly in relation to visible structural elements and height. In my view, an important topic for the future will be how to use timber sparingly. Solid timber constructions can be justified in terms of high static requirements; however, I don't think it is sensible to unthinkingly deploy timber in every situation. As the proportion of timber used in the construction industry grows, we need to become more efficient with the material, otherwise - like any material - it will run out. Digital and intelligent production will certainly help here; however, my aim - aside from the sparing use of materials - is, above all, simplification. An important detail is how moisture protection functions in connection with plumbing and heating. Here, robust and constructive details still need to be worked out. After all, it is important to design planning processes in accordance with timber construction law, meaning that new cooperation models for prefabricated construction should be developed with all involved, from the architectural design to the execution. The fire safety issue has long been

Holzbaus deutlich, der allgemein noch mit Gebäuden bis zu drei Geschossen in Verbindung gebracht wird. Insofern ist der Wettlauf in jedem Falle ein Treiber der Technologie. Das Holz wird sich für die höhere Gebäudeklasse in Bezug auf Wirtschaftlichkeit noch weiter beweisen müssen. Ihr beschäftigt euch im Büro ZRS und am Natural Building Lab an der TU Berlin mit Lehmbau und klimasteuernden Konstruktionen. Welche Rolle spielt der Holzbau für Lowtech-Gebäude?

ER: Der Holzbau wird in der Regel heute als diffusionsoffene Konstruktion ausgeführt. Wenn wir feuchteaktive Naturdämmstoffe und Oberflächen zum Beispiel aus Lehm einsetzen, steuern die Gebäudehüllen die Raumluftfeuchte. So können wir trotz höchster Dämmstandards bei zweimaligem Stoßlüften am Tag im Wohnungsbau auf Lüftungsanlagen verzichten. Auch im sommerlichen Wärmeschutz wirkt sich die Feuchteaufnahme und -abgabe sehr positiv aus. Wir plädieren deshalb für klimaangepasste Gebäudehüllen aus Naturbaustoffen und empfehlen, auf Lüftungstechnik möglichst zu verzichten oder sie nur sehr begrenzt einzusetzen. Das Prinzip lässt sich auch auf Produktions-, Verwaltungs- und Schulbauten übertragen. Trotz des Trends bleiben oft technische Bedenken. Welche Lücken muss die Forschung noch schließen?

HK: Der Brandschutz ist in Bezug auf Sichtkonstruktionen und Höhe sicher noch ein Thema. Aus meiner Sicht ist das Zukunftsthema der sparsame Umgang mit der Ressource Holz. Holzmassivbau hat bei hohen statischen Anforderungen seine Berechtigung. Ihn aber, ohne nachzudenken, überall einzusetzen, halte ich für sinnlos. Wenn der Holzanteil im Bauwesen wächst, müssen wir effizienter mit dem Material umgehen, sonst geht die Ressource zur Neige. Digitale Produktion und intelligente Produkte werden da sicher helfen, wobei mein Ziel – neben der Materialersparnis – vorrangig die Vereinfachung ist. Ein wesentlicher Punkt ist außerdem der Feuchteschutz im Zusammenhang mit Sanitär und Heizung. Hier müssen robuste konstruktive Details entwickelt werden. Schließlich gilt es, Planungsprozesse holzbaugerecht zu gestalten, also neue Kooperationsmodelle für vorgefertigtes Bauen mit allen Planenden von Architektur bis Ausführung zu entwickeln. Der Brandschutz wurde lange über die Bekleidung mit Gipsplatten gelöst. Ihr arbeitet gern mit sichtbaren Konstruktionen. Was realisiert ihr im Moment und was erwartest du für die Zukunft?

ER: Seit ein paar Jahren werden Holzkonstruktionen auf Abbrand gerechnet. Das ermöglicht sichtbare

resolved by cladding timber with gypsum. You tend to like working with visible construction elements. What are you working on at the moment, and what do you expect for the future?

ER: For around two years, timber constructions have been rated for their combustibility. This has made it possible to include visible timber elements, right up until the level of high-rise construction. Timber has become a design tool, which at the same time saves costs for fire protection cladding, which has hitherto been very complex. Our aim is to implement, as soon as possible, a seven-storey building entirely from timber including the elevator shaft and staircase - with the exception of the foundation. The Berlin headquarters of Flexim GmbH could also have been built completely of wood. A timber-concrete hybrid construction was only settled on for cost reasons. And in conclusion: what is your vision for the future of timber construction?

HK: In his day, the timber pioneer Konrad Wachsmann announced a "turning point in construction"; although he was 60 to 80 years too early, today we are probably ready. My hope is that the increase in demand will produce a positive development in competence and clout, both on the part of planners and on the side of production and execution. In the future, timber construction should stand for high architectural and construction quality, durability and maximum comfort.

Holzkonstruktionen bis zur Hochhausgrenze. Holz wird Gestaltungsmittel, was parallel auch Kosten für die bislang aufwendigen Brandschutzbekleidungen einspart. Unser Ziel ist es, möglichst bald einen Siebengeschosser bis auf die Gründungswanne komplett, inklusive Aufzugsschacht und Treppenhaus, als sichtbare Holzkonstruktion umzusetzen. Im nächsten Jahr bauen wir in Bremen in dieser Art fünfgeschossig. Der Berliner Firmensitz der Flexim GmbH hätte ebenfalls komplett in Holz errichtet werden können. Nur aus Kostengründen wurde ein Holz-Beton-Hybridbau realisiert. Zum Schluss die Frage: Was ist deine Vision zum Holzbau?

HK: Der Holzbaupionier Konrad Wachsmann hat seinerzeit den „Wendepunkt im Bauen" ausgerufen. Damit lag er sechzig bis achtzig Jahre zu früh. Heute sind wir wahrscheinlich so weit. Meine Hoffnung besteht darin, dass die steigende Nachfrage eine positive Entwicklung bei der Kompetenz und Schlagkraft sowohl aufseiten der Planenden als auch der ausführenden Holzbaufirmen erzeugt. In Zukunft soll der Holzbau für hohe Architektur- und Bauqualität, Dauerhaftigkeit und höchsten Komfort stehen.

-> Case Study 04 pp. 310 ff. Flexim headquarters

Reboot Architecture!

Circular Building for a Post-fossil World

The question of what sustainable building means in developing a sustainable architecture has been the focus of the Black Forest and Berlin-based architecture office Partner and Partner from its inception; their practice has made it a point to develop simple solutions to complex construction questions, with the caveat that "technology should support but not determine natural potential." Here, Partner and Partner co-founder and managing director Jörg Finkbeiner argues that architecture must fulfil its societal responsibilities through a necessary paradigm shift towards circular building in the coming post-fossil world.

The world today is undergoing the biggest transformation in human history. Population explosion, climate change, the velocity of change in economies and forms of life, digitilisation, etc. – this is all familiar. It is undeniable that the built environment plays a key role in all of these issues. The question of whether the application of circular principles in construction is just a trend that will merely fill a niche (in even the best-case scenario) becomes superfluous on a closer examination of the facts: materially speaking, the earth is a closed system. At the same time, in the coming years and decades, new mega-metropolitan regions will arise worldwide in forms that will individually resemble the world population of 1930. The demand for resources will be immense and will lead to distribution problems and to price increases in the globally interdependent resource markets. European cities will also continue to grow and will, for the most part, need to be refurbished and adapted. How will we deal with already scarce resources? A transition from the current, linear economic model to a circular system – one of using and reusing – will be inevitable.

It is, however, necessary to look closely: raw materials already used in construction, which can in part be reclaimed through urban mining, are only of very limited suitability to be recycled for circular construction. They were not produced with a later reuse in mind. This applies above all to buildings from the post-war era. Most construction materials simply cannot be separated and made useful. They are often contaminated with

Reboot Architecture!

Reboot Architecture!

Zirkulär hat Zukunft

Die Frage, was nachhaltiges Bauen bei der Entwicklung einer nachhaltigen Architektur bedeutet, stand von Anfang an im Mittelpunkt des Schwarzwälder und Berliner Architekturbüros Partner und Partner. Ihre Praxis hat es sich zur Aufgabe gemacht, einfache Lösungen für komplexe Baufragen zu entwickeln mit dem Vorbehalt, dass „Technik das natürliche Potenzial unterstützen, aber nicht bestimmen soll". Jörg Finkbeiner, Mitbegründer und Geschäftsführer von Partner und Partner, argumentiert hier, dass die Architektur ihre gesellschaftliche Verantwortung in der kommenden postfossilen Welt durch einen notwendigen Paradigmenwechsel in Stadtplanung und Architektur erfüllen muss, indem sie sich der Kreislaufwirtschaft annähert.

Die Welt befindet sich in der größten Transformation der Menschheitsgeschichte. Bevölkerungsexplosion, Klimawandel, Dynamisierung der Wirtschaft und Lebensmodelle, Digitalisierung usw. sind hinlänglich bekannt. Dass die gebaute Umwelt bei diesen Fragen eine wesentliche Rolle spielt, ist unstrittig. Die Frage, ob zirkuläres Bauen lediglich einen Trend darstellt, der bestenfalls eine Nische besetzen wird, erübrigt sich bei der genauen Betrachtung der Fakten: Die Erde ist ein stofflich geschlossenes System. Gleichzeitig werden in den kommenden Jahren und Jahrzehnten weltweit neue Mega-Metropolregionen in einem Umfang entstehen, der in etwa der Weltbevölkerung von 1930 entspricht. Der zusätzliche Ressourcenbedarf ist enorm und wird bei global vernetzten Rohstoffmärkten zu Verteilungsfragen und Preissteigerungen führen. Auch die europäischen Städte werden weiterwachsen, im Wesentlichen aber umgebaut und angepasst werden müssen. Wie gehen wir mit den dort jetzt schon gebundenen Ressourcen um? Ein Übergang vom derzeitigen linearen Wirtschaften zu einem zirkulären System der Wieder- und Weiterverwertung wird unvermeidlich sein.

Allerdings ist es notwendig, genau hinzuschauen: Die bereits verbauten Rohstoffe, die sich teilweise als „urban mining" wiedergewinnen lassen, eignen sich nur sehr eingeschränkt für eine echte Weiterverwendung im Sinne des zirkulären Bauens. Sie wurden nicht für eine spätere Wiederverwendung erzeugt. Dies gilt vor allem für die Bauten

Reboot Architecture!

poisonous or undefinable substances. Upcycling with these materials will therefore only delay the problem of resource scarcity. Sooner or later these materials reach the end of their life and become rubbish in the most rudimentary sense.

-

Non-circular facts: far divorced from the circular future

The requirements for action in building a circular future are self-evident: buildings and cities must be transformed into raw material storage sites, in which all building materials can move and be reused in cycles while retaining their original quality. In addition, regenerative construction materials will have a far greater significance in order to cater to additional needs in an environmentally sound way. Our energy supply must be organised to be 100 percent regenerative. Today, we are far from that future. The overwhelming majority of buildings currently being planned and constructed do not come close to meeting these requirements. Instead, every new building creates "non-circular realities" for several decades to come. For this reason, our architectural practice is devoted to the question of how holistic, circular construction could become possible today. We pursue an integrative planning approach and set significant parameters. The aim is to conceptualise resource-positive buildings that are maximally capable of circularity. This means that the primary building structure requires the highest degree of flexibility, while it should be possible to dismantle the structure without affecting the static and constructive characteristics of building components, with the aim to be able to use them again. Even at the end of their useable life, building parts should be capable of being fed back into the appropriate cycle. Façades and/or roofs must be designed to generate energy! The natural potentials of the building contribute to more streamlined building services and increase its operational resilience.

-

(Pre)building for the post-fossil epoch

After an extensive life cycle assessment and careful ecological bookkeeping, we can say that resource-positive building is possible: our project "Woodscraper" - two high-rise buildings made out of timber - provides the proof.

der Nachkriegszeit. Viele Baustoffe lassen sich nicht sortenrein voneinander trennen. Sie sind oftmals schadstoffbelastet oder enthalten undefinierte Inhaltsstoffe. Upcycling aus diesen Rohstoffen wird deshalb das Problem der Ressourcenknappheit lediglich verzögern können. Früher oder später erreichen diese Baustoffe ihr End of Life und werden Abfall im klassischen Sinne sein.

-

Nicht-kreislauffähige Fakten: Von der zirkulären Zukunft weit entfernt

Die Handlungsanforderungen für eine zirkuläre Zukunft liegen auf der Hand: Gebäude und Städte müssen zu Rohstofflagern transformiert werden, in denen sich alle Baustoffe in gleichbleibender Qualität in Kreisläufen führen lassen. Zudem wird den nachwachsenden Baustoffen eine wesentlich höhere Bedeutung zukommen, um die zusätzlichen Bedarfe umweltverträglich bereitstellen zu können. Unsere Energieversorgung muss zu hundert Prozent regenerativ organisiert werden. Davon sind wir heute weit entfernt. Der überwiegende Teil der aktuell in Planung und Bau befindlichen Gebäude wird diesen Anforderungen nicht gerecht. Stattdessen schafft jedes neue Gebäude „nicht-kreislauffähige Fakten" für mehrere Jahrzehnte. Unsere Architekturpraxis widmet sich deshalb der Frage, wie ganzheitlich zirkuläres Bauen heute möglich ist. Wir verfolgen einen integralen Planungsansatz und legen wesentliche Parameter fest. Das Ziel ist es, „ressourcen-positive" Gebäude zu konzipieren, die maximal kreislauffähig sind. Dazu gehört die größtmögliche Flexibilität der primären Gebäudestruktur, der zerstörungsfreie Rückbau der wesentlichen Gebäudekomponenten (ohne Minderung der statischen und konstruktiven Eigenschaften) mit dem Ziel, diese wiederverwenden zu können: Bauteile sollten am End of Life wieder in die jeweiligen Kreisläufe rückführbar sein. Fassaden- und/oder Dachflächen müssen zur Energiegewinnung geeignet sein! Natürliche Potenziale des Gebäudes tragen zu einer schlankeren Haustechnik bei und steigern seine Resilienz im Betrieb.

-

(Vor-)Bauen für die postfossile Epoche

Nach einer umfassenden Lebenszyklusbetrachtung und Ökobilanzierung können wir sagen, dass ein ressourcen-positives Gebäude möglich ist: Unser

Reboot Architecture!

The hurdles for implementation do not lie in a lack of technical solutions or building materials. Far more problematic is the fact that an entire system is not set up for a circular future: the over-reliance on certain paths, established planning and construction processes and the current - even if well-meaning - legislative structure prevent true innovation. The transformation from a linear to a circular system is fundamental and far-reaching and creates a huge challenge for our society and for construction. It affects planners as well as the building materials industry, waste disposal companies, legislation, building contractors and investors. Because aside from a circular construction process, reusable material cycles must be developed and established more generally, and for this, new business models must come into being. A holistic planning culture needs to come to the fore that can function both integrally and between disciplines.

A world organised according to circular systems will play a key role in the coming post-fossil epoch. "Reboot Architecture" stands, in our view, for a necessary paradigm shift. For this to take place, a sweeping debate is necessary - as was made possible in the framework of the MakeCity Festival, for example. We understand this process as a major opportunity to invest the built environment with new meaning and a fundamental integrity. Only in this way can architecture fulfil its societal responsibilities.

Projekt „Woodscraper" – zwei Hochhäuser aus Holz – liefert den Beweis.

Die Hürden in der Umsetzung liegen dabei nicht an fehlenden technischen Lösungen oder Baustoffen. Problematischer ist vielmehr ein Gesamtsystem, das für eine zirkuläre Zukunft nicht gedacht ist: Pfadabhängigkeiten, etablierte Planungs- und Bauprozesse und eine – wenn auch gut gemeinte – Gesetzgebung verhindern echte Innovation. Die Transformation von einem linearen zu einem kreislaufgerechten System ist grundlegend und umfassend und stellt unsere Gesellschaft sowie das Bauen vor große Herausforderungen. Sie betrifft Planer*innen genauso wie Baustoffindustrie, Entsorgungsunternehmen, Gesetzgebung, Bauherr*innen und Investor*innen. Denn neben einer kreislauffähigen Konstruktion müssen Wertstoffkreisläufe entwickelt werden, sich etablieren und dafür neue Geschäftsmodelle entstehen. Erforderlich ist eine ganzheitliche Planungskultur, die integral und transdisziplinär funktioniert.

Eine zirkulär organisierte Welt wird in der kommenden postfossilen Epoche eine wesentliche Rolle spielen. „Reboot Architecture" steht aus unserer Sicht für den notwendigen Paradigmenwechsel. Dafür ist eine breite Debatte notwendig, wie sie zum Beispiel im Rahmen des MakeCity Festivals möglich war. Wir verstehen diesen Prozess als eine große Chance, der gebauten Umwelt eine neue Sinnhaftigkeit und inhaltliche Tiefe zu verleihen. Nur so kann Architektur ihrer gesamtgesellschaftlichen Verantwortung gerecht werden.

Stripped down to the bare infrastructure and refined into contemporary social housing: 530 units transformed for 45,000 euros each in the Cité du Grand Parc, Bordeaux

Rückgebaut auf das Minimum und veredelt zu zeitgemäßem sozialen Wohnungsbau: 530 Einheiten für je 45.000 Euro wurden in der Cité du Grand Parc in Bordeaux umgebaut

Architecture Extended

Lacaton & Vassal's Strive for the Maximum

Situationen verwerten

Wie Lacaton & Vassal nach dem Maximum streben

The architect and writer Florentine Sack formulates criteria for architecture and planning, publishing across many platforms. For Make City, she spoke to Jean Philippe Vassal of Lacaton & Vassal about the architecture duo's landmark projects and their key role in advancing a cyclically oriented construction culture in which building material is made up of pre-existing situations and demolition is seldom the best option. Instead, Lacaton & Vassal opt to preserve sites, to highlight and expand on their histories - and, sometimes, to have the courage to do nothing at all. Theirs is a case for doing only what is necessary to maximise the quality of life improvements.

"In order to transform the city, we must first change our perception of the city - understanding it as a collection of capacities that can be expanded, and not as a passive and malleable mass." Lacaton & Vassal emphasise extending the use of pre-existing materials in order to reveal their previously hidden qualities. The use of ready-made situations feeds into generous and sustainable urban development, which arises from a combination of improved quality of life and densification. In the development of their buildings, the architects place value on precision, sensitivity and attention to everything that is already at hand, and that which has the potential to generate something new - to captivate and enchant. They are careful to retain existing qualities, namely the atmosphere and capacities of the city. It's also about saving money while considering public interest and strengthening democracy. All projects by Lacaton & Vassal therefore meticulously weigh transformation costs against the cost of a potential demolition and rebuilding. In addition, they ask themselves fundamental questions: what is really necessary here? what is missing?

The courage to do as little as possible

The concept the architects put forward for the improvement of Place Léon Aucoc in Bordeaux went so far as to propose doing nothing at all. The square was charming enough as it was.

Die Architektin und Autorin Florentine Sack formulierte in mehreren Publikationen Kriterien für Architektur und Raumgestaltung. Für Make City sprach sie mit Jean-Philippe Vassal über die Meilensteinprojekte des Architektenduos und deren Signalwirkung für eine zirkulär gedachte Baukultur, in der vorgefundene Situationen zum Baumaterial werden. Abriss ist selten die bessere Alternative. Lieber erhalten Lacaton & Vassal die Orte und ihre Geschichte, bauen sie aus, bringen sie erst zum Vorschein und haben manchmal sogar den Mut, nichts zu tun. Ein Plädoyer dafür, nur das Nötigste zu tun, um die Lebensqualität maximal zu verbessern.

„Um die Stadt zu verwandeln, müssen wir zunächst unseren Blick auf sie verändern, sie als eine Sammlung von Kapazitäten zur Erweiterung betrachten und nicht als träge Modelliermasse." Für Lacaton & Vassal geht es darum, Bestehendes weiterzuverwenden und Verborgenes freizulegen. Vorgefundene Situationen sind ihr eigentliches Baumaterial, mit dem sich eine großzügige und nachhaltige Stadtentwicklung schaffen lässt. Sie entsteht aus der Kombination von gesteigerter Lebensqualität und Verdichtung. Bei der Entwicklung ihrer Gebäude legen die Architekt*innen Wert auf Genauigkeit, Sensibilität und Aufmerksamkeit für alles, was bereits existiert und das Potenzial hat, etwas Neues zu ermöglichen, zu führen und zu verzaubern. Sie sind darauf bedacht, die vorhandene Qualität, Atmosphäre und Kapazität der Stadt zu erhalten. Es geht ihnen aber auch darum, Geld zu sparen – aus Rücksichtnahme auf das öffentliche Interesse und zur Stärkung der Demokratie. Allen Projekten von Lacaton & Vassal geht deshalb immer eine akribische Gegenüberstellung der Erweiterungskosten einerseits und der Kosten für den Abriss andererseits voran. Dazu stellen sie sich einfache Fragen: Was wird wirklich benötigt? Was fehlt?

Vom Mut, so wenig wie möglich zu tun

Der Vorschlag der Architekt*innen zur Verschönerung der Place Léon Aucoc in Bordeaux ging so weit, gar nichts zu tun. Der Platz war charmant

Full disclosure: stripped to the max, the skeleton of Palais de Tokyo, Paris

Freigelegt und auf das Maximum reduziert: Das zerrissene Skelett des Palais de Tokyo, Paris

The clients were able to be convinced, and the square was left as it was.

A similar attitude informed the refurbishment of the Palais de Tokyo in Paris: the existing, sumptous ruins of the building's interior were kept. The result was to do as little as possible in order to make the space hospitable – with the smallest budget. Minimum fittings for light, heating, safety and stairs connecting the building's levels brought the spatial beauty and poetry of the building to the fore. As in a poem, in which just the right number of words are deployed with precision, only the barest necessities are used to make space resonate. It is because of this that the Palais offers artists and visitors maximum freedom, where they can bring the space to life in endless different ways.

Strive for the maximum, spend the minimum

In Dunkirk in northern France, Lacaton & Vassal were commissioned to rebuild the shipyard of a former harbour quarter into a centre for contemporary art: the FRAC Nord-Pas de Calais. Because the spatial experience in the so-called cathedral was so incredible, the duo added a "twin", preserving the beauty and strength of the original hall. Building a doppelgänger was additionally the more economical option as it was simpler than renovating the original. For Jean-Philippe Vassal, this created a cornucopia of possibilities.

genug. Die Auftraggeber konnten überzeugt werden, und der Platz blieb so, wie er war.

Ähnlich die Haltung im Projekt zur Umgestaltung des Palais de Tokyo in Paris: Die existierende, prächtige Innenraumruine sollte erhalten bleiben. Das Resultat war, so wenig wie möglich zu tun und einfach Leben im Innenraum zuzulassen – mit kleinstem Budget. Ein Minimum an Licht, Heizung, Sicherheit und Treppen erlaubt jetzt die Verbindung der Ebenen und bringt die räumliche Schönheit und Poesie des Gebäudes zum Vorschein: So wie in Gedichten die richtige Anzahl und Präzision von Worten entscheidend ist, bringt auch hier nur das Nötigste den Raum zum Klingen. Gerade deshalb bietet das Palais den Künstler*innen und Besucher*innen ein Maximum an Freiheit. Sie können den Raum auf vielfältigste Weise immer wieder neu bespielen.

Nach dem Maximum streben – weniger Geld ausgeben

In einem ehemaligen Hafengebiet in Dunkerque in Nordfrankreich sollten Lacaton & Vassal eine Werfthalle in ein Zentrum für zeitgenössische Kunst umbauen: das FRAC Nord-Pas de Calais. Weil das Raumerlebnis in der sogenannten Kathedrale so fantastisch war, fügten sie einen architektonischen Zwillingsbruder hinzu und erhielten so die Schönheit und Kraft der Halle, wie sie war.

It was only through the decision to work with the given situation that a new scenario opened up: two buildings in dialogue with one another.

Surrounding natural elements, too, can provide the basis for a construction: sea, air, sun, sand, water and trees contribute 90 percent of the components of a private dwelling in Cap Ferret. Only 10 percent of steel, concrete and glass were added in order to make the home on the windy coast livable. In both cases - Dunkirk and Cap Ferret - the consistent and fundamental approach was first to understand and then to amplify what was already there.

Don't demolish – expand and densify!

The 16-level residential highrise Bois le Prêtre in Paris was on the verge of being demolished before Lacaton & Vassal suggested that the building from the 1960s simply be expanded: with the aid of a self-sustaining construction, they managed to create more space, generous views and new spatial configurations that envelop the building, offering new possibilities. During the construction period, the residents of all one hundred units were able to continue living in the building. Spaces for play for children, hammams, saunas, a communal laundry, social gathering-points, places for dancing, sun terraces - all of these improve quality of life.

The same principle, on a grander scale, was applied in Bordeaux in the Cité du Grand Parc, for 530 families with over 2,000 rooms. Additionally, new lifts, electric infrastructure and sanitary facilities were introduced. For Jean-Philippe Vassal, the strategy was simple: "Add possibility that is four metres deep - and immediately, life blooms with pleasure, generosity, light, opportunities for multiple use, space for plants and furniture." Instead of demolishing the building, three times less money was spent on making more space available - and without ousting residents. On the sixteenth storey, new flats were expanded, and additional living space was created.

At Tour La Chesnaie, a site with 40 apartments, Lacaton & Vassal went one step further. Here, not only was the pre-existing inventory expanded upon, but there was an addition of two new assemblages with 20 new apartments each. This densification made new situations possible: where there were 40 families, now there are 80 -

Der Doppelgänger war zudem ökonomischer: Draußen neu zu bauen, war einfacher als der Umbau des Originals. Für Jean-Philippe Vassal liegt hier der Reichtum. Erst die Entscheidung, die Situation weiterzuverwenden, schuf eine neue Situation von zwei miteinander korrespondierenden Gebäuden.

Auch die Natur wird bauliches Element: Meer, Luft, Sonne, Sand, Wasser und Bäume sind zu neunzig Prozent Baubestandteile für den Entwurf eines privaten Wohnhauses in Cap Ferret. Was lediglich und feinfühlig hinzugefügt werden musste, waren zehn Prozent Stahl, Beton und Glas, um den Ort an der windigen Küste bewohnbar zu machen. Beide Fälle – Dunkerque und Cap Ferret – stehen für die konsequente Grundhaltung, das Vorhandene zu verstehen und zu verstärken.

Ergänzung und Verdichtung statt Abriss

Wohnungsbau upcycled: Der 16-stöckige Pariser Wohnturm Tour Bois-le-Prêtre im 17. Arrondissement war schon zum Abriss freigegeben worden, bevor Lacaton & Vassal vorschlugen, das Architekturrelikt aus den 1960ern einfach zu erweitern: Mithilfe einer selbsttragenden Konstruktion schufen sie mehr Raum, großzügigere Ausblicke und neue Raumkonfigurationen, die sich wie eine Hülle um das Gebäude legen und neue Möglichkeiten bieten. Spielräume für Kinder, Hamams, Sauna, Waschküchen, soziale Treffpunkte, Orte zum Tanzen, Sonnenterrassen – all das erhöht die Lebensqualität. Die hundert dort ansässigen Familien konnten während der Bauzeit im Gebäude bleiben.

Das gleiche Prinzip – in größerem Maßstab – wurde in Bordeaux, in der Cité du Grand Parc, für 530 Familien mit über 2.000 Räumen umgesetzt. Auch hier stellten die Architekt*innen Fassadenelemente mit neuen Fenstern, Wintergärten mit Schiebetüren und Balkonen als Gerüst vor die ehemalige Fassade. Zudem wurden neue Aufzüge, Elektrizitätsversorgung und Sanitärräume eingeführt. Für Jean-Philippe Vassal ist die Strategie einfach: „Vier Meter Möglichkeiten hinzufügen, und sofort blüht Leben auf, leicht, mit Vergnügen, Großzügigkeit, mehr Licht, Nutzungsmöglichkeiten, Pflanzen und Möbeln." Statt abzureißen, wurde hier nur ein Drittel des Geldes ausgegeben, um mehr Raum bereitzustellen – und das, ohne die Bewohner*innen zu verdrängen. Im 16. Stock ließen sich sogar neue Wohnungen mit Terrassen ergänzen und somit zusätzlicher Wohnraum schaffen.

Greenhouse effect XXL: the twin concept of FRAC Nord-Pas de Calais

Treibhauseffekt XXL: das Zwillingskonzept des FRAC Nord-Pas de Calais

Landscape as building material growing through the beach house in Cap Ferret

Landschaft als Baumaterial, das das Strandhaus in Cap Ferret durchwächst

without a loss of space, and with enjoyable living conditions for everyone.

It is often said that social housing from the twentieth century was lacking in key qualities. Although often written off as a discredited heritage of building culture, social housing can be valuable: through the expansion and densification of pre-existing building structures, generous and contemporary living space can be created and living quality improved. This is not only sustainable but maintains the history of a place and its inhabitants.

City of 1000 situations

For Jean-Philippe Vassal, the city consists of invisible situations that, while rich in potential, are not visible in construction blueprints. For this reason, there is, he declares, no need for new streets, networks, properties and demolition. "We should simply work precisely and carefully in relation to inhabitants and make the best of what is already there." For Berlin, he recommends that the "border zone and free spaces of Tempelhofer Feld, as with the city's other open spaces, should not be touched. There are so many other incomplete, pre-existing sites that could be expanded, overlaid and transformed." From the train station at Südkreuz to abandoned industrial sites, to the refurbishment of highrise apartment buildings or the potentionial redensification of Europacity - an abundant array of possibilities awaits.

All quotes are from a keynote lecture by Jean-Philippe Vassal from the panel "Re-Use Total", MakeCity Festival 2018, Berlin, 15 June 2018.

Beim Tour La Chesnaie mit vierzig Wohnungen in Saint-Nazaire gingen Lacaton & Vassal noch einen Schritt weiter. Hier wurde nicht nur der Bestand ergänzt, sondern zwei Anbauten mit jeweils zwanzig weiteren Wohnungen hinzugefügt. Diese Verdichtung schuf wieder neue Situationen: Wo zunächst vierzig Familien waren, sind nun achtzig Familien – keine Raumverschwendung und gute Lebensbedingungen, Lebensfreude für alle.

Dem sozialen Wohnungsbau aus dem 20. Jahrhundert wird oftmals mangelnde Qualität attestiert. Als baukulturelles Erbe steht er in Verruf und ist doch wertvoll: Durch Ergänzung und Verdichtung vorhandener Gebäudestruktur kann großzügiger und zeitgemäßer Wohnraum entstehen und die Wohnqualität gesteigert werden. Das ist nachhaltig und erzählt die Geschichte des Ortes und seiner Bewohner*innen weiter.

Die Stadt der tausend Situationen

Für Jean-Philippe Vassal besteht die Stadt aus unsichtbaren Situationen, die, wenngleich reich an Möglichkeiten, auf Bebauungsplänen nicht ersichtlich sind. Daher gibt es für ihn eigentlich keinen Bedarf an neuen Straßen, Netzwerken, Grundstücken und Abbruch. „Wir müssen einfach präzise und sorgsam sein im Umgang mit den Bewohnern*innen und aus dem Bestehenden das Beste machen." Er spricht sich beispielsweise dafür aus, die „Grenze und Leere des Tempelhofer Feldes – wie auch anderer Freiflächen in Berlin – nicht anzutasten. Es gibt so viele unvollständige, unfertige Orte, die erweitert, überlagert und verwandelt werden könnten." Vom Bahnhof Südkreuz über verlassene Industrieareale bis zur Umwandlung von Plattenbauten oder der möglichen Nachverdichtung in der Europacity reicht das reiche Feld.

Alle Zitate aus dem programmatischen Vortrag von Jean-Philippe Vassal, Podium Re-Use Total, MakeCity Festival 2018, Berlin, 15.06.2018

Care & Repair

Maintaining Our Cities' Social Relations

With contemporary urban development driven by competing forces of fast-paced growth, consumption and innovation, there exists an urgent need to engage with longer-lasting dynamics in the production and reproduction of space. In this interview, architect Rosario Talevi discusses the potential of architects and urbanists to act as caretakers in the ongoing recuperation of climate and communities with urban researcher Elke Krasny and artist Teresa Dillon.

Part one: architecture and urbanism on this damaged planet

Rosario Talevi: Your recent research focuses on "architecture and urbanism for a damaged planet". What role should architects and urbanists play on this damaged planet?

Elke Krasny: As humans inhabiting the planet Earth, we are making our home uninhabitable. Our bodies are also part of this environment we have created, which has entered the geological epoch of the Anthropocene or, to use Donna Haraway's terms, the Capitalocene or Plantationocene. We are part of this broken environment. Every day on the news there are dire warnings about the future of the planet - that there won't be a future of our planet unless we change.
The 1948 UN Declaration of Human Rights states that "everyone has the right to a standard of living adequate for the health and well-being of himself and of his family, including food, clothing, housing and medical care and necessary social services, and the right to security in the event of unemployment, sickness, disability, widowhood, old age or other lack of livelihood in circumstances beyond his control." Architects and urbanists have a responsibility to contribute as best they can to the provision of adequate housing.

Given the condition of our planet, architects and urbanists can and should do everything possible to sustain the life of this planet by building with the environment. This would be a very different

Achtsam instand setzen

Wie unsere Städte ihre sozialen Beziehungen behalten

In Zeiten, in denen die Stadtentwicklung von den rivalisierenden Kräften kurzlebigen Wachstums, Konsums und schneller Innovationen bestimmt wird, besteht dringender Bedarf an einer langfristigeren Dynamik für die Produktion und Reproduktion von Raum. Im Interview diskutiert die Architektin Rosario Talevi mit der Stadtforscherin Elke Krasny und der Künstlerin Teresa Dillon über die Potenziale, die Architekt*innen und Urbanist*innen als Beschützer*innen des Klimas und der Gemeinschaft haben.

Teil 1: Architektur und Urbanismus auf diesem versehrten Planeten

Rosario Talevi: Ihre jüngste Forschung beschäftigt sich mit „Architektur und Urbanismus für einen versehrten Planeten". Welche Rolle sollten Architekt*innen und Urbanist*innen für den Planeten spielen?

Elke Krasny: Als Menschen, die die Erde bewohnen, sind wir gerade im Begriff, unser Zuhause unbewohnbar zu machen. Unsere Körper sind Teil dieser Umwelt, die wir geschaffen haben und die die geologische Epoche des Anthropozäns oder – wie Donna Haraway es nennt – des Kapitalozäns oder Plantationozäns beschritten hat. Wir sind Teil dieser kaputten Umwelt. Jeden Tag hören wir furchtbare Nachrichten über die Zukunft des Planeten – nämlich, dass er keine Zukunft haben wird, wenn wir uns nicht ändern.
In der Allgemeinen Erklärung der UNO-Menschenrechte von 1948 ist festgehalten, dass „Jede/r [...] das Recht auf einen Lebensstandard [hat], der ihm/ihr und seiner/ihrer Familie Gesundheit und Wohl garantiert, einschließlich Nahrung, Kleidung, Wohnung, ärztliche Versorgung und notwendige soziale Leistungen sowie das Recht auf Sicherheit im Falle von Arbeitslosigkeit, Krankheit, Invalidität oder Verwitwung, im Alter sowie bei anderweitigem Verlust seiner/ihrer Unterhaltsmittel durch unverschuldete Umstände". Architekt*innen und Urbanist*innen haben die Verantwortung, sich dem bestmöglich zu verpflichten und angemessenen Wohnraum bereitzustellen.

ethical approach to architecture than the one dominated by capital and speculation. Neither the legal dimension of laws, or the political dimension of climate negotiations nor the economic dimension through social and environmental inventing have so far produced radical change in response to climate change.

RT: You argue that this challenge has to be met "with care". How might we understand architecture and urbanism as a practice of care and why do you think this is fundamental?

EK: I think it is crucial to remember feminist ethics of care as defined by Joan Tronto and Berenice Fisher, where "caring should be viewed as a species activity that includes everything that we do to maintain, continue and repair our 'world' so that we can live as well as possible. That world includes our bodies, ourselves and our environment, all of which we seek to interweave in a complex, life-sustaining web."[1]
Care, empathy, commitment – these are values that transgress policy, politics, economy or law. They form part of an ethics of care most relevant to practising architecture and urbanism for the Anthropocene. From a perspective of care, architecture and urbanism are situated both in locally specific conditions and in a planetary context. If architecture and urbanism are to take care seriously then these professions must adopt ways of working that will do everything possible to maintain, continue and repair our world – ranging from the provision of housing to the well-being of our planet.

Part two: how to move forward

RT: In 2018 you initiated the Repair Acts Network in response to policies that call for circular and restorative approaches to manufacturing, such as the UN Global Sustainable Development Goals (2016) and New Urban Agenda (2016), Defra, UK reports (2013) and various EU Directives (2008, 2012). Can you describe the network?

Teresa Dillon: Repair Acts is an international network of interdisciplinary experts and activists

1 Berenice Fisher, Joan C. Tronto: "Toward a Feminist Theory of Care", in "Circles of Care: Work and Identity in Women's Lives", edited by Emily K. Abel and Margaret K. Nelson, Albany: State University of New York Press, 1990.

Angesichts des Zustands unseres Planeten sollten Architekt*innen und Urbanist*innen alles ihnen Mögliche unternehmen, um das Leben auf diesem Planeten durch umweltgerechtes Bauen zu erhalten. Dies setzte einen ganz anderen ethischen Ansatz der Architektur voraus als denjenigen, den Kapital und Spekulation bestimmen. Weder auf der rechtlichen Ebene der Gesetze noch auf der politischen Ebene der Klimaverhandlungen oder auf der ökonomischen Ebene der Investitionen in soziale und ökologische Projekte ist es bisher gelungen, einen radikalen Wandel als Antwort auf den Klimawandel anzustoßen.

RT: Sie argumentieren, dass man sich dieser Aufgabe „fürsorglich" widmen muss. Wie können wir uns Architektur und Urbanismus als fürsorgliche Praxis vorstellen und warum glauben Sie, ist das so bedeutend?

EK: Es ist wichtig, sich an die feministische Ethik der Fürsorge zu erinnern, wie Joan Tronto und Berenice Fisher sie beschrieben haben, die „Care-Arbeit als eine Aktivität unserer Spezies" ansieht, „die all das beinhaltet, was wir tun, um unsere ‚Welt' zu erhalten, weiterzubringen und zu reparieren, damit wir so gut wie möglich leben können. Diese Welt besteht aus unseren Körpern, uns selber und unserer Umwelt. Und all dies sollten wir in einem komplexen, lebenserhaltenden Netz zusammenweben."[1] Fürsorge, Empathie, Engagement; diese Werte verändern Richtlinien, Politik, Ökonomie und Recht. Sie sind Teil einer Ethik der Fürsorge, die sehr wichtig für die Architekturpraxis und den Urbanismus des Anthropozäns ist. Aus der Perspektive der Fürsorge sind Architektur und Urbanismus sowohl in den lokalen als auch in den globalen Bedingungen verankert. Wenn Architektur und Urbanismus Fürsorge ernst nehmen, müssen sich diese Berufe einer Arbeitsweise annehmen, die alles Mögliche unternimmt, um unsere Welt zu erhalten, fortzuführen und zu reparieren. Das reicht von der Versorgung mit Wohnraum bis hin zum Wohlergehen unseres Planeten.

Teil 2: Vorwärtskommen

RT: Im Jahr 2018 haben Sie das Repair Acts Network gegründet, als Reaktion auf Strategien, die Kreislaufwirtschaft und Restauration in der Produktion fordern – so wie die Ziele für nachhaltige Ent-

1 Berenice Fisher, Joan C. Tronto: „Toward a Feminist Theory of Care". In: „Circles of Care: Work and Identity in Women's Lives", hg. von Emily K. Abel und Margaret K. Nelson, Albany: State University of New York Press, 1990.

who are interested in questions relating to repair, care, maintenance, restoration and recuperation of the material world and built environment. The network is rooted within the arts and has the immediate goal of bringing together different fields of activity and expertise, such as policy, design, academia and activism, as well as environmental industries, charities and NGOs. The aim is to work globally, connecting to colleagues outside of Europe and North America such as those in New Delhi, India and Accra, Ghana. By bringing together members from different groups and countries, we hope to develop a series of practices for the reuse of objects, materials, buildings, systems, relations and processes.

RT: You propose that repair is an act that does not happen once but can be repeated. How do you imagine the network evolving? How can it reach policy makers for systemic change?

TD: Ideally, yes, it can be repeated. At the policy level, positive changes are happening. Once it passes, the European Commission Circular Economy Package will change how we manufacture goods and address issues relating to planned obsolescence and is likely to have effects in other countries and regions. The Right to Repair movement is becoming a global one with organisations like ifixit.org changing minds and policy. If we are to reach UN Sustainability goals, urgent and radical policy change is needed.
There are multiple meanings in relation to the word "act". To act is to hold a certain type of energy. It is forward moving, it means to do something but it also relates to process, drama, legalities, ways of behaving and participating. Our use of the word "act" reflects all those things.

RT: Processes of repair are sometimes necessary but you propose using the word recuperation instead of repair. Can you tell us more?

TD: Like all words, "repair" has strengths and limitations. It implies something is broken, which is not always a useful way of thinking. Repair can also assume a return to a prior order of stability, which can be normative. "Restoration" is also slippery, particularly when we speak in relation to the heritage sector, where to repair something is often seen as an inferior job, while restoring something implies a return to its supposed former glory. When we discuss all these terms, it's necessary to examine their use in a different context - this is part of the immediate work.
What I'm more interested in exploring is notions of care and recuperation, the latter referring to

wicklung der UNO (2016), die New Urban Agenda (2016), die UK Reports des britischen Umwelt-, Ernährungs- und Landwirtschaftsministeriums (2013) sowie verschiedene EU-Richtlinien (2008, 2012). Können Sie das Netzwerk beschreiben?

Teresa Dillon: Repair Acts ist ein interdisziplinäres Netzwerk von Expert*innen und Aktivist*innen, die sich für Fragen im Bereich Reparatur, Fürsorge, Erhaltung, Restauration und Wiederherstellung der materiellen Welt und der gebauten Umwelt einsetzen. Das Netzwerk hat seine Wurzeln in der Kunst und verfolgt das Anliegen, verschiedene Tätigkeitsbereiche und Expertisen zusammenzubringen: Politik, Design, Wissenschaft und Aktivismus, aber auch die Umweltbranche, Wohlfahrtsverbände und Nichtregierungsorganisationen. Der Anspruch ist eine globale Arbeit, die Kolleg*innen außerhalb Europas und Nordamerikas miteinander vernetzt, zum Beispiel in Neu-Delhi oder in Accra in Ghana. Dadurch, dass wir Menschen aus verschiedenen Gruppen und Ländern zusammenbringen, hoffen wir, eine Vielfalt von Methoden zu entwickeln, mit denen sich Gegenstände, Materialien, Gebäude, Systeme, Verbindungen und Prozesse wiederverwerten lassen. 2018 haben wir dies mit einer Reihe von Workshops erreicht.

RT: Sie werben dafür, das „Reparieren" als eine Tätigkeit, die nicht einmalig, sondern wiederholt geschieht, zu betrachten. Wie können Sie für einen solchen Systemwandel Entscheider*innen in der Politik erreichen?

TD: Idealerweise ist sie wiederholbar, ja. Auf der politischen Ebene finden positive Veränderungen statt. Wenn es verabschiedet ist, wird das Kreislaufwirtschaftspaket der Europäischen Kommission die Güterproduktion verändern und Probleme wie die „geplante Obsoleszenz" angehen. Das wird wahrscheinlich auch Auswirkungen auf andere Länder und Regionen haben. Die Right-to-Repair-Bewegung wird global und ändert mit Organisationen wie iFixit.org Einstellungen und Politik. Wenn wir die Nachhaltigkeitsziele der UN erreichen wollen, ist ein schneller und radikaler Politikwechsel gefragt. Das Wort „handeln" hat viele Bedeutungen und Implikationen. Um zu handeln, braucht man eine bestimmte Art Energie. Es muss nach vorne gehen. Das bedeutet, dass man etwas tun muss, das auch in Verbindung mit Prozess, Abläufen, Rechtmäßigkeit, Verhaltensmustern und Teilhabe steht. Unser Gebrauch des Wortes „handeln" schließt all diese Dinge ein.

RT: Reparationsprozesse sind manchmal notwendig. Aber Sie machen sich dafür stark, den Begriff

"Care Walk" with Elke Krasny at the Nordbahnhof, Vienna: what is the interplay between the new buildings, the remembrance of concentration-camp deportations and the green urban wilderness?

„Care Walk" mit Elke Krasny am Nordbahnhof, Wien: Welche Wechselwirkungen gibt es zwischen den Neubauten, der Erinnerung an die Deportationen zu Konzentrationslagern und der grünen urbanen Wildnis?

how we recover from sickness or exhaustion. We are living within an earthly condition in which we have over-exhausted our natural resources and ecosystems. How do we move forward from this damaged state? Care, maintenance, recuperation and repair, each in their different ways may provide a hopeful language from which to work, without losing sight of the reality of our situation.

„Wiederherstellung" anstelle von „Reparatur" zu nutzen. Können Sie uns das erläutern?

TD: Wie alle Begriffe hat auch das Wort „reparieren" Stärken und Grenzen. Es impliziert, dass etwas kaputt ist – und das ist ein weniger nützlicher Gedanke. „Reparation" kann außerdem auch die Rückkehr zu einer alten, möglicherweise normativen Ordnung bedeuten. „Restaurierung" ist ebenfalls knifflig, insbesondere, wenn wir über das kulturelle Erbe sprechen. Da werden Reparaturen als niedrige Arbeiten angesehen, während „Restauration" impliziert, dass etwas zu alter Pracht zurückkehrt. Wenn wir über diese Begriffe sprechen, ist es also wichtig, ihren unterschiedlichen Einsatz in verschiedenen Kontexten zu betrachten. Dies ist Teil der unmittelbaren Arbeit.
Ich persönlich finde es spannender, die Bedeutungen von Fürsorge und Wiederherstellung zu betrachten – Letztere gedacht als Genesung von Krankheit und Erschöpfung. Wir leben in einem Zustand der Erde, in dem wir die natürlichen Ressourcen und Ökosysteme über-erschöpft haben. Wie können wir aus diesem beschädigten Zustand herauskommen? Fürsorge, Erhaltung, Wiederherstellung und Reparatur können – alle auf ihre Art – eine hoffnungsvolle Sprache formen, mit der wir arbeiten können, ohne die Realität unserer Situation aus dem Blick zu verlieren.

Designing Ruins

The Third-Generation City

The architect, environmental artist, architectural theorist and professor of architecture Marco Casagrande outlines urban acupuncture, a bio-urbanist theory that combines sociology and urban design with the idea of the punctural intervention. Here, Casagrande revisits Treasure Hill in Taipei, Taiwan, Casagrande Laboratory's first urban acupuncture research site and the catalyst for the development of the ongoing Ruin Academy (2010-), where the laboratory continues to learn from the ruins of the city.

In 2003, the Taipei City government decided to destroy the unofficial settlement of Treasure Hill. It was a remarkable organic hillside settlement, with a root cleaning system for grey water weaving its way through patches of jungle. The settlement's residents, mainly elderly Kuomintang veterans and illegal migrant workers, composted organic waste into fertiliser for nearby farms and used electricity stolen from the official grid. The bulldozers began by knocking down the first layers of the terraced settlement, and once the houses were too high for the bulldozers, the city deployed two more coordinated tactics: first, it destroyed the farms and gardens along the banks of the Xindian River, and second, it cut the circulation - bridges, steps, stairs and pathways - between homes. Treasure Hill was left to die slowly, cut off from its life sources.

I began to tour local universities, giving speeches and recruiting students, gathering 200 students from Tamkang University Department of Architecture, Chinese Culture University, and National Taiwan University. A team of students made a deal with neighbouring construction workers, and from trucks passing by, they began to offload some of the construction cargo to us. Armed with people and material, we rebuilt connections between the houses and restarted the farms. Miss Chen, whose house was the soul of the settlement, came to advise us on farming while offering us food and Chinese medicine. Children came to share dinner. Rumours began to spread in Taipei: things are happening in Treasure Hill. More people arrived for volunteer work. The media arrived. Then the politicians. Mayor Ma Ying-jeou came by with television crews and

Ruinen gestalten

Die Stadt der dritten Generation

Der Architekt, Künstler, Architekturtheoretiker und -professor Marco Casagrande skizziert die urbane Akupunktur, eine biourbanistische Theorie, die Soziologie und Städtebau mit der Idee der punktuellen Intervention verbindet. Hier besucht Casagrande erneut Treasure Hill in Taipeh, Taiwan, den ersten Forschungsstandort des Casagrande Laboratory und damit Katalysator für die Entwicklung der laufenden Ruin Academy (2010–), wo das Labor weiterhin von den Ruinen der Stadt lernt.

2003 beschloss die Stadtregierung von Taipeh, Taiwan, die inoffizielle Besiedlung von Treasure Hill abzureißen. Es handelte sich um eine bemerkenswerte organisch gewachsene Hügelsiedlung mit einem Wurzelklärsystem für Grauwasser im angrenzenden Urwaldboden. Die Bewohner*innen der Siedlung – vornehmlich ältere Kuomintang-Veteranen und illegalisierte migrantische Arbeiter*innen – kompostierten organische Abfälle zu Düngemitteln für die nahe gelegenen Farmen und zapften das offizielle Stromnetz an. Die Bulldozer begannen ihre Arbeit. Sie zerstörten die erste Ebene der Terrassenbebauung. Wo die Häuser zu hoch standen, setzte die Stadt zwei weitere Taktiken ein: Erst zerstörte sie die Felder und Gärten an den Ufern des Xindian-Flusses, dann unterbrach sie die Verkehrsverbindungen zwischen den Häusern – Brücken, Treppen, Wege. Sie schnitt Treasure Hill damit von seinen Lebensquellen ab und überließ die Siedlung einem langsamen Tod.

Ich begann, in den lokalen Universitäten Vorträge über die Situation zu halten und Studierende zu mobilisieren. So kamen 200 Studierende der Architekturfakultät der Tamkang-Universität, der Chinesischen Kulturuniversität und der Nationaluniversität Taiwan zusammen. Eine Gruppe von ihnen sprach sich mit Leuten aus der Nachbarschaft ab, die auf Baustellen arbeiteten. Diese schafften bei Transporten kleine Mengen Baumaterial für uns auf die Seite. Mit den vielen Menschen und dem Material bauten wir die Wege zwischen den Häusern wieder auf und nahmen die Farmen wieder in Betrieb. Frau Chen, deren Haus das Herz der Siedlung darstellte, kam hinzu, um uns über den Gemüseanbau zu beraten, und bot uns Essen und chinesische Medizin an. Kinder aus der Stadt kamen zum gemeinsamen Abendessen. In Taipeh sprach sich herum: Am Treasure

gave us his blessing. Suddenly, the city government claimed this was exactly why they had invited me from Finland to work with Treasure Hill – the same city government that had been bulldozing the settlement away just three weeks earlier.

Urban acupuncture as ground work

Our simple construction work acted like an acupuncture needle, penetrating the veneer of the official city until it touched a pressure point underneath, in the collective topsoil of Taipei, where it found and released local knowledge. Urban acupuncture is not a metaphor or an academic invention: it is a bio-urbanist theory that combines sociology and urban design with the theory and practice of traditional Chinese medicine's acupuncture. As a design methodology, urban acupuncture is focused on tactical, small-scale interventions within the urban fabric, aimed at triggering cascading effects throughout the larger urban organism. Through these discrete points, urban acupuncture accesses site-specific local knowledge, relieving stress and industrial tension in the urban environment, directing the city towards the organic. Urban acupuncture produces small-scale but ecologically and socially catalytic development within the built human environment; in Taipei, urban acupuncture's needle is local knowledge.

After the breakthrough in Treasure Hill, we continued our research, utilising multi-disciplinary working methods in collaboration with Tamkang University Department of Architecture, where we were later joined by Aalto University's Sustainable Global Technologies Research Centre. In 2010, we launched the Taitung Ruin Academy with the assistance of the JUT Foundation for Art and Architecture. Operating as an independent research centre in an abandoned Japanese-Taiwanese sugar factory, the academy and its participants moved freely within the general framework of the built human environment, somewhere between art and science, its efforts focused on accessing the third-generation city.

The first-generation city is one where human settlements are in direct connection with – and dependent on – nature. The Taipei Basin region once provided a fertile environment for such a settlement, with its four main rivers, the Tamsui, Keelung, Dahan and Xindian, used for transpor-

Hill passiert etwas. Noch mehr Menschen halfen mit. Auch die Medien kamen. Dann die Politik: Bürgermeister Ma Ying-jeou brachte Fernsehteams mit und gab uns schließlich seinen Segen. Plötzlich aber behauptete die Stadtregierung, dass sie mich nur aus Finnland eingeladen hätte, um am Treasure Hill zu arbeiten – dieselbe Regierung, die gerade einmal drei Wochen zuvor die Bulldozer geschickt hatte.

Urbane Akupunktur wühlt den Boden auf

Unsere einfache Bauarbeit wirkte wie eine Akupunkturnadel. Sie drang in die Fassade der Stadtverwaltung ein, bis sie einen tiefer liegenden Punkt im kollektiven Humusboden von Taipeh berührte, wo sie lokales Wissen aufstöberte und freisetzte. „Urbane Akupunktur" ist keine Metapher oder akademische Erfindung: Es ist eine biologisch-urbane Theorie, in der Soziologie und Stadtgestaltung mit der Theorie und Praxis der Akupunktur in der Traditionellen Chinesischen Medizin zusammenkommen. Als Gestaltungsmethode konzentriert sich urbane Akupunktur auf taktische, klein angelegte Interventionen im städtischen Gewebe, die lawinenartige Folgen im gesamten größeren Stadtorganismus auslösen. Durch diese einzelnen Punkte hat urbane Akupunktur Zugang zu örtlichem Wissen und kann Stress und industrielle Belastungen in der städtischen Umgebung abbauen und die Stadt in eine ökologische Richtung bewegen. Urbane Akupunktur bringt kleine, ökologisch und gesellschaftlich wirkende Katalysatoren in die gebaute menschliche Umgebung; in Taipeh war das lokale Wissen die urbane Akupunkturnadel.

Nach dem Durchbruch am Treasure Hill setzten wir unsere methodisch-multidisziplinäre Forschung fort. Wir arbeiteten mit dem Architekturinstitut der Tamkang-Universität zusammen. Später schloss sich auch das Forschungszentrum für Nachhaltige Globale Technologien der finnischen Aalto-Universität an. 2010 eröffneten wir mit Unterstützung der JUT-Stiftung für Kunst und Architektur die Taitung Ruin Academy, die als unabhängiges Forschungszentrum in einer verlassenen japanisch-taiwanesischen Zuckerfabrik untergebracht ist. Die Akademie und ihre Teilnehmer*innen bewegten sich frei in der gebauten menschlichen Umgebung, irgendwo zwischen Kunst und Naturwissenschaften. Wir bemühten uns um eine Annäherung an die „Stadt der dritten Generation".

In der Stadt der dritten Generation ist die menschliche Besiedlung direkt mit der Natur verbunden und

tation and food production, while the Xueshan mountain range buffered the farmed plains below from the brunt of frequent typhoons. The second-generation city is also known as the industrial city, a built environment that seems to provide humans with everything that they think they need. In the second-generation city, nature is seen as something that is not necessary and, sometimes, even hostile. In the second-generation city, local knowledge and practices are shared and, when practised, hold the potential to tune the industrial city into an organic machine – the desired third-generation city. The third-generation city is the organic ruin of the industrial city.

Local Knowledge: Learning from the Grandparents

It is often open in form, and although it is assembled by local knowledge, it must be held together by self-organised community action.

It is in the community gardens of Taipei where fragments of third-generation urbanism are taking hold, co-existing with their industrial surroundings. The citizens ruin the centrally governed, official city with their unofficial networks of urban farms and gardens. They occupy streets for night markets, activating idle urban spaces for karaoke, gambling and collective exercise. They build illegal extensions to apartment buildings

von ihr abhängig. Die Region des Taipeh-Beckens bot einst eine fruchtbare Umgebung für eine solche Besiedlung mit ihren vier großen Flüssen Tamsui, Keelung, Dahan und Xindian, die als Transportwege und Nahrungsquelle dienten, während die Xueshan-Bergkette die bepflanzten Tiefebenen vor der Wucht des regelmäßigen Taifuns schützte. Die Stadt der zweiten Generation hingegen ist auch als Industriestadt bekannt: eine gebaute Umgebung, die die Menschen scheinbar mit allem versorgt, was sie zu brauchen meinen. Sie erachtet die Natur als entbehrlich, manchmal sogar feindlich. Die Stadt der zweiten Generation teilt lokales Wissen. Wenn sie es praktisch anwendet, hat sie das Potenzial, die industriell geprägte Stadt in eine organische Maschine zu verwandeln – eben in die gewünschte Stadt der dritten Generation. Sie ist die organische Ruine der Industriestadt: überwiegend offen in ihrer Form und muss – obwohl aus lokalem Wissen zusammengesetzt – durch selbstorganisiertes kollektives Handeln zusammengehalten werden.

Lokales Wissen: Lernen von den Großeltern

In den Gemeinschaftsgärten von Taipeh etablieren sich Fragmente des Urbanismus der dritten Generation, die mit ihrer industriellen Umgebung koexistieren. Die Bürger*innen ruinieren die zentral verwaltete, offizielle Stadt mit ihren inoffiziellen Netzwerken aus urbanen Farmen und Gärten. Sie besetzen Straßen mit Nachtmärkten und beleben den brachliegenden urbanen Raum mit Karaoke,

The metropolis as an organic machine: puncturing urban fabric with tactical, small-scale interventions for a third-generation city

Die Metropole als organische Maschine: Akupunktur der Stadtlandschaft mit taktischen Mikro-Eingriffen für eine Stadt der dritten Generation

and dominate the urban no-man's-land through self-organised, unofficial settlements like Treasure Hill. The official city is the source of pollution, while traditional, local knowledge-based activities are humbler in terms of material energy flows. Local knowledge is present in Taipei City, and its anarchist grandmother gardeners are the professors.

The third-generation city is realised when the city recognises its local knowledge and allows itself to be part of nature. The third-generation city is a city of cracks, where the thin surface of the second-generation city is sometimes pierced and sometimes shattered. New bio-urban growth emerges in the ruination of the second-generation city. If a ruin occurs when the human-made has become part of nature, then in the third-generation city, we aim to design ruins.

Spielen und Sport. Sie bauen illegal an Wohngebäude an und beherrschen das urbane Niemandsland durch selbstorganisierte, inoffizielle Siedlungen wie Treasure Hill. Die offizielle Stadt ist die Quelle der Verschmutzung, während traditionelle Aktivitäten, die auf lokalem Wissen beruhen, hinsichtlich ihrer materiellen Energieflüsse bescheidener sind. Lokales Wissen ist in Taipeh vorhanden. Die anarchistischen, gärtnernden Großmütter der Stadt können es lehren.

Die Stadt der dritten Generation ist möglich, wenn die Stadt ihr Wissen anerkennt und sich darauf einstellt, ein Teil der Natur zu sein. Die dritte Generation ist eine Stadt der Risse, die die dünne Oberfläche der zweiten Generation manchmal durchbohrt und zerbricht. Neues Wachstum entsteht aus den Ruinen. Wenn das dadurch gelingt, dass das Menschengemachte zum Teil der Natur wird, dann ist es unser erklärtes Ziel, Ruinen zu gestalten.

-> Case Study 10 pp. 262 ff. The Ruin Academy

Mapping and pinpointing interventions across the urban organism of Taipei

Kartierung von Interventionen im Stadtorganismus von Taipei

Producing from Consumption

Digital Revolution and Circular Thinking

Fab City is an international initiative started by the Institute for Advanced Architecture of Catalonia (IAAC), MIT's Center for Bits and Atoms (CBA), the Barcelona City Council and the Fab Foundation to develop locally productive and globally connected self-sufficient cities – currently with 28 cities including Seoul, Amsterdam, Shenzen, Santiago and even the Kingdom of Bhutan. Fab City is connected to the global Fab Lab (Fabrication Laboratory) Network and comprises an international think tank of civic leaders, makers, urbanists and innovators working to change the paradigm, from an industrial economy where the city operates on a linear model of importing products and producing waste, to a spiral innovation ecosystem in which materials flow inside cities, and it is the information on how things are made that circulates globally. Here, Tomás Díez, Fab City Research Lab Director, explores how the Fab City scales the ideals of the Fab Lab – the connectivity, culture and creativity – to the city.

The rapid urbanisation of the twentieth century was due, in large part, to the Industrial Revolution and the introduction of the assembly line, which allowed the reproduction and replication of infrastructure, products and urban patterns in cities around the world. The resulting urban development, following the same economic principles of infinite growth and efficiency, produced standard morphologies, dynamics and forms of living, all of which are the result of the mechanical and rational systems that make our current occupation of territories possible. With standardised manufacturing came the centralisation of production, and over the last century, urban development and the global economy depended on the construction of an infrastructure to extract and process natural resources, moving the finished products around the world. Airports, ports, railways and roads are all part of the same industrial urban paradigm, built in the service of increasing profit under the guise of efficiency. That claim to efficiency has been exposed as a falsehood.

Konsequenzen des Konsums

Digitale Revolution und zirkuläres Denken

Fab City ist eine internationale Initiative, die vom Institute for Advanced Architecture of Catalonia (IAAC), dem Center for Bits and Atoms des MIT, der Stadtverwaltung von Barcelona und der Fab Foundation ins Leben gerufen wurde, um lokal produktive und weltweit vernetzte autarke Städte zu schaffen. Momentan sind 28 Städte dabei, darunter Seoul, Amsterdam, Shenzhen, Santiago und sogar das Königreich Bhutan. Fab City ist mit dem globalen Fab Lab (Fabrication Laboratory) Network verbunden und umfasst eine internationale Denkfabrik aus Vertreter*innen der Zivilgesellschaft, Macher*innen, Urbanist*innen und Pionier*innen, die an einem Paradigmenwechsel arbeiten: weg von einer industriellen Ökonomie, in der die Stadt als lineares Modell Produkte importiert und Müll produziert, hin zu einem spiralförmigen Ökosystem, in dem die Materialien durch die Stadt fließen. Der einzige globale Fluss ist der Informationsaustausch darüber, wie die Dinge besser gemacht werden können. Tomás Díez, Direktor des Fab-City-Forschungslabors, erklärt wie Fab City Konnektivität, Kultur und Kreativität für die Stadt übersetzt.

Die schnelle Urbanisierung im 20. Jahrhundert ist zu großen Teilen der industriellen Revolution und der Einführung des Fließbandes geschuldet. Sie ermöglichte die Reproduktion und Replikation von Infrastruktur, Produkten und urbanen Mustern in Städten auf der ganzen Welt. Die daraus resultierende urbane Entwicklung folgte den gleichen ökonomischen Prinzipien von unbegrenztem Wachstum und Effizienz. Sie produzierte standardisierte Morphologien, Dynamiken und Lebensformen: Alle sind das Resultat eines mechanischen und rationalen Systems, das unsere derzeitige Besetzung von Territorien möglich macht. Mit den Herstellungsstandards kam die Zentralisierung der Produktion. Im vergangenen Jahrhundert waren urbane Entwicklung und globale Wirtschaft von einem Konstruktionsverständnis geprägt, bei dem natürliche Ressourcen abgebaut, aufbereitet und die fertigen Produkte durch die ganze Welt bewegt werden. Flughäfen, Häfen, Schienen und Straßen sind Teil des gleichen urbanen Paradigmas, das im Dienst der Profitsteigerung und unter dem Vorwand der Effizienz gebaut wurde.

The assumed efficiency has turned out to be untrue

Today, cities consume most of the world's resources and generate most of the world's waste; they import products, energy and food to satisfy local needs, and, upon digesting these resources, they produce the trash that makes its way back into our landfills, water supplies and air. These same cities and their infrastructure, however, can open up to a new form of globalism, based on local capacities, resources, values and skills, while being connected within the largest open global network of human innovation that has ever existed. To do this, we need to reinvent our cities and their relationship to people and nature by re-localising production so that cities are generative rather than extractive, restorative rather than destructive and empowering rather than alienating, where prosperity flourishes, and people have purposeful, meaningful work that they enjoy, that enables them to use their passion and talent. We need to recover the knowledge and ability to make things in our cities, by connecting citizens with the advanced technologies that are transforming our everyday life.

The first Fab Lab in Europe opened about eleven years ago in Barcelona's Poblenou, a post-industrial neighbourhood that was once known as the Catalan Manchester for its manufacturing presence and the strength of its labour union organisers. Like many other historically industrial neighbourhoods, Poblenou was hit hard by the deindustrialisation processes in the last quarter of the twentieth century. The 2008 economic crisis dramatically reduced available options for capital investment in Barcelona, and the real estate market in Poblenou did not boom as expected, putting in jeopardy the city's 22@ urban renovation plan, devised by the council to stimulate real estate investment in the area. But then, in-between, creative industries such as design studios, small architecture firms, design schools and digital production businesses began to pop up. Art galleries and collectively occupied buildings soon followed, and the identity of the neighbourhood began to change, with Poblenou garnering comparisons to Brooklyn, New York, Wynwood in Miami and Berlin's Mitte district. And just like those other neighbourhoods, Poblenou began to experience gentrification with all its afflictions.

Die angenommene Effizienz hat sich als Unwahrheit entpuppt

Städte verbrauchen heute die meisten Ressourcen der Welt und erzeugen den meisten Müll. Sie importieren Produkte, Energie und Lebensmittel, um den Bedarf vor Ort zu befriedigen, und mit dem Verbrauch dieser Ressourcen produzieren sie Müll, nutzen unsere Wasservorräte und beeinträchtigen die Luft. Diese Städte und ihre Infrastrukturen könnten sich jedoch einer neuen Form von Globalismus öffnen, die auf lokalen Kapazitäten, Ressourcen, Werten und Fähigkeiten gründet, während sie im größten offenen weltweiten Netzwerk menschlicher Innovation, das es je gegeben hat, verbunden wären. Um dies zu erreichen, müssen wir unsere Städte und ihre Beziehung zu Mensch und Natur neu erfinden: indem wir die Produktion zurück in die Stadt bringen. Städte wären dann generativ und nicht mehr extraktiv, regenerativ statt destruktiv und würden ermächtigen, statt zu entfremden. Sie wären Orte, an denen Wohlstand floriert und die Menschen sinnvolle und sinnstiftende Arbeit haben, die ihnen Spaß macht und sie befähigt, ihre Leidenschaften und Talente einzubringen. Wir müssen das Wissen und die Fähigkeit wiedererlangen, wie man Dinge in den Städten produziert, indem wir die Bürger*innen mit der modernen Technologie vernetzen, die unser alltägliches Leben verändert.

Das erste Fab Lab in Europa eröffnete vor ungefähr elf Jahren in Poblenou in Barcelona, einem postindustriellen Viertel, das dank einer starken Produktion und seines gewerkschaftlichen Engagements einst als katalanisches Manchester galt. Wie viele andere Städte wurde Poblenou stark vom Deindustrialisierungsprozess im letzten Viertel des 20. Jahrhunderts getroffen. Die Finanzkrise im Jahr 2008 verringerte die Möglichkeiten für Investitionen in Barcelona massiv, und der Immobilienmarkt in Poblenou boomte nicht wie erwartet, sondern brachte 22@ – den städtischen Erneuerungsplan, den die Stadtverwaltung entwickelt hatte, um Investitionen im Immobilienbereich anzukurbeln – in Gefahr. Aber in der Zwischenzeit waren kleine Firmen der Kreativbranche aufgetaucht: Designstudios und -schulen, Architekturbüros und digitale Produktionsfirmen begannen, sich anzusiedeln. Kunstgalerien und gemeinschaftlich genutzte Gebäude folgten bald, und die Identität des Viertels fing an, sich zu wandeln. Poblenou wurde plötzlich mit Brooklyn und Berlin-Mitte verglichen. Und genau wie diese Bezirke erlebte auch Poblenou das ganze Elend der Gentrifizierung.

Poblenou is an urban ecosystem which is gaining a new, unplanned identity through a dizzying array of initiatives. The neighbourhood now has a private-initiative association (Poblenou Urban District) which brings together most of the area's creative industries, maintains communication among its members, organises events and promotes Poblenou's potential to the city and beyond. In Poblenou, Fab Lab Barcelona and Fab City found the perfect context in which to settle and grapple with the future of technology and its potential impact on society. It was at Fab Lab Barcelona and Poblenou that the Fab City Global Initiative started.

In 2014, the mayor of Barcelona challenged other leaders of the world to develop a new urban model: cities that produce locally everything they consume while sharing knowledge globally. Inspired by this call to action, the Fab City Global Initiative established a 40-year roadmap in which Fab City brings the impact of digital technology to cities and connects globally distributed networks of hyper-local and productive ecosystems which enable the mass distribution of goods and resources. By adopting these principles, cities can radically transform the way production and consumption happen within their metropolitan regions, replacing standardisation with smart customisation, focusing on interconnected processes instead of isolated products and, more importantly, empowering citizens and communities while reducing the environmental impact of urbanisation.

Cities can radically change models of production and consumption

The Fab City Global Initiative envisions and constructs possible urban futures by synchronising philosophies, visions and objectives together with existing distributed innovation ecosystems, to consolidate and nurture a knowledge-based economy that has been developed during the past decade around open source innovations, digital fabrication technologies and distributed digital networks in Fab Labs, maker spaces and open communities. Fab City is about radical transformation and rethinking and changing our relationship with the material world in order to continue living on this planet.

Poblenou ist ein urbanes Ökosystem, dem eine Vielzahl von Initiativen eine neue, ungeplante Identität verleiht. Der Bezirk besitzt heute eine Vereinigung privater Initiativen (Poblenou Urban District), die die meisten Firmen der Kreativbranche in der Gegend zusammenbringt, die Kommunikation ihrer Mitglieder ermöglicht, Veranstaltungen organisiert und Poblenou in der Stadt und darüber hinaus bekannt macht. In Poblenou haben Fab Lab Barcelona und Fab City den perfekten Kontext gefunden, in dem sie sich ansiedeln konnten, um die Zukunft der Technologie und ihrer möglichen Auswirkungen auf die Gesellschaft anzupacken.

Im Jahr 2014 drängte der Bürgermeister von Barcelona andere führende Politiker auf der ganzen Welt, ein neues urbanes Modell zu entwickeln: Städte, die alles, was sie konsumieren, vor Ort produzieren, und das Wissen darüber weltweit teilen. Von diesem Aufruf inspiriert, entwickelte Fab City Global einen Fahrplan für die nächsten vierzig Jahre, in dem Fab City die Bedeutung von digitaler Technologie herausarbeitet und global verteilte Netzwerke hyperlokaler und produktiver Ökosysteme zusammenbringt, die die Massendistribution von Gütern und Ressourcen möglich machen. Wenn sie diese Grundsätze umsetzen, können Städte die Produktions- und Konsumweisen in ihren Metropolregionen radikal transformieren und Standardisierung durch smarte Personalisierung ersetzen. Sie können sich auf vernetzte Prozesse statt isolierte Produkte konzentrieren und Bürger*innen und Gemeinschaften stark machen. Damit verringern sie zugleich die Auswirkungen der Urbanisierung auf die Umwelt.

Städte können die Produktions- und Konsumweisen radikal transformieren

Die Initiative Fab City Global entwirft und konstruiert die mögliche urbane Zukunft. Sie verbindet Philosophie, Visionen und Ziele mit bereits existierenden innovativen Ökosystemen. Sie vertieft und nährt eine wissensbasierte Wirtschaft, die sich in den vergangenen zehn Jahren rund um Open-Source-Innovationen und digitale Produktionstechnologien entwickelt und digitale Netzwerke in Fab Labs, offenen Werkstätten und offenen Gemeinschaften verbreitet hat. Fab City steht für die radikale Transformation, neues Denken und Veränderungen in unserer Beziehung zur materiellen Welt. Damit wir weiterhin auf diesem Planeten leben können.

01.

Project:

Stadtwerken / Pretty Plastic Plant / People's Pavilion

City: various
Client: various
Planning: Superuse Studios, Bureau SLA and ReFunc
Status: 2017/2018

A World of Flows
Reversing the Design Process

A circular economy is a system of flows. These flows move through circuits that can be adjusted to connect one circuit with another. Companies within the circular economy are able to leverage both closed loops and tap into open networks. The Dutch architecture offices Superuse Studios, Bureau SLA and ReFunc have developed methods to work backwards and have redesigned the construction chain process - the circuits - first, by examining projects and their environments and, second, by locally sourcing available materials to minimise transportation.

These studios have worked on their own and together to develop installations focused on their reuse and recycling strategies. During the 2018 MakeCity Festival, they worked together to develop and install "Stadtwerken", an exhibition that provided visitors with an overview of their work. The exhibition highlighted their trial-and-error approach, with which they discovered the potential of material and energy use and waste flows, developing innovative solutions and workflow processes that continue to evolve.

The story of the plastic tiles used in the exhibition began when Bureau SLA installed machines at a DIY recycling assembly line in Amsterdam Noord, one of the city's marginalised neighbourhoods, by connecting with a local community project involved in collecting plastic waste. Machines for recycling plastic are simple: "The main problem is the process itself - collecting, sorting, moulding and producing new items. These processes do not tend to be connected." The fragmentation in process flows means companies and initiatives do not effectively communicate with each other. To address this, Bureau SLA and Belgian design studio Overtreders built the Pretty Plastic Plant. Assembling four units entirely out of waste, they are now producing fireproofed recycled plastic tiles for cladding buildings.

The recycled plastic tiles were also used to clad the exterior walls of the People's Pavilion for Dutch Design Week 2017. By sorting plastic waste by colour, they produced a range of tile colours, from pastel to vibrant. Borrowed materials formed the entirety of the structure, including wooden components that were returned after use and glazing left over from an office building

Welt der Ströme
Den Designprozess umkehren

Eine Kreislaufwirtschaft ist ein System aus Strömen. Diese Ströme bewegen sich zirkulär und können so angepasst werden, dass mehrere Kreisläufe miteinander verbunden werden können. Unternehmen, die innerhalb der Kreislauflogik arbeiten, können sowohl zirkulär agieren als auch offene Systeme anzapfen. Die niederländischen Architekturbüros Superuse Studios, Bureau SLA und ReFunc haben Methoden entwickelt, mit denen sie rückwärts arbeiten können, und haben dabei den Prozess der Konstruktionsketten – der Kreise – überarbeitet. Zuerst, indem sie Bauprojekte analysiert und vor Ort nach verfügbaren Materialien gesucht haben, die den Transport minimieren.

Die Architekturbüros beschäftigten sich alleine und im Team mit der Entwicklung von Installationen, die sich auf Wiederverwertung und Recyclingstrategien konzentrieren. Während des MakeCity Festivals 2018 entwickelten sie die Installation „Stadtwerken", eine Ausstellung, die den Besucher*innen einen Überblick über ihre Handlungsfelder bot. Die Ausstellung beleuchtete ihren Ansatz des Ausprobierens, indem sie das Potenzial von Material- und Energieverbrauch und von Müllflüssen ausmachten und innovative Lösungen und Workflowprozesse vorschlugen, die sich fortlaufend weiterentwickeln.

Die Geschichte der in der Ausstellung verwendeten Kunststofffliesen begann damit, dass sich die Mitarbeiter*innen des Bureau SLA an einem lokalen Gemeinschaftsprojekt zur Sammlung von Plastikmüll beteiligten und bei einer DIY-Recyclingsammlung in Amsterdam-Noord, einem marginalisierten Stadtbezirk, Maschinen aufstellten. Maschinen zur Wiederverwertung von Plastik sind simpel: „Das Hauptproblem ist der Prozess selbst – das Sammeln, Sortieren, Formen und das Produzieren neuer Gegenstände. Diese Prozesse sind in der Regel nicht miteinander verbunden." Die Stückelung des Prozessflusses bedeutet, dass Firmen und Initiativen nicht effektiv miteinander kommunizieren. Um das zu thematisieren, bauten Bureau SLA und das belgische Designstudio Overtreders das Pretty Plastic Plant. Das vierteilige Projekt wurde ausschließlich aus Müll errichtet und produziert mittlerweile feuerfeste recycelte Kunststofffliesen zur Verkleidung von Häusern.

Die recycelten Kunststofffliesen wurden außerdem zur Verkleidung des Besucherpavillons bei der

in nearby Utrecht. After Design Week, the materials were used in other projects.

These experimental - and successful - circuits provide us with a glimpse into the future of the circular economy of the construction industry by demonstrating that coveted forms, buildings and urban infrastructure can be created from materials that would otherwise be considered - and discarded - as waste.

"Second-hand materials lead the design process. Not in an eco-garbage-collage building, but with an entirely different architectural language. The structure itself has almost no ecological footprint."
„Gebrauchte Materialien leiten den Designprozess. Nicht mit Gebäuden aus Öko-Müll-Collagen, sondern in einer komplett anderen architektonischen Sprache." Die Struktur selbst hat fast keinen ökologischen Fußabdruck."

Peter van Assche

Dutch Design Week 2017 genutzt. Da der Plastikmüll zuvor nach Farben sortiert wird, ist die Herstellung einer ganzen Palette bunter Fliesen möglich, von pastellfarben bis intensiv leuchtend. Die gesamte Konstruktion war aus geliehenen Materialien zusammengesetzt, darunter Holzteile, die nach dem Gebrauch zurückgegeben wurden, und Reste der Verglasung eines Bürogebäudes im nahen Utrecht. Nach der Design Week wurden diese Materialien in anderen Projekten weiterverwertet.

Diese experimentellen – und erfolgreichen – Kreisläufe geben uns einen kleinen Einblick in die Zukunft der Kreislaufwirtschaft in der Bauindustrie. Sie zeigen, dass Formen, Gebäude und urbane Infrastruktur aus Materialien konstruiert werden können, die anderswo als Müll betrachtet – und entsprechend entsorgt – werden.

"We took the circular idea to a maximum level."
„Wir haben die Kreislaufidee auf die höchste Stufe gehoben."

Peter van Assche

The Pretty Plastic Plant: DIY tools and systems address the fragmentation in the process flows between industrial production and recycling

Das Pretty Plastic Plant: DIY-Werkzeuge und -Systeme thematisieren die Fragmentierung von Prozessabläufen zwischen industrieller Produktion und Wiederverwertung

People's Pavilion for Dutch Design Week 2017: recycled plastic on the façade, borrowed materials for the structure - all slated for further reuse

People's Pavilion auf der Dutch Design Week 2017: Recyclingkunststoff an der Fassade, geborgtes Baumaterial für die Konstruktion – nach dem Abbau für andere Projekte wiederverwendet

02.

Project: **Superuse.org & Harvestmap.org**

City: global
Client: Open access platform
Planning: Superuse Studios with Lettow Studios
Status: Ongoing

Reintegrating Waste
A Platform for Reuse

Over the last two decades, Dutch architecture studio Superuse Studios have become pioneers in circular economies and sustainable design by focusing on developing and providing open source methods and tools for the design community.

When Superuse first set up their agency, they intended to create all-inclusive architecture. Every design task was considered as part of a system with flows to be analysed. Each flow was in a cyclical relationship with its environment. At the time, sustainable architecture focused on energy and water system designs - with little attention to materials. This inspired the development of the Superuse method: from waste to building materials with minimal transportation. They developed a web platform, Oogstkaart (Dutch for "harvest map"), that allows users to access information about materials - wood, plastic, textiles, metal, glass, electronic components, brick and stone, chemicals, organic, paper and cardboard - and how they might be reused.

An important factor for designing waste is an understanding of each material with its specific technical and aesthetic properties. When design is determined by material properties, the construction process becomes dynamic. The platform allows users to post questions or successes, with any images which might tell a story, locations, pricing, supporting documentation and user comments. By building an open source platform that is under continuous development, Superuse, its collaborators and its users, learn how to improve their online community together, making the sharing and reusing of resources simple and accessible, building a more connected society.

Just over ten years later, the platform - charting reuseable materials and connecting like-minded enterprises and industry - has led to a far-reaching network, operating in the Netherlands, Austria, Belgium, China, France, Italy and Spain, that supersedes the linear material-to-waste economy with its circular thinking.

Müll neu einsetzen
Eine Plattform für Wiederverwertung

In den letzten zwei Jahrzehnten ist das niederländische Büro Superuse Studios zu einem Vorreiter der Kreislaufwirtschaft und nachhaltigen Gestaltung geworden, indem es sich auf die Entwicklung und Verbreitung von Open-Source-Methoden und -Werkzeugen für die Design-Community spezialisierte.

Die Gründung von Superuse Studios als Firma war von dem Wunsch geleitet, eine gesamtheitliche Architektur zu schaffen. Jede Gestaltungsaufgabe wurde als Teil eines Systems verstanden, dessen Abläufe es zu analysieren galt. Jeder Ablauf stand in einer zyklischen Beziehung zu seiner Umwelt. Nachhaltige Architektur konzentrierte sich damals auf die Gestaltung von Energie- und Wassersystemen – und schenkte Baumaterialien kaum Aufmerksamkeit. Daher wurde die Superuse-Methode entwickelt: Mache mit minimalem Transportaufwand aus Abfall Baumaterial. Superuse Studios entwickelte die Onlineplattform Oogstkaart (Erntekarte), die Nutzende sowohl über Materialien informiert – Holz, Plastik, Textilien, Metall, Glas, elektronische Bestandteile, Ziegel und Stein, Chemikalien, organische Abfälle, Papier und Karton – als auch über Möglichkeiten, sie wiederzuverwenden.

Für die bauliche Gestaltung mit wiederverwendeten Materialien ist ein Verständnis des Materials mit seinen spezifischen technischen und ästhetischen Eigenschaften wesentlich. Wenn Design von Materialeigenschaften bestimmt ist, dann wird der Konstruktionsprozess dynamisch. Die Plattform ermöglicht es Nutzenden, selbst Fragen oder Erfolgsgeschichten einzubringen, wobei jeder Beitrag Bilder, Orte, Preise, unterstützende Dokumentation und weitere Kommentare umfasst. Superuse und alle Beteiligten lernen, wie sie ihre Online-Community gemeinsam verbessern können, wie sie das Teilen und Wiederverwenden von Wertstoffen einfach und zugänglich machen können und wie sie somit an einer verbundeneren Gesellschaft arbeiten.

Nur rund zehn Jahre später hat die Plattform – die wiederverwendbare Materialien kartiert und gleichgesinnte Unternehmen und Industrie zusammenführt – zu einem weitreichenden Netz geführt, das in den Niederlanden, Österreich, Belgien, China, Frankreich, Italien und Spanien operiert und mit seinem Kreislaufdenken über die lineare Material-wird-Abfall-Wirtschaft hinausweist.

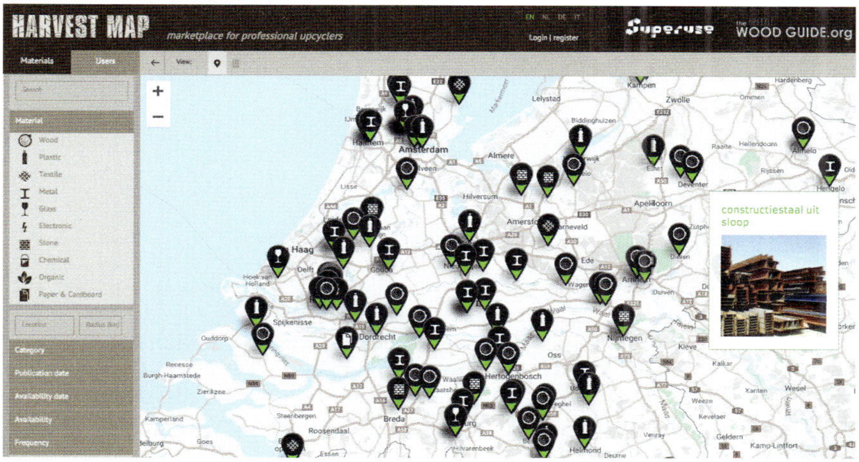

Online platform maps reusable materials and connects users, superseding the linear economy with circular thinking

Die Onlineplattform kartiert wiederverwendbare Materialien, bringt Nutzer*innen zusammen und ersetzt lineare Ökonomie durch zirkuläres Denken

The façades made from one thousand wooden cable bobbins marked for disposal, the load bearing structuremade from the metal components of a textile machine: Villa Welpello by Superuse Studios and En-fer, Enschede, 2006–2009

Die Fassade aus eintausend Holz-Kabelspulen, die entsorgt werden sollten, die Tragstruktur aus den Metallresten einer Textilmaschine: Villa Welpeloo von Superuse Studios und En-Fer, Enschede, 2006–2009

"Nature is a cyclical and dynamic system. Our society is a linear and rigid system, typified by homogeneity and a desire to fix existing connections. This leads to huge amounts of waste and to a waste of resources."

„Die Natur ist ein zyklisches und dynamisches System. Unsere Gesellschaft ist ein lineares und starres System, versinnbildlicht in Homogenität und im Wunsch, bestehende Verbindungen zu fixieren. Das führt zu enormen Abfallmengen und zu einer Verschwendung von Ressourcen."

Superuse Studios

"Unemployment, mountains of rubbish and energy loss are the accepted downsides of our current system."

„Arbeitslosigkeit, Berge von Abfall und Energieverlust sind die akzeptierten Schattenseiten unseres gegenwärtigen Systems."

Superuse Studios

03.

Project: **Berlin Metropolitan School**

City: Berlin
Panning: Sauerbruch Hutton
Client: Berlin Metropolitan School
Status: Completed 2018

The New Wood
From Plattenbau to Timber Construction

Due to a pressing need for additional space, the Metropolitan School in Berlin-Mitte needed to expand: architectural office Sauerbruch Hutton designed and proposed the construction of an addition onto the German Democratic Republic (GDR) former East Berlin prefab building, thereby closing the adjacent vacant lot to produce an additional 4,700 square metres to be used by the school.

It was decided that the choice of building material would be wood: the high degree of prefabrication of the box girder ribbed elements and veneer plywood components would significantly reduce the construction time - an advantage since the construction work had to take place while the school was in operation and the expansion areas could only grow gradually alongside the demand. Although using timber in construction and manufacturing processes is becoming increasingly standardised, this does not mean it is necessarily reflected in standardised design language: in contrast to industrially manufactured construction processes, extensions and spatial additions were articulated fluently and differently. The wooden frames in the attic storey became spatially defining elements while elucidating the auditorium in a visual and haptic manner - the overall indoor climate benefits from this.

The notion that wood as a raw material is highly sustainable is not new. It is, however, innovative that the light weight of the wooden frames would allow for such a slim construction, without additional strengthening of the foundations or interventions on the supporting structure. In its working with pre-existing bulky architectural structures, the project has effected a visible signal in Baukultur (German for building culture): when it comes to urban densification and rooftop extensions, wood represents a real alternative to the otherwise universal solution of reinforced concrete while also being environmentally sensitive.

Neues Holz
Vom Plattenbau zum Holzbau

Weil das Flächenangebot ausgeschöpft war, sollte die Metropolitan School in Berlin-Mitte erweitert werden: Der Vorschlag des Architekturbüros Sauerbruch Hutton sah vor, den aus DDR-Zeiten stammenden Plattenbau aufzustocken und die angrenzende Baulücke zu schließen. Das Ergebnis sind zusätzliche 4.700 Quadratmeter für die Schule.

Die Baustoffwahl fiel auf Holz: Der hohe Vorfertigungsgrad der verwendeten Hohlkasten-Rippenelemente und Furnierschichtholzbauteile reduzierte die Bauzeit signifikant – ein großer Vorteil, weil die Baumaßnahmen während des laufenden Schulbetriebs stattfinden mussten und die Erweiterungsflächen stufenweise mit dem Bedarf mitwachsen sollten. Holzbau wird im Fertigungsprozess immer standardisierter, was sich jedoch nicht in normierter Formensprache zeigen muss: Der Auf- und Zubau artikuliert sich im Gegensatz zum industriell gefertigten Bestandsbau fließend und differenziert. Die Holzrahmen im Dachgeschoss sind raumbildend und definieren die Aula visuell und haptisch – auch das Raumklima profitiert davon.

Dass es sich beim Rohstoff Holz um ein Material mit hoher Nachhaltigkeit handelt, ist nicht neu. Richtungsweisend ist, dass das geringe Gewicht eine derart schlanke Konstruktion erlaubte, dass keine zusätzlichen Fundamente und Eingriffe am Bestandstragwerk nötig waren. So hat das Projekt im Umgang mit sperrigem Architekturbestand baukulturelle Signalwirkung: Holz stellt in der urbanen Nachverdichtung eine ernst zu nehmende Alternative zur vermeintlichen Universallösung Stahlbeton dar – und das ressourcenschonend.

Timber meets Plattenbau: low weight and time efficient due to prefabricated frames

Holz auf Platte: Geringes Gewicht und Zeitersparnis durch vorgefertig-te Rahmen

04.

Project: **Flexim headquarters**

City: Berlin-Marzahn
Client: Flexim GmbH
Planning: ZRS Architekten
Status: Completed 2016

Timber Construction Made in Marzahn Renewable, Urban, Economic

Unexpected urbanity: in an industrial area between prefabricated buildings and railway lines, the Berlin office of Ziegert Roswag Seiler Architekten Ingenieure has built a new company building housing the meter manufacturer Flexim. Two of the six planned courtyard buildings were completed in 2017, while the rest will gradually follow in the coming years. The urban design concept refers to the traditional Berlin block, with its adjoining courtyards and emblematic mix of uses and production. The wood-concrete hybrid construction relies on a low-tech strategy, further reflected in a building envelope that allows for a minimum of building services engineering, such as heating and ventilation systems.

The proficiency of using wood as a building material has also convinced the client

While the staircase cores, joists and columns are made of concrete, the ceiling elements, insulating structures and the diffused and climate-responsive exterior façade consist of renewable raw material, aesthetically defining the outer appearance of the building.

30 percent less consumption than required by the Energy Saving Ordinance

Combined with adequate glass content, shading and night-time cooling elements, as well as regenerative energy sources, the sophisticated mix of materials provides a pleasant indoor climate in both summer and winter, reducing both seasonal cooling and heating costs.

Building with wood pays off!

The Flexim building sends a strong message to the construction and architecture community, demonstrating to medium-sized entrepreneurs that the employment of wood as a building material is more than an aesthetic decision: resource-friendly construction also has economic advantages.

Holzbau aus Marzahn Nachwachsend, urban, ökonomisch

Unerwartete Urbanität: Im Gewerbegebiet zwischen Plattenbauten und Bahntrassen liegt das vom Berliner Büro Ziegert Roswag Seiler Architekten Ingenieure entwickelte neue Firmengebäude des Messtechnikherstellers Flexim. Zwei der geplanten sechs Hofgebäude wurden 2017 fertiggestellt. Der Rest folgt Schritt für Schritt in den kommenden Jahren. Das städtebauliche Konzept bezieht sich auf den Berliner Block mit seinen hintereinandergeschalteten Höfen und dem ihm typischen Nutzungs- und Produktionsmix. Der Holz-Beton-Hybridbau setzt auf eine Lowtech-Strategie, die sich in der optimierten Außenhülle zeigt und zu einer stark reduzierten Gebäudetechnik führt.

Die Leistungsfähigkeit des Baumaterials Holz hat auch die Auftraggeber*innen überzeugt

Während die Treppenhauskerne, Unterzüge und Stützen aus Beton gefertigt wurden, bestehen die Deckenelemente, die Dämmkonstruktionen und die diffussionsoffene und klimaaktive Außenfassade aus dem nachwachsenden Rohstoff, der auch das Erscheinungsbild des Gebäudes bestimmt.

Dreißig Prozent weniger Verbrauch als in der Energieeinsparverordnung vorgeschrieben

In Kombination mit einem angemessenen Glasanteil, Verschattungs- und Nachtauskühlungselementen sowie regenerativen Energiequellen ermöglicht der ausgeklügelte Materialmix sowohl im Sommer als auch im Winter ein angenehmes Raumklima und senkt Kosten für Kühlen und Heizen.

Bauen mit Holz zahlt sich aus!

Das Flexim-Gebäude sendet ein starkes baukulturelles Signal an mittelständische Entrepreneur*innen und zeigt, dass der Werkstoff Holz weit mehr ist als eine ästhetische Entscheidung: Ressourcenfreundliches Bauen hat ganz klar unternehmerische Vorteile.

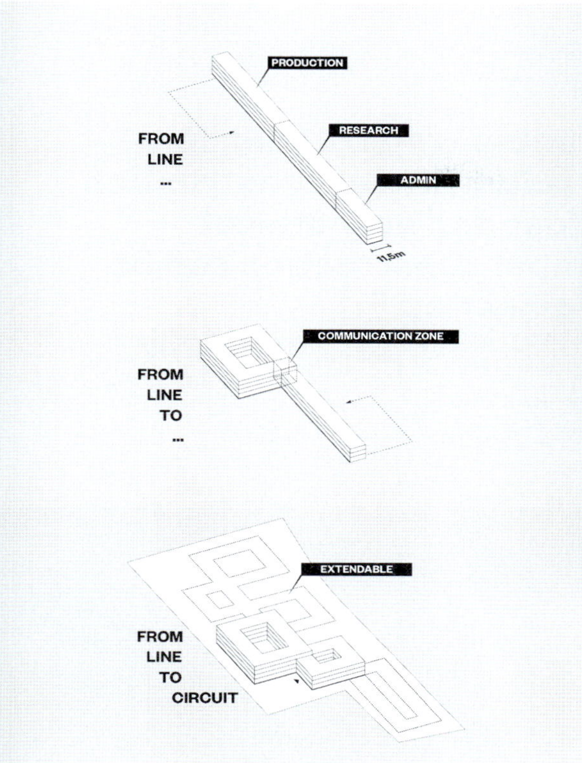

Expandability as an urban planning principle

Erweiterbarkeit als städtebauliches Prinzip

The Flexim building: unexpected urbanity in the industrial park, between prefabricated buildings and railway lines

Das Flexim-Gebäude: urbane Überraschung im Gewerbegebiet, zwischen PLattenbauten und Bahntrassen

Flexim building packed in an efficiently insulating wooden envelope

Flexim-Gebäude gehüllt in eine hochwärmedämmende Holzfassade

"Timber construction is circular. Timber construction is fast and economical. Timber construction can be engineering!"

„Holzbau ist zirkulär. Holzbau ist schnell und wirtschaftlich. Holzbau kann Ingenieurbau!"

Eike Roswag-Klinge

Good working climate: wood in the production workspace

Gutes Klima: Holz im Produktions- und Arbeitsalltag

Light, air and circulation: a sequence of courtyards serve as indoor and outdoor lounges and connecting elements

Licht, Luft und Erschließung: Eine Sequenz an Höfen dient als Aufenthaltsraum und Verbindungselement

05.

Projekt: **Green Roofs and Façades**

City: global
Client: N/A
Planning: N/A
Status: Proposal/concept

Green Is the New Black
Lavish Roofs and Façades

Globally, approximately 800 square kilometres of vegetation are lost daily as the result of deforestation, urbanisation and desertification; this corresponds to an area the size of the city of Berlin. With the loss of vegetation, our environment is losing its evaporation mechanisms, leading to a loss in the global cooling effect. The overheating of urban landscapes is due to an increased use of glass in new building façades and encasements: cities reflect up to three times more heat into the atmosphere than so-called natural landscapes. The universal panacea of air conditioning continues unchecked with detrimental economic and environmental costs. A rethinking towards climate-friendly architecture is long overdue and it is high time for the development of viable alternatives. The German Federal Government's climate plan is to work towards a completely climate-neutral building stock by 2050.

Berlin, June, 2:00pm, sunshine:
Surface temperature of black roof: 55°C
Surface temperature of green roof: 30°C

According to experts, including Marco Schmidt, a specialist for energy optimised construction at the Technical University (TU) of Berlin, green façades and roofs counteract the urban heat island effect, making a viable contribution to the cooling of buildings and even reducing costs. A study at the Institute of Building Physics at Humboldt University shows that the maintenance and repair of a standard façade with external sun protection cost about 16,500 euros per year - compared to just 1,300 euros per year for the irrigation and maintenance of a green façade. The result: better performance and lower investment costs - a win-win situation for planning, users and the environment.

Grün ist das neue Schwarz
Sprießende Dächer und Fassaden

Global gehen täglich etwa 800 Quadratkilometer an Vegetation durch die Zerstörung von Wäldern, Urbanisierung und Ausbreitung der Wüsten verloren. Das entspricht etwa der Fläche Berlins. Mit dem Vegetationsverlust und dem Verlust an Verdunstung schwindet der globale Kühlungseffekt. Zudem reflektieren Städte bis zu dreimal so viel Hitze in die Atmosphäre wie natürliche Landschaften. Die Überhitzung von Stadtlandschaften ist auch dem zunehmenden Glasanteil in Gebäudehüllen geschuldet. Das vermeintliche Allheilmittel Klimaanlage verursacht untragbare ökonomische und ökologische Kosten. Alternativen müssen daher entwickelt werden, und ein Umdenken hin zu klimagerechter Architektur ist längst überfällig. Auch das Klimakonzept der Bundesregierung fordert bis 2050 einen nahezu klimaneutralen Gebäudebestand.

Berlin, Juni, 14:00, Sonnenschein:
Oberflächentemperatur schwarzes Dach: 55°C
Oberflächentemperatur begrüntes Dach: 30°C

Grüne Fassaden und Dächer wirken den sogenannten urban heat islands entgegen, leisten einen veritablen Beitrag zur Gebäudekühlung und reduzieren sogar die Kosten, erklärt Marco Schmidt, Experte für energieoptimiertes Bauen an der TU Berlin: Eine Studie am Institutsgebäude für Physik der Humboldt-Universität zu Berlin weist nach, dass die Wartung und Reparatur einer Standardfassade mit außen liegendem Sonnenschutz im Jahr rund 16.500 Euro kostet – im Vergleich dazu beläuft sich die Bewässerung und Pflege einer Grünfassade auf lediglich 1.300 Euro pro Jahr. Bessere Performance und geringere Investitionskosten: eine Win-win-Situation für Planung, Nutzer*innen und Umwelt.

Green, cool and cost-effective: façade of the Institute of Physics of the Humboldt University Berlin

Begrünt, cool und kostenextensiv: Fassade des Instituts für Physik der Humboldt-Universität zu Berlin

"Greening façades means lower investment costs, lower operating costs, better performance for the building and an improvement to the environment!"

„Fassadenbegrünung bedeutet niedrigere Investitionskosten, geringere Betriebskosten, bessere Performance für das Gebäude und ist besser für die Umwelt!"

Marco Schmidt

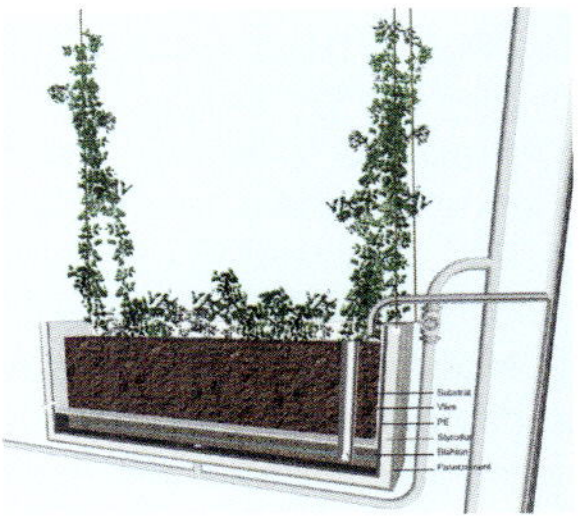

The façades of the Institute of Physics of the Humboldt University in Berlin host biodiversity in 150 buckets irrigated with rainwater harvest:

Fassade des Instituts für Physik Humboldt-Universität zu Berlin: Biodiversität in 150 bewässerten Kübeln mit Regenwassernutzung:

- Actinidia kolomikta
- Akebia quintata
- Aristolochia macrophylla
- Aristolochia tomentosa
- Campsis radicans
- Campsis tagliabuana "Mme Galen"
- Clematis orientalis "Bill Mac-Kenzie"
- Clematis paniculata
- Clematis tangutica "Helios"
- Clematis vitalba
- Hydrangea petiolaris
- Hydrangea arborescens
- Lonicera periclymenum
- Parthenocissus inserta
- Parthenocissus quinquefolia
- Vitis coignetiae
- Vitis vinifera "Phoenix"
- Wisteria sinensis "Alba"
- Wisteria sinensis "Prolific"

06.

Project: **BlueCity**
RotterZwam, formerly Tropicana
City: Rotterdam
Client: City of Rotterdam
Planning: Siemen Cox, Mark Slegers
Status: Ongoing

Blue Economy
A Third Space of a Different Kind

In 2010 the subtropical swimming paradise in Rotterdam known as Tropicana closed its gates, was abandoned and left to decay. Two entrepreneurs, Mark Slegers and Siemen Cox, came together and founded BlueCity, the start-up that bought the vacant property in 2015 for 1.7 million euros on an antikraak (anti-squatting) lease. Slegers and Cox saw an opportunity to draw on the model of nature to transform the complex into a blue economy. Unlike a circular economy, a blue economy is a dynamic and multi-directional network that links processes by using waste from one process for another.

The connections that exist inside Tropicana resemble the intricate mycorrhizal networks of their key product: mushrooms. The Aloha Bar's coffee grounds provide the growing medium for RotterZwam's oyster mushrooms. The CO2 released during the growing process is used by Spireaux to produce spirulina. The mycelium from the mushrooms is used to develop packaging materials. And the 20 to 50 kilograms of fungi that are produced each week? They are on the menu at Aloha, as well as at local bakeries, restaurants and food trucks. Cardboard and organic waste is composted in the basement, while the aquaponics system provides BlueCity with fresh air.

Since its inception, BlueCity has worked closely with the municipality while coordinating with other hubs in the city. Leveraging their early success, BlueCity was able to convince municipal and public institutions and companies in Rotterdam to give their blue economy a prominent place in city planning, thereby turning the former swimming complex into a vibrant, dynamic example of entrepreneurship, reuse and sustainability that can be - and is being - applied elsewhere.

Blaue Ökonomie
Ein dritter Raum der anderen Art

Im Jahr 2010 wurde das Rotterdamer Schwimmparadies namens Tropicana geschlossen und dem Leerstand und Verfall überlassen. Die zwei Unternehmer Mark Slegers and Siemen Cox taten sich zusammen und gründeten BlueCity, ein Start-up, das 2015 die leer stehende Immobilie für 1,7 Millionen Euro im Rahmen einer Anti-Squatting-Pacht bezog. Slegers und Cox sahen hier die Möglichkeit, den Komplex nach dem Vorbild der Natur in eine Blue Economy zu verwandeln. Anders als bei einer Kreislaufwirtschaft ist eine blaue Ökonomie ein dynamisches und mehrdirektionales Netzwerk, das Prozesse miteinander verknüpft, indem Abfallprodukte des einen Prozesses in einem anderen Prozess genutzt werden.

Die Verbindungen im Inneren von Tropicana erinnern an die feinen Mykhorrhiza-Netze von BlueCitys Hauptelement: der Pilze. Der Kaffeesatz der Rotterdamer Aloha Bar bietet den Nährboden für die Austernpilzkulturen von RotterZwam. Das CO_2, das die Pilze im Wachstumsprozess ausstoßen, wird von der Firma Spireaux genutzt, um Spirulina (Mikroalgen) zu produzieren. Das Myzel der Pilze wird eingesetzt, um Verpackungsmaterial zu entwickeln. Und die zwanzig bis fünfzig Kilogramm Pilze, die wöchentlich produziert werden? Die gibt es auf der Speisekarte im Aloha sowie in lokalen Bäckereien, Restaurants und Food-Trucks. Die Verarbeitung von Karton und organischen Abfällen, die nicht nutzbar sind, übernehmen die Würmer, die im Keller leben. Ein aquaponisches System versorgt BlueCity mit frischer Luft.

Von Anfang an arbeitete BlueCity eng mit der Kommune zusammen und stimmte sich mit anderen Projekten in der Stadt ab. Dank des frühen Erfolgs konnte BlueCity die lokalen öffentlichen Institutionen und Unternehmen in Rotterdam davon überzeugen, der Blue Economy einen Platz in der Stadtplanung einzuräumen und das ehemalige Spaßbad zu einem lebendigen und dynamischen Beispiel für unternehmerisches Handeln, Wiederverwertung und Nachhaltigkeit, das auch anderswo anwendbar ist, werden zu lassen.

From foot fungus to food fungus: the blue economy inside the ex-swimming pool complex Tropicana resembles the mycorrhizal networks of their key product, oyster mushrooms

Von Fußpilz zu Speisepilz: Die Blue Economy im Tropicana ähnelt den komplizierten Myzelien des Austernpilzes, dem wichtigsten Produkt im ehemaligen Bad

"In this building we hardly ever buy a thing, because every material or nail is already here."

„In diesem Gebäude kaufen wir fast nie etwas, weil alles, was wir brauchen, schon hier ist."

Siemen Cox

Between 1988 and 2010, the swimming paradise Tropicana was a popular leisure attraction; declaring bankruptcy in 2010, Tropicana closed its gates and was left to decay

Von 1988 bis 2010 galt das Spaßbad Tropicana als Freizeitattraktion, mit der Insolvenz im Jahr 2010 begann der Verfall

07.

Project: **Heinrich 73|36**

City: Berlin
Client: Baugruppe Heinrich 73 GbR
Planning: roedig.schop architekten
Status: Completed 2016

The Genesis of a Redundant Space From Unused to Cityscape

"The façade does not necessarily belong to the owners of a house. Not even on the ground floor!" In line with this claim, the architects roedig.schop reinterpreted redundant urban space in their design for a Baugruppe (German for a building group based on ownership of residential units) in a way that enriches residents, pedestrians and the neighbourhood.

So as not to burden the subway tunnel below, the staircase walls of the building had to be removed from the edge of the street, creating a 75-centimetre-wide space between the house and property boundary. Rather than accommodating the obligatory garbage room with a closed-façade area in this space, the planners convinced the co-investors to take another route and they developed a small and elegant alternative. When a local shopkeeper in the house bought a mere 3 x 2 metres of space, they agreed to use it as a mini showroom: an art showcase for passers-by, with vernissages held on the sidewalk. Since its completion, the gallery has been used by various artists, - including exhibiting works during Make City Festival 2018, when it functioned as a MiniHub.

"We must deal responsibly with areas and spaces that are in direct contact with the streetscape!" A point that is emphasised by the architects, who demand that private property commit to a varied and inspiring cityscape.

Die Genese einer räumlichen Redundanz Aus unbenutzt wird Stadtbild

„Die Fassade gehört ideell nicht unbedingt den Eigentümern eines Hauses. Schon gar nicht im Erdgeschoss!" Diesem Anspruch folgend, deutet das Architekturbüro roedig.schop in seinem Entwurf für eine Baugruppe eine redundante Restfläche in einen Raum um, der Bewohner*innen, Fußgänger*innen und Nachbarschaft bereichert.

Um nicht zusätzlich auf dem darunterliegenden U-Bahn-Schacht zu lasten, mussten die Treppenhauswände des Gebäudes von der Straßenkante zurückspringen – dadurch entstand ein 75 Zentimeter schmaler Freiraum zwischen Haus und Grundstücksgrenze. Statt an dieser Stelle den obligatorischen Müllraum mit geschlossener Fassadenfläche unterzubringen, konnten die Planer*innen die Baugruppe überzeugen, einen anderen Weg zu gehen, und entwickelten eine kleine, aber feine Alternative. Ein Gewerbetreibender im Haus kaufte die nur drei Quadratmeter große Fläche und erklärte sich bereit, diese als Miniausstellungsraum zu nutzen: ein Kunstschaufenster für Passant*innen mit Vernissagen auf dem Gehweg. Seit der Fertigstellung wird die Galerie von wechselnden Künstler*innen bespielt – unter anderem auch während des MakeCity Festivals in Form eines MiniHubs.

„Mit Flächen und Räumen, die in direktem Kontakt zum Straßenraum stehen, muss verantwortungsvoll umgegangen werden!", betonen die Architekt*innen und fordern ein abwechslungsreiches und inspirierendes Stadtbild: Eigentum sollte auch dazu verpflichten.

Vernissage on the pavement:
a redundant space becomes
a mini gallery

Vernissage auf dem Bürgersteig:
Eine Restfläche wird zur Minigalerie

08.

Project: **Sala Beckett**

City: Barcelona
Client: Institut de Cultura de Barcelona + Fundació Sala Beckett
Planning: Flores & Prats, Barcelona
Status: Opened 2016

A Dialogue with the Past
Poetic Revitalisation

"The challenge of the project was to adapt the building to its new uses without banishing the old spirits embedded in its history." In line with this claim, Barcelona architects Flores & Prats tell the story of the Cooperativa Paz y Justicia. An industrial building dating back to the 1920s, it was in urgent need of restoration. The brief: refurbish into a site for production and experimental theatre projects. The response: the architects redesigned the space as an assemblage of memories.

The design process was preceded by a meticulous research and analysis of the history of the building: renewal was a journey through time. In countless drawings and study models, Ricardo Flores and Eva Prats visualised the past of the building and thereby managed to interweave the past with the future: "The ruin we found was of no interest because we wanted to restore it, we wanted to take the ruin with us and make it part of the building - unfinished, as one of many layers, and as the foundation of a new reality."

From the outside, a sweeping new roof unites the buildings of the old co-operative while a spacious vestibule connects the three levels. The poetry becomes apparent in the details: faded colours of doorframes and panels, polychrome tiles, battered stucco rosettes and exposed plaster layers - each element, whether old or new; a relic telling a story and contributing to the new dramaturgy of the theatre building, both spatially and emotionally.

Im Dialog mit der Vergangenheit
Poetische Umnutzung

„Die Herausforderung des Projekts bestand darin, das Gebäude an seine neue Nutzung anzupassen, ohne seine alten Geister zu verbannen." Gemäß diesem Anspruch erzählt das Architekturbüro Flores & Prats aus Barcelona die Geschichte der Cooperativa Paz y Justicia weiter. Das aus den 1920er Jahren stammende, dringend restaurierungsbedürftige Industriegebäude sollte als Produktions- und Experimentierstätte für Theaterprojekte neu genutzt werden. Das Ergebnis ist ein Stück Erinnerungskultur.

Erneuerung als Zeitreise: Dem Entwurfsprozess ging eine akribische Analyse der Geschichte des Gebäudes voran. In unzähligen Zeichnungen und Studienmodellen machten die Architekt*innen Ricardo Flores und Eva Prats die Vergangenheit des Gebäudes sichtbar und schufen so die Basis, um Vergangenes mit Zukünftigem zu verweben: „Der ruinöse Zustand, den wir vorfanden, war nicht von Interesse, weil wir ihn wiederherstellen wollten. Wir wollten die Ruine bewahren und sie zu einem Teil des Gebäudes machen – unvollendet, als eine von vielen Schichten – und als Grundlage für eine neue Realität."

Von außen vereint ein neues großes Dach die Baukörper der alten Kooperative zu einer Einheit, während innen ein geräumiges Vestibül die drei Ebenen miteinander verbindet. Die Poesie liegt jedoch im Detail. Verblichene Farben auf Rahmen und Türen, polychrome Fliesen, ramponierte Stuckrosetten und freigelegte Putzschichtungen: Jedes Element, ob alt oder neu, erzählt eine Geschichte und trägt zur neuen Dramaturgie des Theatergebäudes bei – sowohl räumlich als auch emotional.

From dilapidated factory to architectural gem: the elaborate spaces of Sala Beckett, a showcase of how architects can thoughtfully and sensitively work with heritage architecture

Von der verfallenen Fabrik zum architektonischen Juwel: Die kunstvollen Räume der Sala Beckett, ein Vorzeigeprojekt für den architektonischen Umgang mit baukulturellem Erbe

Bar and vestibule with remnants of the past; performance space lightened up and extended with ornamental details

Bar und Vestibül mit Versatzstücken der Vergangenheit, Bühnenraum in neuem Licht mit ornamenthaften Details

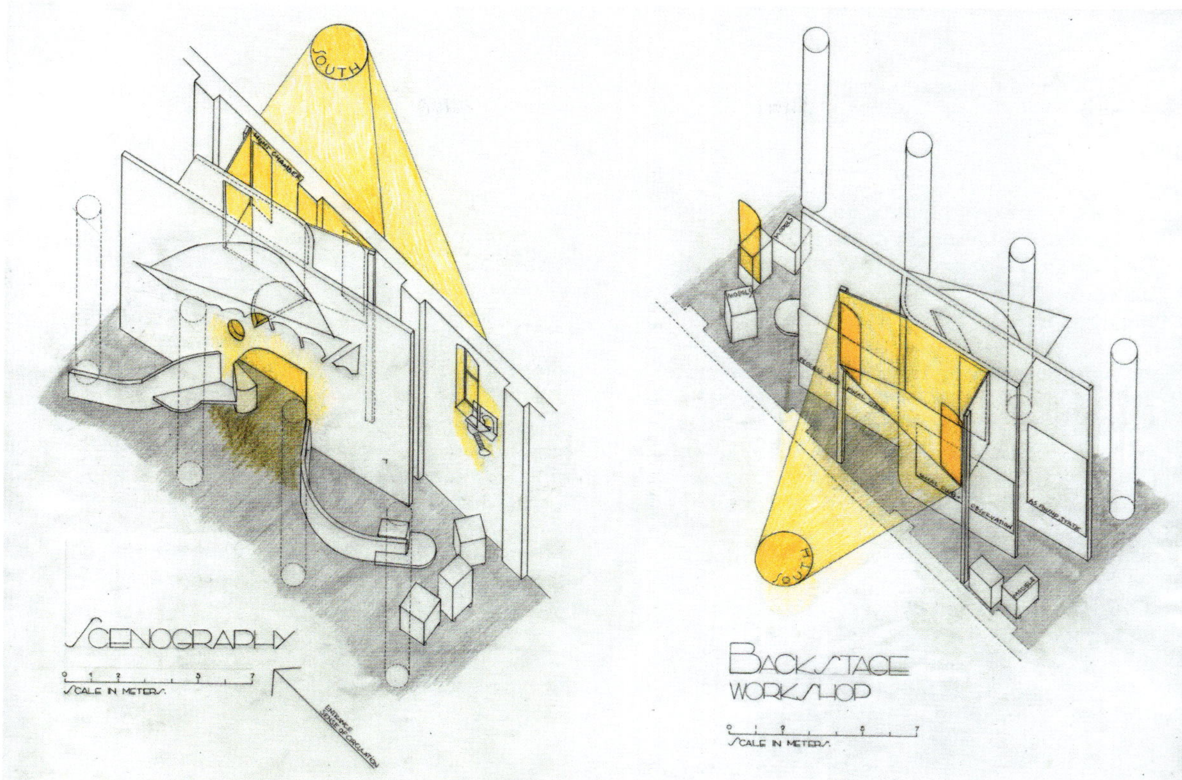

Design as research: the genesis, evolution and socio-spatial condition of the existing building bleeds into its renovation through rigorous and comprehensive processes

Design als Forschungsarbeit: Entstehung, Entwicklungsgeschichte und sozialräumlicher Zustand des Bestandsgebäudes fließen umfassend in seine Renovierung ein

09.

Project: **Her(r)bergskirchen**

City: various places in the Thuringian Forest
Client: Protestant Church in Central Germany (EKM), International Building Exhibition (IBA)
Planning: studioetcetera Berlin, Minkus Architekten Leipzig
Status: 2017-current

Building Reuse Culture
Heritage Resources Reinvigorated

In light of demographic changes and declining church membership, more and more religious buildings in Germany are being left empty. In 2017 alone, over 350,000 Germans left the Catholic and Protestant churches. In the heart of the Thuringian Forest, the increasing challenges for the future preservation and management of underused church buildings were recognised early on, with the Protestant Church of Central Germany (EKM), the International Building Exhibition (IBA) Thuringia and young architects coming together with local associations and residents to form new prototypes for future reuse: an operational model to be tested out in other rural areas.

A fresh interpretation of heritage building culture emerged: since the summer of 2007, the small parish church of Neustadt am Rennsteig has seen unexpected hybrids of spiritual and secular uses brought to life. On the famous Rennsteig trail, cyclists or hikers can now not only stay overnight in the so-called Her(r)bergskirchen, but they can also browse through the newly established village library, enjoy a meal or a film night with the village community, or take part in the weekly yoga class.

With this new symbiosis of ecclesiastical, communal and civic actors, the small town is making a strong statement: concrete proposals are needed in order to reorient the rural area - which is impacted by emigration - towards the future. The church is a third space: the reuse of freed-up spatial resources not only contributes to the maintenance of historic buildings, but also represents an entrepreneurial and cultural opportunity for communities and residents. In the coming years, the project is to be extended and developed in other church parishes.

Umnutzungskultur aufbauen
Neue Aufgaben für das Bauerbe

Angesichts der demografischen Entwicklung und abnehmender kirchlicher Mitgliedszahlen stehen immer mehr Sakralbauten in Deutschland leer: Alleine im Jahr 2017 sind über 350.000 Deutsche aus der katholischen und evangelischen Kirche ausgetreten. Inmitten des Thüringer Waldes wurden die zunehmenden Herausforderungen beim zukünftigen Erhalt und Umgang mit wenig genutzten Kirchengebäuden frühzeitig erkannt. Gemeinsam mit der Evangelischen Kirche in Mitteldeutschland (EKM), der Internationalen Bauausstellung (IBA) Thüringen sowie Fachleuten aus Architektur wurden im Zusammenwirken mit lokalen Vereinen und örtlicher Bevölkerung neue Prototypen für zukünftige Quernutzungs- und Betreibermodelle von Kirchen im ländlichen Raum erprobt.

Baukulturelles Erbe neu interpretiert: In der kleinen Gemeindekirche Neustadt am Rennsteig sind seit Sommer 2017 unerwartete Hybride aus geistlichen und weltlichen Nutzungen erlebbar. Entlang des Rennsteigs können in den sogenannten Her(r)-bergskirchen Radfahrer*innen und Wander*innen nicht nur mit traumhaftem Blick in den Kirchenhimmel übernachten, sondern beispielsweise auch in der neu eingerichteten Dorfbibliothek stöbern, mit der Dorfgemeinschaft Filmabende verbringen, ein ausgiebiges Abendessen oder den wöchentlichen Yogakurs genießen.

Mit dieser neuen Symbiose aus kirchlichen, kommunalen und zivilgesellschaftlichen Akteur*innen setzt der kleine Ort ein starkes Statement: Konkrete Lösungsvorschläge sind nötig, um den von Abwanderung geprägten ländlichen Raum zukunftsorientiert zu gestalten. Die Kirche als dritter Raum: Die Umnutzung von frei werdenden Raumressourcen trägt dabei nicht nur zur Instandhaltung historischer Bausubstanz bei, sondern stellt auch eine unternehmerische und kulturelle Chance für Gemeinden und Bewohner*innen dar. In den kommenden Jahren soll das Projekt auf weitere Kirchengemeinden ausgedehnt und weiterentwickelt werden.

Secularising consecrated grounds: from sermons to third spaces for local communities

Säkularisierung geweihter Böden: von der Predigt zum dritten Raum für die Dorfgemeinde

From church pews to bunk beds

Kirchenbank wird zum Stockbett

Absalon in Copenhagen: a former church became the centre for the local community again; 180 people from the neighbourhood come to supper every night

Absalon in Kopenhagen: Eine ehemalige Kirche wurde wieder zum Zentrum für die Nachbarschaft; bis zu 180 Personen kommen täglich zum gemeinsamen Austausch und Abendessen

10.

Project: **ICCC**
International Center for Contemporary Culture Berlin
City: Berlin
Client: N/A
Planning: Something Fantastic, Bureau N
Status: Concept/ongoing

From ICC to ICCC The Total Transformation of an Architectural Mega-icon

One of the most distinctive contemporary landmarks in Berlin, the Internationales Congress Centrum (ICC) was designed and built in 1979 by architects Ralf Schüler and Ursulina Schüler-Witte. Situated in the district of Charlottenburg-Wilmersdorf, between a highway interchange and the Messe Berlin fair grounds, the ICC is a building so tailored to its planned use that it has been called a Gesamtkunstwerk, a space-station and a machine for culture. In 2014 it was closed for the removal of asbestos and remains closed until further notice.

As a response to its state of limbo, a team that included Bureau N and Something Fantastic, developed a vision for the next iteration of the ICC and Berlin: the International Center for Contemporary Culture (ICCC). Their proposal allows the icon to unfold in all of its glory as a public and cultural engine for the city. Grounded in an intensive week-long assessment of the 30,000-square-metre building, their concept is based upon existing conference facilities reconfigured to future needs. In the near future, the ICCC will be a place where art, culture, politics and science and research come together in a venue that includes a multi-purpose concert hall; art, film and media production and exhibition spaces; university labs, co-working spaces and studios; a market place; a bookshop; apartments; a hotel; as well as restaurants and cafés.

Although such architectural megastructures - and their need for repair - can be indicative of the social, infrastructural and financial challenges contemporary cities face, they can also be a catalyst for experimentation. The ICCC looks to its own past and future, gathering vital cultures and landmarks together as a step towards re-shaping the identity of an urban district.

Vom ICC zum ICCC Die totale Transformation einer architektonischen Megaikone

Das 1979 eröffnete Internationale Congress Centrum (ICC) wurde von Ralf Schüler und Ursulina Schüler-Witte geplant. Es ist eines der architektonischen Wahrzeichen Berlins, gelegen zwischen Autobahnkreuz und Berliner Messegelände im Bezirk Charlottenburg-Wilmersdorf. Das Gebäude des ICC ist derart auf seine vorgesehene Nutzung zugeschnitten, dass es als Gesamtkunstwerk bezeichnet wird, als Raumschiff und als Kulturmaschine. 2014 wurde eine Asbestsanierung begonnen, das Gebäude ist seither ohne weitere Ankündigungen geschlossen.

In Reaktion auf diesen Schwebezustand hat ein Team aus Bureau N und Something Fantastic einen Entwurf für eine Neuauflage des ICC in Berlin vorgelegt: das International Center for Contemporary Culture (ICCC). Ihr Vorschlag soll das markante Bauwerk in all seiner Pracht als öffentlichen Ort der Kulturproduktion entfalten. Auf Grundlage einer intensiven einwöchigen Begehung der 30.000 Quadratmeter Veranstaltungsfläche gestaltet das Konzept die bestehenden Konferenzinfrastrukturen für künftige Bedarfe um. In naher Zukunft wird das ICCC ein Ort, wo Kunst, Kultur und Politik sowie Wissenschaft und Forschung an einem Ort zusammenkommen, der vieles umfasst: einen Mehrzweckkonzertsaal, Räume für Kunst-, Film- und Medienproduktion sowie Ausstellungsflächen, Universitätslabore, Gemeinschaftsbüroräume und Studios, einen Marktplatz, eine Buchhandlung, Wohnungen, ein Hotel sowie Restaurants und Cafés.

Obwohl solche architektonischen Megastrukturen – und ihr Instandsetzungsbedarf – die gesellschaftlichen, infrastrukturellen und finanziellen Herausforderungen, mit denen zeitgenössische Städte konfrontiert sind, deutlich machen, können sie zugleich Katalysatoren für Experimente sein. Das ICCC blickt auf die eigene Vergangenheit und Zukunft – es versammelt lebendige Kulturen und Architekturen für eine Neugestaltung der Identität eines Stadtbezirks.

Touching down in the 70s: the ICC's iconic architecture is now a disused megastructure between the city's highways and Berlin's Messe

Gelandet in den 70er Jahren: Die ikonische Architektur des ICC ist heute ein stillgelegtes Megabauwerk zwischen den Autobahnen der Stadt und der Berliner Messe

Retro futurism: the original signage and lightning systems of the 1970s are still intact

Retro-Futurismus: Die ursprünglichen Beschilderungs- und Beleuchtungssysteme der 1970er Jahre sind immer noch nutzbar

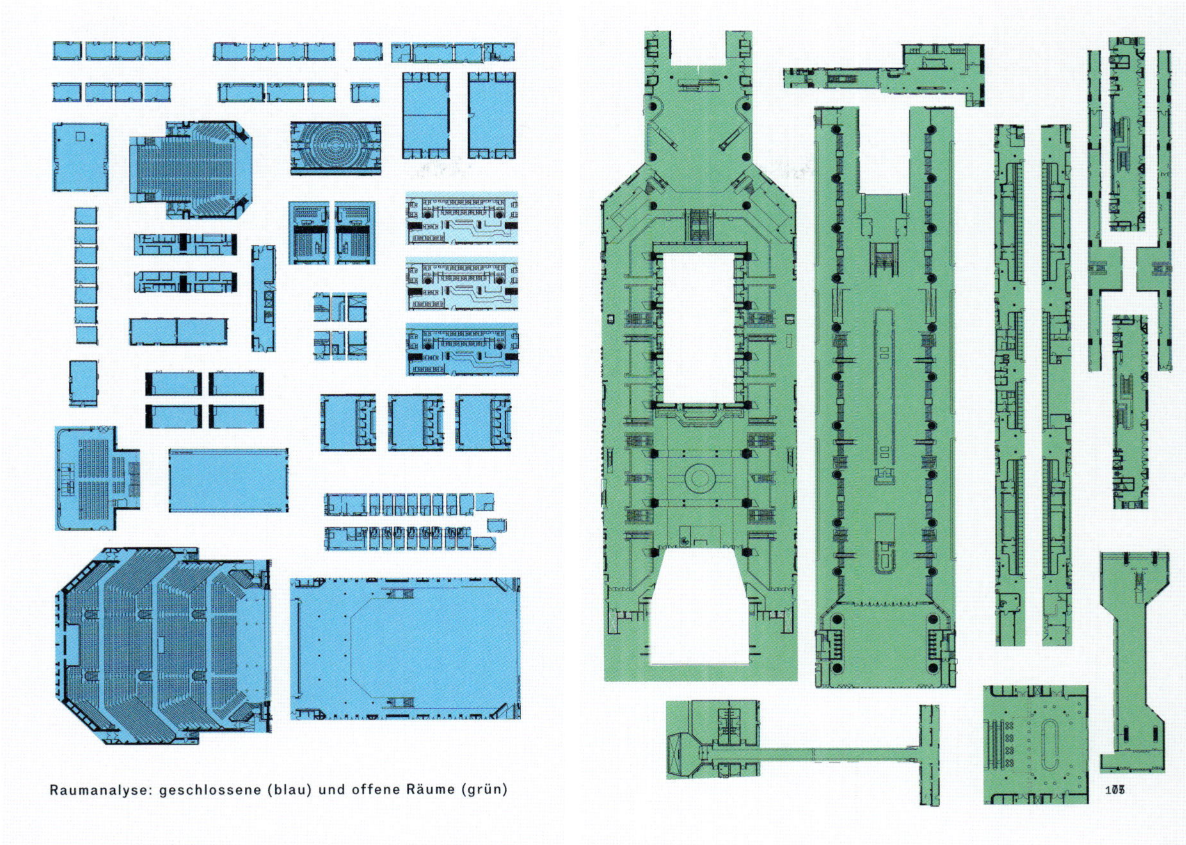

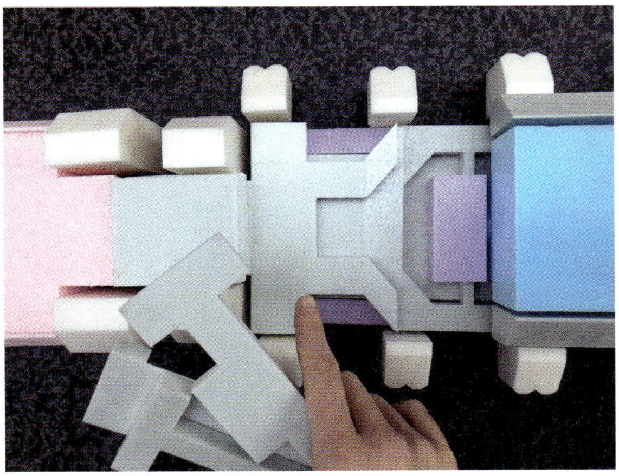

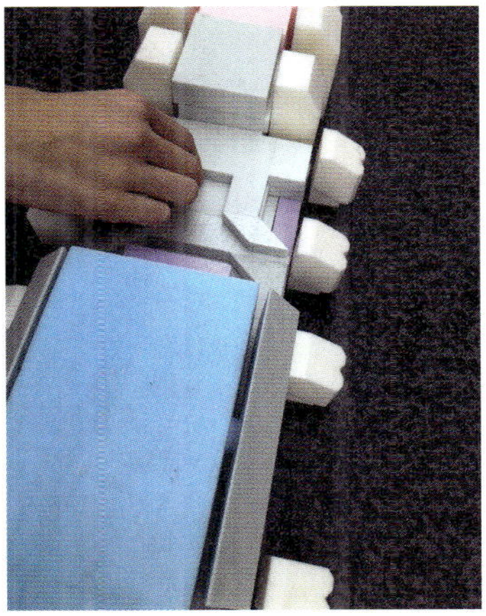

Disassembling and programmatic reconfiguration of the ICC's 30,000 square metres of facilities and spaces

Zerlegen und programmatische Neukonfiguration der Nutzungen und Räume des 30.000 Quadratmeter großen Konferenzgebäudes

Borsi, Katharina

Dr Katharina Borsi is associate professor at the University of Nottingham. Her research focuses on the intersection between housing, domesticity and the urban; the agency of architecture in urbanism; and environments for life/work, learning and innovation. She is involved in design research and consultancy and writes about housing and urbanism from historical and theoretical perspectives.
Dr. Katharina Borsi ist Professorin an der University of Nottingham. Ihre Forschungsschwerpunkte liegen an der Schnittstelle zwischen Wohnraum, Häuslichkeit und Stadt, auf der Wirkungsweise von Architektur im Städtebau und den Kontexten Leben/Arbeit, Lernen und Innovation. Sie ist in der Designforschung und -beratung tätig und schreibt über die Geschichte und Theorie des Siedlungswesens und Städtebaus.

Braun-Feldweg, Benita

Benita Braun-Feldweg is an architect who studied in Dortmund, Stuttgart and New York City. Since 1997, she has run the bfstudio-architekten office together with her husband Matthias Muffert, with a focus on living and working in inner-city areas. Through their additional responsibility as city developers, builders and designers, they utilise their concepts for mixed-use programming in working together to develop and realise what they call Metropolenhäuser.
Benita Braun-Feldweg ist Architektin (Studium in Dortmund, Stuttgart, New York). Seit 1997 führt sie zusammen mit Matthias Muffert das Büro bfstudio-architekten mit dem Fokus auf Wohnen und Arbeiten im innerstädtischen Raum. Gemeinsam entwickeln und realisieren sie – in erweiterter Verantwortung als Stadtentwickler*in, Bauherr*in und Gestalter*in – die sogenannten Metropolenhäuser mit ihren programmatischen Nutzungskonzepten.

Bria, Francesca

Francesca Bria is a senior researcher and advisor on information and technology policy. She has a PhD in innovation economics from Imperial College London, and a MSc in digital economy from Birkbeck, University of London. As senior programme lead at Nesta, she led the EU D-CENT project, the biggest European project on direct democracy and digital currencies. She is currently the new commissioner of digital technology and innovation for the City of Barcelona.
Francesca Bria ist Senior Researcher und Beraterin für Informations- und Technologiepolitik. Sie studierte Digitale Wirtschaft an der University of London, Birkbeck, und promovierte in Innovationsökonomie am Imperial College, London. Als Programmleiterin bei Nesta leitete sie das EU Projekt D-CENT zur Förderung der direkten Demokratie und digitaler Währungen und ist derzeit die neue Beauftragte für digitale Technologie und Innovation der Stadt Barcelona.

Burgdorff, Frauke

Frauke Burgdorff is a spatial planner and founder of BURGDORFF STADT – an agency for cooperative urban development that creates neighbourhood development concepts and designs new starting points for urban building components. Previously, she was founding director of Montag Stiftung Urbane Räume gAG, Urbane Nachbarschaft Samtweberei gGmbH and the initiative Stadtbaukultur NRW. She is co-chair of the Soil Policy Committee of the German Academy for Urban and Regional Planning.
Frauke Burgdorff ist Raumplanerin und Gründerin von BURGDORFF STADT – einer Agentur für kooperative Stadtentwicklung, die Quartiersentwicklungskonzepte erstellt und die Phase 0 für neue Stadtbausteine konzipiert. Vorher war sie Gründungsvorständin der Montag Stiftung Urbane Räume gAG, der Urbane Nachbarschaft Samtweberei gGmbH und der Initiative Stadtbaukultur NRW. Sie ist Ko-Vorsitzende des Ausschusses für Bodenpolitik der Deutschen Akademie für Städtebau und Landesplanung.

Casagrande, Marco

Marco Casagrande is a Finnish architect, biourbanist, social theorist and professor of architecture at Bergen School of Architecture, Norway. He is principal of the multi-disciplinary architecture and innovation office Casagrande Laboratory, with 79 realised projects in 15 different countries. He has been selected for the Venice Biennale five times and awarded prizes in several international competitions, including the UNESCO and Locus Foundation Global Award for Sustainable Architecture.
Marco Casagrande ist ein finnischer Architekt, Biourbanist, Sozialtheoretiker und Professor für Architektur an der Bergen School of Architecture, Norwegen. Er ist Leiter des multidisziplinären Architektur- und Innovationsbüros Casagrande Laboratory mit 79 realisierten Projekten in 15 verschiedenen Ländern. Er wurde fünfmal für die Biennale in Venedig ausgewählt und bei mehreren internationalen Wettbewerben und Preisen wie dem von der UNESCO und der Locus Foundation verliehenen Global Award for Sustainable Architecture 2015 ausgezeichnet.

Dahm, Daniel

Dr J. Daniel Dahm is the founder of the United Sustainability Group and initiator of the project 'Integrative Living Spaces' with Hirschmüller Schindele Architekten. He is also senior advisor to the World Future Council, member of the German Association Club of Rome, fellow at the Institute for Advanced Sustainability Studies IASS, and member of the Council of Economy for the Common Good. His new book "Benchmark Nachhaltigkeit: Sustainability Zeroline" ("Benchmark sustainability: sustainability zeroline") will be published in early 2019.
Dr. J. Daniel Dahm ist Gründer der United Sustainability Group, Initiator des Vorhabens „Integrative Lebensräume" mit Hirschmüller Schindele Architekten. Er ist Senior Advisor des World Future Council, Mitglied der Deutschen Gesellschaft Club of Rome, Fellow am Institute for Advanced Sustainability Studies (IASS), Ratsmitglied der Economy for the Common Good (ECG). Sein neues Buch „Benchmark Nachhaltigkeit: Sustainability Zeroline" erscheint Anfang 2019.

Díez, Tomás

Tomás Díez is a Venezuelan urbanist specialising in digital fabrication and its implications for future cities and society. He is the co-founder of Fab Lab Barcelona, director of the Fab City Foundation and director of the master in design for Emergent Futures study programme at the Institute for Advanced Architecture of Catalonia (IAAC) in Barcelona. Tomás is co-founder of other initiatives, including the Smart Citizen and Fablabs.io projects.
Tomás Díez ist ein venezolanischer Urbanist, der sich auf die digitale Fabrikation und deren Auswirkungen auf die zukünftigen Städte und die Gesellschaft spezialisiert hat. Er ist Mitbegründer des Fab Lab Barcelona, Direktor der Fab City Foundation und Direktor des Studiengangs Master in Design for Emergent Futures am Institute for Advanced Architecture of Catalonia (IAAC) in Barcelona. Díez ist Mitbegründer weiterer Initiativen wie Smart Citizen und Fablabs.io-Projekten.

Dillon, Teresa

Teresa Dillon is an artist, professor and researcher whose work focuses on the techno-civic – the relationships between technology, infrastructure and people. She curated HACK THE CITY in Dublin (2012) and "Anxious to Make" at the transmediale/digital cultural festival in Berlin (2016). Since 2013, Teresa Dillon has directed the international programme Urban Knights. She is currently professor of City Futures at the School of Art and Design, University of the West of England, Bristol.
Teresa Dillon ist Künstlerin, Professorin und Researcherin, deren Arbeit sich auf das „Techno-Civic", die Beziehungen zwischen Technologie, Infrastruktur und Menschen, konzentriert. Sie kuratierte HACK THE CITY in Dublin (2012) und „Anxious to Make" beim transmediale/digital culture festival (2016)

in Berlin. Seit 2013 leitet Teresa Dillon das internationale Programm Urban Knights. Derzeit ist sie Professorin für City Futures an der School of Art and Design der University of the West of England, Bristol.

Edmaier, Christine

Christine Edmaier has been president of the Berlin Chamber of Architects since 2014. She studied architecture and urban planning at the Berlin University of the Arts and has run her own studio for architecture and urban planning since 1992. Since 2015, she has also been a partner of S.E.K. Architects. She continues to strive for a more active role for architects, urbanists and landscape architects, in view of an increasingly overwhelmed Berlin administration.
Christine Edmaier ist seit 2014 Präsidentin der Architektenkammer Berlin. Sie studierte Architektur und Städtebau an der Universität der Künste Berlin und betreibt seit 2015 als Partnerin von S.E.K. Architektinnen ein eigenes Studio für Architektur und Städtebau. In ihrer Arbeit setzt sie sich für eine aktivere Rolle von Architekt*innen, Urbanist*innen und Landschaftsarchitekt*innen vor dem Hintergrund einer zunehmend überlasteten Berliner Stadtverwaltung ein.

Ferguson, Francesca

Francesca Ferguson is a curator, critic and founder of MakeCity. Coming to Berlin in 1989 as a journalist, she developed a transdisciplinary curatorial approach to architecture and urban design, with urban drift projects. She curated the festival Urban Drift in Berlin in 2002. In 2004, she curated the German pavilion at the Venice Architecture Biennale. From 2006 to 2009 she was director of the Swiss Architecture Museum in Basel, and she is currently artistic director of the Stiftung Stadtkultur in Berlin.
Francesca Ferguson ist Kuratorin, Kritikerin und Gründerin von MakeCity. Als Journalistin kam sie 1989 nach Berlin und entwickelte mit urban drift projects einen transdisziplinären kuratorischen Ansatz für Architektur und Stadtgestaltung. 2002 kuratierte sie das Festival urban drift in Berlin, 2004 den Deutschen Pavillon auf der Architekturbiennale Venedig. Von 2006 bis 2009 war sie Direktorin des Schweizerischen Architekturmuseums in Basel und ist derzeit künstlerische Direktorin der Stiftung Stadtkultur in Berlin.

Finkbeiner, Jörg

Jörg Finkbeiner is an architect who has completed an apprenticeship in carpentry and holds an architectural degree from the Technical University of Berlin. Since 2006, he has been co-director of Partner und Partner Architekten. The office specialises in timber construction and sustainable construction according to C2C. Jörg Finkbeiner has been a Cradle to Cradle consultant since 2011, making him one of the pioneers of the C2C idea in the field of architecture in Germany. He is also a speaker on sustainability.
Jörg Finkbeiner ist Dipl.-Ing. Architekt und absolvierte eine Ausbildung zum Schreiner sowie ein Architekturstudium an der TU Berlin. Seit 2006 ist er Ko-Geschäftsführer von Partner und Partner Architekten. Das Büro ist spezialisiert auf Holzbau und nachhaltiges Bauen nach C2C. Seit 2011 ist Jörg Finkbeiner Cradle to Cradle Consultant und gehört damit zu den Pionieren der C2C-Idee im Bereich Architektur in Deutschland. Er ist außerdem Referent zum Thema Nachhaltigkeit.

Fröhlich, Anja

Anja Fröhlich is an architect who holds a doctorate in engineering. Since 2012, she has been professor of architecture and design at the Faculty of Architecture, Civil and Environmental Engineering of the École polytechnique fédérale de Lausanne (EPFL). Together with Martin Fröhlich, she runs Atelier EAST at the Institute of Architecture and Urban Planning. She also engages in practical work as part of AFF Architects in Berlin.
Anja Fröhlich ist Architektin und Doktorin der Ingenieurwissenschaften. Seit 2012 ist sie Professorin für Architektur und Entwurf an der Fakultät für Architektur, Bau- und Umweltingenieurwesen der École polytechnique fédérale de Lausanne (EPFL). Dort leitet sie gemeinsam mit Martin Fröhlich das Atelier EAST am Institut für Architektur und Stadt. Die Brücke zur praktischen Tätigkeit schlägt sie im Team von AFF Architekten in Berlin.

Frohn, Marc

Marc Frohn is co-founder of FAR frohn& rojas, an architectural practice that operates between Berlin, Santiago and Los Angeles. His work has been exhibited internationally. Marc Frohn has been awarded the RIBA National Award, the Architectural League Prize for Young Architects and the DETAIL-Preis. He has taught at SCI-Arc in Los Angeles and the Royal College of Art in London. Since 2014, he has been a professor at the Karlsruhe Institute of Technology.
Marc Frohn ist Mitgründer des Architekturbüros FAR frohn&rojas, welches als vernetzte architektonische Praxis zwischen Berlin, Santiago de Chile und Los Angeles operiert. Seine Arbeiten werden international ausgestellt. Marc Frohn wurde mit dem RIBA National Award, dem Architectural League Prize for Young Architects sowie dem DETAIL-Preis ausgezeichnet. Er unterrichtete an der SCI-Arc in Los Angeles und am Royal College in London. Seit 2014 ist er Professor am Karlsruher Institut für Technologie.

Gil-Fournier, Mauro

Mauro Gil-Fournir is an architect based in Madrid and co-founder of estudio [SIC] Architecture and Urbanism, a multidisciplinary practice focused upon architecture, city and urban territory, and civic engagement.
Mauro Gil-Fournir ist Architekt mit Sitz in Madrid und Mitbegründer von estudio [SIC], einem Studio mit multidisziplinärer Praxis, das Architektur, Stadtentwicklung und bürgerschaftliches Engagement verbindet.

Grau, Dieter

Dieter Grau is a landscape architect and Managing Partner of Ramboll Studio Dreiseitl. For more than 25 years, he has been committed to realising sustainability and outstanding design in his landscape architecture projects - which received the German Design Award in 2018. Dieter Grau lectures worldwide and is the author of several books including "Recent Waterscapes: Planning, Building and Designing with Water".
Dieter Grau ist Landschaftsarchitekt und geschäftsführender Partner von Ramboll Studio Dreiseitl. Seit über 25 Jahren ist es ihm ein Anliegen, Landschaftsarchitektur, Nachhaltigkeit und herausragendes Design in seinen Projekten zu verwirklichen, welche mit dem German Design Award 2018 ausgezeichnet wurden. Dieter Grau hält weltweit Vorträge und ist Autor diverser Publikationen, wie dem Buch „Recent Waterscapes: Planning, Building and Designing with Water".

Grawert, Olaf

Olaf Grawert studied architecture and urban planning with a focus on theory and urban research. He lives and works in Zurich and Berlin as a planner and author and teaches at the Department of Architecture at ETH Zurich. Since 2015 he worked with Brandlhuber+ on various projects, including the film series "Legislating Architecture". Olaf Grawert is co-editor of the WIA platform and has spoken at numerous events about the social role of architects.
Olaf Grawert studierte Architektur und Städteplanung mit den Schwerpunkten Theorie und Stadtforschung und ist Planer und Autor. Er lebt und arbeitet in Zürich und Berlin und lehrt am Departement Architektur der ETH Zürich. Seit 2015 arbeitet er mit Brandlhuber+ an verschiedenen Projekten wie der Filmreihe „Legislating Architecture". Olaf Grawert ist Ko-Redakteur der Plattform WIA und sprach im Rahmen zahlreicher Veranstaltungen über die gesellschaftliche Rolle der Architekt*innen.

Griffin, Matthew

Matthew Griffin is an architect, curator, artist, programmer, project developer, urban planner and co-founder of Deadline Architects. He studied architecture at McGill University in Montreal and the Architectural Association in London. Matthew Griffin is co-founder of the gallery URBAN Issue and the blog LocallyGrownCity.net and has been involved in various initiatives – including TeamEleven and Stadt Neudenken.

Matthew Griffin ist Architekt, Kurator, Künstler, Programmierer, Projektentwickler, Stadtplaner und Mitbegründer von Deadline Architekten. Er studierte Architektur an der McGill University in Montreal und an der Architectural Association School of Architecture in London. Matthew Griffin ist Mitbegründer der Galerie URBAN Issue und des Blogs LocallyGrownCity.net. Außerdem ist er in verschiedenen Initiativen tätig, unter anderem TeamEleven und der Initiative Stadt Neudenken.

Hansen, Simikka

Simikka Hansen is a Berlin-based city planner with an interest in sustainable mobility. With a background in city planning and communication from Roskilde University in Denmark, she focuses on how transport planning affects the public space in cities around the world. Recently, amongst other organisations, she has worked for the German cycling federation ADFC advocating for cycling in Berlin.

Simikka Hansen ist eine Berliner Stadtplanerin, die sich für nachhaltige Mobilität interessiert. Mit einer Ausbildung in Stadtplanung und Kommunikation an der Roskilde Universität in Dänemark konzentriert sie sich auf die Auswirkungen der Verkehrsplanung auf den öffentlichen Raum in Städten auf der ganzen Welt. Kürzlich arbeitete sie für den Allgemeinen Deutschen Fahrrad-Club, um den Radverkehr in Berlin zu fördern.

Hofmann, Susanne

Susanne Hofmann is an architect, professor and founder of the Berlin-based architectural office Baupiloten BDA. She studied architecture at the Technical University of Munich, the Architectural Association School of Architecture in London as well as the Technical University of Berlin. In 2013 was the recipient of a Villa Massimo scholarship. She has taught as a visiting professor in London, Melbourne and Sheffield. In 2014 she published the handbook "Partizipation Macht Architektur".

Susanne Hofmann ist Architektin, Professorin und Inhaberin des Berliner Architekturbüros die Baupiloten BDA. Sie studierte Architektur an der Technischen Universität München und an der Architectural Association School of Architecture in London sowie an der TU Berlin. 2013 war sie Stipendiatin der Villa Massimo. Als Gastprofessorin unterrichtete sie unter anderem in London, Melbourne und Sheffield. 2014 erschien ihr Handbuch „Partizipation Macht Architektur".

Hunchuck, Elise

Elise Hunchuck is a Berlin-based independent researcher, designer and editor with an academic background in landscape architecture and philosophy. Her research develops cartographic, photographic and text-based practices to explore and communicate the agency of disasters through continually configuring and reconfiguring infrastructures of risk. Elise Hunchuck has taught at the University of Toronto, she is a 2019 Azrieli Visiting Critic at Carleton University's Azrieli School of Architecture and Urbanism and a member of the editorial board of Scapegoat Journal: Architecture | Landscape | Political Economy.

Elise Hunchuck ist eine unabhängige Forscherin, Designerin und Editorin mit einem Universitätsabschluss in Landschaftsarchitektur und Philosophie. Ihre Forschung entwickelt kartografische, fotografische und textbasierte Praktiken zur Erforschung und Kommunikation der Auswirkungen von Katastrophen durch die kontinuierliche Konfiguration und Rekonfiguration von Risikoinfrastrukturen. Elise Hunchuck hat an der University of Toronto gelehrt, ist 2018 bis 2019 Azrieli Visiting Critic an der Carleton University und Mitglied des Editorial Board der Zeitschrift Scapegoat: Architecture | Landscape | Political Economy.

Jessen, Nadine

Nadine Jessen has worked as a dramaturge and curator at Kampnagel since 2007, including a short tenure at the Vienna Festival in 2017. She initiates and realises spaces and projects in various constellations, including Hamamness (with Jens Dietrich), Akademie des Verlernens (with Johannes Maile) and Migrantpolitan (with Larry Macaulay), and she founded the independent media group New Media Socialism (with Judith Rau).

Nadine Jessen arbeitet seit 2007 als Dramaturgin und Kuratorin für Kampnagel mit einem kurzen Ausflug an die Wiener Festwochen 2017. Sie initiiert und realisiert Räume und Projekte in unterschiedlichen Konstellationen: Hamamness (mit Jens Dietrich), Akademie des Verlernens (mit Johannes Maile), Migrantpolitan (mit Larry Macaulay). Sie ist die Gründerin der freien Mediengruppe New Media Socialism (mit Judith Rau).

Jürgens, Britta

Britta Jürgens is an architect and co-founder of Deadline Architects. After studying architecture at Technical University of Berlin, she worked in Melbourne for Norman Day Architects and in London for Alsop & Lyall Architects. The "self-made city" has been the focus of Jürgen's work ever since, both in the context of initiatives such as the URBAN issue gallery, and with her own project developments including the current Frizz23 industrial building group project.

Britta Jürgens ist Architektin und Mitgründerin von Deadline Architekten. Nach dem Architekturstudium an der TU Berlin arbeitete sie in Melbourne bei Norman Day Architects und in London bei Alsop & Lyall Architects. Die „selbst gemachte Stadt" ist seither der Fokus von Jürgens' Arbeit sowohl im Rahmen von Initiativen, wie der Galerie URBAN Issue, als auch mit eigenen Projektentwicklungen, aktuell dem Gewerbebaugruppenprojekt Frizz23.

Kaufmann, Hermann

Hermann Kaufmann is an architect. The central theme of his work is the search for comprehensive answers to the topics of sustainability in building and the exploration of the possibilities of modern wood construction. Together with Christian Lenz, he founded the architectural office of HK Architects in Schwarzach, Austria, in 1983. Since 2002, he has been professor at the Department of Design and Wood Construction at the Technical University of Munich.

Hermann Kaufmann ist Architekt und Professor. Zentrale Themen in seinen Arbeiten sind die Suche nach umfassenden Antworten zu den Themen Nachhaltigkeit des Bauens und das Ausloten der Möglichkeiten des modernen Holzbaus. 1983 gründete er das Architekturbüro HK Architekten gemeinsam mit Christian Lenz in Schwarzach, Österreich. Seit 2002 ist er Professor am Lehrstuhl für Entwerfen und Holzbau an der Technischen Universität München.

Klerk, Eva de

Eva de Klerk is a cultural entrepreneur, independent expert on participative urban development and the engine behind the self-organised Art City/NDSM shipyard in northern Amsterdam. Together with 100 companies, shipyards, developers, gastronomy companies and cultural entrepreneurs, she founded NDSM Energie – a cooperative for renewable energy. Eva is the author of the book "Make Your City: De Stad als Casco/The City as a Shell", published by Trancity.

Eva de Klerk ist Kulturunternehmerin, selbstständige Fachfrau für partizipative Stadtentwicklung und die treibende Kraft hinter der selbstorganisierten Art City/NDSM-Werft

im Norden von Amsterdam. Zusammen mit hundert Unternehmen, Schiffbauer*innen, Entwickler*innen, Gastronomiebetrieben und Kulturunternehmer*innen gründete sie NDSM Energie, eine Genossenschaft für erneuerbare Energie. Eva de Klerk ist Autorin des Buches „Make Your City: De Stad als Casco / The City as a Shell".

Knie, Andreas

Dr Andreas Knie is a social scientist, professor, and head of the Science Policy Research Group of the Social Science Research Centre Berlin (WZB), where he focuses on the areas of mobility research, technology policy, science policy and innovation research. He founded the Innovation Centre for Mobility and Social Change (InnoZ) in 2005 and has taught sociology at the Technical University of Berlin since 2000.
Dr. Andreas Knie ist Sozialwissenschaftler, Professor und Leiter der Forschungsgruppe Wissenschaftspolitik des Wissenschaftszentrums Berlin für Sozialforschung (WZB). Thematisch setzt er sich mit den Schwerpunkten Verkehrsforschung, Technologiepolitik, Wissenschaftspolitik und Innovationsforschung auseinander. 2005 gründete er das Innovationszentrum für Mobilität und gesellschaftlichen Wandel GmbH (InnoZ) und lehrt seit 2000 am Fachbereich Soziologie an der TU Berlin.

Krasny, Elke

Dr Elke Krasny is a cultural theorist, urban researcher, curator and professor at the Academy of Fine Arts Vienna. She holds a PhD from the University of Reading, England. Her curatorial work includes "Critical Care: Architecture and Urbanism for a Broken Planet" (2019) with Angelika Fitz, and "Hands-On Urbanism: The Right to Green" at the 2012 Venice Biennale. She recently published "Citizenship and the Museum: On Feminist Acts" and "Modernist Green: Changing Regimes of Labour".
Dr. Elke Krasny ist Kulturtheoretikerin, Stadtforscherin, Kuratorin und Professorin an der Akademie der bildenden Künste Wien. Sie promovierte an der University of Reading in England. Zu ihren kuratorischen Arbeiten gehören: „Critical Care: Architecture and Urbanism for a Broken Planet" (2019) mit Angelika Fitz und „Hands-on Urbanism: The Right to Green" bei der Biennale in Venedig 2012. Jüngst veröffentlichte sie „Citizenship and the Museum: On Feminist Acts" und „Modernist Green: Changing Regimes of Labour".

Kühne, Manfred

Manfred Kühne is an architect, urban planner and since 2008, the head of urban planning and projects for the Berlin Senate Department for Urban Development and Housing. After studying architecture in Kaiserslautern and Berlin, he worked as a freelance urban planner in Berlin. He later worked as head of urban planning for Stralsund and at the Supreme Monument Protection Authority in the Senate Department for Urban Development and Housing in Berlin. He is a member of the German Association for Town, Region and State Planning (SRL) and the German Academy for Urban and Regional Spatial Planning (DASL).
Manfred Kühne ist Architekt, Stadtplaner und seit 2008 Leiter der Abteilung Städtebau und Projekte der Senatsverwaltung für Stadtentwicklung Berlin. Nach seinem Studium der Architektur in Kaiserslautern und Berlin war er als freiberuflicher Stadtplaner in Berlin tätig. Danach arbeitete er als Leiter der Stadtplanung von Stralsund und der Obersten Denkmalschutzbehörde in der Senatsverwaltung für Stadtentwicklung in Berlin. Er ist Mitglied in der SRL und der DASL.

Künast, Renate

Renate Künast has been a member of the nineteenth German Bundestag since September 2017. She was federal minister for consumer protection, food and agriculture from 2001 to 2005 and was the top candidate of the Green Party in Berlin for the parliamentary elections of 2013. Renate Künast led the parliamentary group of the Green Party for two legislative periods. Her work was awarded the Rachel Carson Prize in 2001 and the Michael Kay Award in 2005.
Renate Künast ist seit September 2017 Mitglied des gewählten 19. Bundestages. Sie war von 2001 bis 2005 Bundesministerin für Verbraucherschutz, Ernährung und Landwirtschaft und ging als Spitzenkandidatin der Berliner Grünen in die Bundestagswahl 2013. Renate Künast führte die Fraktion über den Zeitraum von zwei Legislaturperioden. Ihre Arbeit wurde unter anderem mit dem Rachel Carson Prize 2001 und Michael Kay Award 2005 ausgezeichnet.

Kundoo, Anupama

Since 1990 Dr Anupama Kundoo's architecture practice has been focused on material research to achieve architecture with a low environmental impact, and on the development of building technologies that have clear socio-economic benefits. Her work extends to urban design and planning projects, drawing on her background in development issues related to rapid urbanisation about which she has written extensively. She is currently professor at the University of Applied Sciences, Potsdam.
Das 1990 gegründete Architekturbüro von Anupama Kundoo zeigt einen starken Fokus auf die Materialforschung zur Realisierung einer umweltfreundlichen Architektur und die Entwicklung von sozioökonomisch nachhaltigen Bautechnologien. Ihre Arbeit erstreckt sich auf Urban Design und Städtebauprojekte. Sie setzt sich mit Entwicklungsfragen einer rapide zunehmenden Urbanisation auseinander, worüber sie ausführlich publizierte. Derzeit ist sie Professorin an der Fachhochschule Potsdam.

Lompscher, Katrin

Katrin Lompscher is a city planner involved in Berlin's development since 1987 and she has been senator for urban development and housing in Berlin since 2016. Between 2006 and 2011, she was senator for health, environment and consumer protection.
Katrin Lompscher ist seit 2016 Senatorin für Stadtentwicklung und Wohnen in Berlin. Sie ist Stadtplanerin und begleitet seit 1987 die Entwicklung Berlins. Von 2006 bis 2011 war sie Senatorin für Gesundheit, Umwelt und Verbraucherschutz.

Lotter, Wolf

Wolf Lotter is a business journalist and author. He is one of the co-founders of the business magazine Brandeins (1999), where he has been responsible for features since 2000. He has been describing the transformation from industry to a science-based society for three decades. His current book "Innovation: Streitschrift für barrierefreies Denken" ("Innovation: polemic for barrier-free thinking") was published in April 2018.
Wolf Lotter ist Wirtschaftsjournalist und Buchautor. Er gehört zu den Mitbegründern des Wirtschaftsmagazins Brandeins (1999), für das er seit 2000 die Leitartikel verantwortet. Er beschreibt seit drei Jahrzehnten den Wandel von der Industrie- zur Wissensgesellschaft. Sein aktuelles Buch „Innovation: Streitschrift für barrierefreies Denken" erschien im April 2018.

Ludloff, Jens /
Fogarasi-Ludloff, Laura

Ludloff Ludloff Architects was founded in 2007 by Laura Fogarasi-Ludloff and Jens Ludloff in Berlin. Their projects are part of a research-based practice and contribute to the discourse on a new vision policy in which building can succeed as a social practice. Their embassy for children won the BDA Prize Berlin in 2018, has been nominated for the Mies van der Rohe Award 2019 and is on the shortlist for the DAM Prize 2019.
Ludloff Ludloff Architekten wurde 2007 von Laura Fogarasi-Ludloff und Jens Ludloff in Berlin gegründet. Ihre Projekte sind Teil einer forschenden Praxis und tragen zum Diskurs über eine neue Bildpolitik bei, mit der Bauen als soziale Praxis gelingen kann. Für ihre Botschaft für Kinder wurden sie 2018 mit dem BDA Preis Berlin ausge-

zeichnet, das Projekt ist nominiert für den Mies van der Rohe Award 2019 und auf der Shortlist für den DAM-Preis 2019.

Marijnissen, Robert

Robert Marijnissen is an urban geographer and planner. As a Board member of The Rotterdam Council for Art and Culture he advises on art policy issues that integrate cultural, social, economic and urban development. Currently, he is working on the principles and practices of co-creative urban development.
Robert Marijnissen ist Stadtgeograf und Stadtplaner. Als Vorstandsmitglied des Rotterdamer Rates für Kunst und Kultur berät er zu kunstpolitischen Themen, die kulturelle, soziale, wirtschaftliche und städtische Entwicklungen integrieren. Derzeit arbeitet er an den Prinzipien und Praktiken der ko-kreativen Stadtentwicklung.

Niedenthal, Clemens

Clemens Niedenthal was born and raised near Marburg, Germany, and works as a journalist and cultural critic in Berlin. His passion lies in objects and the circumstances surrounding them – in food, above all else. He is editor-in-chief of the food section of the Berlin magazine Tip.
Clemens Niedenthal ist geboren und aufgewachsen bei Marburg und lebt als Journalist und Kulturwissenschaftler in Berlin. Seine Leidenschaft gilt den Dingen und den Verhältnissen darum herum, vor allem den Lebensmitteln. Für das Berliner Stadtmagazin Tip betreut er als leitender Redakteur das Food-Ressort.

Pouzenc, Joanne

Joanne Pouzenc is an architect, curator and lecturer. Some of her curatorial projects include Berlin Unlimited, festival for arts, architecture and urban research in 2014, and as co-curator of the conference "Public Space: Fights and Fictions", a collaboration between the Akademie der Künste and the Goethe Institute in 2016. From 2017 to 2018, she coordinated and curated the programme projekt bauhaus in collaboration with Arch+. Since 2006, she has taught at the École nationale supérieure d'architecture (ENSA) in Toulouse, France.
Joanne Pouzenc ist Architektin, Kuratorin und Dozentin. Zu ihren kuratorischen Projekten zählen: 2014 Berlin Unlimited, festival for arts, architecture and urban research in Berlin und 2016 (als Ko-Kuratorin) die Konferenz Public Space: Fights and Fictions, eine Kooperation der Akademie der Künste mit dem Goethe-Institut. 2017 bis 2018 koordinierte und kuratierte sie das Programm projekt bauhaus in Zusammenarbeit mit Arch+. Seit 2006 lehrt sie an der École nationale supérieure d'architecture (ENSA) in Toulouse, Frankreich.

Prosser, Sarah

Dr Sarah Prosser currently works for the Department of Urban Planning, Oslo Municipality. She founded the community incubator Tøyen Unlimited and is a key voice in the wider national development of the fields of social innovation, co-creation and participation. She previously founded the film festival Human Rights Human Wrongs and worked as Director for the British Council Norway.
Dr. Sarah Prosser ist Gründerin von Tøyen Unlimited und ist derzeit in der Stadtplanungsabteilung der Stadtverwaltung Oslo tätig. Sie gründete den Gemeinschaftsinkubator Tøyen Unlimited und ist eine maßgebliche Stimme bei der landesweiten Entwicklung der Bereiche soziale Innovation, Ko-Kreation und Partizipation. Zuvor gründete sie das Filmfestival Human Rights Human Wrongs und arbeitete als Direktorin des British Council Norway.

Rein-Cano, Martin

Martin Rein-Cano is a landscape architect and founder of Topotek 1. The office is rooted in the design of urban open spaces, the development of urban projects, as well as the conception and realisation of architectural projects and installations. A number of studies have been published on the work of Topotek 1, which has received numerous awards. Martin Rein-Cano currently teaches at the Dessau Institute of Architecture.
Martin Rein-Cano ist Landschaftsarchitekt und Gründer des Büros Topotek 1. Das Büro ist im Feld der Gestaltung urbaner Freiräume und der Bearbeitung städtebaulicher Themen verwurzelt sowie in der Konzeption und Realisierung von Architekturprojekten und Installationen tätig. Etliche Fachliteratur wurde speziell über die Arbeit von Topotek 1 publiziert, die auch mit verschiedenen Preisen ausgezeichnet wurde. Zurzeit unterrichtet Martin Rein-Cano am Dessau Institute of Architecture.

Robel, Steffan

Steffan Robel is a landscape architect and founder of A24 Landschaft. After studying landscape planning at the Technical University of Berlin and then in the Netherlands, he worked as a research assistant at the the Technical University of Dresden. He founded A24 Landschaft in 2005, receiving the IAKS Gold Award 2017 and a German Urban Development Award in 2016. Steffan Robel's writings have been published by Topos, Anthos and Paysage, among others.
Steffan Robel ist Landschaftsarchitekt und Gründer von A24 Landschaft. Er studierte Landschaftsplanung an der TU Berlin und in den Niederlanden. Er arbeitete als wissenschaftlicher Mitarbeiter an der TU Dresden und gründete 2005 das Büro A24 Landschaft, welches mit dem IAKS Award Gold 2017 und dem Deutschen Städtebaupreis 2016 prämiert wurde. Steffan Robel publiziert umfangreich bei verschiedenen Verlagen.

Roswag-Klinge, Eike

Eike Roswag-Klinge is an architect and professor at the Technical University (TU) of Berlin. He founded the Natural Building Lab at TU Berlin in 2017 and co-founded ZRS Architekten Ingenieure in 2003, where he is currently managing director. With his teams, he undertakes research, planning and built projects in diverse global contexts with a focus on holistic, climate-adaptive design solutions that allow for the reduction of technology.
Eike Roswag-Klinge ist Architekt und Professor an der TU Berlin. 2017 gründete er das Natural Building Lab an der TU Berlin und 2003 die Architektengemeinschaft ZRS Architekten Ingenieure, wo er bis heute Geschäftsführer ist. Mit internationalen Netzwerken erforscht, plant und realisiert er Projekte in unterschiedlichen Kulturen als klimaangepasste Gebäude aus Naturbaustoffen, um weitestgehend auf Gebäudetechnik verzichten zu können.

Saaby, Tina

Tina Saaby has been chief city architect of Copenhagen since September 2010. She inspires, facilitates, advises and coaches politicians and city administrators. As chief city architect, she supports the agenda of developing a sustainable and liveable city by engaging in the creation of a resilient strategic framework for future city development. Tina Saaby is chairwoman of the think tank Green Identity and Urban Nature in Copenhagen.
Tina Saaby war vor 2010 bis Ende 2018 Chefplanerin der Stadt Kopenhagen. Sie unterstützt, berät und coacht Politiker*innen und die Stadtverwaltung. Als Chefplanerin zeichnet sie für die Agenda zur Entwicklung einer nachhaltigen und lebenswerten Stadt verantwortlich und setzt sich für die Schaffung eines widerstandsfähigen strategischen Rahmens für die Stadtentwicklung ein. Tina Saaby ist Vorsitzende des Think Tanks „Green Identity and Urban Nature" in Kopenhagen.

Sack, Florentine

Dr Florentine Sack is the founder of the research and design studio open house and an independent architect, theorist and author. She is interested in the relationships between people and the environment in architecture and their influence on our quality of life. Her numerous publications reveal just how diverse the possibilities are for realising these relationships in international

works of architecture and how they can be compared through the use of design criteria. She lectures internationally and teaches at various European universities.
Florentine Sack ist Gründerin von open house und selbstständige Architektin, Theoretikerin und Autorin. Sie interessiert sich für die Bezüge zwischen Mensch und Umwelt in der Architektur und ihren Einfluss auf unsere Lebensqualität. In mehreren Publikationen zeigt sie, wie vielfältig diese in internationalen Beispielen umsetzbar und mit Gestaltungskriterien vergleichbar sind. Sie hält international Vorträge und lehrt an verschiedenen europäischen Hochschulen.

Schmidt, Florian

Florian Schmidt is an urban sociologist, construction city councillor for Friedrichshain-Kreuzberg, head of the Department for Construction, Planning and Facility Management and founder of the initiative Stadt Neudenken. He coordinated the department of sustainable urban development of the Bildungswerk Berlin – part of the Heinrich Böll Foundation – and directed the project office Kreativquartier Südliche Friedrichstadt. In addition, he was atelier representative for Berlin and head of the Atelierbüro of bbk-kulturwerk.
Florian Schmidt ist Stadtsoziologe, Baustadtrat für Friedrichshain-Kreuzberg, Leiter der Abteilung für Bauen, Planen und Facility Management und Gründer der Initiative Stadt Neudenken. Er koordinierte den Bereich nachhaltige Stadtentwicklung des Bildungswerks Berlin der Heinrich-Böll-Stiftung und leitete das Projektbüro Kreativquartier Südliche Friedrichstadt. Außerdem war er Atelierbeauftragter für Berlin und Leiter des Atelierbüros im bbk-kulturwerk.

Srock.Stanley, Nicole

Nicole Srock.Stanley is co-founder of the dan pearlman Group (1999), a group of owner-led, strategic creative agencies. Within the agency group, she is CEO of dan pearlman Markenarchitektur GmbH and is responsible for brand and corporate strategy. As a speaker at conferences, she provides answers to the question of how stationary retail can be transformed with the mechanisms of the modern leisure industry.
Nicole Srock.Stanley ist Mitgründerin der dan pearlman Group (1999) – einer Gruppe inhaber*innengeführter, strategischer Kreativagenturen. Innerhalb der Agenturgruppe ist sie als CEO der dan pearlman Markenarchitektur GmbH tätig und verantwortet übergeordnet die Bereiche Marken- und Unternehmensstrategie. Als Referentin auf Konferenzen gibt sie Antworten auf die Frage, wie sich der stationäre Handel mit den Mechanismen der modernen Freizeitindustrie revolutionieren lässt.

Staudinger, Lukas

Lukas Staudinger is an architect, sociologist and urban communicator. He has taught at universities for several years. In 2018 he founded the Berlin practice Poligonal Office for Urban Communication together with Dr Christian Haid. In that capacity he plans and moderates workshops, seminars, city walks and architectural events. He is an expert in historical and contemporary housing, post-war urban planning, architectural heritage and everyday urban life.
Lukas Staudinger ist Architekt, Soziologe und Stadtvermittler. Er hat an mehreren Architekturuniversitäten gelehrt und gründete 2018 zusammen mit Christian Haid das Berliner Büro Poligonal Agentur für Stadtvermittlung, in dessen Rahmen er Workshops, Seminare, Stadtführungen und Architekturveranstaltungen plant und moderiert. Zu seinen Themenschwerpunkten zählen historischer und zeitgenössischer Wohnungsbau, Städtebau der Nachkriegszeit, Baukulturerbe und urbanes Alltagsleben.

Steiger, Tina

Tina Steiger has a master's in urban studies and most recently worked as associate curator for MakeCity Festival 2018, for the UN Refugee Agency (UNHCR) and as external lecturer at Copenhagen University and HafenCity University Hamburg. Based in Denmark, she is involved in a number of cultural projects exploring concepts of autonomy, migration and urban politics throughout Europe.
Tina Steiger hat den Titel Master of Arts in Urbanistik inne und war zuletzt als Associate Curator beim MakeCity Festival 2018, der UN-Flüchtlingsorganisation (UNHCR) sowie als externe Dozentin an der Universität Kopenhagen und der HafenCity Universität Hamburg tätig. Sie lebt in Dänemark und ist an mehreren kulturellen Projekten beteiligt, die sich mit den Themen Autonomie, Migration und Stadtpolitik im europäischen Raum beschäftigen.

Talevi, Rosario

Rosario Talevi is a Berlin-based architect interested in critical spatial practice, transformative pedagogies and feminist futures, which she applies through various spatial, editorial and curatorial strategies. She has held teaching and research positions at the Technical University of Berlin and the University of Buenos Aires. She is currently acting as a research associate at the Space Production Studio at the Berlin University of the Arts.
Rosario Talevi ist eine in Berlin arbeitende Architektin, die sich für kritische Raumpraxis, transformative Pädagogik und feministische Zukunft interessiert, die sie durch verschiedene räumliche, redaktionelle und kuratorische Strategien anwendet. Sie war in Lehr- und Forschungspositionen an der Technischen Universität Berlin und der Universität Buenos Aires tätig. Derzeit ist sie wissenschaftliche Mitarbeiterin im Raumfahrtproduktionsstudio der Universität der Künste Berlin.

Unger, Nora

Nora Unger studied applied cultural sciences and urban design in Lüneburg, Arles, Hamburg and Brussels. As an urban researcher, she deals with practices of participation, collective urban design and water surfaces as public space. She collaborates with a number of projects and artistic collectives that operate between art, architecture and urban design (such as HALLO: Festspiele, geheimagentur). She is a visiting lecturer at Hamburg HafenCity University.
Nora Unger studierte Angewandte Kulturwissenschaften und Urban Design in Lüneburg, Arles, Hamburg und Brüssel. Als Stadtforscherin beschäftigt sie sich mit Praktiken der Teilhabe, kollektiver Stadtgestaltung und Wasserflächen als öffentlichem Raum. Gemeinsam mit künstlerischen Kollektiven arbeitet sie an Projekten, die zwischen Kunst, Architektur und Stadtgestaltung agieren (zum Beispiel HALLO: Festspiele, geheimagentur). Sie lehrt an der HafenCity Universität in Hamburg.

Vassal, Jean-Philippe

Jean-Philippe Vassal is an architect and has been a professor at the Berlin University of the Arts since 2012. He worked as an urban planner in Niger from 1980 to 1985. Together with Anne Lacaton, he opened the office Lacaton&Vassal in 1987, which has an international practice and works on various programmes of public buildings, housing and urban planning. With Lacaton & Vassal, he has won several awards such as the Grand Prix National d'Architecture, France, 2008.
Jean-Philippe Vassal ist Architekt und seit 2012 Professor an der UdK Berlin. Von 1980 bis 1985 arbeitete er als Stadtplaner in Niger. Zusammen mit Anne Lacaton gründete er 1987 das Büro Lacaton & assal, das international praktiziert und an verschiedenen Konzepten für öffentliche Gebäude, Wohnungen und Stadtplanung arbeitet. Sein Büro hat mehrere Preise gewonnen, darunter 2008 den französischen Grand Prix national d'Architecture.

Vlassenrood, Linda

Linda Vlassenrood is an architectural historian and an independent curator, programme manager, writer and consultant on architecture, urban planning and design. At Het Nieuwe Instituut, she curated a multi-year cultural programme (2015 to 2017) on data and the smart society in

collaboration with the City of Eindhoven. She is also programme director at the International New Town Institute in Rotterdam, and in charge of a multi-year research and exchange programme in Shenzhen, China.
Linda Vlassenrood ist Architekturhistorikerin und unabhängige Kuratorin, Programmmanagerin, Autorin und Beraterin für Architektur, Stadtplanung und Design. An Het Nieuwe Instituut kuratierte sie in Zusammenarbeit mit der Stadt Eindhoven ein mehrjähriges Kulturprogramm (2015–2017) zu Daten und der Smart Society. Sie ist außerdem Programmdirektorin am International New Town Institute in Rotterdam und verantwortlich für ein mehrjähriges Forschungs- und Austauschprogramm in Shenzhen, China.

Zogolovitch, Roger

Roger Zogolovitch is a developer and the creative director of Solidspace, the latest project of which – 81–87 Weston Street, London – is an award-winning development of gap sites, including winning the World Architecture Festival for "Best small completed housing project". He is honorary surveyor to the Royal Academy of Arts, London and chairs the Southwark Design Review. He is the author of the book "Shouldn't we all be developers?", which was printed in a second edition in September 2018.
Roger Zogolovitch ist Entwickler und Kreativdirektor von Solidspace, dessen neuestes preisgekröntes Projekt, 81–87 Weston Street, London, die Entwicklung von Gap Sites zeigt („Bestes kleinmaßstäbliches Wohnungsbauprojekt" beim World Architecture Festival). Er ist Ehrengutachter der Royal Academy of Arts, London, und leitet den Ausschuss Design Review Panel im Londoner Stadtbezirk Southwark. Er ist der Autor des Buches „Shouldn't we all be developers?", dessen zweite Auflage im September 2018 veröffentlicht wurde.

p.1 © Jenna Dallwitz
p.2 © Jenna Dallwitz
p.3 © Nomadic By Choice
p.4 © Nomadic By Choice
p.5 © Anna Vera Lengyel
p.6 © Nomadic By Choice
p.7 © Anna Vera Lengyel
p.8 © Anna Vera Lengyel, © Florentine Sack
p.9 © Anna Vera Lengyel, © Levente Pavelka
p.10 © Nomadic By Choice, © Florentine Sack
p.11 © Florentine Sack
p.12 © Anna Vera Lengyel
p.13 © Nomadic By Choice, © Florentine Sack
p.38 © nineties berlin
p.51 © VIC, Zuloark, Lys Villalba, Sodeste / supported by Intermediae
p.64 © Muck Petzet Architekten, © Arch+ / photograph by David von Becker, © jnwnklmnn
p.65 © Arch+ / photograph by David von Becker, © Olivia Reynolds
p.67 © Raber Umphenour, © Eric Levin, © Ryuli Suzuki, © Nicole Aquillano
p.69 © Margot Canizzo, © Chloé Priou, © Plateau Urbain, © Yes We Camp, © Dounia Mahjoubi
p.71 © ARGE ifau / HEIDE & VON BECKERATH
p.72 © David von Becker, © Andrew Alberts, ARGE ifau / HEIDE & VON BECKERATH
p.73 © Andrew Alberts
p.75 © Keystone / Andrea Helbling, © Istvan Balogh, © Maja Dickerhof, © 296 Quartierverein Zwicky-Areal / artwork by David Keist, wrkstadt, © Kraftwerk1
p.77 © Alexandre Nunis, © Marco Antônio, © Marcelo Ferraz / drawing by Lina Bo Bardi
p.102 © cam.cop media / Andreas Klug
p.106 © Christian Mang
p.111 © AnjaBeutler, © KerstinBehrendt
p.113 © Every One Every Day
p.115 © Every One Every Day
p.117 © Elise Hunchuck, © Levente Pavelka, © BSM / Gregor Lehmann
p.119 © ZKB
p.121 © Mari Vass
p.123 © Research and Teaching Programme Urban Design, HCU Hamburg / photographs by Daniel Wolcke, Sarah Hablützel
p.125 © Werner Huthmacher © Ludloff Ludloff
p.127 © Werner Huthmacher © Matthias Jankowski, Wohnstadt Carl Legien, licensed under CC BY-SA 3.0 (available at https://creativecommons.org/licenses/by-sa/3.0/, image at http://architectuul.com/architecture/view_image/wohnstadt-carl-legien/499), © Gertrud Kanu, © Jörg Brüggemann / Ostkreuz
p.129 © Christoph Wiedemann
p.131 © We Are City Plaza Photo Project, photographs by Sierra, Anna K, Samir, Christian, Jamie, Ali
p.133 © Theresa Hwang
p.142 © Jan Willem Groen, © Ronald Tilleman
p.149 © Deadline
p.151 © F.L.C / VG Bild-Kunst
p.152 © James Wines / SITE New York
p.154 © Friedrichshain-Kreuzberg Museum / p.T.E.R.N. GmbH Berlin
p.155 © Zentral- und Landesbibliothek Berlin, Übersichtskarte des Bebauungsplans der Umgebungen Berlins, Ferdinand Boehm, (available at https://digital.zlb.de/viewer/resolver?urn=urn:nbn:de:kobv: 109-opus-104224)
p.156 © Gustav Assmann / Bibliothek der Technischen Hochschule Nürnberg Georg Simon Ohm
p.159 © Katharina Borsi, © Lukas Staudinger
p.160 © timeline classics / Timeline Images, via Wikimedia / photograph by Phil Stanziol
p.162 © Rainer Gollmer, © Diego Vásquez
p.164 © Bergfried Center
p.165 © Karsten Thielker, © The Green Market Berlin / Anne Freitag, © Fab Lab Berlin, © Industrie Schöneweide
p.170 © die Baupiloten
p.172 © Thomas Mayer
p.175 © C.F. Møller Architects / photograph by Nikolaj Jakobsen, © Arkitema Architects / Niels Nygaard, © Arkitema Architects / Kontraframe
p.176 © Dawin Meckel / Ostkreuz
p.180 © AFF architekten / Sven Fröhlich
p.181 © AFF architekten / Sven Fröhlich
p.183 © Verstas Arkkitehdit / Anders Portman / Kuvatoimisto Kuvio, © helen&hard
p.185 © Virginia Garfunkel, © Praeger Richter Architekten, © Andreas Friedel
p.186 © FAR frohn&rojas
p.187 © FAR frohn&rojas
p.189 © Jan Bitter
p.190 © Deadline, © JanBitter
p.191 © Deadline
p.193 © Virginia Garfunkel, © Irene Yamaguchi Beyer, © plus 4930 Architektur
p.195 © Kunst in den Gerichtshöfen, © Geoportal Berlin, © Günter Ries
p.196 © Joanna Kosowska / Ex-Embassy
p.197 © degewo / Tina Merkau, © degewo / Wolfgang Stahr
p.199 © Alexander Christie
p.201 © Wien 3420 aspern Development AG, © Aspern Shopping / Robert Fritz
p.202 © ppag architects, © Wolfgang Thaler
p.203 © tschinkersten fotografie
p.208 © Patrick Bingham-Hall, © Ornella Orlandini
p.211 © Hanns Joosten

p.212 © Ramboll Studio Dreiseitl
p.215 © Ramboll Studio Dreiseitl
p.216 © Uday Andhare
p.220 © Randy Risling / Toronto Star
p.222 © picture-alliance / dpa / photograph by Moesch
p.223 © Reindeer Renderings, © paper planes e.V.
p.224 © Hanns Joosten
p.228 © BIGH, © Filip Dujardin
p.234 © Roof Water-Farm
p.235 © Marc Brinkmeier / Roof Water-Farm
p.236 © Markthalle Neun
p.237 © Markthalle Neun
p.238 © Markthalle Neun
p.239 © Markthalle Neun
p.241 © Berlinfoodstories, © Christian Haid, © Christian Haid / Poligonal
p.243 © Imke Woelk und Partner
p.245 © Indigo Architects
p.246 © Indigo Architects
p.247 © Indigo Architects
p.249 licensed under CC BY-SA 2.0 / photograph by Comrade King (license available at https://creativecommons.org/licenses/by-sa/2.0/legalcode, image at https://www.flickr.com/photos/56380734@N05/5898855207/in/photostream/), © Ramboll Studio Dreiseitl
p.251 © Ossip van Duivenbode, © Urbanisten
p.252 © Urbanisten
p.253 © Urbanisten
p.255 © Pool is cool
p.257 © Hendrik Lietmann, © Landesarchiv Berlin / photograph by Waldeman Titzenthaler, © Annette Hausschild, © Axel Schmidt, © Stefanie Loos
p.259 © Lukas Staudinger, © Nomadic By Choice
p.260 © Nomadic By Choice
p.261 © Michael Berger
p.263 © AdDa Zei, © Marco Casagrande
p.265 © Berliner Kurier, licensed under CC BY 2.0 / photograph by Allie Caulfied (license available at https://creativecommons.org/licenses/by/2.0/legalcode, image at https://www.flickr.com/photos/28577026@N02/7486388630)
p.270 © AK Architects, © Javier Callejas, © Blas llamazares
p.275 © AK Architects, © Sebastiano Giannesini
p.284 © Philippe Ruault
p.286 © Philippe Ruault
p.288 © Philippe Ruault
p.289 © Philippe Ruault
p.294 © Elke Krasny
p.297 © Treasure Hill
p.298 © Ruin Academy, © Isis Kang
p.303 © Bureau SLA / Overtreders W / photograph by Filip Dujardin
p.304 © Bureau SLA / Overtreders W / photograph by Filip Dujardin
p.305 © Bureau SLA / Overtreders W / photograph by Filip Dujardin
p.307 © Harvest Map (available at https://www.oogstkaart.nl/), © Erik Stekelenburg
p.309 © Sauerbruch Hutton, © Jan Bitter, © Florentine Sack
p.311 © ZRSArchitekten, © GeoportalBerlin
p.312 © ZRSArchitekten
p.313 © ZRSArchitekten
p.315 © Marco Schmidt
p.317 © BlueCity, © Felicia Alberding, © Arie Kievit
p.319 © Stefan Müller, © Alexander Christie
p.321 © Adrià Goula
p.322 © Adrià Goula
p.333 © Flores & Prats, © Adrià Goula
p.325 © Hannes Langguth, © Sebastian Latz, © Alastair Philip Wiper
p.327 © Mila Hacke
p.328 © Mila Hacke
p.329 © Something Fantastic
p.340 © Virginia Garfunkel
p.341 © Mari Vass
p.342 © Virginia Garfunkel
p.343 © Ishka Michocka
p.344 © Anna Vera Lengyel
p.355 © Nomadic By Choice
p.346 © Nomadic By Choice, © Michael Berger
p.347 © Florentine Sack, © Levente Pavelka
p.348 © Jenna Dallwitz
p.349 © Florentine Sack
p.350 © Markthalle Neun
p.351 © Markthalle Neun
p.352 © Anna Vera Lengyel

This publication was made possible by the Senate Department for Urban Development and Housing, Berlin.
/ Diese Publikation wurde gefördert von der Senatsverwaltung für Stadtentwicklung und Wohnen, Berlin.

Editor in chief / Herausgeberin
Francesca Ferguson

Editorial concept / Publikationskonzept
Francesca Ferguson, Laura Bernhardt, Lukas Staudinger, Nora Unger

Editors / Redaktion
Elise Hunchuck, Lukas Staudinger, Nora Unger

Copy writers / Textbearbeitung
Stephanie Bernoully, Sonja Hornung, Richard Pettifer, Tina Steiger

Editorial advisory / Redaktionelle Beratung
Stephanie Bernoully, Olaf Grawert, Doris Kleilein

Editorial assistance / Redaktionsassistenz
Asha Tomlin-Kent, Laura Koch, Gregory Then

Images / Bildredaktion
Asha Tomlin-Kent

Thanks to / Dank an
Alexandra Beer, Irene Beyer Yamaguchi, Giulia Carones, Laura Castillo, Ece Demir, Charlotte Drache-Lambert, Heba Elhanafy, Simikka Hansen, Frederick Leinfelder, Bea Mensing, Rani Charlotte Pabst, Graham Pugh, Mateusz Rej, Eva Spangenberg

Translators / Übersetzer*innen
Janna Düringer, Sonja Hornung, Tina Steiger, Jennifer Sophia Theodor

Copy editing / Lektorat
Michael Thomas Taylor, Jutta Ziegler

Curatorial board / Festival-Kuratorium
Benita Braun-Feldweg, Nanni Grau, Matthew Griffin, Bastian Lange, Florian Niedermeier, Martin Rein-Cano, Kristien Ring, Steffan Robel, Eike Roswag-Klinge, Gudrun Sack, Frank Schönert, Rosario Talevi, Jan Wurm

Cover design / Umschlaggestaltung
Büro Otto Sauhaus (based on Erik Spiekermann's MakeCity-CI / frei nach der MakeCity-CI von Erik Spiekermann)

Graphic design and typesetting / Gestaltung und Satz
Büro Otto Sauhaus

Lithography / Lithografie
Bild1Druck, Berlin

Bibliographic information published by the Deutsche Nationalbibliothek: The Deutsche Nationalbibliothek lists this publication in the Deutsche Nationalbibliografie; detailed bibliographic data are available on the internet at http://dnb.d-nb.de.
/ Bibliografische Information der Deutschen Nationalbibliothek: Die Deutsche Nationalbibliothek verzeichnet diese Publikation in der Deutschen Nationalbibliografie; detaillierte bibliografische Daten sind im Internet abrufbar über http://dnb.d-nb.de.

MAKE_SHIFT gGmbH,
Oderberger Str. 9
10435 Berlin
www.make.shift.info

jovis Verlag GmbH
Kurfürstenstraße 15/16
10785 Berlin
www.jovis.de

jovis books are available worldwide in select bookstores. Please contact your nearest bookseller or visit www.jovis.de for information concerning your local distribution.
/ jovis-Bücher sind weltweit im ausgewählten Buchhandel erhältlich. Informationen zu unserem internationalen Vertrieb erhalten Sie von Ihrem Buchhändler oder unter www.jovis.de.

Printed and bound in the European Union.
/ Gedruckt und gebunden in der Europäischen Union.

ISBN 978-3-86859-567-3

HUB_22/06/18_19:00_Architecture, Art and Cashflow
@ Bar Kosmetiksalon Babette

ST_22/06/18_19:00_Wood Is the New Good with Sauerbruch Hutton
@ Berlin Metropolitan School

HUB_23/06/18_14:00_Design and Build: Children's Workshop
@ Danish Embassy

HUB_23/06/18_11:00_Stadtwerken Exhibition with Superuse Studios, ReFunc & Bureau SLA
@ Lichtenberg

MCO_24/06/18_12:00_Direct Democracy Ride with TU Berlin
@ Tempelhofer Feld

HUB_26/06/18_10:00_Regrow Berlin Symposium with DieNachwachsendeStadt
@ CRCLR House

MCO_26/06/18_17:00_Sleeping on Top of the Highway with Poligonal
@ Schlangenbader Straße

HUB_27/06/18_09:30_playVoid & PLUG-IN Home Not Shelter Initiative with Hybrid Space Lab
@ Embassy of the Netherlands

MCO_28/06/18_18:00_First the Dialogue, then the Design with Deadline architects
@ Frizz23

MCO_28/06/18_16:00_Touring a Sleeping Industrial City
@ Industriesalon Oberschöneweide

ESLY
ESLY
ESLY

MCO_29/06/18_07:00_A Visit to Berlin's Wholesale Market with Markthalle Neun
@ Großmarkt Berlin

HUB_01/07/18_13:00_Who’s Joining Us on a Trip to the Countryside? With Hütten und Paläste @ Hof Prädikow